CLIMBING THE CORBETTS

CLIMBING THE CORBETTS

Scotland's 2,500 ft Summits

by

HAMISH M. BROWN

LONDON
VICTOR GOLLANCZ LTD
1988

First published in Great Britain 1988
by Victor Gollancz Ltd,
14 Henrietta Street, London WC2E 8QJ

Maps drawn by James Renny

British Library Cataloguing in Publication Data
Brown, Hamish M., *1934–*
   Climbing the Corbetts : Scotland's 2,500ft.
   summits.
   I. Scotland. Hill walking — Visitors' guides
   I. Title
   795.5'22

ISBN 0-575-04378-4

ACKNOWLEDGEMENT

The short extract from *Torridon Highlands* by Brenda
Macrow is reprinted on page 265 by permission of the
author and the publishers, Robert Hale Ltd

Typeset at The Spartan Press Ltd,
Lymington, Hants
and printed in Great Britain by
St Edmundsbury Press Ltd, Bury St Edmunds, Suffolk
Colour illustrations printed by
BAS Printers Ltd, Over Wallop, Hants

CONTENTS

Appendices

ABBREVIATIONS

BFMC	Braes o' Fife Mountaineering Club
c.	*circa* (around, approx.)
CIC	Charles Inglis Clark
MBA	Mountain Bothy Association
NCC	Nature Conservancy Council
NTS	National Trust for Scotland
ON	Old Norse
OS	Ordnance Survey
SMC	Scottish Mountaineering Club
UC	Ultimate Challenge

SOME USEFUL ADDRESSES

Atholl Estates, Blair Atholl, Perthshire, telephone 079681–211/230

Gerry Howkins, Achnashellach Hostel, Craig, Achnashellach, Strathcarron, Wester Ross, telephone 052–06232

The Mountain Bothies Association, General Secretary, 2 North Gardner Street, Glasgow G11

Nancy Smith, Fasgadh, Fersit, Roy Bridge, Perthshire (no telephone)

Rhum: The Chief Warden, White House, Rhum by Mallaig, telephone 0687–2026

LIST OF ILLUSTRATIONS

Following page 192

LIFE AFTER THE MUNROS

WITH MORE AND more hill-walkers actively climbing all the Munros and scores now completing their list each year, one begins to wonder what happens after the Munros are done. Do all these walkers quietly fade away, ice axes hung on the wall and the old boots mouldering in the loft, or is there some drug, some Royal Jelly, to lift their eyes once more to the hills?

You'd think there would be something about Munroists that would show, some visible mark of the miles and footage they've put in. This would be useful for Munroist-spotting but, alas, they come fat and thin, old and young, blonde and brunette, hairy and bald. You can usually tell Siamese cat owners by their haunted, persecuted look; but Munroists, against all expectation, appear just an ordinary cross-section of society. What do they do when they have finished ticking off the list?

I've a good friend, Charles from Sheffield, who was a dedicated Munro-bagger in a way I could never be. I could not take all that motoring for a start. Most of his Munros were done at weekends, from Sheffield, because holidays were saved for climbing, ski-touring and trekking in the far corners of the globe. It was the dedication I found staggering, his single-minded application to scaling those hills. I don't know how he puts up with me, for I am easily deflected by historic sites, wildlife and a natural laziness which has saved me from many a meteorological hammering. Another mutual friend based in London was also heading towards completing the Munros and the two of them slogged it out in hectic rivalry. Donald just got there first but Charles had been doing the "Tops" — the hundreds of subsidiary summits — as well as the separate mountains that are the Munros. Donald was tragically drowned in Knoydart but Charles went on to complete the 3,000-ers of England, Wales and Ireland and the 2,000-ers of England and Wales. He was running out of lists!

Quite a few people cheerfully start all over again and repeat the Munros. I've done this myself because, if you are wandering the Scottish hills, you willy-nilly accumulate Munros, and when you reach over halfway, well, you can't resist tidying them. I may be lazy but I am tidy!

Munro's *Tables* also contain two other eponymous lists: the Donalds which list all the Scottish hills *in the Lowlands* which exceed 2,000 feet (Galloway, the Borders, Ochils and such delights), and the Corbetts which list all the 2,500-foot summits. Life after the Munros, for walkers in Scotland, often means doing the Corbetts, and Charles, having cleared off all the other possibilities, had a resurrection into Scottish activity by joining the Corbett-baggers. I suspect there are quite a few of his breed flitting about but, being more solitary and nesting away from the busy hills, the status of the species is hard to estimate. They are not listed, as are the successful Munroists.

The Corbetts have a separation of 500 feet (the Munros are not so defined) which gives them an individuality frequently missing in the Munros. There are fewer "dull" Corbetts than there are "dull" Munros, though dull is a word I would use of no hill (it is usually a comment on the person rather than the setting). The views from Corbetts frequently surpass the views from Munros and there are plenty of them which are magnificent hills in their own right: The Cobbler, Ben Loyal, Clisham, Goat Fell, The Merrick or Garbh Bheinn of Ardgour are each worth a score of Geal Charns of over 3,000 feet. I advocate doing the Corbetts *simultaneously* with the Munros, but often this advice falls on unbelieving ears.

However, one weekend Charles admitted I'd been right, there was an English Bank Holiday and a fair proportion from that country migrated northwards. The Munros were crawling with Sassenachs yet, over the long weekend, Charles, the dog and I never met one person on our Corbetts. Charles climbed many more than I did — having done the Corbetts years ago (and having topped up with all the new ones from the map revisions) I could enjoy *not* having to try and match Charles's *blitzkreig*.

I drove up to Glen Shee on the Friday afternoon and had a pleasant evening of reading, writing and music. Being in bed before midnight was a treat. At 1.30 a.m. Charles found me and bedded-down alongside my Dormobile. At 7 a.m. I took him a mug of tea. We planned for the days ahead over breakfast and then drove over the Cairnwell to pitch a camp in Glen Clunie. Braemar camp-site was full, and dozens of tents were pitched in the glen as well. At every spot where people park for Munros there were cars. In Braemar we nearly ran over Jim Donaldson, editor of the *Tables*, which would have been rough injustice.

We cycled up to Derry Lodge (wickedly being allowed to decay, like so much property on upper Deeside) and on up the Luibeg till too rough for comfort. Sgor Mor was our objective: the Corbett above the Dee/Geldie junction. It gave a walk over gentle moorland, the heather full of dwarf birch, to a granite knobbliness of summit — and a mighty view. It was so typical a Corbett view, all the better for its isolation and facing the sweep of Cairngorms rather than being jostled in their crowdedness. We were back at the car by lunchtime and I knew what would come next. "I may as well do Morrone," Charles suggested. So we drove up to its path starting above Braemar, and after Charles set off I drove round to meet him off the Clunie side. I managed three hours of work before he arrived. A hard frost whitened the camp that night but the snell weather was great for walking. Charles shifted into top gear next day.

Carn na Drochaide above the Quoich was our initial summit, and the dog and I then explored the Quoich and had a pleasant low-level day before going down to meet Charles at the old Bridge of Dee (1752) at Invercauld. This old military bridge, in its wooded setting, with Lochnagar behind, forms a classic view. Photographers in droves were taking pictures of it, a dangerous game with the holiday traffic. Charles came back with the two Culardoch scalps and a sun-wind-burnt bald bit on his head.

Monday I had to do other things in the morning so Charles climbed the Corbett above Glen Clunie and we met at coffee-time on the Cairnwell Pass before dropping down to Glen Shee for Ben Gulabin, the peak that so dominates that green oasis. We went up a burn to the col behind it and then pigged ourselves on blaeberries for the 500 feet to the summit. I'd forgotten just how fine a viewpoint it was. This is the refrain you will hear from all Corbetters: the view! the view!

I was home for teatime but Charles set off for upper Glen Isla, bent on adding Monamenach; three Corbetts in a day again. In case you think this normal, it is not. Only because Braemar itself is 1,000 feet up, can you romp over several like this. Two in a day usually entails quite enough work and often driving between. Three or more is very seldom possible. But Charles is dedicated, and he completed his Munros on 30 December 1987.

It only seems right, then, to dedicate this book of Corbett days to him, in gratitude for many good shared ploys at home and abroad. Slainté! Tearlaich. What will you do now with the Corbetts completed?

INTRODUCTION

IN HAPPY DAYS of youthful ignorance I climbed and walked wherever fancy led — which was over most of Scotland. Munro's *Tables* (with their threefold listings) were not yet known to me. When I discovered this slim but seductive volume it was all too easy to tick off many hundreds of names in all three tables, which is really not a thing to do if one wants to retain a sane and casual freedom.

Like so many before me (61 to be precise) completing the Munros became a most desirable objective and, fulfilled, repeated (six times over), while the Corbetts and Donalds followed. Now, I am not basically a Munro-bagger, as they are called, for proportionately the time I give to Munros is probably far lower than that of most walkers, especially those avowedly seeking these hills. Months, in any year, may be spent abroad; I canoe, ski, botanise, bird-watch, sail, take photographs and sketch, and I have other hobbies, other interests. I don't think mountains alone, listed or unlisted, any more than climbs, should be a person's *only* interest. That they can be a vast blessing and provide contentment is just one of life's rich bonuses. By all means tick off the Munros, the Corbetts and the Donalds. No one has any call, beyond sour grapes, to criticise you for seeking pleasure in so doing.

The Munros have obviously dominated the lists, but there are only a few walkers, I'm sure, who are so ensnared by them that they do not also happily charge off to the odd Corbett, Donald or unlisted nothing at all when fancy or chance takes them. You cannot just skip Suilven or Stac Polly or plenty of others. Beauty of form and the joy of being there is not restricted to any particular height. Munros are climbed because they contain a spark of magic and that magic remains even when the last 3,000-er is sclimmed. The good news is that there is life after the Munros: the Corbetts.

At once let me plead with active Munroists to be equally busy with the Corbetts, *simultaneously*. Whenever a Munro is on the schedule, check if it has a Corbett possible on the same walk. (Ben Aden can be linked with Sgurr na Ciche, Auchnafree Hill with Ben Chonzie and so on.) Doing Munros and Corbetts together is more practical in the long run (the economics of hill going is a subject in search of a thesis) and also more satisfying, even if it means the Munros may take another year or two to complete. It is not a race! There is a false idea that climbing Corbetts is, somehow, a poorer game. This is nonsense. The Corbetts are every bit as satisfying as the Munros — for reasons I hope you can find for yourself. By definition the Corbetts are much more solitary and individualistic. You will not find seven of them lined up on any easy ridge. As well as being more independent in character and setting (and partly because of it) they frequently command finer views than the majority of Munros. They are at the height from which mountain views are at their best. Corbetts are more widely scattered geographically than the Munros so they ensure a widening of the exploratory factor. Galloway and the islands would alone sell me the Corbetts, and some of my best-loved areas are not covered by any of the lists. However, all the lists give a spur, an incentive, to visit new territory. Walking, for walking's sake, for mere exercise, for "training", hardly appeals to someone as lazy as myself; I need the spur of something like a set of tables to bully me on to my hind legs. The *Tables* both lead and drive like a good schoolmaster.

Information on the Corbetts is often difficult to obtain, and while this, to me, is no liability as I seldom swot an area before a first visit, for those with short holidays and a brief ration of weekends it can be annoying. Nobody, after all, is forced to read a guidebook, so those who object to such are hardly being logical, or fair to others, when they voice displeasure. *Chacun à son goût.* . . . This is not a guidebook, then; at least not in the accepted sense. It is one man yarning about his Corbetts and therefore there is no standard presentation; of some hills I write extensively, of others briefly; it is a very subjective game after all. The practical information is there but it has to be discovered. Instead of a bold guide statement like "Do not try to cross the Allt a' Tobrect in its lower reaches in wet weather. It can flood for several miles from its entry to Loch Numor", you will find the story of the mess we made of crossing at that notorious spot — and can draw your own conclusions!

While giving largely first-hand accounts of expeditions over the Corbetts I have woven into the text most of the practical information needed for these hills. Going to the hills (Munros, Corbetts or any other) should be fun, and part of that fun is in the dreaming and planning as well as in the execution. So you will not find statistics of miles and hours laid down for you. That is something you should be working out yourself, anyway, and *on the map*, not just at second hand.

I originally planned to write this book chronologically, but details of many of my earliest ascents are forgotten while more recent escapades are fresh in mind as well as recorded in carefully kept log-books. If it is to be of practical help I feel the day-to-day story should also have a solid core of useful information and its lay-out would be more helpful if following that of the present *Tables* — they are due for revision within the next few years. Most people will want to dip into this book for specific hills rather than read a continuous narrative. We don't "do" the Munros or Corbetts very logically or efficiently anyway.

I would recommend the practice of keeping a hill log-book. Memory is fickle, and often it is the small details that make a day; these are so easily forgotten unless written down at the time. One friend of mine, who keeps complaining he is so "useless at names", would find them easier to recall if he had regularly noted them down. I started this habit only in 1960, using notebooks with a small, close-lined format, but am now on notebook number 178. In these I stick postcards, illustrations, even stamps — any related material — as well as contact prints of all black and white pictures and some colour prints from slides. They are a treasure-chest for degenerating brain cells!

J. Rooke Corbett is number four in the Munro list (1930) but his own list of the 2,500-foot summits, which he had also climbed, was published only posthumously. With a re-ascent of 500 feet on all sides the hills were listed with a cold logic lacking in Munros — not that that has stopped the alterations and amendments and revisions due to Ordnance Survey re-mapping and a certain editorial whim. The present sections are far too large, and using the list is often difficult. Having completed the Corbetts long before the re-mapping/metrification landmark there was some topping-up to be done and a sad farewell to be given to others, demoted to obscurity, or promoted to the notoriety of Munro status. Being naturally iconoclastic there is something satisfying in seeing the logical clarity of the Corbett list suffering the effects of man's natural talent for chaos. For better or for worse this book closely follows the list as set forth in the last, 1984, edition of Munro's *Tables*.

As most walking is done using the 1:50,000 OS maps the appropriate sheet is given for each hill and ideally this should be dug out and *studied in conjunction with the text*. Each heading gives the Corbett section number, followed by the number of the peak within the section, the peak name, its height in metres, the 1:50,000 sheet number(s), its six-figure reference and the translation of the Gaelic name. Where heights do not agree with the 1:50,000 sheets they will be from the 1:25,000 sheets or more recent OS information.

Many of the Gaelic names of geographical features are now only preserved on the map, for local keepers and shepherds (nearly all English-speaking now) have long replaced most of them with their own practical "convenience-namings" — which is the whole point of names. Names are a lively, changing subject and it is only we slaves of the map, rather than any residents, who use the early Victorian fossilisation of the centuries of Gaelic namings. So many names have stories behind them which are now quite lost. Why is it "stone of weeping"? Who is William and why did he leap?

The pronunciation of Gaelic names is often difficult and I've given a few helps where possible. Translations are not always obvious, as many original names have been simplified or Anglicised out of recognition. There is a useful Gaelic guide in the 1984 Munro's *Tables* — which are worth buying for this alone. For a score of the more difficult derivations I must thank Iseabail Macleod and Ian Fraser for their researches. Topographical Gaelic, with a bit of study, soon becomes fascinating rather than frightening. I'd also like to thank Don Green and Brenda Macrow for permission to use extracts from their accounts of some days. My thanks too must go to Sheila Gallimore who has had to cope with typing this work; Gaelic names I'm sure were not made easier by my handwriting.

As most people are now car-owners or approach their hills by car this is kept in mind when describing approaches. Some private estate roads may be available, but with complicated negotiations I find it easier to be completely independent and either walk or use a push bike which, in Scotland, is "an aid to pedestrianism", not a vehicle. Many remote glens can be reached by post buses from the nearest town, often a railhead, and there are other train, bus or boat services which can be useful. The annual *Getting Around the Highlands and Islands* is a valuable publication.

Cutting free from a car is a blessing rather than a disaster, and it is not for nothing that the annual Ultimate Challenge coast-to-coast event has its "high-level" route pinned to doing twelve Munros and/or Corbetts. My previous *Mountain Walk* and *Groats End Walk* books tell of the extremes of being car-free. This is a much more prosaic collection of odd days and holidays, such as we all take, and can therefore associate with. "The sun always shines on the days you describe", is a criticism I hear now and then. But weren't summers always sunnier in the days of youth? Plodding through the rain makes for soggy prose as well as sodden feet and memory recalls more clearly the very good days — or the diabolically bad ones — so if I've been on a Corbett several times, as I have many, a good day is quite likely to be described. I make no apology for this. I've gone out on far too many miserable days when I should have known better.

About 150 different people have been with me on Corbett days — I must have been persuasive over the years — and I hope I can convince you that this is one of the better games to play in the Scottish hills. Be warned, though, once you start ticking the list it will soon have you in thrall. The dedicatory piece before this Introduction appeared in the *Glasgow Herald*, and several other days have been described in this, Scotland's oldest national newspaper; I thank the *Glasgow Herald* for permission to reprint them here. I would also like to thank all the people who have been with me on the Corbetts. One of the pleasures of hill days is the people involved. I just wished I'd been able to meet the man responsible for this game.

J. Rooke Corbett was a District Valuer, based on Bristol, but several times a year he would be in Scotland, exploring its hills, often with Scottish Mountaineering Club friends. He joined the SMC in 1923, attended nearly all its meets, served on the committee and was a joint editor of the *Northern Highlands* general guidebook. He was the second person to complete the Munros and Tops, in 1930, one of a small gang of eight pre-war Munroists, of whom four also did the Tops, a proportion not maintained in these slack times. He also made the ascent of every 2,000-foot hill in Scotland, still a very rare feat. He accomplished this just before a heart attack in 1943 which curtailed his activities somewhat, and presumably his tables of the 2,500-foot summits, which now bear his name, were compiled from this experience. They were not published during his lifetime. Corbett was a quiet, retiring man of cheerful inner strength. He walked again after his heart attack and few knew of a growing paralytic affliction. He died, aged 72, a few years after the war.

There are only two full-scale articles of his in the *SMC Journal*: one on the Paps of Jura (one Corbett!) and the other on "Aneroids and Munros", which reflects his interest in things scientific, and accounts for many short notes on topographical observations — they were finding new Munros even in the 1930s. Corbett had a distinguished education at Cambridge but even then he was a powerful long-distance walker. He once walked home from Cambridge to Manchester. Later he was an original member of the Rucksack Club and took delight in such ploys as all-night expeditions.

The list of Corbetts was passed by his sister to the SMC and soon incorporated into Munro's *Tables*. With a few minor amendments it is as he left it, Corbetts being more clearly defined than the Munros. Corbett never stated that there had to be a 500-foot re-ascent, but it is implied and employed, distance and difficulty being ignored. Subsidiary "Tops" were not listed. Just how much alteration there has been to the mapping of the landscape came out in the new metrical era. Jim Donaldson checked the maps, and the result was 17 new Corbetts and 11 Corbetts removed, leaving 223 Corbetts. There was a thunderous silence following this event, but Corbetteers are probably older and wiser than mere Munroists and have learnt to live with the vagaries of the OS and SMC during their Munro apprenticeships. Various comments on status changes, Corbett names and other odd features are made in my text but the summary at the start of the 1984 tables gave 19 new Corbetts and 13 deletions, still a total of 223.

That however was not the end of the story. Since then Beinn Teallach has been promoted to Munro status and Cook's Cairn has been eliminated, so the tally is really 19 promoted, 15 removed, making 221 Corbetts. Those who possess only the 1981 edition of the tables should be careful. Charles, with only a score to go, was given a jolt when I told him of two unobtrusive extra Corbetts in the 1984 list, Beinn Each 2:14 and Sron a' Choire Chnapanich 4:9. It is worth comparing Sron a' Choire Chnapanich as it appears on the First and Second Series maps (Sheet 51). You will see why I emphasise the importance of the latter. Since starting on this book I am glad to say nearly all Corbetts (except those on Sheet 37) are now on Second Series sheets.

There are anomalies in the heights of Corbetts which I have given up trying to fathom. One day the *Tables* may be definitive but not until the OS has sorted out some problems. Hopefully the SMC will tidy up the sections, too, but this book follows what we have at present, imperfect though it be.

No list of Corbett-completers has been kept, though a few names appear in the notes in the *SMC Journal*. Maybe this is a good thing. In 1985 (one of the wettest years ever) Craig Caldwell from Milngavie did a continuous bike and hike trip over all the Munros *and* Corbetts, an astonishingly gritty feat. Not long before finishing this book Craig looked in and we had a grand chat. Just looking at his map with the route shown on it could have kept us talking all night. There were not many bits of Scotland left untouched, and that, in the end, is the richest reward of doing Munros and Corbetts and Donalds and uncle Tom Cobbleys and all: you come to know the land in a quite unique way, a knowledge which cannot but be transformed into a lifelong love affair. This book is a tale of 221 flirtations — and one rockfast marriage.

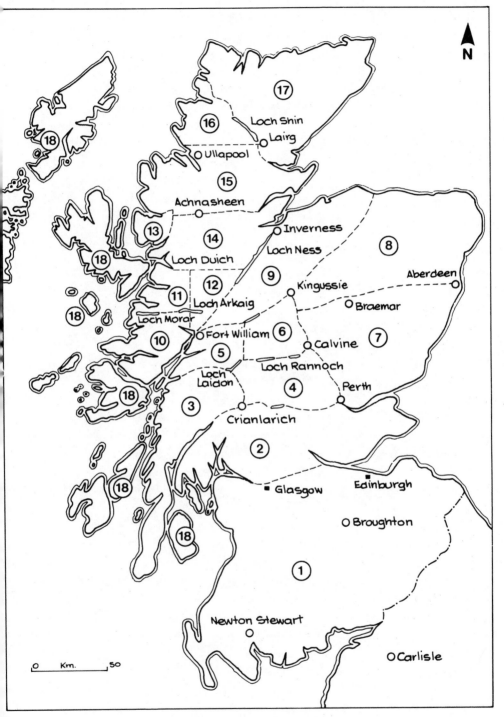

CORBETT SECTIONS

SOUTHERN SCOTLAND

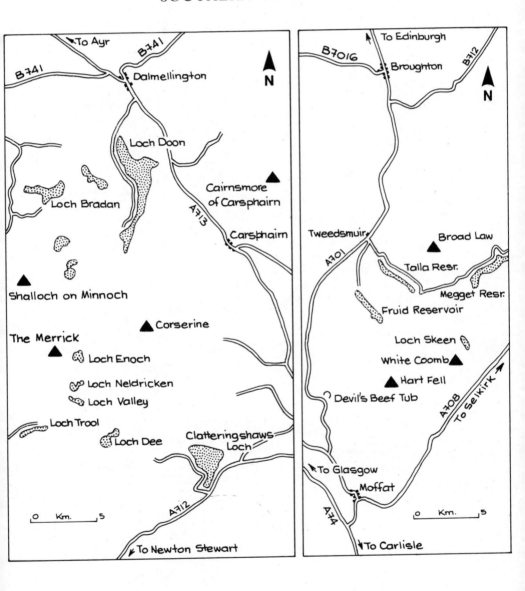

Section 1:   1. SHALLOCH ON MINNOCH   768 m   OS 77   405907
  The heel of the Minnoch ridge

Section 1:   2. THE MERRICK   814 m   OS 77   428855
  The branched finger

BACK IN THE days when we had counties The Merrick was the highest
point in Kirkcudbrightshire, at 2,764 feet. Of Scotland's 33 counties
all had highest points over 1,000 feet, and 25 of them had highest
points over 2,000 feet. We tend to forget how hilly Scotland is *over all*.
The division into Highlands and Lowlands is misleading; we have
Highlands and Notsohighlands! The Merrick Hills, or The Awful
Hand as they are also called, tend to be neglected partly because of this
misconception. On a Bank Holiday, Glen Coe will be swarming with
visitors (half of whom drove up the A74, a squirt east of Dumfries),
yet you could walk for days over the Galloway Hills and meet no one
else, which is daft seeing they have the wildest scenery and the
roughest landscape south of Rannoch.

Kirriereoch Hill a mile north of The Merrick has been removed as a
Corbett, but as Shalloch on Minnoch is north again you will still
traverse it in linking the two Corbetts. The Awful Hand has a split-
level system: a high-level highway linking the Corbetts and a lower-
level clearway to the east (Mullwharchar, Dungeon Hill and
Craignaw). They are about all that is clear. The rest of the area seems
to have been drowned in a flood of forestry. Only the highest summits
rise, *nunatak*-like, from this clammy choke of conifers. Now and then
the trees can actually enhance the scenery, and the prime example is
Glen Trool, with its remnant of natural forest, which is also the
customary starting-off point for The Merrick.

Glen Trool is a bit like Wasdale: "round the back" of all the hills, a
bit remote. The comparison ends there; for Trossachs-like Glen
Trool, in the words of Ken Andrew, one of the South West's
champions, is "a superb little glen . . . a scene of astonishing variety
with its woodlands and broken slopes. Meadows on the valley floor
merge with the coarser grasses, heather and bracken, natural
woodlands merge with planted, larch with pine, pine with spruce . . .
sheep, cattle and even goats dot the rugged landscape which maintains
a wide variety of birds and other small creatures." Driving up one
early morning in colourful mid-October I had to dodge a roe buck, a
red deer hind and a gambol of goats, all in the time it took to pass the

length of Loch Trool to the car park by the Bruce's Stone, a monument to a clash in 1307 when Bruce was starting his bid for the Scottish throne. Some of the goats have learnt to scrounge food off the tourists. The adders are much more wary; I've never seen one despite many visits to the area. The Rev. Thomas Grierson in his *Autumnal Rambles among the Scottish Mountains* (in the 1840–1850s decade) has this warning on adders: "As serpents are common, long worsted stockings should be worn and no person should attempt roughing it without a pair of Horrell's best double-soled shoes." He thought Glen Trool "perhaps the most romantic spot in the south of Scotland".

The path for The Merrick is clearly signposted and heads north up by the Buchan Burn past Culsharg (a shepherd's house in Grierson's day) to the slopes of Benyellary, *the hill of the eagle*. It is all thoroughly planted now, so there is a feeling of relief on gaining the breezy open slopes of the hill. A dyke leads all the way up to the top of Benyellary, and when I reached it the subtle, early morning colours had turned the many lochs to the east into burnished silver.

The swell of The Merrick fills the north (over a dip, the Neive of the Spit), and gives an easy, grassy walk up to the highest point, after Goat Fell, in all Scotland south of Ben Lomond. The dyke hits the corrie of Black Gairy half a mile west of the summit, and its rim can be followed up to the trig point. The OS First Series crag symbols are vastly exaggerated, often being little more than broken ground. The dog and I traversed over to the springs of Gloon Burn for a drink and cut straight up to the summit with its cairn, scattered erratics and trig point.

A good ridge leads down to the col (with Loch Twachtan to the east) and then pulls up to Kirriereoch Hill, which gives the best view of The Merrick. Then it drops steeply to the broad saddle of Carmaddie Brae with its collections of lochans, rises and falls over Tarfessock to the Nick of Carlach before the grassy cone of Shalloch on Minnoch is reached. These summits are the knuckles of the colourful Hand, with fingers pointing west, and Benyellary the cocked thumb. Some of the summits and braes are stony but the walking is exhilarating — and worth saving for a good day. The peaks of Cumbria, Northern Ireland, Jura and Arran are all visible, as is Ailsa Craig (Paddy's Milestone) in the Firth of Clyde while, below and to the east, lies a remarkably wild landscape which can give an excellent return to base.

This return I describe is long and rough so should only be tackled by experienced hillgoers. It is not advisable in really wet weather. Most walkers will be happy to descend westwards off Shalloch on Minnoch to the car park at Laglanny or north west to the Straiton road at

Pilnyark Burn. This needs some arranging of transport or, as I did on one occasion, the use of a cycle which I'd left there in readiness. On this autumn occasion I took another option and, returning to the Nick of Carclach, I dropped down east to Tunskeen, which is half a building that was turned into a primitive bothy in 1965, the very first such building to be saved by the nascent Mountain Bothies Association.

From there you can name-drop back to Glen Trool: Castle on Oyne, Rigg of Millmore, Eglin Lane, Mullwharchar, Dungeon Hill, Craignaw, Loch Neldricken, Loch Valley and the Gairland Burn. The "Murder Hole" shown on Loch Neldricken has been transposed from its real site elsewhere by the novelist S. R. Crockett in his most famous book *The Raiders*, which captures this wild area very effectively. I think he could not resist the names. Who could, with places like Craigmawhannal and Craigmasheenie, Lump of the Eglin, The Wolf Slock, Clatteringshaws Loch and Curley Wee? There isn't room here to describe this wilderness of granite, bog, heather and water, the real heart of these hills, but they are well covered in the SMC's *Southern Uplands* and in several older books. *Classic Walks* and *The Big Walks* (both by Ken Wilson and Richard Gilbert) also cover the area, though The Merrick is the only hill appearing in both these lavish publications which perhaps indicates its challenging qualities.

Section 1: 3. CORSERINE 814 m OS 77 497871
The crossing of the ridges

Corserine is the second highest summit in Galloway and is just one of many summits topping a long, continuous north-south ridge which is separated from the Merrick range by a long valley running from Clatteringshaws Loch to Loch Doon (the Doon of Burns's "Bonnie Doon"). This valley, from the Dungeon lochs to Loch Dee, is known as the Silver Flowe and is a notorious bog only to be crossed in drought conditions or when frozen solid.

The Big Walks gives the outline of a route from Glen Trool over Benyellary, The Merrick, then across Gala Lane to Corserine and the Rhinns of Kells ridge and back by Loch Dee but this is rather charging about for the sake of charging about and misses too many interesting points. Corserine is quite awkward enough to reach by itself, at least if one is going to make a good expedition rather than a mere Corbett raid. The usual problem is of transport when traversing a long ridge, but here, for once, there is a useful bus service along the A713 east of the Kells range (Ayr–Castle Douglas service) which allows long days on the hills. There is a Youth Hostel just off the A713 (Kenloon 616883) which can make a jumping-off point for several days of hill and bothy wandering. An example, which gave me a perfect trip, began at Polmaddie Bridge. I walked up to Shiel of Castlemaddy for the night, traversed the Rhinns of Kells to White Laggan (Loch Dee), traversed the Dungeon Hills to Tunskeen, topped The Merrick on the way to Back Hill of Bush and went out to Dalry over Meikle Millyea — Donald/Corbett-bagging at its very best.

To keep to the autumn visit above (1:1, 2) I'll describe the simpler attack on Corserine. It was all new country to me then. I motored a couple of miles along the side of Clatteringshaws Loch to the locked gate where the forestry road branches off, then used a cycle. The dog was sometimes carried, and sometimes ran behind. There were so many new plantings and forestry roads to add to the map that I was constantly stopping. (Make sure you have a Second Series map.)

Back Hill of Bush was a fairly luxurious bothy. It even had an armchair which, on another occasion, I hauled outside the door to enjoy a dram in the evening sun; I was sitting half asleep when there was a crash on the window behind my head and a stunned wren fell on to my lap. Someone in the bothy book had warned of meeting a brontosaurus in the Silver Flowe bogs. I *think* he was joking.

The old path over the ridge behind the bothy had largely gone, so perforce I used the wiggly forestry road to gain height. There was not even a stile on the top deer fence. It had rained hard overnight and my legs were soon saturated from the grass; on the lazy ascent to Corserine the fuggy dankness left the hairs on my cheeks silvered with water droplets. The dog looked like a drowned rat. Corserine is a rounded, grassy dome with five ridges criss-crossing the main north-south line (hence the name). The easiest route from the east is to drive up to the bridge before Forest Lodge then walk on by Fore Bush, Loch Harrow and the North Gairy ridge. When staying at Shiel of Castlemaddy I followed the forest road to Goat Craigs and on over Carlin's Cairn. An entry in the Shiel bothy book was amusing. A lad had made a bivvy in a firebeater shelter, not knowing of the bothy. "I lay all night with a fence post to hand, scared stiff and expecting to be attacked at any time by pumas or something which prowled around making their grunting calls. At first light I fled and was glad to find this safe place." (Roe deer *do* sound a bit like large felines.)

Living in Carlin Craig I naturally had to go on to Carlin's Cairn, a mile north of the Corbett and not much lower. It is topped by a big *chorten*-like cairn which, legend has it, was built by a miller's wife who was granted land by the Polmaddy, a reward for aiding the fugitive Robert the Bruce. The cairn gave shelter for a snack and we then headed south for the shaly tops of Millfire, Milldown and Meikle Millyea, the last a bald flat summit with its highest point to the south west, not at the trig point to the north east. On the Hawse Burn is a memorial to a 17-year-old shepherd who died of exposure there in 1954. Another blizzard, on the main ridge above, once caught a funeral party carrying the wife of a shepherd and they had to abandon the coffin for several days. An old dyke joins the ridge before Milldown and runs all the way to Little Millyea. Millyea is murdered Gaelic: Meall Liath or grey hill. Gaelic, lost long ago in Galloway, has led to a real corruption of place names.

We skirted Milldown to gain the Downie's Burn corrie and so back to Back Hill, soaked to the thighs by then and glad to put on the kettle. A forestry vehicle dropped some firewood off for the bothy but I dried out while cycling the nine miles back to the car at Clatteringshaws Loch.

The road on to Newton Stewart is full of interest. Another Bruce's Stone by the loch, just after we'd joined the A712, celebrates the Battle of Raploch Moss in 1307. Half a mile on is the Galloway Deer Museum, and near Murray's Monument there is a particularly attractive bit of country with good walks, waterfalls, viewpoints etc., an area where the feral goats are allowed to roam free, but out of the forest. Murray, of the monument, was a local shepherd lad who ended up as Professor of Oriental Languages at Edinburgh University, where he died in 1813 still only thirty-seven. He had learnt 28 languages by then. He once had to translate a letter addressed to George III by the King of Ethiopia. He was the only person in the country capable of doing so.

Section 1:   4. CAIRNSMORE OF CARSPHAIRN   797 m   OS 77
                 594980

> "There's Cairnsmore of Fleet,
> And Cairnsmore of Dee;
> But Cairnsmore of Carsphairn
> Is the highest of the three."

— so a Corbett which will take the hill-wanderer into a pleasant part of the South West which he might otherwise miss. On my first visit I thought the ochrous domes a bit like the Ochils. Having abandoned a planned day on the Kells range the weather improved so I simply parked by the Water of Ken and headed up the Craigengillan Burn to reach Cairnsmore over Beninner. That rather casual walk would need some re-routing now as vast areas up the Water of Ken have been drowned with conifers. The farm road from Craigengillan Bridge up to Moorbrock is now the obvious line of access.

The most popular route starts from outside the village of Carsphairn at the Green Well of Scotland. Follow the track on the east bank of the Deugh to the Benloch Burn, a hollow locally called Midge Ha', skirt Willieanna, then simply head up Dunool and on to the Black Shoulder from which an easy walk leads to the summit. From Knochgray (east of the village) a path to Moorbrock and the Ken can be followed and Cairnsmore reached over or round Beninner. The two combine for a pleasant day's walk. From the top you realise just how vast is the extent of the Galloway hills.

What I saw on my first visit made me plan a proper visit to these hills. There was a bothy locally which would be fun for a night out, and besides its Corbett, Carsphairn has a cluster of "Donalds", those Lowland 2,000-foot hills of the third list in the *Tables* which I'd been pecking away at while motoring to and from the south. The next visit came while driving back from a trip to Morocco and Corsica; I quote from my account written at the time (1978):

. . . from friendly Dumfries I motored up to Thornhill and Penpont and then by the wee road up Scaur Water where we lunched and packed under some big trees. The bird life was varied: bullfinch, sandpiper, warbler, blackbird, kestrel, cuckoo. A shepherd with two dogs stopped for an hour's blether then I continued along the twisty upper glen. The trees finish and a grassy sweep of hills was about me when I parked at the road end. During the rest of the day only one other car came up, turned and went off without stopping — so they missed hearing the curlews, thrushes, pipits, redshanks, snipe, and hoasty sheep. It rained most of the time but I was able to keep the sliding door open and drink in the sounds and scents of "my ain countrie". A contrast to Peakirk and the Fens two days ago and even more so to the Atlas or jagged Corsica. The glen is almost a mirror of our geographical history: ruined castles, holiday homes, forestry plantings, hills of sheep and the grey sadness of rain.

Thursday 22 June: a good day and delighting to be on home hills once more. I was stiff by the day's end. Departure was at 8 a.m., up Polskeoch Rig. All day I was stopping to add new features on the map. Forestry workers drove up and set off to work on Fortypenny Hill opposite. I skirted by Ryegrain Rig to reach outliers Blacklorg Hill and Blackcraig which lie above the Afton Water, "sweet Afton" of Burns' song. Donalds of course. Curlews down below and skylarks up above made the day's *continuo*. There was a spacious feel to the tawny hills with little sign of cultivation, other than the invasion of forestry and fences everywhere. Back at my rucker I had tea and while fetching water found a meteorological balloon. Going up Meikledodd Hill a loud bang made me jump and, looking back, I saw a pillar of smoke rise out of the Kello Water glen. (A good route not to be on!) Between Alwhat and Alhang I passed the source of the Afton. The Holm Burn, leading south to the Ken, had an amazing array of little bumps like moraines, but are more likely to be old mining tips, and beyond the Ken, and beyond ken, were ugly blanketing trees again.

A col led to the second block of hills, higher and rougher than where we'd been. Windy Standard had a stark trig-point. The vast Carsphairn Forest rolled away beyond. The outlier Trostan Hill had such spongy grass that it was tiring to walk on, like soft snow. Dugland was the last Donald addition and then it was brutally down to Clennoch, an old shepherd's house now saved as a primitive bothy. It was only 2.30 but the rest of the day went with a book while rain on top of rain rattled on the flat roof. I actually took to the bedshelf at 8.30 and woke thinking I was in a *bergerie* back in Corsica. . . .

Friday 23 June: An early start (6.15) to use the grey but dry morning, a wise move as the afternoon broke down again and was "gey weet". We wandered up the Bow Burn, and some rocks on the watershed made a recognisable spot to leave the rucksack. We set off up into the saturated mist, and a fence did likewise but then sloped off southwards. The ground steepened but we were almost disappointed to find the huge cliffs marked were simply small crags and scree. We went straight up and landed just 20 m from the summit trig-point of Cairnsmore. The granite-strewn summit is reminiscent of the Cairngorms.

The summit was left on a bearing for 600 paces and at that precise spot there was a big cairn. My second bearing led me down, and up on to Beninner. (I wasn't sure if I'd come over it on the previous occasion.) The back bearing took me down to the col and from there a fence dutifully led me down to my rucksack.

In thicker cloud I went up the other side to find Moorbrock Hill and carefully, with map, compass, altimeter and dead-reckoning made my way over its NW Top, a col, another Alwhat and Keoch Rigg, the last of the dotty Donalds. I'd worked back to be almost above Clennoch again and planned to exit by the path that crossed the hills from it down to the Holm–Ken valley. I paced off what the distance should have been and began to go uphill. No path. So we followed the compass down the Bawnhead ridge and never saw a path anywhere. [It has gone from the Second Series map.]

Nether Holm of Dalquhairn was still lived in and had sheep and cows pastured round it. The Water of Ken was a bit grubby so a clear side stream provided the brew water. The tarmac was reduced to two strips, the grass between making a kind surface for feet, then it became just a footpath — until cut by new forestry work. Forestry activities up the Polvaddoch Burn were responsible for the muddy Ken. The gentlest of watersheds led us back to Polskeoch and the Dormobile. An hour of tidying up and we drove off, singing with content, back to Thornhill and on for the Dalveen Pass and Moffat where John Cairney did his "Robert Burns" presentation. He is a good look-alike. The show was nicely done, sad in a way, but not sentimental and the poetry was treated as it deserves. What a grand "welcome home" day.

Section 1: 5. HART FELL 808 m OS 78 114136

Section 1: 6. WHITE COOMB 822 m OS 79 163151

Section 1: 7. BROAD LAW 840 m OS 72 146235

I am glad the Border Hills have a scattering of Corbetts for there is a suspicion that they would be less-visited without these specific lures. My conscience is clear, for all my motoring life I have purposely taken time off to explore the Borders when travelling to and from England or the continent. It may be a grabbed hour for one historic site or it may be a week trekking across the wilds of Galloway, but persistence paid off. It was one area I did not need to raid when completing the Corbetts became an obsession (doing the Donalds is another story), and I have long sung the praises of a hill landscape, still peopled and proud, a contrast to the desert that laps so much north of the Highland Line. Like Orkney, the Borders can feel like another country. Even the hills are different and, after crossing Rotten Bottom between White Coomb and Hart Fell, there may be a temptation to give thanks for that.

In February 1891 the young and lusty Scottish Mountaineering Club held its first official meet at the Crook Inn, Tweedsmuir, and Broad Law was climbed by all and sundry. There had been informal meets before then, of course, and it was only three months later, on the Queen's birthday, that a party traversed White Coomb and Hart Fell. To show how little has changed I summarise the note in the journal about their day on the Moffat hills.

The party left Moffat about 9.30 a.m., driving up Moffatdale to below the Grey Mare's Tail. A cold wind was blowing down the valley and they were not sorry to leave the trap "and set legs in motion". Starting at 11.10 they climbed quickly up the roughish ground by the fall, crossed the burn, and continued till in view of Loch Skeen, a loch created by the natural dam of moraine debris. Lochcraig Head, with its screes falling to the margin of the loch, was their objective and this was reached by a right-flanker up steep grass, arriving at 12.40. The biting wind had them scurrying round the crags that circle Loch Skeen, a "lovely little loch, lying in a veritable cradle of bare stony slopes topped by precipitous crags". It brought them to White Coomb, "the highest point in Dumfriesshire". From there they made for the long flat ridge of Hart Fell, keeping to the watershed between the Moffat–Annan drainage and the Tweed.

Oddly enough the Tweed is to the west, but runs to the east coast while the Moffat waters enter the western Solway — and the upper reaches of the Clyde are not so distant. Burns wrote of

"Yon wild mossy mountains, sae lofty and wide,
   That immerse in their bosom the youth o' the Clyde."

Hart Fell gives a good view over to Queensberry and the Lowther Hills, perhaps my favourites outwith Galloway, because they are not so wild and mossy. This gang pointed out the aptness of the name Rotten Bottom on the map, and there still are some quality peat hags. Hart Fell was reached at 3.20, the clouds broke up and they took a longer break to admire the view.

Keeping along the ridge towards Swattlefell (Swatte Fell to us) they admired the steep, scraggy trench of the Blackhope Burn before striking down the Birnock Water to reach Moffat at 5.40. "A most enjoyable tramp" was the verdict on the day.

Some things have changed of course. The Grey Mare's Tail has become such a popular tourist attraction that careful work has had to be done to counter the track erosion that had developed. The NTS however have tried to keep the car park and approaches as natural as possible. The fall is still a fine sight, and its waters, frozen, have become popular as a climbing route. What would the 1891 party have thought of that? I don't think they would approve of the conifer plantings up Moffatdale.

From the head of Loch Skeen it is quite easy to climb up to the col between Lochcraig Head and Firthybrig Head, or White Coomb can be approached more directly up the Midlaw Burn. There is no way of avoiding Rotten Bottom between the Corbetts. Hart Fell offers several ways down to Moffat or elsewhere, and Moffat itself is a delightful wee town to finish in. There is a famous statue of a ram in the square (the sculptor forgot to give it ears) which points to the importance of that creature in Border economics. Moffat was something of a spa back in Victorian times, as Moffat Well on the Birnock descent indicates.

If you descend off Hart Fell to the south west over Arthur's Seat, you come to Hartfell Spa, a chalybeate well, not sulphur like Moffat Well. Higher up the Annan valley is the deep hollow of the Devil's Beef Tub and the road from the top of the pass, and on to Tweedsmuir is another good starting or finishing point for a traverse of these hills.

The grandest scenery is not on the tops but rather in the glens which bite back into the grassy plateau above Moffat Water: the Blackhope, Carrifran and Loch Skeen glens. It was a bleak February day that first took me up by Loch Skeen and down by the Blackhope Burn. I'd forgotten my ice axe, had a white out on White Coomb and never a car came to offer a lift back up the A701. I'd still offer this as a worthwhile alternative. They are impressive glens and add considerably to the character of the range. The old county boundary is marked by a wall which was most useful for navigation that day. Doing the Donalds has meant further visits to the prows between the glens.

From Firthybrig Head an easy walk leads north to Moll's Cleuch Dod and down to the Megget Stone (452 m) at the top of the pass between Talla Reservoir and Megget Reservoir, which offers another alternative traverse: Megget to Moffat. As Broad Law, the highest of the Manor Hills, lies north of this pass all three Corbetts could be linked easily enough if one could arrange to be dropped off at the Megget Stone. Ah, for the days of simply hiring a trap. Heading south I once drove up from Talla Reservoir (a 1-in-5 hill) to enjoy a windy walk up Broad Law over Porridge Cairn. The first wheatears were probably wishing they were back in Africa. The wind screamed through the fences and washed over the grass, plovers were pleading and the blue-brown landscape seemed to move with the gale. A wig of white cloud fell down the nape of Broad Law, covering Cramalt Craig, a Corbett now deleted. That night I camped in Langdale.

There is now a radio beacon on top of Broad Law which would no doubt surprise the members of that first SMC Meet were they to be whisked back today. Forests, dams, tracks, fences have really changed the hills quite a bit — but the fun of the game remains. Being based at the Crook Inn they took the natural line up the Hearthstane (Heystane) Burn and on by Glenheurie Rig, rather dull now as it is the line of the radio station's maintenance road (but then, all the Tweed spurs and glens are planted and/or tracked). Broad Law has a broad view: of hills beyond the Highland Line, of the English Lakeland fells, of the Cheviot. The SMC had absolutely no view as there was thick mist on top.

They descended (unintentionally) to Meggethead and had to return over by Talla (no reservoir then) to Tweedsmuir, quite a long round; but the next day saw new arrivals, Douglas, Munro and Stott, intentionally repeat the misty crossing to Meggethead, then they ascended the Winterhope Burn to the hag country leading over to Loch Skeen and the Grey Mare's Tail, from where, in wind and rain, they tramped along to Moffat in their big hobnailers. Border Corbetts can be as demanding as any others.

LOCH FYNE, STRATHYRE & LOCH EARN

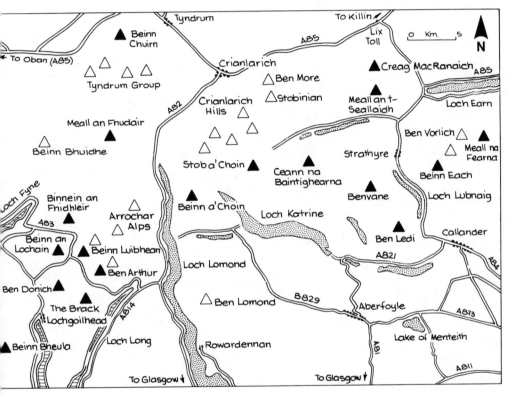

NOTE: Black triangles indicate Corbetts, White triangles Munros.

THE NAME BEINN BHEULA always struck me as sounding like something out of *Pilgrim's Progress*. It became a Promised Land to me as a boy in wartime, staying at Carrick Castle on Loch Goil. Boats, woods and hills were a magnificent playground — and quite a contrast to being bombed out of Singapore or staying as a refugee in South Africa. Not that Carrick was entirely safe. When Greenock was heavily bombed the friendly hills were dark against a sky of flames. A wee steamer, the *Comet*, would take us to and from Carrick (or you rowed to Portincaple for a train) but now there is just a bus which makes the long haul round over the Rest and Be Thankful. Between Lochgoilhead and Carrick it runs under the "home" hills: Cruach nam Miseag and its big brother Beinn Bheula.

The Cruach (606 m) was the first hill I ever climbed in Scotland, tacking along behind my big brother Ian and an older girl who knew the area well. Racing down, Margaret turned to warn us of some "deep irony pools" and promptly ran right into one, landing up to her waist. We boys thought this very funny.

Beinn Bheula, two miles west of the Cruach, had to wait some years, but it never lost its special place in the imagination. Much later still Fife opened Ardroy, its outdoor centre, at Lochgoilhead and, as County Adviser, I managed to stay there occasionally and renewed my love of this corner of Scotland. Ah, if only we could have west coast mountains with east coast weather!

After a morning rock climbing, a companion, Ian, and I had leave for the afternoon so we slipped off to go up Beinn Bheula. From Lettermay a forest road runs up the glen for a mile, then we broke out of the plantations (a silvicultural despond) to scramble up the burn coming down from Curra Lochain, a charming lochan in an old pass through to Strachur on Loch Fyne. The stream cascades down in a series of falls so we played Mr Bold and Mr Old on its greasy rocks. After inspecting the remains of a crashed aircraft we set our faces to the rough NE Ridge and the several schisty bumps that led to the summit. There we took a brief ease to look over the Delectable Mountains, till Ian pointed out that supper was being served in an hour's time. So we set ourselves for a sprint. We could see the sailing boats heading in to the centre, stowing sail and everyone rowing ashore. We just made supper.

Beinn Bheula is a good hill to have above an outdoor centre. It is a varied hill with plenty of complex ground, interesting corners, a rich flora and, as the highest peak in Cowal, a grand view over the woods and waters of the west. It has corries to east, south and west and clear-cut ridges. There are some caves on its NW spur, Carnoch Mor. Next time, however, I want to link it to Cruach nam Miseag, for old time's sake, descending to Coromonachan or Cuillimuich and on to Carrick Castle. There's so much I want to do before passing on, permanently, to Bheula land.

Section 2:   2. BEN DONICH   847 m   OS 56   218043

Section 2:   3. THE BRACK   884 m   OS 56   245031

Ben Donich and The Brack are hills I've climbed several times in several combinations and, as I can't decide which is best, I'll briefly summarise the route options. Few Corbetts are quite so accessible, for there is a northerly arc of road round them from Lochgoilhead to Coilessan on Loch Long and these places are linked by a footpath cutting across just south of the Corbetts.

The forestry have a road (not open to vehicles) all the way down Loch Long but it is only the branch up the Coilessan Glen which concerns the Corbetts. The southern end of the Ardgoil wedge between Loch Long and Loch Goil is known as Argyll's Bowling Green, a humorous touch which is quite accidental, for it is simply the murder of the Gaelic *Buaile na Greine* (sunny cattle fold) which originally applied to one place on the south east of the peninsula.

Ben Donich is in the rough form of a cross and the north, east and south ridges are all reasonable routes. It is a grassier hill than The Brack but there are some crags. Perhaps the North Ridge is the most satisfying in ascent (it is the shortest). I went up it the day after Beinn Bheula for this reason. The dog was not well and had to be left in the car and I wanted him to be at the vet's that afternoon. I found a convenient firebreak up on to the North Ridge from near the top of the Rest and Be Thankful, which also gave a 300-m start. It is pleasant to descend the South Ridge to Lochgoilhead because you are looking on to the sea and the village. Last time I counted over 100 boats on the loch.

My old friend W. K. Holmes, of *Tramping Scottish Hills*, once combined Beinn an Lochain and Ben Donich one sweltering summer day, and on the descent began having fantasies about being offered tea by a party he could see picnicking down in Glen Croe. The bright red and white frocks of the girls could even be seen but, alas, as he descended, the picnic party turned into a roadworkers' dump and the colourful frocks were only painted barrels!

The Brack, though lower and more compact, is rugged and has some real cliffs on its north flank and the hill is really very hemmed in by trees. One way to avoid them is to take the route up Coilessan Glen to gain the SW Ridge. If ascending on the Glen Croe side it is worth studying the breaks from the A83 before setting off. This is perhaps the most interesting route as you can see the cliffs on the way. Follow the forest road on the south bank of the Croe past Creagdhu and up the hill until, beyond a double bend, you can follow up the east bank of the burn descending from The Brack. The path from Lochgoilhead up by the Donich Water and on for Coilessan also allows access to the SW Ridge. Some of these routes have been signposted or marked by the Forestry Commission.

The two hills can be combined from either Lochgoilhead or Ardgartan. At the latter there is a camp site and a modern youth hostel right on the shore of Loch Long. The hostel has panoramic windows looking out to the loch, with The Cobbler seemingly peering over its roof. An early start makes for a pleasant walk up Glen Croe, on the forest roads, and then the old motor road which is still occasionally used for rallies. Look out for the Rest and Be Thankful stone on the pass. This also allows the peaks to be traversed in a "homeward" direction. An anti-clockwise circuit from Lochgoilhead is the easiest combination, descending Ben Donich's South Ridge and then making for the bridge over the River Goil. The peaks are nowhere difficult. All crags can easily be bypassed; but it is still typical Arrochar Alps country of lumps and bumps and false summits, which can be very confusing in mist. And if you want something different, you can always have a night out in "Cobbler View", a howff (shelter) under one of the big boulders which have crashed down from the precipice on The Brack (250036). The big gully in the cliffs is "Elephant Gully" which is "likely to appeal more to the botanist than the climber". Much of it is subterranean and the climber finally emerges through a hole on to the hillside, "the hole in the elephant's bottom" so to speak.

Section 2:   4. THE COBBLER (BEN ARTHUR)   884 m   OS 56
259058

The Cobbler was the first Corbett I ever climbed. It was one of the first hills of any sort I ever climbed. The peak has a stature and an allure far beyond mere lists. I had been up it many times before I knew what

"Munro" or "Corbett" meant. For a couple of years, as a young man, I lived in Paisley and having just acquired my first climbing rope — a new-fangled (fankled) nylon rope — it was hardly surprising that the Arrochar Alps in general and The Cobbler in particular became familiar and friendly ground. My introduction to The Cobbler was not so friendly.

Having cycled across Scotland to the old Ardgartan youth hostel (during schooldays) the sight of The Cobbler was too much for one reared on the couthy humps of the Ochils. (John Leyden said The Cobbler had "the appearance of a ruptured volcano", and Dorothy Wordsworth wrote, "the singular rocks on the summit were like ruins — castles or watch towers".) The bike was abandoned next day when I wandered along Glen Croe then angled up in a direct line for that weird jumble of crags. Above the trees I was on to soggy snow, which became something of an effort. An old photograph, sharper than my memory, shows a boy in short trousers leaning on a shepherd's crook, school scarf blowing in the wind.

The South Summit is a great hunk of crag and my route brought me face to face with it. Without much hesitation I began to wend up the crag but there was soon a new feel of nothing much below my feet and ever-steepening rock ahead. I did not like the thought of going on, but going back down was even more discouraging. It is a situation we all find ourselves in periodically — at least I hope so — the core of climbing lies in the balance of fear and frolic. My course of action was soon enough settled. I saw a brass plaque fixed to the rock and when I scrabbled over to it I read something about someone having fallen or died on that spot. "RIP".

The meaning of Rip eluded the young tyro, but I took the hint and slithered down and flanked up past the South Summit. It was separated by a distinct col and looked anything but easy. My eye traced hopeful lines, marked in snow, but I realised that descending it, unsighted, would have been a different matter. "Experience", as the French saying goes, "is the sum of near misses".

The shocks of the day were not over, for The Cobbler has a sting in its tail. Like the Inaccessible Pinnacle in Skye, though on a much reduced scale, the mountain top has a rocky (15-foot) protuberance which actually rears higher than the expected summit. In Pin and Cobbler require *climbing* to stand on their real tops. I looked at the frost-hoary, split hunk of schist with some surprise but had scrambled enough on rock to study it with practical hope. There was this great split in the top rock and by scrambling into that one could surely wriggle up and out on to the summit. The feasibility of this route depends on the body circumference of the assailant. It was no problem to a young lad but, ooh, it was cold on fingers and knees. My yell of glee was probably heard in Glasgow. My moans as I thawed out frozen fingers I kept to myself.

The easiest way up the final rock is to go right through the split and out the other side where an easy ledge curls up to give access to the top. The scramble is quite exposed and, like the Inaccessible Pinnacle, can frighten off the walker who has avoided all scrambling. In those cases a rope can be a most reassuring article of equipment. Later on it was roped climbs that brought us back again and again to that triptych of crags that can be seen so temptingly from Arrochar.

The name of the hill goes back some hundreds of years and supposedly derives from a fanciful picturing of the North Peak being the cobbler leaning over his last, the Central Peak, while his wife Jean, the South Peak, looks on. I've never heard it referred to as Ben Arthur. Being so close to Glasgow it became hallowed ground to those pioneers of the depression days who escaped to the hills. Jock Nimlin, John Cunningham and others were hero–names to me when I came to know it. Alistair Borthwick's classic book *Always a Little Further* has a chapter called "The Cave" which gives the feel of those days. The Arrochar Alps are riddled with caves. One I discovered by falling into it when what I thought was firm ground proved to be a hole covered with heather. Some of these places have been swallowed up by forest plantations but the popular route of access to The Cobbler up the Buttermilk Burn was diplomatically left clear and, if overgrown a bit, it is now a well trodden path.

The convex slope keeps The Cobbler hidden for a long time and its sudden appearance is a grand bit of mountain swank. The Narnain Boulders ("Shelter Stone" on the map) have seen generations of climbers sleeping under them and practising on them. Narnain is the Munro on the opposite side of the Buttermilk Burn to The Cobbler, and it, too, has plenty of climbing and scrambling interest. You can actually enter a rift in it and climb right through and out the other side of the hill. The Arrochar Alps were lure enough that, even when teaching in Fife, our school gangs would often be wending up the Allt a' Bhalachain towards The Cobbler.

If the South Summit is the hardest to climb, the North Summit is the most spectacular to be *on* for the top juts out in an overhanging prow of rock. The Cobbler has a good view to Ben Lomond and the waters of the Clyde. It is altogether a very fine mountain. What a lucky chance led a young boy to within sight of its dramatic profile.

Section 2:   5. BEINN LUIBHEAN   858 m   OS 56   243079
Hill of the little plant

Keeping some form of personal record is advisable for those busy
ticking off lists. One forgets otherwise. Some years ago I parked at
the Butterbridge end of the Rest and Be Thankful pass and traversed
Ben Ime to Narnain at the behest of my Munro-bagging dog Storm.
I then put in a claim for The Cobbler which doesn't have to be
anything to beguile visitors. It was crawling with people, being July,
so we soon headed off for the Bealach a' Mhaim. I then did a bit of
checking and realised Beinn Luibhean was a Corbett, so we diverted
to take it in as well. This is actually a satisfying round of four
interesting peaks and one I'd recommend. It was only later, checking
my record, that I discovered I'd already been up Beinn Luibhean a
decade earlier. Memory can be a fickle thing, for the previous visit
had obviously been as good, as I could tell from reading the log book
of the period. Hence my advocacy of keeping some form of report *at
the time.*

Nearly half of this Corbett's height has gone by the time one
drives up to the Rest and Be Thankful so it could be done in the same
day as Binnean an Fhidhleir (2:7) or Beinn an Lochain (2:6) or, if still
Munro-bagging, in the round mentioned above. That first visit saw
us lingering in Glasgow on the Saturday morning after a wild night
of storms but the thought of *seeing* The Cobbler in new snow took us
off up the familiar Loch Lomond road to Arrochar and, being that
distance, well, we might as well go up something. Beinn Ime is a
good old standby. We set off up the burn that edges the wood on the
NW flank of Luibhean (a path is now worn up it) with the new snow
rather heavy until we rose above the freezing level.

The four lads with me would benefit from a bit of responsibility so
I decided they could do Beinn Ime alone while I'd wander up Beinn
Luibhean (unaware of its Corbett status) from where I could keep an
eye on their progress. We parted after a snowball fight across the
burn. I went as directly up as I could, rather than by the Corbett's col
with Beinn Ime, so as to watch the others and also to use the NE
facing rocks for some sport. In those days one cut steps in snow and I
raised a good sweat hacking up a gully. There are only minor,
avoidable, crags on the Corbett. Some showers and spindrift came
and went but it was quite pleasant and I made a lazy descent down
the North Ridge. The tiny dots on Beinn Ime eventually made the
top — and vanished. (Thoughts of Mallory and Irvine!) The snow
fell more solidly as I went down by the wood, back to the

Dormobile. Half an hour later the lads swam in, "wet below the waist line" as one of them misquoted T. S. Eliot, and looking like snowmen, and in high glee at their winter climb of the biggest of the Arrochar Alps.

Our camp that night was rocked by storms and at some black hour we had to crawl out and tighten guy lines.

> "At two o'clock in the morning, if you open
> your window and listen,
> You will hear the feet of the wind that is
> going to call the sun."
>
> Kipling

Section 2: 6. BEINN AN LOCHAIN 901 m OS 56 218079
    The hill of the lake

As a deleted Munro, Beinn an Lochain has gone into eclipse but it always occupied something of a maverick position. I grew up with it being 2,992 feet on the One Inch map but 3,021 feet in Munro's *Tables*. The map's spot height was not the summit, and Munro & Co. enjoyed working it out with their aneroids and filling Notes pages of the *SMC Journal*. The 901 m given on the metric map *and* in the latest *Tables* is the real height, the OS assures me. It was a pleasant hill as a Munro, and remains such, despite the bureaucratic messing-about with altitudinal mathematics.

Having early connection with Carrick Castle has meant a lifetime of travelling over the Rest and Be Thankful: Beinn an Lochain has been climbed summer and winter, alone or with friends, and several times with school parties. It has character enough to be a proud part of the Arrochar Alps. The slightly concave east face above Loch Restil is what everyone sees and this, being craggy and broken, can give some good sport in winter when the greasy schist and wet gullies are all safely frozen. Walkers are advised to reach the summit by the ridges that bound this face, up the NE Ridge and down the South Ridge being the best combination. There is plenty of room to park at the head of the pass.

The NE Ridge is fairly broken by steps and crags and becomes narrower above the northern corrie (with its debris of a stupendous rockfall) then a succession of false summits leads eventually to the real one. There is a bird's eye view down Glen Croe with its twin roads and geometrical plantings, The Cobbler above and Ben Lomond beyond. Arran, Jura and the western seascape is of special interest, for the seaboard is arrayed more than usual. Any hill view has an extra satisfaction for "old hands"; one looks to *known* peaks and glens and islands where one has wandered the golden years away.

There are few problems descending southwards and once the cliff edge disappears there is just the big, steep skirt of grass to angle down back to the Rest and Be Thankful. If the day has hours left then there is always Beinn Luibhean across the road or Ben Donich across the other road.

Southey, on tour in 1819, gives a description remarkably straight-forward for the period. "Leaving the inn at Cairndow (Loch Fine) the road almost immediately begins to ascend Glenkenlas, a long, long ascent between green mountains sloping gradually from the stream which fills the bottom. On the right is a remarkable streak, or ridge, of large stones, appearing as if forced out like a torrent from a large hole in the hill above [the rockfall?]. The road turns to the right; the mountains green to the summit of the pass, and to their own summits also; and large loose crags are lying about in numbers, and in all directions. On the summit is a seat looking down Glencroe bearing the inscription 'Rest and Be Thankful'."

Section 2:   7. Binnein an Fhidhleir   817 m   OS 56/50   230109
              The fiddler's peak

This name is given to the peak that forms the central tower (811 m) of the battlement of hillside north of Glen Kinglas while the Corbett is nameless and 1½ km further east, above Butterbridge. Personally I feel this hijacking of any convenient neighbouring name should be avoided.

Glen Kinglas is a classic "glaciated trough" of a valley with both sides presenting continuously steep, wet, scraggy slopes which give little variety on any ascent. The views are restricted going up. I should imagine the summits give good views to Beinn Bhuidhe and the Lui group but on my single ascent it rained all the way up and the cloud was down on the tops. I bagged the Corbett only because I was there, wandering home after some good days on Islay and Jura. You can't win them all.

I just went up from Butterbridge to the Corbett and down again. Had the day been clear it might have been pleasant to walk along the ridge to the trig point on the lower summit, Binnein an Fhidhleir, or to wander in the other direction to the 597 top from which the complex of hydro roads and catchments for the Loch Sloy dam can be studied. Walking back down the upper Kinglas Water you pass Abyssinia. This slightly disappointing hill could be combined with

Beinn Luibhean and/or Beinn an Lochain to make a clean sweep of the Rest and Be Thankful Corbetts.

Years ago when acting as student courier to a bus-load of American sailors we stopped in Glen Kinglas to let the visitors see some Highland cows on the slopes of Binnein an Fhidhleir. Being assured they were safe, several lads walked up the hillside for photographs. Highlanders are docile, but nosey: they began to amble forward out of curiosity. The sailors stopped. The cows came on. The sailors retreated, the cows came on the faster. A minute later the rout was complete with the sailors splashing down in full flight with some excited cows lumbering after. I received no tips that day.

Section 2:   8. MEALL AN FHUDAIR   764 m   OS 50   271192
      Gunpowder hill

Meall an Fhudair was a return to normality, the first week home after a ski holiday under the array of the Eiger and Jungfrau when we had days of the deepest powder snow I've ever tried to drown myself in. The very day of returning I was off to Fife's outdoor centre at Lochgoilhead instructing potential leaders, some of whom were old friends anyway. Seven of us had a day on Meall an Fhudair as part of the training. Surprise, surprise, it was a Corbett I had not been up before. Perhaps because it was such a contrast, my memories of the day are very clear.

If the Alps impressed with their bigness and grandeur, the home delights lay in a host of little things: the daffodils in flower at Inverarnan, or the brace of mallard which kept complaining up the burn ahead of us, or the pheasant that exploded from our feet in a shower of feathers (feathers with the most jewel-like markings), or the tang of spring gale, or the view across Glen Falloch to the Ben Glas Falls — a whisper at that distance and so white against the tawny slopes of winter-colouring. We followed the Allt Arnan, a cheery, tumbling burn with one worthy waterfall and a score of splendid pools. As the water level was low we scrambled up on the rocks wherever possible, always good training for several skills.

Over a lip we joined a hydro road which ended at a small dam half a mile further up the Allt Arnan. The dam was simply an intake — presumably the water is piped west over the watershed to the reservoir that has drowned most of the Allt na Lairige Glen. This name *stream of the pass* indicates an ancient regular route and it is in fact the easiest line from the north end of Loch Lomond through to Glen Fyne and the sea. The slopes of Troisgeach have peculiar rocky, lumpy ribs, but rather than go up straight away we followed our burn to its source in a round lochan just below the spongy watershed. After a snack we headed up for Meall an Fhudair, scrambling on such rock as lay in our path. We spent forty minutes on top hoping for a view but the clouds would not roll away. The grandstand view of the Arrochar Alps, Lui and Beinn Bhuidhe is actually recommended in the *SMC Guide*. While the rest headed down for Glen Fyne, one lad and I, perforce, returned to Inverarnan for the minibus.

East of Meall an Fhudair is a col with an odd proliferation of tiny pools and lochans. There must have been several dozen, far more than can be shown on the 1:50,000 map. We explored them in the passing and grudgingly angled down off the hill. There is a sudden delightful change of view when the lip of the Loch Lomond trench is reached; eyes are suddenly held by the downward richness, a vivid contrast to the sterile heights. There was plenty of expected fauna on the descent: ptarmigan, deer, hares, a mountain blackbird, grouse and the first wagtail of the season. After a brew we drove over the Rest and Be Thankful and met the others at the foot of Glen Fyne. They arrived just as the kettle began to sing.

Section 2:   9. BEINN A' CHOIN   770 m   OS 56/50   354130
            Hill of the dogs (or hounds)

Beinn a' Choin is the peak that dominates the Rob Roy country. It is now well moated by Loch Lomond, Loch Arklet and Loch Katrine, but the last two have been much enlarged by dams (Glasgow's water supply) so the scenery has altered considerably since Rob Roy's day. It was a much wilder landscape then, with more trees and deeper heather, and many more people. About 150 people lived between Loch Katrine and Loch Lomond, for example. The landscape, which we take so much for granted, has a long and continuing history of change. Sadly much of it has been exploited, and the Highlands are now a dying waste of wet desert. Man, supposedly the most intelligent being of all creation, is the only one that cannot live at peace in his niche. Poor world, when we have gobbled it up entirely . . .

These were some of my cheerless thoughts as I left the Dormobile at six in the morning to follow the Snaid Burn up from Garrison of Inversnaid. "Garrison" points to the days of a military presence trying to tame the unruly MacGregors. Rob Roy married his Mary at Corriearklet and had houses in Glen Gyle as well as in the glens to the north. Glen Gyle was quite an important through-route for cattle (legally or otherwise), from Glen Falloch and further west, leading to Strathyre and Crieff.

A heavy shower had me sheltering in the tree-clad gorge of the Snaid but the midges poured out to make a meal of me so I carried on, up the burn by Stob an Fhainne (peak of the Fianna, those mythical Celtic warriors of both Irish and Scottish folklore). The going was soft. The rain was hard. It was disgustingly hot and in the end I stripped to my Y-fronts and just got wet. The rain was quite enjoyable.

A fence runs from Stob an Fhainne to Beinn a' Choin, which was useful as the final cone was in cloud. "Moundy, rough hills", Rennie McOwan calls them. I was less polite. Dog or hound occurs in the name of quite a few hills. This often harks back to the Fianna, who were great hunters, but it can also imply a place where hounds were kennelled for hunting either deer or men — MacGregors as like as not. Either could apply here, I feel.

Across Glen Gyle is a pass with the cheery name Bealach nan Corp, *the pass of the dead*. This was the route taken by MacGregors on their last journeys. (Everyone wanted to be buried on home territory.) The outlawed clan were called "the children of mist". In this wild country with its maze of passes they were never easy to control.

At the summit I ate the one marmalade sandwich which had not become soggy and threw the rest away. Within a minute gulls had appeared through the cloud and were squabbling over their booty. How did they know it was there? They followed me down the hill, grabbing and dropping my apple core in turn before squawking off in disgust.

Given a better day I might have circled to Maol Mor above Loch Katrine which is an even better viewpoint than the Corbett, itself "a magnificent viewpoint" (McOwan). The Arrochar Alps, the Ben Lui group, the Crianlarich hills, Ben Lomond, an inner ring of Corbetts and the various lochs certainly give the view character, but I wrote that evening, "It's the jumbled, shut-in, lumpy, grassy, scabby sort of country that lies across Scotland's midriff — not a patch on the country out in 'the golden remote wild west'." It does not seem to have been the cheeriest of ascents. Was it the rain? Was it me? Was it the background of those old unhappy doings of long ago?

Beinn a' Choin is rather remote, even with a vehicle. The motor approach is by Aberfoyle (not by Loch Katrine) and the road is narrow and slow-going. You can also walk over from Inverarnan in Glen Falloch, up by the Ben Glas Burn and then south by spiky Ben Ducteach and several more "moundy rough hills". Another way would be to take the passenger ferry across Loch Lomond to

Inversnaid. This is signposted and you may have to signal to the other side of the loch for the wee boat to come and fetch you. Many early travellers came this way: James Hogg in 1803, Robert Southey in 1819, the Wordsworths and Coleridge in 1803. With a poor road system, boats and ferries plied everywhere.

James Hogg, as a shepherd, came through these glens several times and in a letter to Sir Walter Scott in 1803 gave some reminiscences of his herding days. A fog once caught them and they spent the night on the hill (probably Maol Mor rather than Beinn a' Choin) waking to a stunning fresh, clear morning. "Loch Katrine with its surrounding scenery stretching from one hand, Loch Lomond on the other. The outline of Ben Lomond appeared to particular advantage, as did the cluster of monstrous pyramids [the Arrochar Alps] on the other side. One hill, in Strathfillan, called Ben Leo [Laoigh] was belted with snow, with a particularly sharp, peaked appearance of a prodigious height.

"Besides all this I had drunk some whisky the preceding evening and had a very indistinct recollection of our approach to that place, and it was actually a good while ere I was persuaded that everything I saw was real. I sat about an hour contemplating the scenes with the greatest pleasure before I awakened my comrade."

The Ettrick Shepherd slept on the same spot twelve years later, "to experience the same delightful feelings", but woke instead to hideous yellings and, throwing off his plaid, found four eagles circling over him. "Go away! I'm not dead yet!" was his reaction.

Section 2:   10. STOB A' CHOIN   865   OS 56   416161
             Dog peak

Section 2:   11. CEANN NA BAINTIGHEARNA   771   OS 57   474163
             Her ladyship's head

There is a fine mountainous area between the Trossachs and the Loch Voil valley which offers good cross-country routes and hill wanderings. Stob a' Choin would be a notable peak were it not so hidden away, and Baintighearna lies in pleasant surroundings. Baintighearna is a convenience name; it really applies to the rocky bluff overlooking Loch Doine and not to the Corbett which, like so many hills, is left nameless by the Ordnance Survey. (Pleas to the OS to name all Munros, etc., fall on deaf ears, but presumably local shepherds have names if the OS cared to enquire.)

With Storm keen to do Corbetts I set out to link these two, a combination which had once before given me a solitary tramp; but the traverse is one where a friendly driver is an advantage. I drove up to the car park before Inverlochlarig intending to leave the push bike, then return eastwards and up to Ballimore in Glen Buckie to start the traverse. However, I realised there was a stiff pull up to Ballimore, and the lochside road was a bit of a switchback: too much "push" for the bike at the day's end. It was also a "bright and beautiful" summer morning which would probably cloud over all too soon. We set off for Stob a' Choin there and then.

The hill thrusts up boldly in a surge of green, with plenty of crags to give it some detail, a knobbliness so typical of the area. The crags are all very obvious and can be avoided and the rocky summit is perfectly easy. More care is needed in descent; the Stob is very much a hill for a day of clear visibility, not only as an aid to safe navigation but to relish the summit panorama. "It is a hill with splendid views", says Rennie McOwan in his *Walks in the Trossachs and Rob Roy Country*, a book covering much of Section 2 and giving interesting historical notes as well as routes of all grades.

There has been a great deal of bulldozing of roads in the area so the Second Series map is useful. There is a road right along (through the middle of the plantations) on the south side of Loch Voil and Loch Doine, and from the bridge over the main river near the car park/picnic place tracks radiate up and round under Stob Breac to the Invernenty glen and westwards towards Stob a' Choin. From Inverlochlarig a track runs up the main valley westwards for four miles. The bridge over the main river, a mile from the farm, is worth remembering but normally the river can be crossed anywhere.

We crossed the bridge near the car park and, from Blaircreach with its clumps of conifers, puffed our way up the lower part of the bold NE Ridge of the Corbett. This, strictly speaking, leads to an eastern top, itself knobbly and with a deal of ups and downs leading to the summit. We cut round into the hollow north side of the mountain: Coire an Laoigh, *the corrie of the calves*, presumably once a favourite deer-calving ground for the area, is now heavily under sheep. We came out at the bealach below the final cone of the Corbett. What an unrelenting ascent — and what a rewarding view, with a gathering of Clan Munro to west and north!

The whole area reeks of real clan history. In the popular imagination it is Rob Roy Country. He was born at Glengyle, lived at Inverlochlarig amongst other places and is buried at Balquhidder. The valleys are full of ruins pointing to a heavy population not so long ago. Glen Gyle to the south was an historic droving route, which also meant reiving and military use as well. Loch Katrine is now the jealous property of Glasgow Corporation who apply a no-go policy to its shores — while they ply a tourist boat on the super-hygienic waters. However one can cycle (or walk) along from the Trossachs public road end, and Stob a' Choin and Ceann na Baintighearna could easily be done from the south.

The Bealach nan Corp (that is known as the *pass of the corpses*) further west was the funeral route into the Lochlarig Glen. The Allt a' Choin, lower in height, leads up to a boggy pass. The Invernenty Glen was used, however, and the Glen Buckie–Glen Finglas link was an important one. Scott, with his *Lady of the Lake* and *Rob Roy*, virtually set the Scottish tourist industry in motion and the Trossachs still buzz in summer. The hills, however, are strangely empty. Back at the car park (now full of cars) there were three parties setting off. Yes, they all agreed, Stob a' Choin was the finest peak in view, but they all streamed off for the Munros to the north — so well seen *from* the Corbett.

We had descended by Coire an Laoigh and boulder-hopped across to the road down to Inverlochlarig. A curlew patrolled overhead, wailing, and young wheatears flitted among the stones. Storm walked through a flock of sheep on the road without paying them any attention, which rather silenced a potential salvo from a shepherd. We had a "crack" instead. They are, perhaps justly, a bit anti-dog for so many visitors bring untrained beasts and let them run uncontrolled. Litter and vandalism were other complaints. I find it surprising (and sad) that the yobbo element is found even among hillgoers. Surely we go to the hills to escape the frustrating urban world, not to bring its attributes and attitudes with us. A quick coffee and we drove back along the lochs to Balquhidder, branched off across the charming old bridge over the loch's outflow and so up Glen Buckie to Ballimore where the Calair Burn runs under another stone span. Just across the bridge is a sign pointing out the right-of-way to Brig o' Turk and the Trossachs.

Glen Buckie is a pleasing corner. The glen is well wooded lower down, has tree-girt pastures round the farms of Ballimore and Immeroin (the only lived-in centres now) and wide sheep-ranges running to its head. Beinn an t-Sidhein (*fairy hill*) and Ben Vane enclose the valley but the major drainage, the Calair Burn, breaks in from the west at Ballimore, its waters fed by the two burns which clasp the eastern aspects of our second Corbett, Ceann na Baintighearna. The view, as one follows the damp path, is to the big ridge descending from the Corbett and separating the Fathan Glen and Gleann Dubh. The extreme northern end of Ben Vane's ridge is a succession of bumps, and Bealach a' Chonnaidh across the lowest gap suggests that the old route cut over there rather than up the wetter valley. The Brig o' Turk path rounds this spur of Ben Vane and runs up to an easy col under Ben Vane itself. The turning was a superb viewpoint, looking over a wide basin, full of free-ranging cattle and a fold of bleating sheep, with Stobinian's characteristic lopped-off summit cone through the gap beyond. The day had clouded over but the afternoon, instead of rain, gave periodic breaks, so sun, showers, clouds, wind and midges came along in a random succession. At times the weather changed quicker than I could unpack a camera to photograph some effect.

Having chased the view round the end of the hill there seemed so little distance to the col that we went up to view the other side (a bulldozed track and a sprawl of reservoir has rather changed the descent route) and from there Ben Vane looked so near that we went up it too. A Corbett at hand is worth two in the book.

The haul up grassy Ben Vane coincided with a sunny spell and was quite a toil. We met a couple of people on top. "Corbett? What's that?" showed they were just normal (sane) visitors. The Stuc a' Chroin–Beinn Each ridge across Loch Lubnaig, and the ridge from Ben Vane to Ben Ledi, looked equally jagged and rough — both excellent traverses. Back at the pass we contoured as much as possible (some bog, some heather) to gain Gleann Dubh which we circled between steep upper flanks and the heathery glen bottom. Dubh is *black*, or *dark*, and in the general green-ness of these hills the heather of the glen does appear dark. ("Glen Dubh" on the map can often be a warning of rough going due to bog and/or heather.)

The Corbett has a trig point even if it does not have a name. A spell of clouds on the *dubh* side of safety (drum rolls of thunder) had us scurrying off fast, dog panting and unhappy. He dislikes thunder and I only enjoy it from safer — lower — altitudes. We descended the big East Ridge but then cut over to pick up the Brig o' Turk path at the viewing corner. It cleared again for the photographs I wanted. Rather than return down the valley we went up to the Bealach a' Chonnaidh. A kestrel perched on a crag decorated with natural *bonsai*. We followed a sheep path along to look down on Glen Buckie. North of Calair Burn the fields were dotted with red deer. They are "farmed" along with the usual sheep and cows.

An alternative recommended route for this Corbett is to start at Balquhidder, cross the bridge and go along past Stronvar (once a youth hostel) and Muirlaggan, then take a path or rake up to the Bealach Driseach to reach the Corbett from the upper Fathan Glen, returning down Gleann Dubh and Glen Buckie. On a winter traverse of the pair I started and finished at Inverlochlarig (no car park then), descending west off Baintighearna down a burn of spring cascades to the Invernenty Burn. That was a very windy trip and my original high camp on Stob a' Choin had to be abandoned and a sheltered nook found at the head of Glen Sgionie. South of Stob a' Choin is the country described in John Barrington's *Red Sky at Night* (Pan Books), an idealistic description of the life of a shepherd.

Section 2:   12. BENVANE   821 m   OS 57   535137
                   White hill

Section 2:   13. BEN LEDI   879 m   OS 57   562098
                   Hill of the gentle slope or *God's Hill*

"Ben Ledi is prominent from Stirling and imposing from Callander", someone wrote at the turn of the century. One wonders what the pioneers would have thought of the view of Ben Ledi from Callander introducing a long-running telly soap opera as it did for *Doctor Finlay's Casebook*? The comment is still true, however, and every time I drive over the hill road from Stirling to Doune I experience a lifting of the heart as Ben Ledi rears ahead, first of the hills beyond the Highland line.

Benvane is a much more retiring hill but, as Rennie McOwan declares, "it therefore has views far more striking than many a higher hill". I find Benvane the more friendly with its green and open northern aspects rising above cheery Glen Buckie while Ben Ledi has been strangled with dank forestry plantings (through which glutinous paths have been gouged) and dotted with grim names like "loch of the corpse", and Stank Glen and the like. I've been up them both by various routes but a traverse of the pair gave me the best day and is the outing I'd recommend for the walker.

Ben Ledi used to be most often climbed from the south but farming on the lower slopes has switched the popular lines to the east flanks: paths go up from the Bridge over the Leny and via Stank Glen. These have had a great deal of use and are in a sorry state. Commission policy chops and changes and waymarking has recently been removed to try and ease the pressure. I think, now, I'd start at Brig o' Turk and wander up to the Glen Finglas reservoir and tackle Ben Ledi from the west. However, on my traverse I went up the Stank Glen (the name comes from the Gaelic *stang*, meaning pool) and had quite an obstacle course as a storm a few years before had flattened many trees. Since then new roads have appeared and the forest has been cleared. The route lies up the south bank of the burn. There are some falls worth seeing but my main memory was of the "Seven Boulders" which lie about the slopes above the treeline. These have some historic howffs and offer sport for the rock climber. I spent half an hour scrambling on the first of them but then realised time was going all too fast so I pushed on for the ragged skyline. The boulders are up left when you escape the trees and a burn leads on to a high, secretive corrie which is another fine feature: a real cauldron of snow on my March day.

It was barely freezing and too hazy for extensive views. One of the tentative derivations of the hill's name is *mountain of God* which perhaps harks back to pagan ceremonies once held on the summit. All round this region the hearth fires were allowed to go out before midnight at the end of April and, on the first day of May, the Celtic New Year, they were renewed with flames kindled in the Beltane fires on top of Ben Ledi. There was feasting, with weird rites and ceremonies, and despite Christian overlayers something of this lingers in the bonfires and May Day ascents of hills even now. Dominating several passes into the Highlands, Ben Ledi is also a natural site for forts — as Dunmore and Bochastle show, the former perhaps Pictish, the latter a Roman outpost.

Lochan nan Corp, by the low point on the switchback traverse to Benvane, commemorates a drowning tragedy at a funeral party. There were some quite dramatic "coffin roads" in the old days: the route to St Bride's Chapel at the south end of Loch Lubnaig was probably their destination, this being the Mackinlay burial ground (one of that scattered clan became president of the USA). Having toiled up Gleann Casaig the bearers laid their burden on the ice of the lochan — which promptly broke under them, with considerable loss of life. I made sure of seeing the lochan but it was black water and only fringed with a wreath of ice.

Loch Lubnaig means the *crooked loch* in the sense of *loch with a kink in it* and Ardnandave Hill makes the bold thrust that creates this feature. The hill dominates the loch much more than the terminal big hills, and grumpy Maccullough, loquacious Sir Walter, the willing Words-worths and plenty of others have all (rightly) commended the view. Having walked *north* to this fulcrum top I turned almost *west* for the continuation to Benvane. It too had a small hidden snow bowl of a corrie near the summit. Ben More and Stobinian were boldly white against a blackening sky. Night and storm were probably on a collision course. I turned down eastwards to the watershed between Glen Buckie and Loch Lubnaig.

You could not do so now; new trees wash well up below Benvane's north east slopes. But you can descend to Creag a' Mhadaidh (*the fox's crag*) and then down the grassy slopes to the old shielings at the head of Glen Buckie, or simply keep to the ridge as far as fancy leads. There are grand views down Glen Buckie. A car can get up to the big farm of Ballimore (*the big township*) which, with Immeroin across the glen, is a survivor of the several "farm-touns" or hamlets in Glen Buckie. So far they have not been swallowed by trees. Brig o' Turk to Ballimore I reckon is now the most attractive traverse.

Above Glen Buckie on the other side is Beinn an t-Sidhein which dominates Strathyre. A path straggles up through the trees to cross its southern shoulders and on down to Immeroin. On one ferociously wet meet of the Scottish Mountaineering Club a party of us crossed this col and back by Balquhidder with evergreen Tom Weir, the then President, setting a cracking pace.

I mentioned Maccullough earlier. He found Ben Ledi rather lacking in charm, writing, "I thought that I had known Highland rain in all its forms and mixtures and varieties in Skye, Mull, Shetland, Fort William, Lawers, Glencoe, but nothing like the rain on Ben Ledi did I ever behold, before or since." His tomes of travel were addressed to Sir Walter Scott and he did not hesitate to take the poet to task, wishing he had laid the "venue" of his "Lady of the Lake" in St Kilda or the wilds of Ross-shire because of the clanjamfray of tourists the work had let loose about the place. What would he make of today's clanjamfray?

My traverse had been made at the end of another SMC Meet. Before dining the previous night in the New Inn at Strathyre I'd taken my push-bike high up a forest road to leave it near the watershed under Benvane, whence we made our way after dealing with one electric fence, and one barbed-wire fence which was decorated with the stinking head of a long-dead fox (Creag a' Mhadaidh was not far above!). The dog went into my rucksack and we whizzed down to loch level. Caulfeild, Wade's successor, had built his military road west of Loch Lubnaig, a line which was also taken by the railway. Axed in the Beeching days, it has reverted to being a road, which was a joy to cycle, in quietness, dodging the frozen dubs, while across the loch came the mosquito drone of holiday traffic.

Callander was busy as a hive but I called in to the chip shop and bore off a supper to eat on the hill road where I could sit and look at that vast panorama of the Highlands, with Ben Ledi boldest of all. The dark colours of the hill reached up into darker clouds, shot through with angry reds, which flared, like a fire, and stuttered out, like dying coals, into night. If Ben Ledi was "prominent from Stirling and imposing from Callander", from half way between the view that evening had a brush with perfection.

Section 2:   14. BEINN EACH   813 m   OS 57   602158
              Horse hill

Section 2:   15. MEALL NA FEARNA   809 m   OS 57   651186
              Alder hill

Beinn Each is a recent entry to Corbett's list and, though still 811 m on the map, the OS assures me it is 813 m in reality. I describe it together with Meall na Fearna because by linking them over the intervening Munros you can have "a splendid day's sport", which means a long, hard but satisfying day's tramp. It was only a few months ago I did this myself, up till then these hills had been visited in various other combinations.

A quarter of a century ago Sam and I, on 27 January, had a frost-touched, river-steaming camp at Strathyre and traversed Beinn Each and Stuc a' Chroin in very icy conditions. A year later, on 27 January, Sam and I with several other friends traversed right on to Ben Vorlich. The next winter the Stuc became my first Munro on skis — and my third *day* on skis. In all I've been on these hills with a score of different friends so there were memories at many places during the recent solitary traverse, made from the head of Glen Artney.

Beinn Each is no great distance from Loch Lubnaig at Ardchullarie More from where a right-of-way goes over and down Glen Ample, but Glen Ample has been given over to massed conifers and thereby loses a great deal. (It was at Ardchullarie that the great explorer James Bruce wrote the story of his travels, having been branded a mountebank by a sceptical press. "Cutting steaks from live cows — ridiculous!" Yet this had occurred in the Highlands not so long before never mind in Ethiopia.) Trees also swarm over the ridge above Loch Lubnaig to fill the Allt Breac-nic corrie south of the Corbett therefore, if heading for the Keltnie, descend the long SE Ridge, a ridge, incidentally quite devoid of anything calling for the crag symbols so generously given on the First Series map. Cars can be driven up from Callander to the end of the tarmac near Braeleny, a useful gain in height, and another alternative approach. The oddly artificial-looking Bracklinn Falls are worth a diversion en route. This rough road goes on to sheep sheds at Arivurichardich (what a resonant name!) from where another rougher road contours round under Tom Odhar to link with the Glen Artney estate road.

Meall na Fearna is basically reached either by Glen Vorlich or by Glen Artney, the latter providing the better combination with the other hills. On driving out of Comrie follow the Braco, then the Cultybraggan Camp signs to gain the road up Glen Artney. A parking place has been left below the small, plain, attractive church up on its knoll, but the tarred road goes on up to the bridge over the Ruchil Water. In summer the glen has a green lushness, a contrast to the heathery northern flanks. The underlying schisty rock creates this richness. It is very much sheep country with free-ranging cows, too, and deer up in the wilder fastnesses. Sir Walter Scott's picture of Glen Artney is highly romantic.

As one follows the estate road up Monadh Odhar the Lodge looks very attractive. What a view it has, down the glen especially! The long ridge running from Meall na Fearna to Glenartney Lodge effectively shuts out all views of the Munros/Corbetts till the Monadh Odhar is passed. (The crest of this ridge is all peat hags, not crags.) Several white garrons came cantering over to Storm and me on top of the rise. The summits were cloud-covered but the whole visible landscape was bright with summer green.

The road twists down, upstream rather than as shown in the First Series map (where a shelter belt of trees has been planted across the river), crosses a sturdy bridge and wends on towards Arivurichardich. We followed track then path up Gleann an Dubh Choirein. The *black corrie* of the name is the one between the Munros, dark with peat hags and crumbling crags, but the path leaves the ruined sheilings at the junction to go on up to the Bealach Dearg (*the red pass*) between Vorlich and Fearna. The pass is reputedly haunted by a ghostly piper and the way the wind was shrilling through it for us one could well imagine weird music not of this world.

Storm and I followed a side stream which led up to the summit of Meall na Fearna with the minimum of bogs. We even managed to stalk some hinds and young calves to about twenty yards but one climbed up on a hag and would soon see us so I stood up and fired, hopefully in that brief moment when they froze in surprise, before galloping off. For once I had the right lens on. I've so many pictures of distant, bobbing caudal patches!

We were below the rip of cloud with the "big top" crest of Ben Vorlich invisible. The flank below the cloud level looked quite formidable, face on. It is steep, too, but by cutting across a bit below the Bealach Dearg and traversing I was able to cut up on to the SE Ridge fairly easily. Blasting rain made for an uncongenial summit. We fled the stark trig point. The welcome snack had to wait till down on the col. Rocky steps led up to what appears a difficult buttress on the Stuc but a path is now well marked up it. For interest I went left and after botanising in a tumble of boulders climbed straight up. The Stuc *is* craggy but Vorlich by no means deserves the crag symbols given to it on the map.

The weather kept hinting at clearances (it was probably quite a pleasant day at valley level) and slowly eased as we followed the many contortions of the zigzag ridge to Beinn Each. There is a connecting fence (ruinous) to help in misty conditions. We tried various outflankings but these seldom paid off (knobbly ridges usually prove easiest along a crest and the final bold thrust leaves only the one option of up). The cloud cleared to give partial views. With the white racing overhead and the dark shadows sprinting over the hill slopes there was the odd sensation that it was Beinn Each that was moving, that Ben Ledi and Benvane, Baintighearna, Ben More and Stobinian were charging at us on some Valkyrian steeplechase.

From the col beyond we descended into Coire nan Saighead (*corrie of the arrows*) but turned out of it to pick up the lie of the land down into the valley. We crossed the burn, as the far side looked less marshy, and to obtain photos back up to the Corbett. Somehow we drifted up the hillside so just went on to cross the old pass of Meall na h-Iolaire (*the bump of the eagles*), part of the Callander–Glen Vorlich–Loch Earn route. We cringed in the lee of one of the decayed peat hags but were rewarded in the end with views both to Each and to Fearna. The eastern slope of the pass spills down in an extraordinary scattering of bog bergs. We rimmed the bumps of the col and angled down to another new sturdy bridge a mile up from the foot of the glen. The legs just began to feel the last miles of tarmac but roadside raspberries, a *white* scabious and grass of Parnassus gave excuses to stop. It had been quite a long day after all. Our brew at the car was abandoned (till we drove a mile down the road) for the car was invaded by dozens of wasps.

When Sam and I had tackled Beinn Each we had gone over the ridge to reach Glen Ample (pre-plantation days), a route that had been followed by Naismith and Thomson on New Year's Day 1894. They came off the morning train, then traversed Vorlich, the Stuc and Beinn Each to descend the Keltnie road to Callander where they reached the station with five minutes in hand for the evening train. Plumb (*Walking in the Grampians*) mentioned staying at Ardvorlich House and drove from there to Callander. When the party was ready to leave again they found their collie had vanished, but by the time they drove the sixteen miles round the dog was home before them —

via the Keltnie, over the Eagles col and through the Bealach Dearg. Beinn Each was to prove Charles's last Corbett, achieved on a flying visit from Sheffield via Dunoon. Horse Hill, for the end of such a gallop, seems appropriate.

LOCH ETIVE, GLEN ORCHY & AUCH

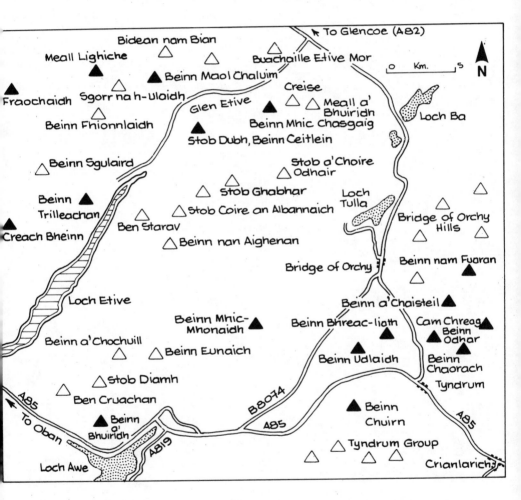

To Glencoe (A82)

Bidean nam Bian

Meall Lighiche

Buachaille Etive Mor

O Km. 5

N

Fraochaidh

Sgorr na h-Uloidh

Beinn Maol Chaluim

Creise

Meall a'
Bhuiridh

Loch Ba

Beinn Fhionnlaidh

Glen Etive

Beinn Mhic Chasgaig

Stob Dubh, Beinn Ceitlein

Beinn Sgulaird

Stob a'Choire
Odhair

Beinn
Trilleachan

Stob Ghabhar

Loch
Tulla

Stob Coire an Albannaich

Bridge of Orchy
Hills

Creach Bheinn

Ben Starav

Beinn nan Aighenan

Bridge of Orchy

Beinn nam Fuaran

Loch Etive

Beinn a'Chaisteil

Beinn Mhic-
Mhonaidh

Beinn Bhreac-liath

Cam Chreag
Beinn
Odhar

Beinn a'Chochuill

Beinn Eunaich

Beinn Udlaidh

Beinn
Chaorach

Tyndrum

Stob Diamh

B8074

Ben Cruachan

A85

Beinn Chuirn

A85

To Oban

Beinn
a'
Bhuiridh

A819

A85

Tyndrum Group

Crianlarich

Loch Awe

BEINN A' BHUIRIDH is on the natural circuit of the grand Cruachan ridge traverse though I must admit to having missed it out on several occasions and when eventually I climbed the hill I was really engaged on other business. But "because it was there", at the end of a sweltering summer's day the summit was a good place to put the day to bed.

The story of that day is fully told in *Hamish's Mountain Walk*: the second of the 112 days spent walking over all the Munros. The day began on the far side of Mull but it ended with a camp high on this Corbett, which made it rather special. Beinn a' Bhuiridh is quite a distinctive hill in its own right, however overshadowed by the Cruachan Munros, and sticks up boldly in the view from the Strath of Orchy and Dalmally. I'd perforce walked up the Hydro road to the shapely dam as my bike was left at a house by St Conan's Church near where the road starts. St Conan's, a church I always find fascinating, had to be revisited. The heat was intolerable and every trickle of water gave the chance of a drink. I took several rests to gaze down Loch Awe. Loch Ness and Loch Lomond may be bigger but Loch Awe is the longest loch in Scotland. The view was clear right down to New York.

A stream comes down from the Larig (*sic*) Torran which separates the Corbett from the Munros and was welcome for its glorious shade. I splashed in it with the gusto of a dipper, then followed up beside the burn to pitch the tent just below the col. "Lairig" usually points to historical use as a pass and Wallace reputedly used this pass to outflank the men of Lorn holding the Pass of Brander. Cattle crossed it to graze in the basin now filled by the Cruachan Reservoir. My side of the pass was comparatively gentle; the eastern side, Coire Ghlais, is much wilder, with bands of cliff on which the early stalwarts of the SMC found the exercise they wanted. I wonder if much climbing is done on these cliffs in winter now?

After setting up the tent and downing several mugs of tea I wended up to the top of Beinn a' Bhuiridh. The summit was all lumps and bumps and scattered melt-water pools. Sunset strode in and the burnished loch soon turned to lead-grey, leaving the world raw and chill. A lone *feadag* (plover) was calling.

The most satisfying route up Beinn a' Bhuiridh is over Monadh Driseig, starting from opposite Kilchurn Castle. Loch Awe is always in view, the Laoigh group shows well and one looks up Glen Strae's trench. Coire Ghlais is also an interesting approach and, if heading towards it, one can utilise a track (once a mineral line) which contours round to the abandoned lead-workings from where a path of sorts leads to the Allt Coire Ghlais–Allt Coire Chaorainn confluence. If a full round of the Cruachan ridges is undertaken the starting and finishing point will probably be the Falls of Cruachan car park. There is a path up the west bank of the burn to the dam. A trip to the underground power station is an unusual extra for a visit to these hills. There is an interesting Hydro display in the visitor centre.

Section 3:   2. BEINN CHUIRN   880 m   OS 50   281292
         Cairn hill

With Ben Lui so near I thought there would be something in old *SMC Journals* about Beinn Chuirn (it is not infrequently taken for Ben Lui by people motoring west along Strath Fillan), but the volumes were silent on Lui's little look-alike. Beinn Chuirn gave me a good return to the hills of home after a summer in Norway.

I'd driven up and found a quiet spot for the van on the old road to Cononish, a site which was a favourite until plantings and locked gates and new tracks changed everything. There was a semi-permanent caravan nearby and its old, bearded owner spent his days panning for gold. He showed me the month's haul. Four poachers arrived in the moonlight and spread their blankets by a wood fire. The cold night led to a breathless, sharp, clear dawn, making an early start a joy in itself.

The hour up to Cononish always seems long and my old dog Kitchy was very slow. I put this down to lack of exercise but later discovered he was not very well — for which a traverse of Beinn Chiurn and Ben Lui was hardly a rest cure. We took the burn that comes down by the farm and followed it, then cut the corner, to reach the steep wee corrie on the east face. A slot of a gully to the left and a top rim of cliffs looked as if they could offer some winter sport. The corrie offered ripe blaeberries which I ate while the midges ate me. The summit has quite a big flat area and when we popped out on to it the dog gave tongue as if to say "Thank goodness that's over". I gave a yelp, too, for in a sudden revelation there was a tone-poem view of Cruachan in the west, rising from a sea of cloud.

I'd chosen my route upwards to explore that eastern corrie but most walkers would find it pleasanter to ascend by the gorge of the Eas Anie, which yields a succession of waterfalls, one of them big and impressive. A path to the old mines and on up the SE Ridge makes for quite easy going. This mine was opened in 1739 — the story of mining at Tyndrum is worth reading. At the time of the Forty-Five an English contractor, Sir Robert Clifton, had leased the mineral rights and had done quite well. He, strangely, was a Jacobite and the Argyll militia took the opportunity to sabotage his works. The Mine Adventurers of England carried on till 1760, then, after various changes (take-overs are nothing new), the Scots Mining Company acquired it and built smelting works near Tyndrum rather than sailing the ore down Loch Lomond to the Clyde. By the end of the century the prosperity had gone. The second Marquis of Breadalbane made a costly gamble rather than any fortune. The last lead extracted was in 1923. V. A. Firsoff's invaluable book *In the Hills of Breadalbane* has several pages about the Tyndrum mines.

In the autumn of 1987 an exploration company (which had already spent £250,000) was making hopeful noises about the findings of their two drills operating on Beinn Chuirn. Who knows, we may yet have a Corbett with a productive gold mine on its slopes.

Kitchy and I wandered over to the 773-m bump, and the casual nature of the day went when we saw how deep a drop led to the Allt an Rudd and how much of Lui there was beyond to be climbed. Black cherry jam pieces on Lui's summit rewarded the hot toil up. It was another six years before I was on top of Lui again and on that visit I also had black cherry jam sandwiches, a coincidence only discovered on referring back to the log account of the day. You can gather I like black cherry jam — and keep a note of trivial pursuits!

Storm did Beinn Chuirn by the shortest reasonable route on a day of dashing winter storms: starting at the vital bridge at Glenlochy crossing (six miles west of Tyndrum) and angling round to go up the Garbh Choirean, which was less rough than the weather — another enjoyable raid.

Section 3: 3. BEINN MHIC-MHONAIDH 792 m OS 50 209350
     Hill of the son of the moor

In *Hamish's Groats End Walk* (p. 71) I describe a walk through from Loch Tulla to Loch Awe by Gleann Fuar and Glen Strae, and either of these glens would be a good approach route to Mhic-Mhonaidh. There is some new planting defending Gleann Fuar, and the path shown ends past the ruins of Druimliart, birthplace of the bard Duncan Ban Macintyre. Further up the *cold glen* there are some fine stands of old Scots pines. There is only a little loss of height by Coire Bhiocar to gain the sweeping ridge of the Corbett.

Looking up Glen Strae the SW Ridge appears as a distinctive cone.

In very wet conditions it might be worth avoiding the Corbett altogether from this side, as the River Strae can become unfordable. In normal conditions you just use the road up the glen, paddle the river and work up to follow the An Sgriodain ridge to the summit levels. The view to Cruachan and Loch Awe will give good excuses for resting.

I've now made two ascents of the Corbett from Glen Orchy, a better choice than the map might suggest with the huge takeover of forestry. From the bridge over the ragged Eas Urchaidh a forestry road swings up by the Allt Broighleachan to end on a little "meadow". When Storm and I went up one autumn we came upon two foresters busy loading a stag on to their vehicle. We met several deer inside the forest over the day — where they are not very welcome. On the meadow great tits, gold crests and a wren all fussed their way down the burnside trees. A go-anywhere vehicle was parked in the clearing and a track, beaten by it, crossed the burn and forked. We took the left fork which wended on, a bit wet in places, to the edge of the trees near the watershed. (On the previous occasion there was just the preparatory ploughing which gave purgatorial progress.) We had a snack by the Arigh Chailleach shieling ruins, where one rowan flamed red among the orange autumn slopes. The day echoed to the roar of stags and the corrie above had several dozen deer grazing across it. By keeping in the slot of the burn we managed to stalk up among them unseen. The wind was blowing down on us. On the uppermost slopes we almost walked into a fine stag which stared in disbelief before giving a croak and prancing off over the snow. We landed right by the cairn which is so large and precisely circular (like a breast) that it might be prehistoric. In its centre stands a nipple of modern cairn.

Most of the big hills were cloudy but Cruachan was displayed in ermine splendour. The Starav–Stob Ghabhar peaks to the north, and the Lui group to the south, are well seen from here — the Corbett superiority of view once again. Conditions were too cold for lingering and we scampered along to the lochan which is surprisingly deep and would make a welcome summer summit swimming-pool. The grain of the strata gives a succession of steps to descend and we circuited round, above all the gullies, to make a direct descent through the trees back to the meadow. There was no problem with the trees as there were plenty of breaks but the grass had grown rank and tussocky so it was hard going. We would have been better off regaining the outward track.

Out of curiosity I looked up the index to early *SMC Journals* and found three entries for Beinn Mhic-Mhonaidh. Several early meets at Dalmally account for them. The latest note was of Hogmanay 1920 when a party was made up for Beinn Mhic-Mhonaidh and reported enthusiastically of its qualities, both as a climb and as a fine viewpoint. The earliest mention was a short article in 1894: ". . . although under 3,000 feet and therefore unclassed as a 'Ben' (i.e. Munro) it is worth a visit from Dalmally for those who have exhausted the 3,000-foot hills in its neighbourhood." Munro-bagging obviously began very early.

The writer, Francis Dewar, was quite wrong in his thoughts on the "apartness" of the Corbett: "I distinguish it by the peculiarity of its standing entirely apart, an unusual circumstance, I think, in hills of its altitude" — where this apartness is, in fact, a hallmark of the sterling quality of Corbetts. He hit the other feature of most Corbetts. "The view from it is a particularly fine one, at least 35 first-class Bens, from Lomond to Bidean and Cruachan to Beinn a' Ghlo. Lochearn's Ben Vorlich is striking and Ben Lui presents a unique appearance." Dewar crossed the Orchy and ascended as we did, "a beautiful walk" on which he saw hares, deer, ptarmigan and an eagle which "caused some disquietude by circling over me in what I considered a too inquisitive spirit".

At the end of the Dalmally New Year Meet in 1901 Maylard, the president, and Sang were alone on the last day and decided to "ring the brow of Beinn Mhic-Mhonaidh with an SMC halo". Sylvan Glen Strae led to a foaming torrent (the Allt nan Guibhas) and an easy victory, but "the glory of this virgin peak was greatly enhanced by half-veiled glimpses of the surrounding mammoths. Only 2,602 feet but it was cold as the North Pole. The hill teemed with stags." Typical Corbett commenting.

The descent was to give some jolly good sport: "The OS sheet showed a bridge over the Orchy close to Larig farm [Lairig Hill is the only name on the map now] but put not thy faith in OS sheets! The farm is a ruin and the bridge is not . . . the road looked so inviting on the other side but the tangle impeded progress and the failing light made hardship harder and the future bleaker still. The River Orchy is deep and wide . . . it was a stormy breast-high crossing and a secret to be kept from insurance agents . . . a mile and a half further down a bridge appeared from nowhere, mockingly spanning the torrent. . . . That night in the Dalmally Hotel we were grieved that the rotameter gave only 21 miles for the day's work." Our round trip from Glen Orchy was a mere eight miles.

Section 3: 4. BEINN UDLAIDH 840 m OS 50 280333
            Dark (gloomy) hill

Section 3: 5. BEINN BHREAC-LIATH 803 m OS 50 304339
            Speckled grey hill

A sub-zero March morning saw me parking at Arinabea in Glen Lochy 2½ miles west of Tyndrum and heading off up the course of a burn in order to avoid the solid plantings of trees. The trees are now considerably bigger and nearly all Glen Lochy has been afforested but this is still the quickest route for these hills, even if it is not the best.

I had some fun getting the dog over the top deer fence. We ended on the col between the speckled grey hill and the wee hill (Beinn Bheag). The Corbett was a big bald bump and we wandered round its rim to see the view. There was a fine symmetry looking over to Auch Gleann with its torque of railway line. Ben Lui and Ben Oss shone like armour in the sun. Cruachan was hidden by Beinn Udlaidh whose eastern flank above deep Coire Ghamhnain looked as if it might produce climbing but just doesn't. Trundling down to the col we set off six stags. They galloped away over the saddle, dark shapes against a lemon brightness of winter sun.

Hard snow all the way up on to Beinn Udlaidh was useful. The second Corbett was an even better viewpoint, for the toothy tops of Cruachan were added to the panorama. It is also a big dome, or plateau, but is crag-rimmed on many flanking slopes while Coire Daimh is perhaps more famous for its winter climbs when the liberal summer leaks freeze into welcome ice. Some of us were once discussing how funny it would be to write a spurious, but very serious, article on some new climbing ground. This would have to be accessible enough to tempt climbers (a lazy breed) but also quite unknown. I suggested Coire Daimh. A few weeks later we were reading about a flurry of new routes in a recently-discovered corrie: Coire Daimh.

The main feature of Coire Daimh (*the corrie of the stags*) is a line of quartzite crags and a top rim of schisty rock. Perhaps the clash of rock causes the copious wetness which can, occasionally, yield good ice conditions. The quartzite crosses the north ridge of the hill as a prominent straight dyke which can be spotted from the Blackmount road. It is continuous enough to be shown on the map.

Last autumn, Sandy, Stan and I left my car a mile south of Bridge of Orchy and drove in Sandy's car up to the big bend near the top of the road to Tyndrum. By following the edge of the wood above Coire

Chailein we had a very easy ascent up Beinn Bhreac-liath but one which gave an ever-widening panorama in quite special fashion. It was a day of magical, crisp clarity. We arrived simultaneously with Andrew, from Inverness, who'd come up from Arinabea and we all went on together up Beinn Udlaidh to picnic by the slabby cairn. Andrew went south, we descended down the North Ridge and then followed the odd quartz dyke down to the Allt Ghamhnain to hit the Glen Orchy road a mile before it joins the A82. With just one car a full circuit from the north would be as good and preferable to the Glen Lochy line. New plantings now stretch two miles down Glen Orchy from the Allt Ghamhnain, so Coire Daimh has become rather isolated. Glen Orchy is a quiet backwater compared to Glen Lochy, and this alone would make the northern approach more satisfying. Glen Lochy's most flattering aspect is the view *down to it* from the col between the Corbetts: a gunbarrel view over Lochan na Bi away to the jumbled hills of Crianlarich.

Section 3:	6.	BEINN ODHAR	900 m	OS 50	338338
		Dun-coloured hill			
Section 3:	7.	BEINN CHAORACH	818 m	OS 50	359328
		Sheep hill			
Section 3:	8.	CAM CHREAG	885 m	OS 50	375346
		Crooked crags			
Section 3:	9.	BEINN A' CHAISTEIL	885 m	OS 50	348364
		Hill of the castle			
Section 3:	10.	BEINN NAM FUARAN	807 m	OS 50	361382
		Hill of the well			

This is probably the only day among the Corbetts which can naturally produce a tally of five ticks for the list. As the day entails nearly 2,000 m of ascent (*c.* 6,500 feet) it will test the fittest muscles, especially as the slopes of this crowd of Corbetts are invariably steep. I've never been over them all on a single expedition but my excuse is that Cam Chreag had not been invented before 1981. I'd already been up some of the others individually before a May romp round the then four Auch Corbetts.

The now five Auch Corbetts have contorted and fascinating watersheds. Cam Chreag is really one of the Glen Lochay peaks, the Forest of Mamlorn, while Beinn Odhar and Beinn Chaorach are Tyndrum hills, much of their drainage running to Strath Fillan and eventually to the east coast by the Tay, and the Auch Gleann and Gleann Coillean both drain to the Orchy, Loch Awe and the western seaboard. All being Corbetts gives them a special entity.

Beinn Odhar appears as a fine cone to the south, a look-alike for Beinn Dorain for which it is sometimes taken. This peak stands boldly above the pass from Tyndrum to Bridge of Orchy and is a good start to the day over these Corbetts. Even the SMC district guide so far forgets itself as to write enthusiastically about Beinn Odhar. "The view encompasses almost all the high mountains of Perthshire and Argyll. Ben Lui stands up grandly to the south west, and to the west Ben Cruachan dominates the horizon . . . the Blackmount peaks make a fine array while, closer at hand, Beinn Dorain, Beinn a' Chreachain, Creag Mhor and Heasgarnich show their bulk. Eastwards there is a glimpse of Ben Lawers and the Tarmachans, and to the south east the familiar outline of the Crianlarich mountains. Ben Lomond and the Arrochar Alps appear in the distant south. Altogether it is a wonderful panorama"; and, one suspects, known because of the hill's tempting shape and easy ascent. Beinn Udlaidh, westward, has a fine view, but whoever has praised it?

My most memorable ascent of Ben Odhar was a winter one. Ernst, Iain, George, Storm the dog and I went up it on a January day that saw some wild and wet weather move on and a cold clarity blow in. As a quick rescue of the day it proved a winner. We went up the normal SSW Ridge route, which gave a portal-view to Loch Tulla and to dramatic sun-cloud effects to the south. On top the wind-chill factor was unpleasantly emphasised. Hands had to be warmed after every photograph taken. George had been coming along slowly and we had to start down before he arrived as it was too cold to linger. George was George Roger, an ever-smiling friendly enthusiast who had had a lifetime of wandering the world's mountains. An ex-president of the SMC he was slowing with increasing years but the tenacity was still there. A year later (again from Bridge of Orchy) he was out in appalling conditions and both he and his dog were hit and killed by a train on crossing the Auch viaduct, grim news that met Charles, Ernst, Belinda and me when we turned up at the Meet from our own pasting on Sgorr na Diollaid (14:6) while staying at Cozac Lodge.

I had a windy ascent at the start of the long day, but Argyll had been singled out for good weather in the forecast. The first two (now three) Corbetts are on the Argyll–Perthshire boundary. On the level shoulder of the SSW Ridge of Odhar, just before the final rise to the summit, there is a tiny lochan which would make an eyrie-like camp spot. Beinn Odhar was my 100th Corbett and old Kitchy's 50th.

On the way off I also looked at the other tarn, drained by the Allt

Choire Dhuibh. The SSE Ridge rather curves off to the south, Coire Thoin to the right being, to translate euphemistically "backside corrie". I left my rucksack at the col before going up and down the steeper flank of Beinn Chaorach, a hill which perhaps deserves its name. Have you noticed how few sheep hills there are in the *Tables*? Goat hills there are in plenty. The dominance of sheep came centuries after hills received their names. (The multiplicity of similar names, often queried, is simply due to local people naming their own hills. They were not aware that, in umpteen other areas, other people were also producing Ben Mores and Sgurr Dubhs.) The sole feature of Beinn Chaorach is its trig point, the only one of the day.

From there to Cam Chreag is the easiest part of the full day. By its recent inclusion we can gather there is only just over 500 feet of re-ascent. Beinn Chaorach does not merit a mention in the SMC district guide, which might be to its credit for Cam Chreag is dismissed as "an undistinguished hill with a flat, mile-long summit ridge, which is rarely climbed for itself but may be included in a traverse from Creag Mhor to Ben Challum". I first climbed it on a traverse from Beinn Chaorach to Ben Challum, the Auchertyre horseshoe. This gave a good view of Ben Challum's north face which, too broken for rock climbing, gave Charles and me some sport one winter when we came up Gleann Choillean from Auch to reach the peak, which peers over the Chaorach–Cam Chreag col as one drives south from Bridge of Orchy. Gleann Choillean is an alternative start for this day's walk; it depends where you want to return to at the end of the day and there is little really to choose between the Auch road end and the top of the pass.

From Cam Chreag there is a long easy ridge down to the Abhainn Ghlas; and the Allt a' Mhaim, which joins it, is the natural continuation up for Beinn nam Fuaran. On my long day I returned west off Beinn Chaorach and then had some miles of glen walking by the Allt Cumhang and the level upper Abhainn Ghlas which, lower, is swallowed by the artificial waters of Loch Lyon. Centuries ago plenty of traffic went through to upper Glen Lyon but now it is trackless and difficult. Even the shepherds use boats.

Beinn nam Fuaran is rather lost in a welter of hills and the pull-up is the longest since the initial ascent of Beinn Odhar, but the view along Loch Lyon is the reward. The biggest col of the day, and the only real saddle, has some peat bogs and leads to a rather heartbreakingly, evenly-angled ascent of Beinn a' Chaisteil. The peak's name is entirely due to its appearance from Auch, for it thrusts westwards as a bold prow, split by a big gully (climbed in 1899) and with curtain-wall flanks running back above Auch Gleann and Gleann Choillean. Beinn

Dorain, quite the wrong shape, still bulks large and high across Auch Gleann.

The 883 height is a spot height and not really the summit. The cairn, too, is 100 m north west of the highest point — all very confusing. The way off is clear: to the south east, along and above Creagan Liath until it is safe to cut down into Gleann Choillean. I've come up more directly but don't recommend that as a descent route. After a day largely on easy grass it is odd to have to escape from a rocky, cliff-guarded keep of a mountain.

My day actually took in Beinn a' Chaisteil before Beinn nam Fuaran (leaving the rucker on the col) and I angled down steeply to As-an t-Sithein in the upper Auch Gleann, to camp inside the old sheep fank and go on over Mhanach–Chreachain–Achallader the next day. I'd only just pitched tent when the first big raindrops introduced an evening and night of heavy rain. The batter on the roof and the plaintive crying of lambs and curlews gave the site a feeling of extreme solitude. Duncan Ban Macintyre, the poet, lived up here at one stage.

Section 3: 11. CREACH BHEINN   810 m   OS 50   024422
Mountain of spoil

"To discover the peace that dwells upon hill tops you need go no further than our Homeland hills. On them, among their rocks and heather, you will be given something that not even the lords of the Himalayas are able to give."

So wrote Frank Smythe in *The Kangchenjunga Adventure* and so Creach Bheinn was to me one restorative weekend when respite from pressure was badly needed. On the way up I had an interesting day with Tom Weir and a TV crew doing a piece about my Munros trip, then I joined a local club meet at Black Rock. While some of them were keen to do the Munro, Beinn Sgulaird, I was left to myself for its neighbour, Corbett Creach Bheinn. Having spent so many days and years not only with others, but in charge of others, a solitary day was always a glad release, a quiet restfulness in which to relish the peace that only the hills can give. A day of fresh spring welcomed me to Loch Creran.

Just along from Druimavuic a useful forestry road led up the Allt Buidhe. The landscape had the lushness of the west. Nearing the end of April the primroses and anemones were in flower and wheatears were setting up homes on the heights. In the car I'd come close to running into a cuckoo, the first of the year. A sparrow-hawk was beating along the upper fringe of forest.

I followed the Allt Buidhe, but the crags to the south were nothing like as dramatic as the map suggested so I cut up to gain height quickly and to escape from the scratchy vegetation lower down. For interest I kept to a burn. The purple saxifrage was just starting to drape the dank banks. There was quite a distinctive NE Top (803 m) and a gentle walk along to the summit of Creach Bheinn. The view is like that from Beinn Sgulaird, with the addition of granity Sgulaird; it is of the west, western, sea-circled hills and oceans of sky.

Creach Bheinn can easily be added to Beinn Sgulaird if it is thought of in time. Curiously some years after this day I was back with Charles and we came up the Allt Buidhe again, then he ascended the Corbett and I went up the Munro for the sake of the dog Storm. Charles had to drive back to Sheffield afterwards. There wasn't time for both of us to do both hills.

Creach Bheinn looks west, down Gleann Dubh to outer Loch Creran, to Eriska and Lismore and the wild Corbett country beyond Loch Linnhe but, sadly, the *black glen* has been swamped with a sprawl of spruce. The corrie can be circled, and a long ridge gives a good high-level walk (on to sheet 49) before one descends fire breaks to South Creagan near the old railway bridge. (Foot/cycle crossings were always permitted and it used to amuse my school gangs to cross the bridge and then watch motorists' expressions as they came on the same group again.) This ridge can be reached by descending slightly north of west to pass above the Eas Garbh (*rough falls*) gorge and its pleasing waterfalls. If a car has been left at the road by the Allt Buidhe it is easier just to contour round and over the ridge to reach the *yellow stream* by a descending traverse that keeps one safely out of the jaws of the forestry.

Creach Bheinn's derivation leaves one speculating. A *creach* was a raid, usually with the pillaging of cattle as its prime objective, so does this name commemorate such a despoiling? Who raided whom? And who gave the name to the silent witness? There is a great deal of social history hidden under the names on our maps. Perhaps some of it is best forgotten. The desert of the past can be the peace of the present. Raiding Corbetts certainly does less harm!

When Charles and I drove off on our visit we had to go round by the drive of Druimavuic House as the main road was under water; high tide, a westerly gale and high streams combining to flood it. Even when you pass under normal circumstances there is often a tangle of seaweed festooning the roadside fences.

Section 3:   12. BEINN TRILLEACHAN   *c.*840 m   OS 50   086439
                  Hill of the sandpipers

A friend once suggested Beinn Trilleachan should be *hill of the sandpaper* but then he was a climber and had been gripped up on the popular Etive Slabs. The granite is indeed rough as sandpaper. The first time I climbed this Corbett I was also to become thoroughly gripped — but on a winter escapade.

I woke thinking it was snowing but it was just my down sleeping-bag that had split open to fill the Dormobile with feathers. I was on a crowded local club meet at Inbhirfhaolain but nobody would condescend to go for a mere Corbett: climbing, skiing and Munro-ing had the priority. Those who set out for Bidean or Starav failed to reach their summits. Big is often bloody in foulest February. Even the frenetic climbers were not contemplating routes on the Etive Slabs, that palette of mighty climbs that looks down on Loch Etive. I sat in the Dormobile by the pier sipping a coffee and trying to become enthusiastic about going up a hill on a dribbly morning. It slowly cleared and I set off to traverse under the slabs, which were running with water. At the foot of the white waste of rocks I found a karabiner.

My route led up and across, avoiding the great face, but I still grabbed some fun, scrambling on granite walls and slabs and gullies. Too soon I was on slobbery snow and my new ice-axe (this was a dozen years ago) was tested for the novelty of being able to bang the pick in and pull on it. With old axes a pull usually meant the axe flew out, and one of the few falls I've had climbing was caused by just that. Fortunately I merely dropped for 30 feet through the air and landed in deep snow, injured only in my dignity.

Somewhere, high up, above Ard Trilleachan, after having several tussles with "problems" I managed to become stuck in a corner. The rock was pushing me out of balance and to move in any direction was hazardous. There was a great deal of nothing below my trembling legs and a snow boss overhead. It was a situation where to do anything was dangerous but to do nothing would soon prove disastrous. The newly-tested axe was swung hard into the frozen turf over the snow eave and I scrabbled and pulled, up and over the bulge, with everything committed to the ice-axe holding. It held, or I wouldn't be writing this. Great stuff, adrenalin.

After some twisting up I hit the summit ridge and the summit storm hit me. Sleet turned to snow, wildly driven by a gale. Fortunately it was blowing from behind so I scampered off along the crest. There are a couple of miles of knobbly granite ridge, with a 767-m top above the slabs, but even the pull up on to this was easier than it looked. There are no escape routes and it is a long way to Meall nan Gobhar. I was all too aware of the great drop on my right. The loch, when it appeared through gaps in the storm, seemed to be directly below. When it was safe to turn down I sat and slid much of the way. Still 1,000 feet up I came on a ship's bucket which presumably had been blown there from the tide line. There are traces of an old path from the head of Loch Etive over to Glen Ure but there is no chance of straying as the massed afforestation drives one down to the sea. Last century a missionary preacher regularly crossed by this path to hold services in Glen Etive. Before the advent of the road across Rannoch Moor, Glen Etive was a very remote spot, generally reached by boat. My weather lower down was just wild and wet but, not for the first time, a Corbett had given good sport while bigger hills were beyond reach.

Trilleachan is best done on a more reasonable day, for the summit is well guarded by cliffs and distance. The country between it and Beinn Sgulaird is boggy and foul enough to discourage any link from there and its southern approaches are beyond the back of beyond. The head of Loch Etive is a grand spot. Another ploy is to walk down through the hazel woods by the loch (path), well past Ard Trilleachan, and then wind up, a circuit always being more rewarding than there-and-back by the same route. The hill is aptly named and the lochside rings to the *willy-needy willy-needy* calls of that bird of summer-welcoming, the uncommon sandpiper.

Section 3:   13. STOB DUBH   883 m   OS 41/50   166488
             The black peak

Inbhirfhaolain, the cosy hut in Glen Etive, is dominated by Stob Dubh. "You'd think it would be climbed more often being so near the hut," someone once suggested.

"Have you seen it from the hut?"

"No."

"Well, those who have can usually find excuses for not climbing it."

The black peak dominates very successfully. It fills the view as one drives up from Loch Etive, a bold prow, cleft by a gorge on its southern flank.

That gorge, or the ridge straight up from Glenceitlein, are perhaps the best routes up Stob Dubh but it is well worth continuing, to make a traverse over Beinn Ceitlein (*the hill of concealment*) to descend to the Allt a' Chaorainn. The last tower of this east ridge is An Grianan (*the bower*) and is one of the many Glen Etive spots associated with the legend of Deirdre of the Sorrows. The Allt a' Chaorainn is a big river of fine granite pools but, in spate, may only be passable a mile upstream. Those who don't mind a yo-yo sort of day can go on and traverse 5:4 Beinn Mhic Chasgaig, the neighbouring Corbett, which is climbed even less often than Stob Dubh.

I must confess to having gone up Stob Dubh only once though I've used its flanking glens on several occasions. During my tramp over all the Munros, the Starav–Meall nan Eun group had given me a desperately hot day and when I was on the col behind Stob Dubh all I wanted was water. Swimming in the Allt a' Chaorainn won easily over any ascent. All too often Stob Dubh is a dark, soaking hulk, as it was on the nasty November day I climbed it, crossing the River Etive at Dalness and going up the north ridge — which is as brutal as the west ridge already mentioned. "A quartzy shambles plastered in snow" was my untechnical description. The SMC district guide tells us the hill is "a complex of mica schist, quartzite, rhyolite and dykes of porphyry almost surrounded by granite".

The best of that day was finding a dead stag, a Royal, and eventually I bore the head off as a trophy. Unfortunately it had died in its prime so the antlers were firmly attached to the — smelly — skull. Even pounding with a hunk of granite could not snap them off, yet, had the beast lived, they would eventually have just fallen off. Had he lived he could have become an Imperial, one of the lords of the mountain. (Deer are judged by the number of points or tines which each antler has: brow points, bay, tray and the threes on top making six a side, the twelve points of a Royal. Fourteen is an Imperial.)

BREADALBANE, GLEN LYON, GLEN ALMOND

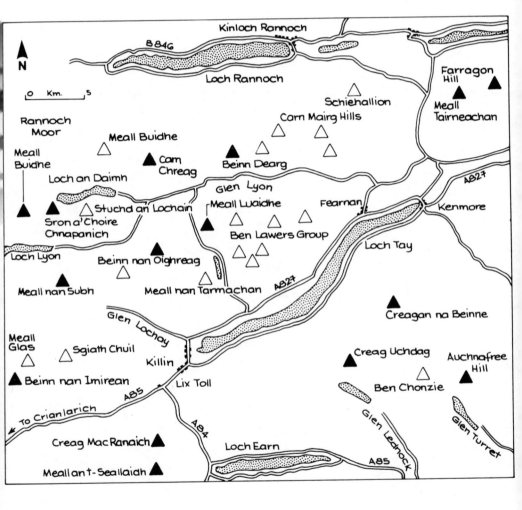

Section 4:   1. BEINN NAN IMIREAN   844 m   OS 51   419309
            Hill of the ridge

FREQUENT MUNRO-BAGGING combinations round the head of Glen
Lochay have ensured several visits to "lowly" Beinn nan Imirean, as
Firsoff calls this Corbett: "The last of the Glen Dochart Hills which
have disintegrated into formless moorland." Poor Beinn nan Imirean.
Strangely it was one of the first Corbetts I ever did, back in 1962,
admittedly when miles and feet were treated rather cavalierly.

A lift south had dropped me at Crianlarich and a mile eastwards I
pitched my tent in a sheltered hollow by a burn, a site we often used
until road improvements simply bulldozed it out of existence — and
also removed a nasty hump-backed bridge which had yielded
entertainment as speeding motorists took off from it and crashed
down beyond in showers of sparks.

A friend and I had traversed Sgiath Chuil the year before, from Glen
Lochay to Glen Dochart; this April day gave me a chance to add Meall
Glas and Ben Challum and, of course, Beinn nan Imirean stands
(in)conveniently between them. No sooner had I climbed up on to the
road than a car offered me a lift to Glen Coe so I took the chance of a
run along to the Auchtertyre road-end and made the conventional
traverse of Ben Challum. The superb snow conditions of the day
before had gone and with the temperature away above freezing, plus
odd showers of rain, there was a penetrating wetness to the walking.
The clouds sank lower and lower and I faced a day of dedicated effort
rather than any carefree rapture.

A long sitting slide (glissade is too grand a term) down Stob
a' Bhiora took me rather far down into Glen Lochay. The slide was no
doubt quicker than walking, but the subsequent peat-rough ascent
round Beinn nan Imirean to reach Meall Glas was exasperating and
exhausting. Meall Glas rewarded with the cloud girdle slipping just
enough to look over the top of the white, out of which rose all the
giants from Ben Lui to Ben More to Ben Lawers. I dumped my sack to
add the East Top (it was Munros *and* Tops that first time round) and
then headed for home. Beinn nan Imirean was rather in the way and
"as there was plenty of time" I traversed over rather than round the
Corbett. I then baled off into the valley cloud rather casually (compass
in pocket) so ended up hitting Loch Essan rather than Loch Maragain
as planned. I felt as if *I* was disintegrating as much as the formless
moorland. An exhausting flounder led to the frustration of being right

opposite my tent but with the unfordable River Fillan between. It took another hour to go round by the Crianlarich viaduct and I stumbled into the hotel to order a vast pot of tea.

"What a wretched end to the day. I spent an hour drying off and doubtless letting lifts go by. Went along to camp and threw out my soup and struck the tent in a downpour. Still, I'd only walked up past the station when a Black's van stopped and took me at a spanking pace to Erskine Ferry where a quick change to a bus allowed me — just — to reach the youth hostel in time. It was far too much for a day. Ben Challum is worth a return visit but the Imirean–Sgiath Chuil country I never want to see again."

My youthful judgment has long been rescinded, for that area has given plenty of good days. On one Ultimate Challenge Tony and I traversed from Crianlarich to Killin, a sort of postgraduate course in bog studies, and on Imirean put up one of the biggest herds of deer I've ever seen. Part of the difficulty of these hills comes from their odd lay-out: on both north and south there is a lower skirt of gentle-angled moorland which, by its very gentleness, has held water and decayed into peat bogs, dubh lochans and wending streams. Auchessan Farm is the easiest approach to the Corbett and the Fillan–Dochart is not a defence to tackle other than by a bridge. If nothing else Beinn nan Imirean is a useful educational Corbett.

Section 4:   2. MEALL AN T-SEALLAIDH   852 m   OS 51   542234
             Hill of the sight

Section 4:   3. CREAG MACRANAICH   809 m   OS 51   546256
             MacRanaich's crag

Tantalising glimpses of these hills can be had when motoring up the A84 between Strathyre and Lochearnhead though the major feature is the huge, uniform slopes of Auctoomore Hill — the Braes of Balquhidder. These have been planted, which does not help with access to the Corbetts.

Glen Kendrum, Kirkton Glen and Monachyle Glen are all passes used in olden times but Kirkton Glen is the only one with a good track all the way from Balquhidder through to Glen Dochart. Edinchip is the home of the MacGregor chiefs and close to Rob Roy's grave at Balquhidder. I decided to start my Corbetting there and finish at the head of Glen Ogle where my newly-acquired folding cycle was securely chained to a tree to await my arrival and whizz me down, and round to Balquhidder again.

The present Balquhidder church dates to 1855, the ruined one from 1631, but is on the site of an older one still. St Angus, the local patron saint, had an oratory nearby. In 1589 the MacGregors had cut off the head of a royal keeper in Glen Artney and they brought the grisly trophy back and laid it on the altar of the church here for a macabre oath-taking. Rob Roy, who lived in several houses hereabouts, his wife Mary and some of his family are all buried in the churchyard. The grave is clearly indicated. There are several historic relics in the church but it was shut at seven in the morning.

Kirkton Glen was a bit claustrophobic on a steamy-warm day in May. I found a firebreak and then a stream course which led me up out of the trees quickly, if sweatily. A crow flew over with something in its claws; I clapped my hands and the startled bird dropped its prize. I had to dodge a big bone.

The summit of Meall an t-Seallaidh was in cloud. Bits of fence were ignored (they lead astray as often as they may help) but I found the cairn easily enough, and the trig point over a bit. The name, it is suggested, celebrates the view, especially of the four lochs: Loch Tay, Loch Earn, Loch Lubnaig and Loch Voil. This is typical schisty country complete with folds, hollows and knobbles. The tiny lochan by the Cam Chreag came as expected. We descended by a gap to the *beallach* and had a second breakfast in lee of a tilted slab of rock. Purple saxifrage was still hanging down in carpets on the crags.

As eating did not bring a clearance I set off up the crags opposite. It was like tackling Bidean a' Choire Sheasgaich from Beinn Tharsuinn, only Creag MacRanaich had to be searched for among the ups and downs. There was a big cairn on one top but I was not convinced it was necessarily the summit. Other tops had other cairns. The hill is apparently named after a "famous" robber — though nothing is known about him now.

I wandered off northwards and then took a rough bearing to the north east. Glen Ogle was a big enough target to hit after all. Half way down, flogging through the heather, I came out the cloud and I also suddenly realised that I'd left the vital wing nut for holding the cycle together back in the car at Balquhidder.

Sunday lunchtime is not the best time for walking down Glen Ogle. I thumbed in self-defence and a car stopped when I was half way down the glen. The driver was going to Lochearnhead but kindly ran me on to Kingshouse, from where I walked along under the Braes by Auchtoo. By the time I'd driven up to collect the bike (still unused!) the rain was falling heavily; so at least acting on the forecast and going early had been the right decision.

Section 4:   4. CREAG UCHDAG   879 m   OS 51   708323
                    Bart, Uigeach: *crag of the hollows*

Section 4:   5. CREAGAN NA BEINNE   887 m   OS 51 (52 for Glen
                    Almond)   744369
                    The hill of the rocks/crags

The resemblance of this area to the northern Pennines recommends it
enough as good walking country. Many books describe it as heathery,
which is misleading, and the ascents of these Corbetts can be made on
easy grass slopes. Western flanks seem to be grassy. There certainly is
plenty of heather; there are peat hags on cols and plateaux, and a lot of
rock breaking through. Some pleasant glens cut deep into these hills
south of the Tay, and a web of old drove roads are still rights-of-way
of character.

    As a teenager most of my holidays were spent in the Highlands,
staying in howffs and hostels (who could find or afford a tent?) and
exploring "by bike and by hike". Quite often the bike and hike were
simultaneous as a clear dotted line on a pre-war map (cost 1/6d)
proved to be a long-forgotten path. Now and then new reservoirs
(with Loch Mullardoch the extreme case) would ambush a route, or
another mountain had been secretly drowned in friendless conifers.
Glen Lednock was just caught in time. Now its dotted line is under
water.

    Most of the nearer roads had been cycled, so part of the fun then was
to find new ways through and over the hills. If I drew the line at
cycling through the Lairig Ghru, Glen Lednock from Comrie to Loch
Tay seemed an obvious line. Loch Lednock dam was going up and the
track over the pass brought home why it is called a push bike. I pushed
it a long way that day.

    Visits to the Munro Ben Chonzie or the area's Corbetts or to Sput
Rolla or the Deil's Cauldron had taken me back to Glen Lednock at
irregular intervals and, each time, rekindled the desire to walk
through to Loch Tay.

    Glen Lednock supports a dwindling number of sheep and an ever-
increasing amount of bracken. Rearguard farming. Despite a long dry
spell Sput Rolla was still attractive: a wide brocade of a fall draped
down gashes cutting across the glen. We drove up to the dam. The
water level was low and the loch was surrounded by a glaring band of
exposed rock, sand and gravel. The water itself was being churned up
by half a gale and the sky was an all-grey composition of rectilinear
shapes. I just hoped we could win through dry.

On a recent autumn day, Storm and I took a rough farm-track along to a small wood, below which a fank was perched on a shelf of spoil into which the waves were biting. The burn of the wood came down a deep cleft with a bridge of sleepers leading to the fank. It was a rumbling bridge. The walls of the cleft were hung with lady's mantle cushions, and heaths, and bluebells and a colour-explosion of rowan berries.

The creation of reservoirs has frequently made the alternative walking very unpleasant. I would have thought the flooding of an old right-of-way would have entailed some moral if not legal obligation to make a substitute but the Hydro obviously don't. The flanks of Loch Lednock are, however, well trodden by sheep and a good enough path has evolved through bestial necessity. We battered along into the wind.

Nearing the top end there was an area of broken schisty rocks where a burn came down, which formed a secretive shelter where we sat out of the wind. A tent-sized flat of grass just asked to be used. Apart from the scars of Hydro it was an idyllic spot and the blaeberry clumps in the rock were a blaze of red autumn tints.

The north west corner of the loch had dried out. The new map shows paths rounding the head of the loch but a walk along the north shore is quicker and easier. Our path heaves out of the loch and over the pass with more cartographical confidence than reality.

I thought I spied a rising path, not far beyond the round dyke of a sheep shelter, that led up a grassy ridge and crossed a bigger burn at a cairn. The burn came down from a band of crag beyond which lay the final bulk of Creag Uchdag. This would be the obvious way up, but I wanted my pass as well, so carried on. There was no obvious path sloping up but a clear one contouring and, as the map one climbed only to have to descend to the pass, it seemed a likely alternative. I took it.

All went well and after a perch with a last view down the loch we entered the narrowing upper glen. It had the real feel of a wild pass (many just don't) and after one bit where my track vanished (as sheep tracks do) we were confronted with a rocky hollow which cut deeply back into our slope as a rotten crag. This effective barrier probably explains why the old path climbs high up. The sheep track went boldly up the heather to round the obstacle. Iron-orange seepage spilled into it and the crags were flame-bright with tinted willow herb, that dedicated coloniser which an old flora of mine describes as "a woodland flower of the Alps which has established a few colonies in the south of England".

Two streams and an old boundary fence come down off the grassy flank of Creag Uchdag to demarcate the watershed. It is a pass of lumps and bumps and sloping down to a gate-gap in the fence-of-no-wires was the green sweep of the old track. At one time it must have been a well-made, well-kept route. Going down on the Tay side it was easy to follow.

First we left the pack and set off up the hill, making a left-flanking move to gain a broad easy ridge and to enjoy having the wind right behind to push me up Uchdag.

Back at the col my first thoughts were of a brew but it was too windy. Where the path crossed the Finglen Burn we seemed more sheltered and on went the tea. Storm brushed past and set his fur on fire! When I was eventually sitting back, cup in hand, to enjoy the break, the wind dropped and the last midges of the season descended on us.

Another great gash of a burn came down the eastern slopes and it was interesting to see, in that sheep-shorn landscape, how this inaccessible gorge was bursting with trees and vegetation. It was quite impassable and sheep tracks went uphill on both sides as well as across the foot. Wise walkers use the wily ways of sheep and deer rather than fighting the landscape.

New boots were rubbing one heel so we stopped on a breezy knoll with a fine view up the Finglen. The first-aid bag had only a long strip of plaster and I had no knife: stone-age tools cut off the strip needed and we chuntered down to the cultivated lands of the Tay. The loch stayed hidden till the last slope.

We managed to lose the line of the path in the pattern of fields but came out to the road where a Scottish Right-of-Way sign pointed to Comrie. Ardeonaig lay 300 yards on.

Ardeonaig is now little more than a popular fishing hotel, but it was once the inn for a trans-Tay ferry. St Adamnan (Eonan) is supposed to have had a cell here. One winter night in the sixteenth century a gang of MacNabb thugs, twelve sons of the chief, landed here with a boat and carried it over the hills I'd just crossed. They used the more westerly glen up, and went down Glen Beich to Loch Earn where they sailed out to surprise their MacNeish enemies on their "safe" island castle. Heads and boat were carried up to the watershed but the boat was then left. It finally rotted away last century. I think I'll stick to hike and bike.

Strong walkers could do Creag Uchdag and Creagan na Beinne in a day from Invergeldie in Glen Lednock. This would still give three uphill sections but the going is much easier than one would expect in that rough landscape. After ascending Creag Uchdag along Loch Lednock descend to Dunan (a derelict house) and climb Creagan na

Beinne up and down by its south ridge then regain Invergeldie by the elusive track west of Dundornie. If you drive up to the dam you then have 600 feet up the road at the end of the day. Creagan na Beinne lies above the Ardtalnaig–Glen Almond right-of-way (well visible) or the Ardtalnaig–Dunan–Invergeldie track could be taken in *en passant* while making a through route. This was more or less what we did, except we cut a corner or two rather than tramp miles of tarmac eastwards.

My first visit was a windy traverse one November, and a good round too: I parked at Ardtalnaig Lodge and went up skirting Beinn Bhreac, traversed Creagan na Beinne to Dunan, "burned-up" Creag Uchdag and returned along Tullich Hill with a pink and grey sunset behind Ben More and Stobinian: a grand day. Coming off Uchdag that day I saw remains of mining which are described in V. A. Firsoff's *In the Hills of Breadalbane*. Welsh miners dug for gold in them there Corbetts!

The wind had died down by the time Storm and I left Ardeonaig and the weather was obviously deteriorating: a worrying prospect with the car on the other side of the mountains. Where the road eastwards began to pull up we took an old green track up a field which soon gave us a big but stormy view along Loch Tay. Huge ash trees lined the track so it must have been very old. There was a ruined village in the top fields and the hillside beyond bore traces of old walls, ditches, tracks and more ruins. If the people have gone it was encouraging to see plenty of free-ranging cattle.

My steady, rising traverse led in to the Allt a' Mheim at the junction of streams just above the wooded level and we tucked in out the wind for a breather. It was a burn of clinging willows and tinted ferns. We crossed and followed the side stream to the col joining Tullich Hill with the Uchdag bulk. It was a satisfying col, looking down into a long valley with the walls of the pass at its head vanishing into the clouds. This "tunnel" was our route. We made a long descending traverse to the col, putting up several parcels of deer. The pass had half a mile with only one contour line and I was glad it was in an unusually dry state. Storm found a bog, though, falling through a covering of heather so only his hind legs and tail were visible. He came out with his face plastered black, looking most indignant.

Dunan lay in a pleasant hollow, backed with a scattering of unusual moraine bumps. In the valley they were symmetrical cones but up on Creagan na Beinne they had been spread and flattened across the hillside. Gleann a' Chilleine, the old drove road to Ardtalnaig, is overlooked by very steep flanks, the Corbett side blushed red with the season's colouring, lit by a momentary stutter of sun. We had a brew at the derelict cottage (it had molehills in the floor) and left the sack there, to wander up Creagan na Beinne. We followed a burn for a while and just ambled on up the easy grass slopes to the peaty dome. In the swirling cloud I was certain the hills to the east were higher. I just hope the summit doesn't move one day!

A blackness swept through (no doubt giving Lawers a drenching) while we scuttled down to eat and drink some ounces off the rucksack weight. Our third uphill lay ahead. I was keen to try and find/use the old route to Invergeldie. It is so sure on the map but I did not find it low down before we broke off on our preferred alternative. If we crossed the col and went down to Invergeldie we would face a 600-foot road-haul back up to the dam, but if we cut over and down more directly, we'd only have half that footage upwards.

We dodged from one stream to another, using their grassy borders or the odd animal track to avoid thrashing up the heather (it was a north-east facing slope). Hares bounded away in all directions. One came haring round a hag and ran right into Storm. If a dog could glare Storm glared. The col was an expanse of decayed peatbog, easy walking, but beyond it was very cut up and only the dryness made it easy as we could walk down the drainage cuttings. The lochan (at 740308) does not exist any more. The peat and heather gave way to grass again and then we hit an estate track which led us down parallel to the Allt Mor. Grey curtains of rain were moving along the loch and we were only two minutes home to the Dormobile when the rain reached us. You can't cut it much finer than that.

Section 4:   6. MEALL LUAIDHE   780 m   OS 51   586436
             Dome of lead

Section 4:   7. BEINN NAN OIGHREAG   909 m   OS 51   543414
             Cloudberry hill

             Note: 4:6 is more correctly MEALL NAM MAIGHEACH,
             Hill of the hare

The frustrations of an office job demanded an escape to the hills for the weekend. Thanks to flexitime I was off reasonably early and arrived at the pass over to Glen Lyon with an hour left of November's grudging daylight. I had a quick snack and we set off there and then for Meall Luaidhe.

There was a layby beside the watershed cairn shown north of Lochan na Lairig and we went from there to Meal nan Eun and along to the Corbett. It is not a good route, however logical, for it is very peaty for most of the way. Dusk and a single star made it feel a lonely summit and then, suddenly, it became magical. The winter cold came down like a tangible thing. Or perhaps a musical one — a ringing triangle, perhaps, as the ground grew a frost and a million stars came out. Warm inside my duvet, Kitchy and I snuggled into the cairn for an hour before I could bear to break the spell. Lawers and her satellites were dark shapes against the stars.

Recently Storm and I went up Meall Luaidhe again and managed to avoid nearly all the peat bogs. We started at the tin shed on the crook of the road where it joins the Allt Bail a' Mhuillin (583416) and did a sweep across the shallow corrie to ascend finally west of the wall that runs up the hill. In descent we followed the wall right down to the road — easiest of all, even if there is more uphill than from the top of the pass. It had been a miserable early morning but cleared on the hill so we had splendid dappled sunlight effects on the Tarmachans up lonely Coire Riadhailt.

Meall Luaidhe would be more interesting if climbed from Glen Lyon. A track goes up the Allt Gleann Da-Eig. (Why is it *the glen of the two eggs?*) It is worth returning via the viewpoint of Creag nan Eildeag which so dominates views up Glen Lyon. Its north flank is a mix of cliff and scrub, so descend southwards into Gleann Da-Eig again. Lead was once mined on the hill, which explains its name. There is another Meall Luaidhe across Glen Lyon in the Carn Mairg hills, and the pass west of Oighreag has this name too. From the shed mentioned above, one spill tip can be seen in lower Coire Riadhailt.

On that night expedition we took a more direct route back to the pass but still floundered in bogs. The torchbeam glittered off the frost and mica particles. My only stumble was falling into the ditch by the roadside. We spent the night in the pass, a cold one in the tin box of Dormobile, but being cold was an aid to rising early. There was an Eastern SMC Meet that morning on the lairig — and I wanted to claim Beinn nan Oighreag first.

I drove to the shed at the crook of the road (see above) and, by torchlight again, slowly traversed up and along to round Meall Buidhe to the Lairig Breisleich. This was a bit of a flounder. The bogs, as on Luaidhe, can be largely avoided by setting off up one of the small streams to gain the higher grassy level and traversing on the green rather than the brown, but this alternative could not be observed in the dark. A stag let out a bellow from very near. The hairs stood up on the back of my neck! Later, in the lairig, Kitchy set up a grouse to give us another fright. Munro and Stott came to the Lairig Breisleich by this route one winter and the latter described it as a "villainous frozen bog, all peat haggs and heathery hummocks". (They were *en route* to Meall Ghaordie.)

The squint of day came as we tramped up the white slopes on to the north ridge of the Corbett. There was one star that put in a deal of overtime before packing in the night shift. The summit fails by only 22 feet in its attempt to become a Munro. In the 1930s there was a brief period when its promotion looked likely and the hill received several visits to try to verify its height; since when it has returned to its slumber. J. Gall Inglis, in 1932, described a peculiar wind when climbing the final slopes. The wind was strong enough to have the party leaning on it at such an angle that on one occasion Inglis fell on his back when it suddenly dropped — which it did frequently, and instantly, then slowly built up to full strength again. The "new" road over the Lochan na Lairig pass was so narrow and without passing places that they preferred to drive right down Glen Lyon rather than risk meeting another vehicle.

There was not much opportunity for me to linger but I kept the 9 a.m. meeting in the Lairig na Lochain and, by placing vehicles at both ends, we had a grand day over the Lawers range. Another car parked beside our collection was not claimed till long after dark — just when I was at coffee and dram stage and wondering if a rescue lay ahead. Out of sheer relief I gave the lads a dram, and kept my fears to myself. They'd been enjoying themselves and who was I to comment on tramps home in the dark? That week had seen me giving thought to what I called "The Long Walk", the non-stop tramp over all the Munros, and it was this weekend, as much as anything else, that dragged the idea from the realm of dreams to become a practical proposition. I'd had enough of the office. The stars and the sun called. The wind on the hill was free.

The next day I added Cam Chreag to the Corbett tally, a day described in 4:11, but I'd also decided that I'd return one day, with more time, to Beinn nan Oighreag and the Lairig Breisleich. The pass lost its one-time importance with the construction of the Lawers road over to Glen Lyon. The Lairig an Luaidhe, west of Oighreag (nothing to do with the Corbett) is another historic link from Glen Lochay to upper Glen Lyon.

It was a decade later, with Charles on the Corbett trail, before the return to Oighreag. My Dormobile was left in Glen Lochay and we drove up the Lochan na Lairig road in Charles's car. It was early March and we had to bash through some drifts on the way up, then, just before the loch, there was one giant drift which stopped Charles driving any further. So we set off on foot and took the same sort of line as I'd done before. Drifts *and* bogs this time. The fence led to the first bump and then to the top of the Corbett, quite helpful in the cloud. It was cold on top, with the thin tunes of winter winds playing on the frosty cairn. We soon headed off southwards down the ridge to reach the Glen Lochay road at Duncroisk. A buzzard flew up from its picnic on a squashed rabbit. The weather had turned mild enough to sit outside over tea, then I drove home to Fife and Charles headed for Sheffield.

Section 4: 8. MEALL NAN SUBH   804 m   OS 51   461397
            Hill of the soo (raspberry)

"West of Meall Ghaordie there is a rather uninteresting group of hills stretching towards the Learg nan Lunn. They can all be climbed easily from the south, but they have no features of interest."

That is all I've noted in the authoritative sources I've looked at, a check I sometimes make, perhaps to balance my own maverick opinions! This time I may seem to be in agreement for my log book of the day girned that it was "a frustrating series of knolls, bogs and detours". I'd started the day camped at Cashlie in Glen Lyon and had been up Meall Ghaordie (a much finer Munro if climbed from the north) and was to go on over Beinn Heasgarnich and Creag Mhor to camp below Ben Challum. As this high-level backpacking expedition was described in *Hamish's Mountain Walk*, I'll give only a brief note on this Corbett.

That day, heavily laden, I took in a majority of the Glen Lochay peaks, so what about someone having a go from Killin to Tarmachan and on over the complete Glen Lochay skyline back to Killin? It would be a notable round. After several weeks of non-stop walking, I wrote that the miles from Meall Ghaordie to Beinn Heasgarnich gave the hardest going up to that time. They are tough enough for "rather uninteresting" to be rather untrue. I found specific interests that wasted over an hour of the morning's floundering.

The going was heavy certainly. "Long miles of very rough and peat-boggy schist with deep heather", was my inelegant log-book summary. Hares and ptarmigan were forever exploding at my tortoise feet. At one stage I sat for a long time watching deer browsing in the Lairig Liaran just below me. Even in mid April there were grunts and groans and a variety of sounds from these supposedly silent animals. I then spent half an hour by a pool which seemed to be only 10 per cent water and 90 per cent frog spawn, and was heaving with frogs who vanished at my tread, but after I'd sat for a while eyes would pop out and after twenty minutes the scene was an entertaining one. Two, gripped together, swam off with immaculately synchronised strokes while another could not co-ordinate his limbs at all and another spent ten minutes battering at a wall of spawn as it tried and failed to fight through. Strange, isn't it, how some areas teem with frogs while others, which look much the same, never seem to have them?

That was all happy procrastination. I was glad to have the chaotic acres above clear of mist for you could never be sure of the exact summit of Meall nan Subh otherwise. It even looks a "frustrating series of knolls, bogs and detours" on the map.

The ascent of Meall nan Subh can be made very easy by motoring up Glen Lochay, a quiet glen of many charms and some good waterfalls, and then up the Hydro road from Kenknock. A locked gate may bar the Learg nan Lunn road over to Loch Lyon at the top of the pass, which seems a bit of cheek considering public monies built the road. This hill could equally well be done from the Glen Lyon side in combination with Meall Buidhe and Sron a' Choire Chnapanich — but perhaps you'd prefer the watershed walk round Loch an Daimh to take in those Corbetts which do not even gain the put-down of "uninteresting". No hill is uninteresting. You canny subh your granny aff the bus!

Section 4:   9. SRON A' CHOIRE CHNAPANICH   837 m   OS 51
              456452 *The nose of the lumpy corrie*

Section 4:   10. MEALL BUIDHE   907 m   OS 51   427449
              The yellow dome (boo-ee)

The *SMC Journal* for 1984 broke the news of "a new Corbett", discovered by Jim Duguid. This was Sron a' Choire Chnapanich, the name being obtained from the 1:25,000 map as was the startling height of 837 m rather than the 686-m contour on the 1:50,000 First Series map.

Only when I started writing up the Corbetts for this book did the oddity of the hill become apparent. The First Series 1:50,000 shows it separated from the Stui hills by a mere four contour lines — 200 feet in old measurements — so how could it be a Corbett? Even accepting the 1:25,000's 837 m, what was the separation? It all became so frustrating that I took the easy answer and went and measured it myself, a good excuse for a day on the hills above Glen Lyon. We set off for Meall Buidhe first, a big Corbett, both in bulk and height.

We parked under the dam, whose outflow explodes upwards like a fountain. The loch's level was low and we initially hopped along the exposed boulders on the north shore to admire the patterns and textures of the well-cleaned rocks, then we angled up steeply to pass under the crags (hanging garden of flowers as they are out of reach of sheep or deer) and on north-westwards across gentler, very featureless grassy moorland slopes to end at a cairn perched above the upper Feith Thalain. This area could be very confusing in cloud. The cloud was coming and going for us, but on the whole we could see what we wanted, topographically if not photographically. The scene was all Whistler tints of grey.

We dipped to the col and then plodded up the ridge, which has the posts of an old fence, to circuit round and up Meall Buidhe, which is not far off being a Munro, though it is probably one of the least-climbed hills in Scotland because of its 8 m shortfall. During the Munro-in-one expedition I could not resist making a high-level traverse from Meall Buidhe to Meall Buidhe — the range north of Loch an Daimh which, when I first knew it, was two lochs, Loch an Daimh and Loch Giorra. In the dry summer of 1984 they became two lochs again, the local keeper told me. The level of the new reservoir joining them was low enough today that they had almost reverted. Our morning reverie was interrupted by the noise of a train and, sure enough, down on the edge of Rannoch Moor, a caterpillar train was eating its way across the wasteland, just as had happened on the Munro trip.

A fresh south-east wind was blowing, allowing us to walk into a herd of deer which was crossing the col east of the Corbett. The deer that saw Storm and me ran, but there were more behind who still cantered up unaware of why the leaders had shot off. They just kept on coming, scores of hinds, with youngsters at heel.

From the Buidhe col I dropped past a peat patch to traverse along the flank of the glen quite easily, ending on the col below the problem Corbett, a real jungle of peat hags and runnels. I had a bite to eat which gave my two altimeters time to settle, then I noted the heights carefully.

The ascent to the Corbett is over as kindly a surface as you will ever find on a hill. The heather or moss-sedge mix seems to have been woven like a carpet — with a deep pile. There is one area (quite clear when coming off Buidhe) where a band of bright green runs down the slope from the seepage of a horizontal fault. This was dotted with mountain violets, looking so delicate in that wild, upland world. Across on the *sron* of Meall Buidhe a long line of deer were clearly seen against the grey sky. A deer track led up at an angle to bypass the crags and obviously linked with the col I'd just crossed. The whole gentle slope of the Allt Phubuill valley is blanketed with peat hags — not a good way to the Corbett.

I was still on the old fence line but I tend not to mention fences as they can be more of a hindrance than a help in bad weather navigation. Perhaps if a fence was clearly following a county boundary, which is marked on the map, I'd give it prominence but not otherwise. I've been led astray too often by trusting fences instead of using map and compass. On these hills there are fences, old and new, all over the place. Cows, as well as sheep (and deer) range over these green domes. Glen Lyon's green is partly from the rich underlying rock but also from the evil-spreading bracken. It is the longest glen in Scotland and this walk is at its western extremity, the uppermost houses having gone under the waters when Loch Lyon was dammed after the war.

The summit of the Sron was a superb one, a real nose (*sron*) jutting out to the north. Our perch gave an eagle's eye view *down* to the slim version of Loch an Daimh and also *up* to the Stui (Stuchd an Lochan), still very dominant in the east. While the altimeters caught up, Storm and I wandered down the green prow a bit. The turf was starred with the flowers of dwarf cornel and cloudberry. How such a soft vegetation survives in such an exposed spot is a puzzle. The cairn is tiny as there is no stone close to hand on that tower of peat. A skylark was in full song overhead.

The *SMC Journal* note goes on a bit about the name of this Corbett, but a walk up the hill would have cleared any theoretical speculation. The summit is such a marked nose that, logically, *sron* has to be in its name. Nor is it the flat sausage shape of the 1:50,000 First Series delineation. The altimeters made the pull up from the col to be 735 feet.

As it was a draughty summit Storm and I ran most of the way down. Deer were grazing under the crags to the east and when I knocked a stone down they heard the clinking sound and fled along the hillside. At the south col we sat among the bobbing hare's tail, over a bit from a forlorn-looking gate, and did some more arithmetic. The difference on that side was 676 feet. My figures were a quick estimate from metric altimeters but the hill clearly had 500-foot clearance, definitely a Corbett.

With no hope of cancelling a Corbett we ambled on again, by Meall an Odhar, for the pull up Stuchd an Lochain (the Stui). The weather was going, however, the east having a cheerless, dark, late-Goya gloom to it as we headed down to Pubil fairly quickly. By the time we had changed sweaty garments, had tea and written up some flower notes the rain had started. For those to whom dates are vital, the car radio was full of Boris Becker being bumped out of his chance of a third Wimbledon title. It was that wet year. The keeper at the house under the dam said the road over to Glen Lochay was not locked. We made our exits over that pass, though we saw nothing.

Section 4: 11. CAM CHREAG 862 m OS 51 536491
      Crooked crag

A second *crooked crag* Corbett (near Tyndrum) came in with the mapping revisions, but Cam Chreag to me is always the Glen Lyon hill for, with Braehead School having a bothy in the Black Wood of Rannoch, it was within our sphere of influence. The hills between Schiehallion and Rannoch Moor we came to know well and, as always, a lasting affection arose from the acquaintance.

If "we captured the rainbow and rode its shining path" on those days at Rannoch there were still good days afterwards as well. Following my November days on Meall Luaidhe (see 4:6) and Beinn nan Oighreag early on the Saturday (4:7), I still kept a 9 a.m. rendezvous with an Eastern SMC Meet for a day traversing the Lawers group. Staying up high in the pass overnight was a wise move as, on the Sunday, when I drove down into the shadowy depths of Glen Lyon the ground was glittering from a hard frost. At seven o'clock I set off for Cam Chreag from the bridge above Gallin.

That November weekend Kitchy and I wandered up the dark heather with its scattering of old pines. The heather eased with height gained and grey rocks occasionally broke through, very much the desolate moorland of much of the area. Cloud was welling up from the glens as the temperature changed and Meall Buidhe soon disappeared — but the Corbett stayed clear, a not unusual state of play. This hill's name presumably comes from the crags that stutter along its eastern face. It is fairly featureless otherwise but gives good views, to Lawers –Tarmachan in particular and to really wild country to north and west.

As the day was young I decided to go on to the Munro Meall Buidhe. The only snag was that my map (One Inch) ran out just west of the Corbett. Where exactly was Buidhe? I sat and tried to recall all I could from previous visits. In a col down the north ridge of Cam Chreag lay Cul Lochan and on one occasion we'd come up the Dall Burn and passed it to a vast wildness below Glas Choire, that symmetrical hollow under the rim of Meall Buidhe. Glas Choire had to be south west from the Cul Lochan and as Meall Buidhe curved round the corrie the east top of the Munro (Meall a' Phuill) had to be more or less directly west of my position. I set off, by compass and memory, in search of the Munro.

The cloud actually cleared on Meall a' Phuill and a grand day evolved so we added the Stui as well, the best of Glen Lyon's hills, before returning to the Dormobile and Monday morning back at the office. I had absolutely no worry at trying this "blind" navigation because, if I became hopelessly mislaid (not *lost*) then I only needed to steer due south and I'd have to come down into Glen Lyon or Glen Daimh.

This basic grasp of lay-out is something which is seldom mentioned in textbooks or classroom, yet I'd say it is one of the essentials of navigational skills. The Black Wood of Rannoch is a fearsome big place but my gangs of young teenagers would cheerfully go off into it for hours at a time, and often did become mislaid (you're only *lost* when you sit down and give up thinking) but could always win out because they knew every stream ran down to Loch Rannoch and its road, beside which the bothy was situated. They just went down to the road and turned right or, if they'd crossed the Dall Burn, turned left. Nothing complicated with map and compass but something better. The confidence engendered was remarkable. Map and compass came easily after that.

If you could arrange it (friend with car, post bus or whatever), Cam Chreag is a good excuse for a walk through from Loch Rannoch to Glen Lyon, rounding or going over the Cross Craigs to the Cul Lochan and on up the north ridge. Do add Meall Buidhe and descend to attractive Loch an Daimh with the Stui ranged as its backcloth.

If strictly Corbetting, the new bulldozed track approaching Cam Chreag up the glen from the east could be used to link on with Beinn Dearg (4:12). Off track, the country between the Corbetts is not recommended.

Section 4:   12. BEINN DEARG   830 m   OS 51   609497
            Red hill (jerrak)

Just west of Beinn Dearg is the Kirk Road or Lairig Chalbhath (Lairig Ghallabhaich), an historic old drove route from the south to Loch Rannoch, which is still tracked and gives the easy route to the Corbett from the north. From our school bothy near Dall, traverses of the Carn Mairg range sometimes began by that route up to Beinn Dearg. So many Corbetts *can be* combined with Munros that this becomes one reason for doing them simultaneously rather than Munros first and Corbetts second.

The only time I went up Beinn Dearg from the south was on a day when crisp winter conditions were sliding into the more usual monsoon that passes for winter in Scotland. The temperature rose quicker than I could. We went up from Camusvrachan, one of those establishments sitting below a complex drainage system so typical of these hills. These bellyfolds of hidden glens above Innerwick,

Camusvrachan and Invervar, are rather attractive: green in their depths, heathery higher and with framed views over pretty Glen Lyon to the Lawers hills. There are some huge herds of deer, and throughout our school days at Rannoch we sometimes spotted a rare "white" stag. Such beasts are never shot and are still viewed with a certain superstitious reverence. On one estate I know, a tenant insisted on shooting a white stag — and was asked to leave the next day.

I followed up the Cul Lairig stream for shelter (this was pre-trees) and then caught the west wind up on to Beinn Dearg. As the west began to chuck down a mushy mix of rain, hail and sleet, I scurried on with the storm to the next col and then rushed down the Dubh Choirein. With only an hour of daylight left there was no time anyway for the logical continuation to Carn Gorm, perhaps the best of the range, to complete the round of the Camusvrachan watershed. All the Glen Lyon hills are under deer so should be avoided from midsummer till the end of October. Given a good day Creag Ard should be taken in. As Firsoff says of Creag Ard and Beinn Dearg they "stand handsomely above Glen Lyon and the system of little glens and corries which divides them from the sprawling massif of Carn Mairg". In 1892 Stott recounted a Glen Lyon trip with Munro and wrote something similar: "A bold bluff hill, well-named, from its red shingly shoulders guarding the west side, the steep green slopes of Carn Gorm on the other." The current SMC guide (with a Munro fixation) says nothing at all about Beinn Dearg.

Section 4:   13. AUCHNAFREE HILL   789 m   OS 52   809309
      Hill of the field of the deer forest

"The wind was loud, the rain was heavy and the whistling of the blast, the fall of the showers, the rush of cataracts, and the roar of the torrents made a noble chorus of the rough musick of nature than it had ever been my chance to hear before." So wrote the ponderous Doctor Johnson when confronted with a wild night in the Highlands. Dave and I had a November camp in those conditions up at the head of Glen Lednock above Comrie when the storm did its best to wipe away a full moon. Whooper swans called on the loch and Sput Rolla down the glen was a solid wall of water instead of its usual braided beauty.

We set off from Invergeldie at 7 a.m. in the first gloom of day, having risen early "in self-defence". Geese were struggling south-wards through the tattered clouds. The first hare went charging off up the icy path and then went head over heels on a frozen puddle. I once counted fifty hares in a look along the dark heather flanks of Ben

Chonzie. It was spring, the snow had gone, but the hares were still parading in their white coats. Most heathery eastern hills have hares, but Chonzie has a world take-over programme under way!

Dave and I followed the old right of way up the Invergeldie Glen and then cut across north of Chonzie to drop to the wide Moine Bheag col and up the other side to reach Auchnafree Hill, the Corbett. The wind bullied us along so it was just a case of reaching out a foot and seeing where it landed us — eventually at the big cairn, a bit south of the long fence running to the south east. Had it been Dave's car rather than mine back at Invergeldie I would have blown on for the fine high-level, but slowly-descending, seven or eight mile walk to Meall Dubh and then either down to Newton Bridge or by the Shaggie Burn to Crieff, to be met there with the vehicle. Ah well, you must always leave something for "next time".

We backtracked to the Moine Bheag and contoured under the crags overlooking Lochan Uaine to keep out of the wind as long as possible. In hard snow it would have been dangerously steep when eventually we climbed up for the summit of the Munro. Loch Turret was sending sheets of water over the dam at the south end. Dave cracked: "They'll think it's raining in Crieff." We were back at Invergeldie by lunchtime.

This is probably as easy a way as any to gain Auchnafree Hill, or traverse it on a walk from Crieff via Glen Turret Reservoir and on by Creagan na Beinne to Loch Tay. Auchnafree is a great barren dome but the flying buttresses holding it up on the Glen Almond side give it a certain architectural merit, which makes that the most aesthetic approach.

There is parking just along from Newton Bridge towards the Sma Glen (Glen Almond is closed to cars) and an hour's walk will see one on the slopes of the Corbett. I've used a folding bicycle to shorten the time if not the distance when I also wanted to see the stone circle further up the glen. If transport can be arranged I'd suggest going up the Corbett from Conichan, then descending to Larichfraskhan. Instead of returning down the glen, a walk up through the scraggy pass of Glen Lochan to the public road at Loch Freuchie is a delightful addition to the day.

From Conichan skirt the Eagle's Rock southwards to Coire Chultrain. You can then search for the Thief's Cave on the way up. This large refuge was once used by a sheep-stealer, Alister Bain, who was eventually apprehended in the cave while roasting part of his booty. He was duly hanged on the gallows at Perth. The upper corrie is steep and craggy but easy enough. The Kirk of the Grove (a natural pile of big rocks at 831311) is an old secret conventicle site where services were held, free of persecution, in covenanting times. You have a choice of sacred or profane routes. Mad cyclists could even take their bikes to within a mile of the summit, for the Second Series map shows new tracks everywhere, even to the 700-m level. Somewhere up here the last wolf in Scotland was supposedly slain but there are as many such claims as there are beds slept in by Mary Queen of Scots. Auchnafree Hill is ringed by an extraordinary number of big waterfalls: Sput Rolla, the Diel's Cauldron and the Falls of Turret, Barvick, Keltie and Monzie. Exploring these on a wet day is a pleasant occupation. The details can be found in Louis Stott's *Waterfalls of Scotland* (AUP 1987).

Section 4:   14. MEALL TAIRNEACHAN   780 m   OS 52   807544
              Hill of Thunder

Section 4:   15. FARRAGON HILL   780 m   OS 52   840553
              Feargain's Hill

These were hills I always had to fight for in our bothy days in the Black Wood of Rannoch: Schiehallion was too near. Considering how visible the Farragons are from the Queen's View, or from the old military road over the hills south of Aberfeldy, they have remarkably little written about them. Detailed books on Pitlochry or Aberfeldy keep silent and even the SMC district guide simply omits this chunk of mountain country. Strange, for Farragon Hill seems a well-kent name.

The only book I've seen mentioning Farragon is *Fair Perthshire* by Hamish Miles, long a favourite of mine; but he only touches on Farragon while describing Grandtully Castle in Strathtay: "From the other [north] bank of the Tay here the ascent of Farragon Hill may easily be made. It is no great matter as climbing but the view from the top is remarkable — better than many far higher peaks reached with greater toil." He mentions MacGregor outlaws living in the recesses of Farragon — and recesses imply a complex country, which is certainly true. Few skylines are more ragged and a clear day is advisable for these peaks.

I had a day clear recently, doubly fortunately, for my day was an unexpectedly tasty filling in a sandwich of diabolical weather — that wildness from which Faldo won his golfing crown at Muirfield in 1987 and, while looking for a biro on the summit to mark in all the new bulldozed roads, plantings, the Foss Mine, etc., I discovered I'd brought the wrong jacket — and my compass was in the other, back in the car near Lick. Escape would never have been difficult: all drainage to my right would have been "home" but in that complexity a mist falling could have cost the Corbetts.

Somewhere east of Frenich Wood is the best place to start. Finding a bit of verge to leave the Loch Tummel road clear is not so easy. Storm and I followed up the first burn east of Lick, rising through a pleasantly wooded hillside. Birch predominated and the burn rushed down a flowery cleft. Over the day I must have spotted nearly every hill-flower that one will readily find in July. Perthshire hills are often rather dismissed for quality, but the schisty rocks produce a flora seldom equalled elsewhere.

The day before had been so wild that I left home only to go and see *Vivat! Vivat Regina!* at the Pitlochry theatre and then to spend the night in the Dormobile. No Holst of stars sang the planet asleep so the midge-calm Sunday morning came as a surprise; the rucker was quickly packed and we set off about ten o'clock.

As the woods thinned out there were some vivid patches of foxglove spires. A lamb with the trembles startled us as we walked through the smother of bracken. We passed by an abandoned sheep fank with the burn ahead held by a quiet corrie full of sheep and deer. Flies were a pest and, sweaty or not, I soon pushed on, taking the east fork in the burn and angling up to gain the ridge behind craggy Sron Mhor. Beinn Eagagach (Eagach usually) appeared ahead as a shapely cone and it was tempting to cut over to add this third of the range's summits.

Instead I circled the next bump on the west; as hoped, we kept coming on parcels of deer, most of the hinds with month-old calves at heel. We cut east of Creag an Lochain and saw the green knobble of Farragon Hill through the gap. Deer tracks in the heather were a great help in picking a route through all the bumps. Lochan a' Chait (*loch of the cat*) appeared, below, from the last col only just before the pull up to the Corbett. A sharp wind drove us into a nook in the summit crags to have some lunch. The flowers of mossy saxifrage lay like confetti on the blaeberry greenness that is such a feature of these ragged crests.

The view was indeed remarkable, even if all the bigger hills were cloud-covered. To Ben Vrackie and southwards I looked over varied tints of blue, shot through, here and there, by wandering bands of sunshine. Below me, the moors above Weem and Strathtay were a patchwork of new corduroy plantings with several roads coming up onto the patchwork. A new road (from Blackhill) comes up to pass Loch Derculich and zigzags up to the col between Farragon and Eagach before turning along the latter and Creag an Fhithich then down to Loch Tummel. This would make the ascent of Farragon from the south very easy, but less interesting than the wilder northern approaches.

St Fheargain was an early Christian missionary in the Pitlochry area and Farragon could well be a corruption of his name. We did not stay long on the summit of Farragon Hill. After a photo of Schiehallion towering over Meall Tairneachan we scurried down out the wind, circling the head of the big Frenich corrie of corries. Lochan Lairig Laoigh (*loch of the calves' pass*) points to an historic crossing point, but the *kylos* must have been athletic beasts in those days. A bulldozed track rounded the northern end of Creagan Loch and led across the top of the next corrie to the rather messy area being mined. A rare quartz rock is the reason for the mining activity though, being Sunday, all was quiet and still till three youngsters on trail bikes, with dogs following after, roared over the moors and off up the access road.

This road zigzagged steeply up from the mine to round a spur, then wended north of the Corbett and down through the solid plantations above Loch Kinardochy to the B846. You could practically drive to the summit. Schiehallion, which smoked like a volcano (a familiar feature), looked very big and bold from the top of Meall Tairneachan (Tarruin'chon on older maps), and the Carn Mairg range was flatteringly arrayed. I could also see Beinn a' Chuallaich above Kinloch Rannoch. Wade's road up from Tummel Bridge was an intrusive straight line in a world of curves. Great cumulus clouds and rags of blue gave a brightness to the scene. My first ascent of Tairneachan had been on skis, from the limekiln at Tomphubil, in a blasting of spindrift. That was pre-plantings. Now the easiest route for the Corbett is to walk up the mine road, not open to vehicles.

That day a poisoned toe was proving troublesome. I'd worn mini wellies for comfort and these were a boon on the descent. Doire Leathan, to the north, is the sharp cone which catches the eye so often hereabouts and along, under it, was a green rake (pointing to a leak-level between rock layers) which would make for soft, if wettish walking. I hobbled along the rake and, from the end of the ridge, had started to descend to the Frenich Burn when the heavens opened. It did not rain so much as just drop water wholesale. This thunderplump left everything saturated, just as we reached bracken level, and the pitted sheep paths became slippery in the extreme. The flies were back too. Well do they say, "Don't praise the day before the evening." In five minutes our dawdle was turned into a struggle, needing care and concentration.

The Frenich flows in a deep cutting which we followed, rather than the heather slopes above, crossing from bank to bank, slithering and being soaked from the thighs down. Eventually we were forced on to the east bank as the burn plunged into a gorge where the west bank is taken over by big forestry plantings. At the fields above Lick the bracken became head-high. We forced a way through it to a stand of big larch-trees which paraded beside an old made path down the side of the burn to a little wicket gate by the bridge on the Loch Tummel road. Frenich House has the burn flowing through its grounds, a bonus in an outstanding garden which I looked at from a seat on the bridge parapet. We'd been on the hill for six hours.

I drove over by the Braes of Foss, stopped briefly at the Foss Mine road-end, passed the Glengoulandie deer park, crossed Wade's Bridge to Aberfeldy and on to Grandtully Castle which was open under the Scottish Gardens Scheme. "Nothing like a circum-motoring of the Farragons to end their traverse," I thought as I sipped welcome tea at what Hamish Miles called "a handsome pile". Farragon, across Strathtay, was hidden by its own opulent lower slopes. The north is the grand side of these hills.

LOCH LINNHE TO GLEN ETIVE TO LOCH TREIG

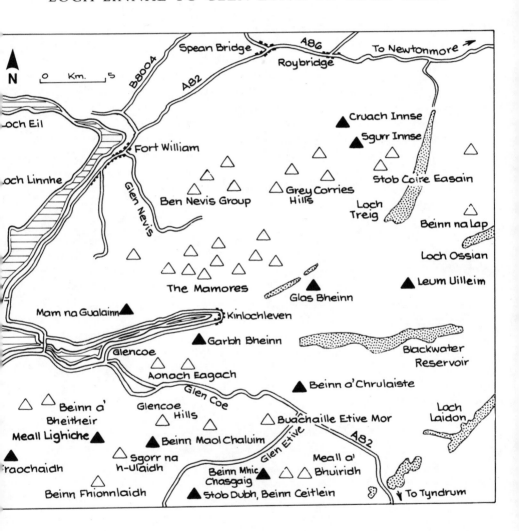

Section 5:   1. FRAOCHAIDH   879 m   OS 41   029517
Heathery hill (free'achy)

AT THE END of 5:3 I mention the fossilising effect our maps have had on Gaelic names. This *heathery hill* would almost certainly have had its name changed to *hill of trees* and probably prefixed by a rude adjective, even before walkers could render it in Anglo-Saxon. You just cannot climb Fraochaidh without having to tackle trees, which may be at any stage from recent planting to recent felling and every nastiness between.

I cycled up Glenduror to the bothy, not easy as there are changes to the forest roads as well, and crossed a bridge over the river (023536) to tackle Coille Dhubh direct. We were soon engulfed by blowing cloud, and the whole round trip is one I'd as soon forget.

From various criss-crossings of the valleys my recommendation, now, would be to start at Ballachulish and take the path up above the River Laroch, then the left fork that crosses over to Glen Creran to its highest point before a long, rather "up and down and in and out" traverse to the Corbett. At least this allows a tree-free ascent and the more aesthetic "walking west". Whatever its sins of forest, heather, bogs and braes (and probably midges) all is forgiven when one reaches the summit of Fraochaidh and looks out over the glitter of the west. It is not only the thought of the trees that makes one postpone the descent. Beinn a' Bheitheir under snow has the curvaceous purity of a Marilyn Munroe.

The quickest, simplest descent is by the west ridge for a mile and then north to Glen Duror through plenty of trees. A better route is to descend the steep south ridge and go on a mile to Beinn Mhic na Ceisich (Sheet 50) where there are two options: south then east to reach Glen Creran without any afforestation to fight, or west then north to reach the forestry road on the Salachan Burn which gives a minimal amount of tree-bashing. The Salachan Glen gives a pleasant walk down to the road along Loch Linnhe (Sheet 49). Whatever route is chosen depends on having someone helping with a car. If you just want to go up and down the same route I'll leave you to choose your own arboreal alternative.

Down in the forest on the south side of the Corbett are some limestone caves, and where Glen Stockdale spills over into the Salachan Glen are some others, including Uamh na Duilean Briste, on the side of a gorge just off the road (982519). When it was "discovered" in modern times an old ladder was found half way along its 300-foot passage. Alan Jeffrey's *Scotland Underground* has notes on all the explorations hereabouts.

Section 5:   2. MEALL LIGHICHE   772 m   OS 41   094528
             The doctor's hill

At one time a third of my life was spent in Glen Coe, either climbing hills or climbing routes, so it is an area I rather tend to avoid now in overcrowded summer. My great joy is being in the wild and lonely places. Glen Coe is wild but it is seldom lonely and the very fabric of the mountains shows the wear of a million tramping boots. Meall Lighiche's late appearance as a Corbett made a visit imperative and, running into that novelty, a dry spell in Glen Coe, we revelled in returning to what is undoubtedly an area of outstanding natural beauty. Traverses of the wee Buachaille and the Aonach Eagach were made for the sake of the dog's Munros, and as Storm also required Bidean we set off for this Corbett over the highest point in Argyll — hardly the conventional route to Meall Lighiche.

   The road up to Gleann-leac-na-muidhe is the normal approach and the road continues up to the junctions of the streams that embrace Meall Lighiche, or Creag Bhan rather, as its craggy northern arm is called. It is probably easier to ascend this bold rump of *white crags* than tackle it in descent, and this route gives an approach to the Corbett along a splendid high crest. That excellent but unjustly ignored hill, Sgorr na h-Ulaidh, fills the view southwards while Beinn a' Bheitheir shows her shapely curves in the west and the Ben bulks over all the jumble to the north. Bidean presents its least prepossessing aspect.

   By setting off at 7 a.m. we ensured having Bidean to ourselves. Clouds boiled up out of the glens to dramatise the summit. We then descended the back side of Bidean to reach Beinn Maol Chaluim (5:3), traversed Sgorr na h-Ulaidh, and climbed up Meall Lighiche direct from the linking col. Three buzzards were mewing and spiralling above the col, and the slope up the Corbett was so virgin that I actually commented on this in my log. Dropping down to that col and descending by the Allt na Muidhe would be a good way to complete a visit to a Corbett which is an excellent addition to the list.

   We met one person on our walk, though we could see tiny dots of figures on Bidean all day. The NTS Centre car park was packed, the favourite visitor pastime being reading the Sunday papers, an interesting spectator sport with periodic visitations from the midges when the breeze died away. Meall Lighiche could be linked with a

traverse of Beinn Fhionnlaidh and Sgorr na h-Ulaidh from Glen
Creran but the tree plantings would have to be taken into account.
You won't find that an overpopulous approach — and Glen Creran is
singularly beautiful.

Section 5:   3. BEINN MAOL CHALUIM   904 m   OS 41   135526
              Callum's bare hill (Bin-mel-halum)

Bidean nam Bian, the highest summit in Argyll, and the giant of Glen
Coe, is one of the very best peaks in Scotland for everything one seeks
on a mountain, whether easy walking, long ridge traverses or climbs
of all grades. In winter it becomes a majestic Alpine peak — and
should be treated with due respect. The gentle walker, merely after
this Corbett, should make its acquisition a summer ambition.

   Like all the hills hidden behind the bulk of Bidean, Beinn Maol
Chaluim suffers an undeserved neglect for it is out of sight and out of
mind from the centrist activity of Glen Coe. The Corbett is really a
Glen Etive mountain and, like everything else above that glen, the
slopes are steep, craggy, and full of character. It just happens to be
attached to Bidean by a high pass, the pleasant Bealach Fhaolain,
which is a lure to the spectacular traverse of Gleann Fhaolain rather
than just a slog up the Corbett. Our first nibble at this area was a flight
from midges.

   With a gang of kids I was camping in Glen Etive where we endured
a night of sheer hell from the piranhas of the insect world. Our morning
porridge turned grey on the spoon between dixie and mouth. In despair
we struck the tents and fled to Glen Coe Youth Hostel by the most
direct route — over the Bealach Fhaolain and down the Fionn
Ghleann. Neither Corbett nor Bidean deflected us from that journey!
The Fionn Ghleann would be the normal route to the Corbett from
Glen Coe. The Bealach Fhionnghoill is overlooked by big crags but
these can be turned on the north and an easier descent made from the
Bealach Fhaolain back to the Fionn Ghleann.

   My most recent visit to Callum's Hill was incidental to climbing
Meall Lighiche, a "new" Corbett (5:2). From Bidean one looks down
on the Corbett, as on nearly everything else, but Beinn Maol Chaluim
is as individual a peak as Stob Coire nan Lochain or Stob Coire
Sgreamhach. The descent off Bidean was the dog's least enjoyable part
of the day. It is steep and largely vile scree, and a right-flanker is
essential to avoid the crags which ambush on the direct line to the col.
In winter this slope can be icy and a slip would probably shoot one
down into the Fionn Ghleann with fatal, Coire Leis-like efficiency.

From the col we had an easy walk along and up the Corbett. At one stage we were sitting quietly when a big dog fox traversed the hill just below us. Foxes are always proclaimed as nocturnal animals but the foxes of the Highlands are often encountered in the daytime, quietly going about their business. They are nocturnal in urban-rural settings, I suspect, purely as a matter of survival. A fox, like us, has no objection to lying in the sun.

Beinn Maol Chaluim is capped with quartzite, which lies on top of the schists that make up the hill. The quartz rocks are on top simply because of the colossal folding of the earth's crust in far off times; normally they are below the schists. The Torridon giants are the extreme example of this folding, and geologists originally gave all sorts of explanations, for even they could not conceive the reality that Liathach had been turned over as if the young world had been ploughed. The lower slopes of Chaluim owe their green brightness to the richer schists which also give a more lavish flora.

As mentioned above, the best route to Beinn Maol Chaluim is the circuit of Gleann Fhaolain. Start at Dalness from where unrelieved steep slopes lead up to the shapely summit of Stob Coire Sgreamhach. There are big views down Glen Etive and down the Lairig Eilde. Any awkward steps on the crest can be turned on the south flank. The ridge sweeps on with a dip to the head of the Lost Valley merges with the ridge coming in from Stob Coire nan Lochain, and reaches the top of Bidean, a viewpoint which for once loses nothing by its superior position. You could probably name off as many peaks from the top of Bidean as you could on any Scottish summit. The continuation to Beinn Maol Chaluim has already been described; the descent is down the long south ridge to the Glen Etive road, just off the map, but there is a wide gap in the trees which have so effectively cut off Gleann Fhaolain itself. (The Etive trees are a plague of almost midge proportion.)

The Corbett name is tautological, for both *beinn* and *maol* mean "hill". *Maol* is always used of a rounded, bald, dome sort of hill, emphasising its shape: Callum's bald dome. A baldy lad called Callum no doubt was the victim of his friends' wit in giving this name. Callum (Malcolm) is long forgotten. The name sticks, fossilised on the map for ever and ever. Keepers and shepherds rarely use map names, which are practical aids, after all. We named all sorts of places above Dollar in our boyhood Ochils — and some of these have been likewise fossilised — they have proved useful. Baldy Callum's grandchildren might well have called the hill something else from their own associations with it. Post Clearances it would have probably been in English too. Names were living things before the Ordnance Survey pinned them, like butterflies, in the map cabinet.

Section 5: 4. BEINN MHIC CHASGAIG 862 m OS 41 221502
(named after a person)

This is rather a forgotten hill, a mere appendage to Clachlet — a Clachlet appendix — which most people manage to live without. Corbett-baggers will eventually come round to it, of course, and gluttons for punishment could well traverse Stob Dubh (Ceitlein) as well in a single expedition (see 3:13), which is a more strenuous day than the circle of Chasgaig–Clachlet–Creise.

A gang of us once did so, but in reverse order, Sron na Creise being easier *in ascent* we'd decided. A box on wires allowed us to cross the River Etive dryshod but when last I looked, this novel "bridge" was all chained up. The River Etive is fordable only in good weather. As Creise's Munro moved south a mile with the major revision, you can still add two Munros easily enough to the Corbett. It would be a waste not to, really, for the huge, lumpy, glen-gouged hills on the Etive side of the Blackmount have an austere, almost Himalayan grandeur to them. Alltchaorunn is the starting point and a path leads up into the Ghiubhasan Ganga. There are fine granite pools in the first mile and a threefold choice of route thereafter: 1. straight up the West Ridge, turning a crag at 400 m; 2. by the burn which curves up on the south side of this ridge; 3. up the Allt Coire Ghiubhasan to mount to the col joining the Corbett to the rest of the Blackmount hills. If willing to paddle the Etive, this col, or its bordering ridge, can be followed from the other side. The amount ascended will still be the same. The summit is a strange saucer of a place and in bad weather it can be difficult to pinpoint.

The best of the Corbett lies in linking it with Clachlet (*Clach Leathad*) and a short diversion can add the Munro of Creise (238507) as well. Rannoch Moor, being 1,000 feet up, has a completely different character to the shadowy depths on the Etive side. The descent from Clachlet to the Bealach Fuar-chathaidh is demanding; the Bealach is the secret link from Glen Etive to Rannoch Moor at its innermost recess of Coireach a' Ba, and you may feel happy just to descend the Ghiubhasan rather than go up again in order to descend the Aonach Mor ridge. Ben Starav and Cruachan look well from this round.

Section 5: 5. BEINN A' CHRULAISTE 857 m OS 41 246567
Rocky hill (croo-las-tay)

This was a convenient outing for 1 January 1968 when a crowd of us were based at Lagangarbh. We'd had some fairly desperate climbs during the previous few days as snow fell on snow and thaw on thaw, and going anywhere on foot (or even by car) was eventually almost impossible. Seeing in the New Year had eaten up several hours of the day, we did not make an early start.

John was from Australia, David from Cambridge, Robbie from East Scotland and Bob from the West: a right mixed bag. Our ages spanned over fifty years. A further delivery of snow had been dropped off overnight and I took my skis for the ascent. An unusual absence of wind meant some fog on the moor, so the view was given suddenly after we'd climbed for half an hour: the Buachaille like a frosted citadel across a pantomime moat of mist. It was a weary flog up, even with skins, for the snow was heavy. Later the snow was powder or worse. The mist rose like smoke and we only had tantalising glimpses from the summit.

Our ascent, which was not difficult, took us up the west ridge from Altnafeidh over Stob Beinn a' Chrulaiste. The main rockiness lies on the south flanks of this approach. I was tempted to ski down the SE Ridge to the Kingshouse but time was a bit short. The Blackwater Reservoir was frozen over and I thought then that skates would be the way to explore it, for the shores are extremely bog-bound. How the drovers coped with the vast herds of cows that came south down the Ciaran and over the hills to Kingshouse is a mystery, even if the Blackwater was then a series of lochs, not the massive barrier it is now. I still want to skate it. There are two good Corbetts on the north side of the Blackwater (5:8; 5:9) which are a bit out of the way from this Rannoch Moor side.

Rannoch Moor is one of the places verbally abused by John Maccullough, who was perhaps the first real explorer of our mountains, and who could charm on one page and rain sarcasm on the next. According to him we looked down on an "interminable Serbonian bog, a desert of blackness and vacuity, solitude and death". He had hired a horse to cross the Moor, which was a mistake. He "might have remained in Glencoe. A ride this was not. I cannot even call it a walk, for half was traversed by jumping over bogs and holes. I may fairly say I jumped half the way from Glencoe to Rannoch."

Those of our gang on foot were glad enough to use their up-furrow on the way down. The skiing was not good. At the end the skis kept balling-up. It was snowing hard by the time we were back at the hut and an hour later, when we set off for the fleshpots, six inches of new snow lay on top of all the rest. Under the circumstances Beinn a' Chrulaiste was quite a successful first summit of the year.

More recently, when I tried to catch up on some friends who had gone off for Chrulaiste from Kingshouse, I set off from Jacksonville and went straight up. A big gully, left of the summit, was left on my left and

I followed a tongue of pink porphyritic rock which gave enjoyable scrambling. It is clearly seen from the road. The west bank of the deep gully would be the quickest and easiest line of all.

Section 5:   6. GARBH BHEINN   867 m   OS 41   169601
              Rough hill

Garbh Bheinn, which is well-enough named, is a secretive hill, for the Pap of Glencoe blocks the view to it from the west and the battlements of the Aonach Eagach loom over it to the south; even seen across Loch Leven it does not stand out. The Corbett is a good hill to stand *on*: it has the Mamores in full array to the north. Unlike many in the list, this is one to be climbed from sea level. The view is earned.

The easiest approach is by the maintenance road up from Kinloch-leven to the town's water-supply reservoir on the Allt Coire Mhorair. Burn-addicts can follow the stream to its source on the slopes south of the summit, those in a hurry can take a direct line up on to the 734-m eastern top and reach Garbh Bheinn that way. Up the valley and down the ridge would be a good combination. The southern slopes are grassier and less hostile than the northern, which are steep and rough. I once went up from Caolasnacon and have an abiding memory of bracken, birch scrub, heather, greasy slate crags, clegs, midges and drizzle. On the summit there was blue sky overhead, but cloud lay all around and I saw nothing. A pile of beer cans and other garbage at the cairn soiled the experience much more than these natural perversities. It was on those northern slopes above the kyle that Stevenson, in *Kidnapped*, had David Balfour lying up in the heather while Alan Breac sought food from Caolasnacon (*the narrows of the dog*). I bet the clegs and midges were as bad then as now.

In a 1914 *SMC Journal* W. Inglis Clark enthusiastically advocates Kinlochleven as a mountaineering centre, comparing it to a Nor-wegian fiord. "How can one reach Kinlochleven?" he asks. "By train to Ballachulish and thence by small steamer. Leaving Edinburgh by early train we reach our destination about 11 a.m. and by returning at 2.30 p.m. it is possible to make the double journey in a single day" — in other words Garbh Bheinn was a day-outing by public transport from Edinburgh.

He also describes the footpath from Glencoe village to Kinlochleven along the south slopes of the loch and its annoying habit of going over crags rather than round them. The road was completed only in 1922, having been started with the labour of German prisoners of war. The narrows themselves were quite a formidable barrier on the sea approach, having bad tides and needing constant dredging. Kinloch-leven still has an air of unreality about it. One does not expect an industrial complex in such a corner. The houses are now colourfully painted to counteract the long weeks when the sun is blocked off from the town. You can blame Garbh Bheinn for that.

Section 5: 7. Mam na Gualainn   796 m   OS 41   115625
Pass of the shoulder

This is a Corbett for a Sunday morning, usefully allowing for a return to a Scottish home the same night. It was the last Corbett I climbed on my final weekend as a normal office worker. The next week I left my job, was laying caches for the Munros expedition and then went off to ski and climb in Poland to gain some fitness for "the Long Walk" as I thought of that 112-day Munro tramp. Because all my maps were packed I could find only one map that had some of this Corbett on it. The missing bit was sketchily drawn on the map margin while in the Kingshouse bar on the Saturday night. Sunday did not dawn so much as drown.

After a late breakfast the weather brightened enough "to go and have a look", a phrase which often heralds an escapade (or justifies a disaster) but here was merely practical fact. I drove round the south side of Loch Leven so as to look across to Mam na Gualainn and pick out a reasonable line. I'm not sure now why I didn't just walk up the path from Callert over to Lairigmor. It crosses high on the Corbett's west shoulder with a branch stalkers' path wending up to 620 m. Eventually this was the way I took Storm up the Corbett. The path now starts a quarter of a mile east of Callert (signpost), with parking just round the corner, and wends up through oakwood to a knoll with fine views, then on up the hillside, avoiding the Callert farmlands. Two miles east of Gualainn lies Beinn na Caillich, 764 m, which dominates Kinlochleven's view. It has a path all the way to the top (very clear) and is a good ascent to start a traverse to the Mam.

Perhaps I'd had enough of the Callert path on that first visit for its status as a right-of-way was disputed all through the decade I was a director of the Scottish Rights of Way Society (a body, incidentally, which I feel every regular hill-walker in Scotland should support with their membership, both out of gratitude for past defences and for the problems still to come). The right-of-way was established in the end, this being an old coffin route, and Callert being the ferry port on the north side of the loch to reach Eilean Munde burial ground. As a boy I was rowed out to the island by a local man of great age and when, in conversation, I mentioned the name Campbell, he glared at me and then turned to spit into the sea.

Maybe he influenced me to drive round by Kinlochleven to park at a cemetery on the north shore. I followed a track up past a sheepfold which contained some big rams. A sparrow-hawk was winging through the trees and buzzards called higher up the hill.

I followed up a hysterical stream, still high with overnight indulgence. The slippery ground at one stage had me going for a slide and when I grabbed the bank in reflex reaction the old bracken gave me a bloody cut.

I'd chosen the roughest line of ascent but everything was too sodden to allow safe scrambling. When I broke up on to the ridge, waterproofs went on to counteract the vicious wind and I funked out of the storm in the lee of the summit crags to study the Corbett, Garbh Bheinn, across Loch Leven. This hill was backed by the white crest of the Aonach Eagach, much whiter on this north side than that overlooking Glen Coe (the north-south differences can be quite important for winter route selection), while the Mamores (south side) were grey and white, a streaky-bacon effect. Between the Corbett and the Mamores is the Lairigmor, part of the old military road from the south to Fort William. I'll never forget a school trip when we walked through the pass during a heat wave. The bare, scree flanks of the lairig reflected the glare and heat, and twice, clothes and all, we flopped into streams only to dry again before long. We were walking from Killin to Skye along old drove roads, this being one of the historic parts of the road from the isles. Now it has a summer flow of West Highlandwaymen. When I last walked through, west-east, two score of them charged past me, then I had the glen all to myself again. The majority did not seem to be enjoying their day very much. "How far to Fort William?" I kept being asked. As they were festooned with maps and guidebooks it seemed an odd question. Every time I replied I added an hour to my estimate — but nobody seemed to notice.

From the summit of Mam na Gualainn the Pap and Beinn a' Bheither were luridly lit in a clash of sun and cloud, but the Ben wore a bunnet of black so my smugness at a dry ascent suddenly seemed misplaced. A desperate romp down failed to beat the next deluge. I was saturated below cagoule level but as the storm went on for the rest of the day I suppose I was lucky. My thoughts were gloomy enough. What if the weather was like that for the big trip? What had I let myself in for? You can read what in *Hamish's Mountain Walk*; however, there is simply no comparison between a big trip like that and merely pecking away at the lists over odd weekends.

The commitment is total. An hour off Mam na Gualainn I'd changed clothes, was dry, fed and enjoying the hospitality of a friend in Fort William.

Section 5:   8. GLAS BHEINN   789 m   OS 41   259641
                The green hill

Section 5:   9. LEUM UILLEIM   906 m   OS 41   331641
                William's leap

New boots in Fort William before the train to Corrour Station and a night at Loch Ossian Youth Hostel gave me Leum Uilleim. The boots hurt so much that they were dumped in the loch to soak overnight. They were then moulded by a pre-breakfast romp up this fine viewpoint. We caught the *morning* train out. That was a pure Corbetting raid, which has one justification: dissatisfaction will ensure a desire for a more leisurely visit. Every time I travel the railway this peak tempts. It is a shapely tent rising over the northern flanks of Rannoch Moor. Corrour is 400 m up but the Corbett still gives a big view of everything from Ben Nevis southwards and, eastwards, along Loch Ossian to the gunsite pass of the Bealach Dubh. Leum Uilleim can easily become a favourite hill, whether skied between trains or sleeping out on it on midsummer's eve. Best, as so often, is the memory of a journey . . .

The alarm failed to wake me and I had a rush to catch the morning train at Bridge of Orchy. The early January snowfall had thawed out to leave the hills with a mottled effect. Leaping off a train at Corrour Station is always exciting. Having a path from it to one's chosen hill is almost overdoing things. The path wanders over the boggy moor and crosses the mouth of Coire a' Bhric Beag to land one on the drier slopes of Tom an Eoin. The Glasgow train grumbled up from Loch Treig but a tongue of cloud reached out from Loch Ossian and hid the "low" ground, then flowed up and over the hill. One gain was almost walking into two unsuspecting stags.

Leum Uilleim is double-topped with Bhric corries to north and south. On the waist of saddle between the tops I dumped my heavy rucksack, quite sure of finding it again as firm footprints were left on the snow. The cloud cleared briefly as I went up the final cone and below, southwards, shone the sprawl of the Blackwater Reservoir, a huge longitudinal moat which, like Loch Quoich, has drowned several once-useful stalking paths. In a strange way it has isolated these Corbetts; access from Corrour or Kinlochleven is easy in theory —

but when did you start a hill day from Kinlochleven? The shores of the Blackwater were created by the devil to break Christian souls; and they are as rough as along the north side of Lochan Fada for A' Mhaighdean.

I sometimes wonder how others plan and approach their hills, be they Munros, Corbetts or whatever, so I was fascinated to read an account of Don Green's in the Grampian Club *Bulletin*. That cheery Dundee club has a large number of list-tickers, the inheritance of Eric Maxwell, perhaps, who once kept the records of those who had done them all. Don drove to Rannoch Station one June and joined the north-bound morning train, meeting a friend and his dog who had joined the train at Crianlarich. They descended at Corrour.

The moorland approach to Sron an Lagain Garbh was remarkably dry and in the frequent sunny intervals the ridges enclosing Coire a' Bhric Beag with its big snowfield presented an inviting prospect. Among the peat hags we flushed a meadow pipit from its nest, which contained four eggs.

The females drew ahead but Misty got a lot of mileage out of returning to check that Gordon and I were following. On the sron which soon became well defined, then rose in rocky steps, we disturbed several stags in velvet. The top of our ridge was marked by a small cairn from which the summit of William's Leap was half a mile to the south-west. Like so many Corbetts, Leum Uilleim is a grandstand for Munros: Schiehallion, Beinn Laoigh, the Black-mount summits, Glencoe, the Mamores, Grey Corries and the Ben Alder forest were spread around us.

Misty soon disposed of her packed lunch plus titbits from her companion's pieces. We watched a north-bound steam excursion train, looking like a Hornby toy, toot and pause at Corrour. With plenty of time before our south-bound train was due the whole party opted — especially Misty — to visit the summit of Beinn a' Bhric.

The intervening bealach was surprisingly dry and a short climb brought us to the cairn. From it there was a striking view across the wetlands of Rannoch to Lairig Gartain's U-shape, with the summits of both Buachailles in cloud. The descent of Tom an Eoin was a canny daunder with expanding views all round. Stob Coire Easain's south ridge, delicately etched in snow, rose temptingly above the end of Loch Treig. As we descended to warmer levels Loch Ossian became the foreground for the Bealach Dubh and the great colourful plateau of Ben Alder.

After the unhurried descent on a sunny afternoon we sat below the track enjoying the dappled view of our sky-line round as we quaffed the carry-out which Gordon had thoughtfully cached in the morning. The south-bound train pulled in just four minutes late and we were soon back at Rannoch. A modest but satisfying venture, it has sown the seeds for further excursions using the same approach.

It sounds familiar, doesn't it?

With my summit view gone I returned to my rucksack on the col and on over Beinn a' Bhric, the lesser western top (872 m). There was a brief glimpse north to Loch Treig from whence comes a path to skirt Loch Chiarain, between Leum Uilleim and Glas Bheinn, and then plunge into the Blackwater. Another path keeps west of Loch Chiarain then splits, one branch going to the Blackwater and then down to Kinlochleven, while the other traverses round Glas Bheinn before going down to the town. At the south end of Loch Chiarain stood the bothy which was my haven that night after I'd spludged down through the thawing snow off Leum Uilleim.

I arrived early enough to be grabbed by Leen to go down to a wood dump by the Blackwater for a big beam each. You had to have a companion: whoever sank through drifts could not rise again without help. Eight others had arrived by the time we returned and people kept drifting in, from Alltnafeidh at the entrance to Glen Coe, from Kinlochleven, even from Ben Alder cottage. The bothy was an upstairs room in the shell of the building and it soon built up its own inimical atmosphere. Officially an MBA committee meeting was being held, but this did not prevent interruptions for brewing punch. Hours, brews and drams later there was relative quiet again, just two rows of sleeping-bag mummies with big daddy Denis in the middle.

A rather manky morning followed and as I'd been up Glas Bheinn not so long before I went out with those heading, via the Blackwater dam, back to Alltnafeidh which also ensured a lift back to my car at Bridge of Orchy. Alltnafeidh had been my approach for Glas Bheinn, while staying at Lagangarbh. Memories of moonlight on Chrulaiste and the wandering beams of passing cars, the familiar black shapes of the Buachailles and the Lairig Gartain, reading Alastair Borthwick's *Always a Little Further* and listening to the last night of the Proms.

Dry weeks had left the normally wet walk through by Lochan na Feithe quite dry. I had been on the watershed for daybreak. The Crowberry Tower looked very spiky from there. I crossed under the dam and then wandered up the hillside for Meall na Cruaidhe (570 m) with its tiny tarn beside the path that angles up from Chiarain. There was little view but it was too raw to sit and wait for a change. A line off southwards to avoid the steep eastern flank led me to the path out from the bothy. It and the Feithe glen and the Lairig Gartain are all in a straight line (a geological fault?) which made for a view inside a view inside a view. The monument is to a London vicar, the Rev. Alexander Heriot Mackonochie, who died there in 1787. This time I crossed the top of the dam before going down to look at the score of graves — the price of building this dam. Dates were from 1905 to 1909, one was a *Mrs* Riley, one "Not Known", others showed what a mix the navies were: Gillies, Hughes, Wilson, J. Smith, McFadden, Johnstone, Dunlop, McKay, Murphy, Dow, Day, Darkey Cunningham, Derry, McKenzie, W. Smith, Wallace, Brady. Borthwick tells a bit about their tough life, but Patrick McGill's *Children of the Dead End* is a vivid novel based on the author's experiences during the construction work. It is still in print.

I took the dam road west for a bit and then cut up on to the old military road to the Devil's Staircase and so back to Lagangarbh. Several people have spoken enthusiastically of the high, level NNE Ridge of Glas Bheinn — that, I think, will be the next way to the top. It would be a good excuse for another cross-country trip starting at romantic Corrour Station.

Section 5: 10. SGURR INNSE   808 m   OS 41   290748
            Peak of the meadow

Section 5: 11. CRUACH INNSE   857 m   OS 41   280763
            Hill of the meadow

I've often wondered which "meadow" these hills are named after. Perhaps at one time the area round the Lairig Leacach was under cultivation, or perhaps it was Coire Laire which is so dominated by Sgurr Innse or maybe just the Spean valley itself. Considering how the Corbetts are surrounded by big Munros they, or at least Sgurr Innse, are remarkably prominent landmarks. I suspect they were named from the early users of the Lairig Leacach. The flat ground there would be a natural resting point for cattle on the move. In the great droving days the Lairig Leacach was an important part of "The Road to the Isles".

For several years our school struggled to try and establish Inverlair as a residential centre before the bureaucratic Fife authorities scuppered those hopes. In the end we were not allowed to sleep in the building (a one-time prison for Rudolph Hess), in case someone was hurt. Yes, we could camp outside, or camp on top of Ben Nevis, but not inside the building. . . . We were stopped doing any restoration work (surely the most genuine, educative practice the kids could have?) because this might take work away from proper joiners. Those Inverlair days, however, gave us a chance to wander and explore the surrounding countryside, to head off on multi-day treks, to botanise, to rock climb and sclim every Munro within a day's walk — Beinn a' Chlachair to Creag Mheagaidh to the Grey Corries was a pretty good classroom! The promotion of Beinn Teallach to a Munro was only inconvenient for my new dog Storm.

Much of our rock-climbing instruction was done on the rocks of the gorge below Inverlair though every now and then we would wander up Coire Laire to climb on Sgurr Innse or the Stob Corries. The two Corbetts are both craggy but our activities were confined to Sgurr Innse which is a much more dramatic wee peak. The easy way up it lies on the side facing Cruach Innse and, in descent, route finding can be tricky, with crag piled on crag and the transverse ledges not always easy to see. Sgurr Innse so dominates with its portly presence that it comes as something of a surprise to find Cruach Innse is the higher hill.

We came to know them from the Coire Laire side but occasionally the keeper (who had lost an arm in the Korean war) would drive up the Lairig Leacach by Land Rover and give us a lift to the bothy. To us it was always Payne's bothy, a good base for the hills and passes round about. The incorporation of these Corbetts with a walk through this fine pass is the day I'd particularly recommend for bagging the Innses.

Start at Corrour Station and take the path and estate track down to Loch Treig and Creaguaineach Lodge. The Easan Dubh is a fine fall in the gorge between the lairig's guardian hills. Follow the east bank up the Lairig Leacach. The Corbetts eventually dominate the pass. The rake up the Sgurr is clearly seen — and best used unless wanting some scrambling or climbing — but the Cruach is a more straightforward traverse. Rejoin the road before it is swallowed in the plantation. Below the trees there are traces of the old miniature railway which followed the British Aluminium pipeline from Loch Treig to the works in Fort William (the so-called tunnel under Ben Nevis). The line, even now, can look confusingly like one of the Parallel Roads. The last few miles to Spean Bridge are by the attractively wooded banks of the Spean, the well-named Grey Corries bold on the southern skyline.

This walk can be done between trains, in either direction, but the actual walk is easier going south-north, as Corrour Station stands at over 1,000 feet. An alternative is to descend Coire Laire after traversing the Innses. Tulloch Station can then be used — or a night may be spent at Nancy Smith's hostel at Fersit (see p. 7), an enjoyable experience in itself. My last two visits were both on through-treks, the last a May Ultimate Challenge, when Nancy's hostel was a welcome haven from the earliest midges I've ever met.

SECTION SIX

LOCH RANNOCH TO LOCH LAGGAN & BADENOCH

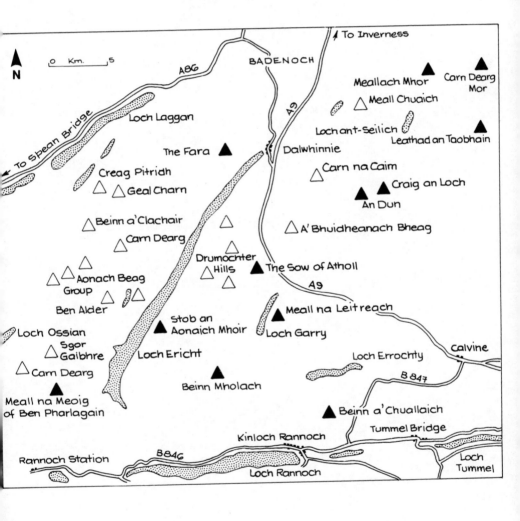

Section 6: 1. Meall na Meoig (of Ben Pharlagain)   868 m
            OS 42   448642
            Hill of whey, Pharlagain perhaps *grassy hollow*

Many years ago I climbed Sgor Gaibhre and Carn Dearg in a circuit from Rannoch Station. I was not then aware these were Munros but I do recall going over Beinn Pharlagain (it sounded just like ptarmigan), such is the lure of a name. When Meall na Meoig of Beinn Pharlagain appeared as a Corbett I could not be sure of having ascended it. I set off to do so — from the CIC Hut.

This is not as crazy as it sounds. I'd just completed a *cycle* link of country summits: Carrauntoohil, Snowdon, Snaefell, Scafell Pike and Ben Nevis, the climax being a stunning sunset from the CIC Hut after traversing the Ben and Carn Mor Dearg. The idea of cycling home did not appeal (main roads in mid-summer) so I left the hut at six the next morning and called in at the Youth Hostel for a shower and my cycle. When I rolled out the bike I found there was a flat tyre; I blew it up and raced for the train.

Good intentions of repairing the puncture on the way failed due to chatting with the guard; I left the bike tethered at Rannoch Station and set off under the viaduct for a floundery crossing to the Allt Eigheach and the useful track all the way up into Coire Eigheach. It was a sticky, hot, hazy day as I followed the side burn up as long as it lasted, drank lengthily and dandered up the penultimate "new" Corbett. The area felt vaguely familiar, that knobbly world with the lochans. Only later did I see the intriguing feature of the lochan east of the Corbett having *two* outflows. Some day I'll have to go back and check if this is really the case.

That valley approach is recommended. Pharlagain is all lumps and bumps and tussock and bog, and the direct line is rather trying. Up the burn and down the ridge would be reasonable. Quite unreasonable would be a direct approach from Ben Alder cottage. The Cam Chriochan runs through unrelieved peat country, both difficult and dangerous.

I went on northwards to add Sgor Gaibhre and Carn Dearg but descended quickly into the corrie as I was desperate for water. I drank some, paddled in some more and then ended having a sort of bath. I was not very keen to descend. Syd Scroggie's words (on Loch Ossian) applied: "Summer seemed in love with idle days." The Mam Ban bogs were cracking in the drought and the views had the paleness of watercolours about them. After tea in the station café I caught a train back to Corrour, pumped the tyre, again, and just reached the Youth Hostel before it was flat once more. Tom Rigg welcomed me in but, though it was hot and the old "range" was blasting away, the windows were kept closed because of the vicious assaults of midges. They were as bad in the morning. I defy anyone to repair a puncture under those conditions. I pumped the tyre and raced for the station, sanity and home.

If travelling by train it is quite possible to break the journey and do these hills from Corrour to Rannoch stations (or vice versa). My doings were a bit complicated by having the cycle but the opportunity was not to be missed. Without puncture or midges I'd planned to cycle east from Rannoch Station to Pitlochry for a train home from there. One last warning. Going direct from the station to the Allt Eigheach track is a dry-weather short cut. Under normal conditions it is best to take the estate road from Loch Eigheach.

Rather sadly, Beinn a' Chumhainm has been deleted as a Corbett as not having a 500-foot re-ascent. It is a natural continuation of this Munro traverse and well worth a visit. Keep it on *your* list.

Section 6:   2. STOB AN AONAICH MHOIR   855 m   OS 42   537694
              Spike of the big crest

Section 6:   3. BEINN MHOLACH   841 m   OS 42   587655
              Shaggy mountain

"The road that leads to Rannoch is the gangrel's royal way."
(Ratcliff Barnett)

My last sortie to these hills led to a near fiasco. Storm just managed to add the shaggy mountain to his list but Aonaich Mhoir was left unvisited. I suspect that "unvisited" — and perhaps unloved — is the state this remote hill long occupies for most Corbetteers. "Speak as they please, what does the mountain care?" (Browning) A difficult cull is Aonaich Mhoir.

Dog and I were in the Rannoch area but, being the stalking season, were keeping off the hills until the weekend when I decided on a quick "raid". There is no stalking on Sundays. Late on Saturday we set off up the old right-of-way that goes from Rannoch to Dalwhinnie via Loch Garry. (The route comes down to Annat, not to Craiganour.) Once above the fields we came on an old village in the hollow of the burn, a stark reminder of departed life all over the Highlands — and on the way back we sat there for an hour of bliss, agreeing with the prophet, "Better is a handful of quietness than two hands full of toil." (Ecc. 4:6)

My plan was to follow the track so far, head up Beinn Mholach and on towards Aonaich Mhoir till too dark to see, sleep out, then, on the Sunday, add the second Corbett and tramp part way down the long Hydro road to Bridge of Ericht (the sane but stultifying "voie normale") — only I'd branch off for the hill track by Meall Garbh and the Killichonan Burn to hit the lochside road just west of Talladh Bheithe. Here I'd left my folding cycle to speed the return to the car at Annat. I had a good sleeping bag (being crisp autumn weather), a stove and food, and a bivvy bag "just in case".

Dandelion days are apt to blow away and as we crossed the rather squelchy moors to the final upheave of Beinn Mholach I knew we were in trouble. Clouds had come rushing over and a sleety rain started when there was about an hour of daylight left. To save weight I had no torch, so even a straight retreat down the road would not be welcome. We needed shelter. A vicious front going through would not be very pleasant on top of the hills while coffined for ten hours in an orange poly-bag.

Less than two miles off I knew of a hut (not on the map) — but it might be locked — while, in the opposite direction, lay a building (on the map) which I'd never seen and feared could just be a ruin. We chose the latter, however, and after struggling up to Mholach's big cairn descended with the rain now sheeting across the hills. (The forecast had said "scattered showers" or something equally innocuous.) "Even if there's a gable standing, at least that would shelter us from the worst of the punishment," I muttered. "It's all your fault anyway, dog, wanting to do the Corbetts!" The building remained invisible till the last moment. But it was a building. And it was open. A most welcome howff.

The rain lashed down all night and on into Sunday morning. There was a certain smugness in standing at the window watching a parcel of deer splashing across the flooded glen. When the rain eventually gave up, so, perforce, did we. A retreat was made back to Annat.

Aonaich Mhoir was shortly after earmarked for a canoeing trip to Benalder Cottage, and Beinn Bheoil set down as our Munro for the "Boots Across Scotland" charity attempt on scaling all the Munros simultaneously. Anything to avoid the long tarred road in from Bridge of Ericht.

Loch Ericht is a strange water and stories persist that there was once an inhabited valley where now we have the loch. The loch is dammed at both ends and when the engineers were working on the dam at the Dalwhinnie end they found evidence of an ancient outflow to the

Truim. Some catastrophe is supposed to have occurred and the ancient parish of Sgireadail was overwhelmed and the loch's outflow changed to the Rannoch end. Off Aonaich Mhoir a fisherman, pulling in his boat's anchor, hauled up a small gravestone inscribed, "Elspet Robertson. Died 1545."

In the summer of 1802 James Hogg, the Ettrick Shepherd, wrote to Sir Walter Scott, from Dalnacardoch, of a sortie through by Loch Garry to Rannoch and back by a peak to the south east of Loch Ericht. He could have climbed one or other or even both these Corbetts. He found a ptarmigan which "fled fluttering to wile us away from her young" so he must have been high. Ben Arlenich (Alder) with remnants of snow was much commented on. He could pick out the far Ochils and eastwards the view "was lost and bewildered amongst the vast ranges that surround the utmost limits of the Bruar and Dee . . . every time the fatigued eye wanders through them they remind one exactly of the billows of the ocean; such a prodigious extent of country is crowded with them, rising and swelling behind one another, and that which the eye fixeth on always appears the largest."

The choices have not changed much since Hogg's day — you enter this "prodigious extent of country" by Annat or Bridge of Ericht on the Rannoch side or through by Loch Garry from the A9. The eight miles of Hydro road from Bridge of Ericht is the one I'd recommend — to my enemies. Sixteen miles of hard road is not my idea of fun.

Section 6:   4. Beinn a' Chuallaich   892 m   OS 42   684618
         Hill of the herding

Beinn a' Chuallaich is the huge but unobtrusive sprawl of hill above Kinloch Rannoch, a spur of which, Creag Varr, so dominates the village. In bad weather the Allt Mor draining the huge western corrie of the hill can also be a dominant feature for, then, it roars down through the woods into the village. This corrie could well be responsible for the name of the hill. It is a huge, gentle hollow which would be the perfect place for summer grazing or for secreting cattle for safety.

Creag Varr was the nearest climbing crag to our school's Black Wood bothy but we never went on to the hill after a climb; I made an ascent some years later when Corbetts began to be a specific interest. I found Chuallaich to be a hill well worth exploring, even if my first visit, on a May afternoon, gave sleet, rain and clouds on top. I parked the car on the road from Kinloch to Trinafour and went straight up, certainly the quickest route as quite a height has been gained even before starting. A few words of warning, though.

There are additional plantings along the southern and eastern flanks so any starting point should utilise one of the paths shown. The most easterly path (over Meall na Moine) is just outside the planted area and is now the best start (706615). This path leads by a hidden hut to a gate in the deer fence. All the streams are captured by an aqueduct, which explains the horizontal line across the hillside. The water is being led along over to the Errochty scheme. By chance a traverse of Chuallaich was my last hill-birthday-outing, a summer tradition I've always tried to maintain. If you are only likely to climb the hill once, then our route is what I'd recommend.

I drove up to the high point and dumped my folding cycle in the bracken, then drove down to park in Kinloch Rannoch itself. We set off up the Allt Mor, up the fall in a literal sense. There was not much water coming down and plenty of slabby rock to scramble on. The rock was a bit too greasy, however, and when we reached the water supply intake we followed a path up the west bank. The zigzags on the map are now an estate road which wends on above the trees to turn east across the Allt Mor above a dyke which runs towards Craig Varr's northern end. There is a footbridge (rather rotten) across the river not far above the wood which could be useful if the burn was in spate. We merely followed the burn.

The woods with the falls (really a long waterslide) had been windless, giving sweaty progress so the breeze on the heathery moors of the Allt Mor corrie was welcomed. There was an extraordinary lack of wild life. Even the hill flowers were past, except for the heather which was just tinting into flower — still pastel tones rather than the garish acrylite to come. Clouds were break dancing out of the west and rolling along the Carn Mairg hills. The burn ran in a slabby slot, its banks providing the first blaeberry feast of the year. I never tire of following streams up into the hills. My first solitary explorations followed them in the Valley of the Thousand Hills in Natal and moving waters have never lost their allure for me. Three days before, I'd been in Edinburgh for the launch of the sumptuous book, *Waterfalls of Scotland*. It lists over 750 falls. Perhaps here is a new list for tickers, something for after the Munros and Corbetts and Donalds and Bridges and Walls and Wainwrights . . .

We eventually followed a side stream and gained the heights north of Creagan Breac. The mass of Beinn a' Chuallaich appeared ahead and then vanished under a tide of cloud. With the good path to Loch Errochty crossed, there was only one wee pull and suddenly, through the murk, loomed trig and cairn. The cairn is a colossal erection for the quartzy rock is perfect for building. Indeed every bump round the corrie coming up seemed to have a "stone man" on it. We sat out of the tearing wind and our patience was rewarded after half an hour when the cloud ripped off and the view was displayed.

"The view is particularly good owing to the long stretches of low country which surround it in most directions, the Cairngorms appearing to special advantage; while on the neck of the NE spur lies Loch a' Caillich where the deer love to wallow." So wrote Charles Plumb in *Walking in the Grampians*, 1935, a book which still retains the freshness of its descriptions and points to an amazingly different world from the one we know. Loch Errochty had not been raised by its dam, then, for instance.

Schiehallion can't have changed, though. It dominates Loch Rannoch and the Tummel valley in unique fashion. Ben Vrackie and the Farragons rose in stark, dark shapes such as D. Y. Cameron loved to paint. The Gaick Pass (with Loch an Duin held between its Corbetts) is one feature to capture the eye. Nearer lie some vast moors, tawny and brown, leading away to Rannoch Moor. With Tony, on one occasion, and Sandy and Claudia on another, I've twice crossed that empty quarter on Ultimate Challenges, on the former going from Loch Ericht to Loch Errochty to the Bruar, on the latter to Kinloch and Blair Atholl. Beinn a' Chuallaich diverted us, north and south in turn, with all the assurance of a super tanker running into a regatta of dinghy sailors. God bless Beinn a' Chuallaich and all who climb on her. It was a satisfying birthday summit.

The view westwards brought back the words of the song: "By Tummel and Loch Rannoch and Lochaber I will go . . . By Ailort and by Morar to the sea." At Braehead school this had inspired a class project on the Road to the Isles, and, as a climax, we trekked the route outlined in the song. The song's origins are local — Marjory Kennedy Fraser's folks came from Tummelside. The tune had been composed by a pipe major and carried various military names as it made its way in the world of piping. A Barra man, Calum Johnson, learnt it from an island tinker and in turn played it on his chanter at a gathering in the Frasers' house. Kenneth M'Leod was, there and then, urged to write words to this splendid tramping tune and so, by Tummel and Loch Rannoch, the generations have gone.

On my birthday visit our route off, due east, ran into more quartzy crags than the map indicates (best turned by first descending south for a quarter of a mile, then off down to the east). There is a lonely corrie hidden up in the sweep of ridge to Meall nan Eun. A crow was croaking above us and we disturbed a mountain blackbird (ring ouzel) and a family of young wheatears — which hints at the bouldery nature of parts of the descent. There was a pipit or two, and a curlew drifting by on its wailing song. I don't know why the ascent route had been so devoid of life. Best of all, when I was retrieving my bike out of hiding, I came on a slow-worm sunning itself on a bank: still and glossy as a sculpture cast in bronze.

A derelict wall was being worked over by the wheatears. Farragon's cone and triple-topped Meall Tairneachan changed colours and weathers in rapid succession. All the showers seemed to keep south of the Rannoch–Tummel valley. We had it dry. The Meall na Moine path angled down to a gate which we were glad to use — and so back to the road.

Minutes later we were whizzing down the brae on the bike, Storm smirking over my shoulder from the rucksack. He dives into the rucksack with the happy expectation of a town dog jumping into a car. Children's faces grinned out the back of the cars that overtook us and, as I dismounted in the village, I noticed the car behind had a ciné camera trained on us. With the bike on board I promptly drove back up to where we'd been and on round to the old Wade road up from Tummel bridge where I parked and waited a fruitless hour for a photograph of our hill. The hill was clear but flat and lifeless under grey skies. While waiting I filled a dixie with blaeberries. I may not have had a birthday cake but Mary's blaeberry pie, once home, was a far nicer end to the birthday hill.

Section 6: 5. MEALL NA LEITREACH   775 m   OS 42   639703
              Hill of slopes

Section 6: 6. THE SOW OF ATHOLL   803 m   OS 42   624741

In 1729 General Wade rode up in his carriage from a "hut" at Dalnacardoch to a site opposite Loch Garry where his 500 Highwaymen, as he called his road-building soldiers, had prepared a feast. "We dined in a tent pitched for that purpose; the Beef was excellent and we had plenty of Bumpers." They'd built 52 miles of road that year and the line of that route is still generally followed by the A9 through the Pass of Drumochter today. If you park near Dalnaspidal Lodge for these Corbetts, wander up the Allt Coire Mhic-sith a bit, you'll find the ruins of this bridge: "Oxbridge" as it was called.

Dalnaspidal is *the field of the hospice* and was obviously a long-established stop for drovers and travellers coming south from Speyside through by Loch Garry to Rannochside. In 1863 Telford's protégé, Mitchell (after years of bureaucratic fighting), saw his Perth–Inverness railway opened. On the Drumochter county march and watershed, at over 1,500 feet, it is the highest mainline railway in

Britain. The new dual carriageway now tends to speed travellers through at twice the speed of seeing anything, which is a pity. Drumochter is an impressive pass and perhaps the best view of it is from the slopes of Meall na Leitreach. Both it and the Sow of Atholl can be climbed conveniently from Dalnaspidal.

I had Leitreach on a crisp, windy March day, setting off from Dalnaspidal and following a very boggy track straight up the lower slopes, a track made by one of the then new go-anywhere tracked vehicles. I was soon above the freezing level and hard snow made an easy ascent; there is less than 400 m to climb. There were deer everywhere and a plover wailing on the summit with its fine view of shapely Schiehallion, rising darkly out of a world of shivery silver tones and blowing a long plume of spindrift across the sky.

Drumochter, from this ascent, is an impressive pass, its depths an incredible jumble of moraines like frozen waves on a torrent, thrown into sharp relief by slanting sun and drifted snow. The intrusive rail–road–pylon lines shrink into their real scale: small works of men. There were deer everywhere when I slid down a gully and walked along a trod above Loch Garry. A parcel of stags splashed across the loch's outflow and the valley echoed to the various calls of spring wading birds. The wind picked up dervishes of snow which danced ahead and suddenly vanished. Anne Murray in a poem has the phrase "where the wind skins Drumochter" and it can certainly blow with flencing ferocity. A friend once combined Leitreach with Mholach (6:3) but had an escapade crossing the stream moating Leitreach opposite — so be warned.

That March day I went on to climb the Boar of Badenoch rather than the Sow of Atholl, being more interested in a botanical rarity than anything else. The Sow is the only site in Scotland for a heather whose normal home is in Norway. I didn't find it on the Boar. Even turning the Sow into a Corbett has not helped with my search. Both Boar and Sow are old friends. The Sow can easily be added to a round of the four Munros west of Drumochter; starting at Dalnaspidal on the south slopes for the Sow and Sgairneach Mhor removes the problem of crossing the Allt Coire Dhomhain to the north.

Torc is the Gaelic for boar and Badenoch is the name of the country to the north. The Sow of Atholl is probably a more recent fanciful name, the pass's watershed being the march between Atholl and Badenoch. The Sow is really Meall an Dobhrachan, *watercress hill*. Both Boar and Sow have steep flanks to Drumochter and it is worth going to the edge to be able to gain the view into the pass. What history it must have seen: Montrose, Argyll, Cromwell, Clavers-house, Johnny Cope, Jacobites and Hanoverians, the clansmen of

Atholl, Speyside and the west, drovers and packmen, Queen Victoria (incognito), the navvies and Hydro workers, right up to the modern juggernauts, stagecoaches and weekenders wending up to Aviemore and Cairngorm.

Driving southwards from Dalnaspidal keep an eye open to the left for Wade's Stone, a monolith set back near the Allt na Stalcair. This has a date, 1729, on it and commemorates where the northward and southward gangs of soldier-navvies met when building the Drumochter road. It was moved during the latest road improvements. I'd rather like to have seen Drumochter before man came here at all; however, these Corbetts give the next best impression of Scotland's Khyber.

Section 6: 7. THE FARA 911 m OS 42 598844
       Presumably *faradh*, ladder

The *SMC Journal*, all six foot of it on a shelf, is a mammoth source for all sorts of hill information but when I looked up its indices, to see what anyone said about The Fara, the name did not occur. This is quite extraordinary for The Fara is a big Corbett which is often climbed on its own merit and not just for ticking off on a list.

The Fara is a hill I've been up five times — on four occasions traversing it during coast-to-coast or other long tramps. Loch Ericht is a bit of a barrier to trans-Scotland routes and you are forced up to Dalwhinnie to reach the A9. After a few times walking the road by Loch Ericht *anything* is a welcome alternative — even traversing The Fara! Quite a few Ultimate Challengers have done just that and been pleasantly surprised by the hill. The Fara is nothing much to look at but the view from the summit is one of the very best in Scotland, while there is also the unusual feature of the Dirc Mhor.

The first time I just ambled up and back from Dalwhinnie having dropped off some friends to blitz Munros east of the A9, but even that easiest of lines is no longer practical thanks to a band of conifer planting which runs from Loch Erichtside to the top of the old Wade road to Laggan (the A889). The easiest route is now to walk down Loch Ericht for a mile and then up the edge of the old plantings which leads on straight to the summit. Even doing that I'd recommend making a circuit to take in the Dirc Mhor and return by the Allt an t-Sluic, forestry or no.

The Dirc Mhor is a boulder-filled slot, hemmed in by crags, silent and dry, a weird spot which I found while walking from Ardnamurchan to Buchan Ness, the widest crossing of Scotland. It was a low-level alternative but has been first choice since. On that grey day it was quite atmospheric and I remember a joyous meeting with the gush of water below the cut where we sat among the birches for a brew. *Dirc* is dirk, the highlander's big dagger, an apt name for this stab-wound of a feature. A good path leads from the River Pattack road up by the Allt Beinn Eilde to finish in a wide basin, west of The Fara, whence an easy wander up the hillside leads to the Dirc Mhor, and a longer, easy wander up leads to The Fara's summit. Whichever side one climbs The Fara there is always a second view suddenly revealed on reaching the summit crest.

The Fara is a long undulating crest, and on another coast-to-coast, which was also linking Banachdich to Mount Keen (west-most and east-most Munros) I took to the slopes above Loch Pattack, making for Meall Cruaidh the first summit, and then relishing the 2½ mile crest to The Fara summit. On the way up I kept taking photos of the Ben Alder hills and it was curious to see them "shrink" as we walked the miles to The Fara. On top the view to the Spey and the Cairngorms was added.

There is a huge cairn on top of The Fara. A wall leaves it, dropping east, and the last time up there, on UC 86, Chris, Tony and I were glad of its shelter: though it was sunny, for the first time in a week, a bitter wind was blowing and snow showers were trailing across the sky. Chunks of ice were blown off the cairn as we sat in the lee with the inevitable brews. On the path up the Allt Beinn Eilde we had found a half-full two-litre bottle of a "well known soft drink", which had been a welcome refreshment too. We left it as it had been left for us. Heading to Culra from a winter traverse I once found a loaf of bread on the path, which was most welcome too, once it had defrosted from nature's deep freeze.

Dalwhinnie has become a bit of a backwater with the new A9 "passing by on the other side" but it is always a good stopping place on these long tramps. There is a shop, a transport café, a useful hotel and pleasant B & B. And there is The Fara, its very own mountain.

Section 6: 8. AN DUN   827 m   OS 42   716802
           The Fort

Section 6: 9. CRAIG AN LOCH   876 m   OS 42   735807
           The cliff of the loch

The word Gaick comes from Gaig (Gaa-ik) meaning a cleft place, a good name for this deep gash that is an historical pass from Speyside to

Atholl. The steepest, wildest mile of the pass lies between these two Corbetts, with Loch an Duin filling the slit and leaving little room one feels for foot-passengers. So far the estate roads have funked this gap. The country boundary bisects peaks and loch and it is an eleven kilometre walk, mostly up an unsurfaced road, to reach the march — the easiest route to the Corbetts.

This is a private road, and one where a cycle could be used to great advantage, but the most pleasing ascent of these hills would be to take them in on a walk right through the Gaick Pass from Dalnacardoch to Tromie Bridge. (The Minigaig Pass shares the northern part of the Gaick, see 7:7.) Some friends and I started at opposite ends to walk the pass and we met at the memorial to the loss of Gaick for lunch and an exchange of car keys — one way of dealing with the car problem. My log at the time recorded the walk being a much more satisfying route than the more famous Corrieyairack which we'd done the day before; and with several visits to both since, I'd not change that opinion.

There is a plantation above Dalnacardoch (a government-built inn of 1774, on the site where Wade was based when building the road through Drumochter) but after that the going is rather bleak up the Edenoch Water to Stronphadruig Lodge, which stands in a rather battered plantation. In 1986 Tony and I were glad to use the shelter of an outhouse to make hot drinks and apple flakes after a gale-blown crossing from Dalwhinnie. An Dun was on our programme then, but, with miles to go and a big wetting due, we left An Dun and descended off Vinegar Hill.

From Stronphadruig, An Dun looks like a colossal, natural *dun*, or fort mound. Where the estate road is shown finishing below An Dun there is a dam on the river, and this captured water flows through the pass and then is tunnelled to Loch Cuaich and so on to Loch Ericht, Rannoch, Tummel and the rest — an amazing re-use of a liquid asset. We stupidly crossed there and so had to paddle over to the abandoned lodge. After our refreshments we traversed a boggier stretch up to the col due east of the lodge (the building up the slope is a water-supply shed) to reach the Glas Choire, but by turning north Craig an Loch is easily ascended. *The cliff of the loch* is followed to a distant bare plateau summit with two cairns. The name is really A' Chaoirnich. The best way off is to the north west, for the whole west flank is a mass of scree, reminiscent of the Pass of Brander.

Loch an Duin's outflow is usually a safe crossing place (a good swimming strand too) and the burn on the hillside gives eyes and feet a feature, which helps relieve the mind for the steep toil up on to An Dun. Its cairn is at the south end of the elongated flat summit area.

Due west is the least brutal way off but it is quicker to head due south.
An Dun gives a steep descent in any direction, but on reasonable grass.

The Gaick path passes along the west of Loch an Duin then swaps
over to become an estate road again by Loch Bhrodain. Unlike Lot's
wife, indulge freely in looking back to the steep vee formed by the
Corbetts. Gaick Lodge is situated on the flats before Loch an t-Seilich
and just north of it is the monument to the "Black Officer" and his
companions who were swept away in an avalanche in 1800. Captain
John MacPherson was a hated recruiting officer, so local sentiment
soon spun myths round the story. The steep contours of the slopes and
the plateaux above create avalanche conditions very readily and there
are several records of massive disasters. One huge avalanche poured
down when the locals were near starvation point and deposited at their
doors 6 stags, 6 brace of grouse, 3 brace of ptarmigan, 20 hares, 1 snipe
and a white horse!

Section 6:   10. MEALLACH MHOR   769 m   OS 35/43   777909
             The big hump

Section 6:   11. CARN DEARG MOR   857 m   OS 35/43   824912
             Big red cairn

These two Corbetts are both on Sheet 35 but for practical purposes
Sheet 43 is also needed and possibly the NE corner of Sheet 42. They
stand in a pleasant bit of the country which is rather neglected as it lies
so close to the bigger Cairngorms. This is to the Corbett-collector's
benefit and I've often noted these hills smiling and sunny while, just a
few miles to the east, the Glen Feshie Munros were having their faces
washed.

The area is riddled with footpaths and bulldozed tracks, as it is
prime sporting estate country. This is a disadvantage for some months
of the year but a great gain for the rest of the time — deep heather is not
the gentlest of walking surfaces. It also gives a huge variety of possible
routes for the clutch of Corbetts in this dark corner of Scotland.
Leathad an Taobhain (7:7) can be done easily enough on a round with
these two; I managed the three together in mid-December, starting at
first light and cycling from Tromie Bridge up the estate road to the
path junction beyond Bhran Cottage.

I dumped the bike and walked along the left fork to the weir on
the Allt Bhran then followed the path on the north bank of this river.
The path swings steadily south (path and stream junctions are right on
the edge of Sheets 42 and 43 so call for a bit of care) and finally flanks up

the eastern slopes of Coire Bhran to the pass of The Minigaig. This is an old drovers' route and the featureless crossing is made at *c.* 830 m (see under 7:7). The Corbett lies less than two kilometres away to the north east and is the nameless, solitary trig point, 912, the list name being hijacked from the lower western top. Here is the sort of place to take people who do not believe Scotland has any "wide open spaces". The bowl of the upper Feshie is an extraordinary "Empty Quarter" and the eye is led away through by the Geldie to the Deeside hills. Schiehallion also looks well.

A track runs northwards from the Corbett, and on the next bump, Meall an Uillt Chreagaich, it has been bulldozed into an estate road. A snow storm caught me there, and as I followed the road in and out the folds of hill my port side became white. The snow went off as I rounded into the deep "sneck" of the pass that holds Lochan an t-Sluic, a blue eye that reflected the great plateau country above Coire Garbhlach — and the ugly bulldozed track up to those heights. A left fork, rather than going down the pass, leads up and then along above a plantation (which is right across the old footpath) and a stalkers' path continues up on to the saddle between the Carn Deargs. I zigzagged up through blowing clouds, meeting a large posse of stags near the col. The wind was cold enough for the dog to curl up in the snow when I stopped at the presumed summit of Carn Dearg Mor. Kitchy helpfully sniffed along our track so, rather than take hands out of warm pockets to navigate over Carn Dearg, I let him lead me down the zigzags to the road — giving the stags another surprise. The dog was white with hoar, as were my beard and my woolly garments.

The track ran along above a second plantation and then swung down northwards through a pass, which was just below the freezing cloud level. A shot rang out away to the north, probably a keeper culling hinds. A grouse going off was much more startling. A straight western walk over a lower bump, Meall an Dubh-chadha, led to the bigger lump of Meallach Mhor, allowing navigation to be fairly casual. Going into the icy blast I was thankful not to need intricate navigation. We hardly broke step for the Corbett and then romped down the burnt patches in the heather out of the murk of cloud into the cloudier murk of dusk. As my cycle lamp died on me the run out was much more exciting than the walking.

Without always going up summits, I've criss-crossed most of the paths in this area and they are all clear and often very useful. One alternative, for this pair of Corbetts, would be to start at Achlean, the end of the public road up Glen Feshie, and walk up the glen, crossing to take the track up by Lochan an t-Sluic and returning to Glen Feshie by the Feith Mhor. And what about a big day, perhaps based up Glen Feshie, walking up past the Eidart to take in Carn Ealar, Beinn Bhreac, Leathad an Taobhain and Carn Dearg Mor? The Ring of Feshie. That's one for a midsummer's ramble!

ATHOLL, GLEN FESHIE, GLEN SHEE, DEESIDE

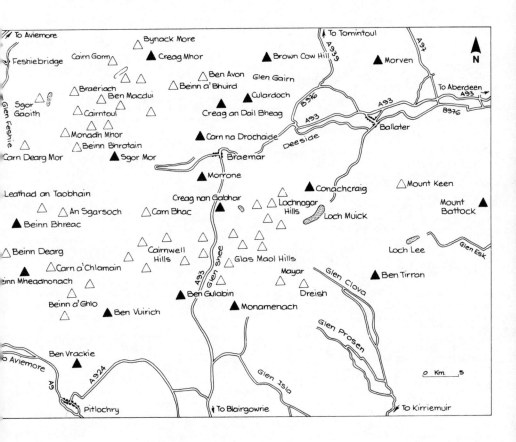

Section 7:   1. BEN VRACKIE (BEN-Y-VRACKIE)   841 m   OS
43/52   951632
The speckled hill

WE WERE A gang of young lads camping at Blair Castle when Ben
Vrackie, in 1956, became my second Corbett, not that I knew
anything of Munros or Corbetts in those days. One climbed, like any
young animal, for the uncontemplative freedom of fitness and
strength. Birds can spread wings; we earthbound creatures seek the
heights. The view is the same.

Ben Vrackie is very much Pitlochry's local hill, and one of the best
views of the hill is from Pitlochry's Festival Theatre with its sylvan
setting by the River Tummel. They are difficult to separate in my
memories and the one can be a pleasant sequel to the other. As a
teenage schoolboy I cycled from my home under the Ochils to make
some show, and the director showed me backstage and treated me to a
meal. I slept in a haystack that night and was home for church parade.
Later, as a teacher, a bus-load and a car-load of us went to see *Hamlet*
and slept out in the heather afterwards up on the slopes of Ben
Vrackie. You can sometimes twin your enthusiasms.

From any high point on the A924 road from Pitlochry to
Kirkmichael you can tramp across the heather moors to Vrackie,
rough going but with the odd sheep track to help. The view from the
summit is tremendous, especially westwards along the Tummel–
Rannoch trench to distant Rannoch Moor and its hills. Beinn a' Ghlo
looms large and, southwards, there is a good view of the Lowland
hills. There is a view indicator to help the visitor unravel the extensive
panorama, a memorial to the Leys School, Cambridge, which was
evacuated to the Atholl Palace Hotel during the war. The materials for
the indicator were carried up by donkey.

The knobbly, craggy, heathery world of the moors and tops is a
stark contrast to the wooded richness of the lower slopes, and to enjoy
Ben Vrackie fully it should be climbed from either Pitlochry or
Moulin or, at least, a descent made to the valley to complete a traverse
from any other starting point. From Pitlochry you can walk up Golf
Course Road to Moulin or you can drive up to this attractive and very
historic village where the path up Ben Vrackie is well signposted.
After a drive up a lane to a car park the walking starts through birch
and pine woods and heads by Loch a' Choire to the final rough
triangle of hill, the screes and crags being passed on the right. The

summit mass is an unusual lava issue in a world of schisty rocks. Ben Vuirich, the Corbett to the north east, just too distant to combine with Vrackie, is granite. Another route is to go or return via Craigower which overlooks the splendid woodland scenery of the Pass of Killiecrankie. You can also follow the burn up from Killiecrankie hamlet towards Loch a' Choire, skirting the crags to the left. This was the route taken by our gang of lads from Blair Atholl.

When I took Storm up recently by the "tourist route" we had a day of tearing wind and dancing snowflakes but the view south had a marvellous clarity. On the slope above the trees a bench gave a comfortable resting place to look down the Tay's gunbarrel view to the twin paps of the Lomonds in Fife. A plaque on the bench read "Terence Toole RAAF 1947–72" and curiosity had me ringing Hugh Campbell, an expert on Pitlochry lore, to find out more. He told me the Tooles came from Perth (Scotland) and often walked up Ben Vrackie; when their son, who had joined the Royal Australian Air Force, was killed in a road accident in Australia, they placed this bench here as a memorial. There was an odd sequel a few winters ago. An estate worker went up to feed the hill sheep and his tractor slipped on the ice. The tractor — and driver — were saved by the vehicle's slide being stopped by the bench.

Section 7:   2. BEN VUIRICH   903 m   OS 43   997700
The hill of roaring (stags?) (voor-ich)

Ben Vuirich is an unobtrusive Corbett and is probably one of the least-climbed hills of its size in Scotland but, as with some shy people, the hill improves with acquaintance. Those drawn by the Henry Moore shapes of Beinn a' Ghlo look over Vuirich from its Munros, when spying out the country to the south; motorists going from Pitlochry to Kirkmichael half-glimpse it when they look north from Glen Brerachan. Perhaps a Henry Moore sculpture on top would be a lure — it would be a worthy setting.

In the very first *SMC Journal* (1891) there is a brief note about Ben Vuirich by Sir Hugh Munro.

Thursday 22 January. Left Blair Atholl 9.10, a glorious day — hard frost, snow on the ground but a tearing wind, to avoid which followed Fender Burn until S and E of Carn Liath when, 10.40, left road and ascended the lee side to the summit, 12 noon. Sun but the wind raised the snow in spiral columns several hundred feet, penetrating everything, filling pockets, and drifting between my waistcoat and shirt, where it melted and then froze into a solid wedge of ice. I have never suffered so from cold. . . . The descent, like the ascent, was steep, and only practicable because of the soft snow. Crossed burn (Allt Coire Lagain) 1 p.m. and easy going to Loch Valican and Ben Vuroch, 2,961 feet, at 3.20, Glen Fernach at 5 p.m. and Dirnanean, two miles before Kirkmichael, at 6.30. Heavy walking all day in soft snow. At Dirnanean they had to scrape me down with a knife to get the frozen snow off me before I could enter the house.

Sir Hugh describes the good view from Vuirich: to the Cairnwell, Tulaichean and Beinn a' Ghlo ranges, but it is another character of those days, in the third volume of the *SMC Journal*, who writes about something some people never learn. Alex Inkson M'Connochie: "The summit of Ben Vuroch is flattish and bare . . . an hour spent there [July] but little to be seen. A happy thought struck us, and a slight descent was made, and then beautiful Glen Fearnach was visible for miles. An excellent view was also got of Beinn a' Ghlo and Loch Loch from a slender eight-foot cairn five minutes down in a northerly direction." On flat summits it is always worth a perambulation round the perimeter as well as freezing or broiling at the viewless summit cairn. It was the view, though, over Loch Loch that I recall from a visit many years ago. More recently, with Tony on UC 86, we had no view at all, when we climbed it more in desperation than delight.

That was the 1986 monsoon crossing, when we'd abandoned our plateau-route by the Tarf to the Cairnwell and Lochnagar, and had escaped south out of the hills east of Drumochter, enjoyed a coffee break at Bruar, a bar-lunch at Blair Atholl and taken the familiar road up to Loch Moraig (a black-headed gulls' Bedlam) and on under the near-perfect cone of Carn Liath. Being a Sunday we met a constant stream of walkers heading home from their punishment on the Beinn a' Ghlo Munros.

Vuirich could be added to the Ghlo Munros for a big but bearable day, which is what I'd once done, after cycling in up the Glen Fearnach estate road. Cars can be taken as far as Loch Moraig on the Blair Atholl side, and of course Ben Vuirich can be climbed from the south, but the moors north of Glen Brerachan are heathery-foul and the going is rough and craggy and altogether a toil. The Ghlo-side is the least *pénible*.

Rather than go all the way round by Shinagag, Tony and I cut the corner, paddled over the Allt Coire Lagain and followed the intermittent path to the bealach (585 m). An estate road is picked up just over the crest of the pass and this flanks along a knobbly spur before dropping down into Glen Loch. Here we left our packs and cut through towards Vuirich. We made a sweeping dip round and across the valley-head on to the flank of Vuirich. After ten days of rain it was a very wet slope but every now and then we found brilliant carpets of purple saxifrage. Tony found a grouse nest with ten eggs — and did the same on Monamenach the next day. The wind blew us up; on the descent we had to fight into it as well as sleety rain. We were rather tired at the end of an eleven hour day but with ten Munros done, Vuirich and Monamenach surely could be added, despite the daily deluge, to give us our twelve for a High Level crossing. So, perforce, Vuirich was done, a two-hour diversion at the supper-end of day.

The only glimpse of a view we had was of Loch Valigan, a grey touch on the dark moors. Had we been car-based at Loch Moraig the loch would have been visited either going to or coming from Vuirich. It would make a secretive camp in that crying emptiness. Ben Vuirich may be unobtrusive but it has the common magic of all mountains.

Section 7:   3. BEN GULABIN   806 m   OS 43   101722
     Hill of the curlew (or whimbrel) or Hill of the beak

This was the last of Charles's three days of liberty one holiday weekend and I can only raise my hat to his dedicated enthusiasm. I'd been quite happy to dander up one hill each day and then do a variety of other things (I've too many interests) but Charles knocked off two, three, and three Corbetts and drove back to Sheffield at the end of his day on Creag nan Gabhar, Ben Gulabin and Monamenach. Such dedication is either admirable or reprehensible — I'm not sure which. To be fair I did not hesitate to egg him on. Time and distance force such a dedication. I'd been through that mill myself. The benefit of having already done all the Corbetts was in relishing a real respite from pressure. I'd eaten my cake and was quietly having it again. Charles was just slaving in the bakehouse.

We had been camping on the Braemar side of the pass, so before driving south over the Cairnwell Charles had bagged Creag nan Gabhar. Though it was mid-August, the car windows were milky with frost. It had been a cold night in the tent with only a summer sleeping bag. We chose the easy way up Gulabin — which is the Glen Shee side.

Ben Gulabin looks its finest as one reaches the Spittal of Glen Shee from the south. It rises above a green corner, beyond the old hump-backed bridge and a cluster of buildings, in a series of steep steps, and that direct route up was one I made the first time. It was hard work. The easier approach is to go up the glen a bit and attack the hill from behind. There is a path shown slanting up from the road to the col behind Gulabin. This is an estate-type road and parking at its foot is neither safe nor welcome if someone wants to drive up. Half a mile further on there is a large layby with a stile to the slopes of the Corbett, the best starting spot — though road improvements may change the situation.

Charles and I angled across to join the burn, which we followed up beside or in this flow. It was banked with an extravagance of flowers. A dipper exploded from under a bank and thereby betrayed the presence of its nest. Storm suddenly jumped on to a tussock of grass and grabbed a field mouse. The burn led up to the track which we took, and then abandoned to go over and inspect the old ski hut. It was in the last stages of decay and a gale will soon blow it to bits, which will be the end of another odd howff. The forlorn posts of ski tows go up on both sides — all that is left of one of the original ski sites in Scotland.

We crossed the dip to continue up our burn: a grassy course through a hillside of clawing heather. The footage was hardly noticed for we *ate* our way up, guzzling handfuls of sweet blaeberries until the burn ended — or started rather — in a sphagnum pool not far from the dip between Gulabin and the Top that appears highest from the Spittal side.

The summit cairn lay in an extensive flatness and I walked its rim taking a series of pictures. The Corbett is a commanding viewpoint. The road could be seen sweeping up out of Glen Shee to the Cairnwell and Glas Maol and Creag Leacach lay beyond. Carn a' Gheoidh (Munro) was not nearly so outstanding as Carn Bhinnein (its Top). Glas Tulaichean lorded it in the west, the big corrie towards us. The Beinn a' Ghlo hills lay beyond the ridge across Glen Lochsie. The highest point of that ridge (Meall Uaine) used to be a Corbett, one of those to have been lost in the new mapping as failing to keep the 500-foot separation. The car radio had reported a Test Match abandoned and the south of England having force 10 gales and torrential rain, yet we lay by the cairn for a good half hour in shirt sleeves, enjoying the sun and shadow play as the great glowing clouds tumbled about the sky.

Coire Shith lay beyond the col joining our hill to the bigger country beyond. I don't think the name is referring to skiers, it is much older. Glen Shee is the Glen of the Fairies and a very old pass for us earthbound creatures. "Spittal" is hospital or hospice in olden times, a tradition carried on by the hotel. The Celtic story of Diarmid and the boar is set in the Glen Shee hills. The romance of Diarmid and Grainne is one of the most deep-rooted legends, and Diarmid's end and Finn MacCool's part in it is usually set on Ben Gulban (Ben Bulben) in the west of Ireland. The legends came with the Celtic invaders and now have Scottish settings.

It is worth wandering round the graveyard beside the old bridge, there are some well preserved eighteenth-century stones, one for a climber avalanched in the Alps. Behind the church there is a standing stone on a knoll, proving the site very ancient. Gulabin Lodge (Dundee Ski Club) has been a "hospice" to us on a couple of Ultimate Challenges. You can't help liking an area after accumulating memories.

We ambled down more or less as we'd come. Charles still had Monamenach to go, *en route* to Sheffield, and I had to return to Fife and then drive to Speyside. After a snack by the cars we went our ways.

Section 7:   4. MONAMENACH   807 m   OS 43   176707
         Middle hill

A bothy under Ben Vuirich is probably not the commonest starting point for Monamenach, but then Tony and I had our reasons. We were doing a high-level version of UC 86, and Ben Vuirich had left us with one Munro or Corbett to go. We had already been driven south by nine days of atrocious weather and were quite happy to forgo the Cairnwell–Lochnagar heights as long as we picked up one more peak. Monamenach was the tempting solution. After that we could spend the night at Kirkton of Glenisla and reach the coast in a day and a half.

Perforce we were away early and eleven o'clock found us enjoying coffee and toasted cheese sandwiches in the Spittal of Glenshee Hotel with several other Challenger friends. I phoned for a forecast and wished I hadn't — another vigorous depression was heading our way. We headed off fast. The first name on the map was hardly an encouragement: Tomb.

Monamenach is probably most often climbed by people driving to Auchavan at the head of Glenisla and then following the path up to the south of the final cone, a whole mile and a half and 1,300 feet of ascent. The hill deserves better and, if a tame driver can be organised, the walk from the Spittal has much to recommend it, even if it starts by Tomb.

Pleasant tracks lead along Glen Shee to the farm, Westerton of Runavey. In May the lambing was not long over and the fields were noisy with the new mutton intake, and a pair of piping oystercatchers were beating the bounds. We turned up a lane which ambled on over empty moors where grouse butts were the only sign of man. We paused for a drink at a stream and, looking away up its course, could see the scree-capped crest of Creag Leacach. Monamenach lay up a valley ahead, Gleann Carnach, a big cone of almost symmetrical contour lines. The track sidles across to pull up into the glen. To the right lay Loch Beanie and a more direct pass down to Glenisla. Tony and I had taken that route on a Challenge five years earlier. One of the joys of that event is the endless variety of routes possible, not only in outline but in detail. Having walked round every side of the hill and up and down it by several routes I began to feel I know Monamenach a bit. Perhaps the biggest insult a hill can have at the feet of a walker is a *single* visit. Time alone I suppose excuses us. We can't repeat everything however much we'd like to.

The previous time up Gleann Carnach had been with Sandy and Claudia in 1984. We had found a gush of water in the upper glen, after the track had ended, and had brewed there. I led Tony to the same spot. We brewed and had a dish of apple flakes, then swung up to the peat-gashed col. With the girls I'd rushed down the snow-edged burn to Tulchan Lodge and on over Mayar and Dreish to Glen Doll; with Tony, Monamenach would ensure our high-level route. We left our rucksacks on the col and followed a derelict fence up to the summit. You could have heard our yells of glee in Montrose.

Chuntering back to the col, we contoured round Monamenach on mixed ground with plenty of peat to drop down to the burn draining to Auchavan. Curlews and peewits were proclaiming spring and the first lamb triplets of the crossing proclaimed the agricultural richness of the east. We crossed to the east bank of the River Isla and the hour of walking down its green roads to Little Forter were a lush contrast to the barren summits. I'd suggest having one's tame driver waiting there rather than at Auchavan, for those three miles of Glenisla are too good to miss. The rest down to Kirkton I'd rather forget. Blistered feet and nappy rash had me waddling like a duck. Kirkside House made up for much, with a bath, dinner and a dram working wonders. We'd managed to put in 22 miles doing Monamenach.

A more sensible round is to park at Dalvanie in Glenisla and go up Glen Beanie and climb, in succession, Craigenloch Hill, Monamenach and Creagan Caise, returning to Dalvanie; or park at Auchavan, climb Monamenach from the south, drop to the col of our ascent and descend to Tulchan Lodge, walking back down the Isla. Monamenach is worth a clear day. It has a good view to the Caenlochan heights and depths, and the view to the Lowlands is an unusual one.

Section 7:   5. BEINN MHEADHONACH   901 m   OS 43   880758
Middle hill

The hill is wedged between two Munros and can conveniently be
added to them on a long day's tramp from Glen Tilt. The road up Glen
Tilt is private for vehicles, but permission is usually granted to drive
up outwith the stalking season (contact the Factor, Atholl Estates, see
p. 7). Beinn Bhreac (7:6) could be added to a walk to Mheadhonach
but is described separately.

Ours was a dusty road when we drove up one May to camp near
Marble Lodge. From there we climbed Carn a' Chlamain, then made
the long bog-walk to Beinn Dearg (a massive pile of granite boulders)
and took in Beinn Mheadhonach on the way "home", a harder day
than map miles might indicate. On a winter attempt at these three,
deep powder so slowed us that we had to escape down the Diridh Glen
in the dark, missing Mheadhonach. Given really good snow cover this
country offers some of the best ski-touring, and with that aid I've done
all four Ring of Tarf Munros in a day easily enough. Weather and
conditions decide so much in areas like this where there is a great deal
of peat bog.

Dotterel and golden plover were calling among the hags as we
wended over from Beinn Dearg. The Tarf country is a fair imitation of
Arctic tundra. This aptly named Middle hill is a wedge of ridge
bounded by Gleann Diridh (*glen of the wood*) to the west and Gleann
Mhairc (*glen of the horse*) to the east, these streams then joining and
dropping into the River Tilt. Both streams rise far north of the
Corbett (Loch Mhairc is almost on the Tarf) which thrusts out south
in what Dr Johnson would call "a considerable protuberance". The
Diridh–Mhairc waters reach the Tilt half way between Gilberts
Bridge and the bridge of Marble Lodge, and either can be used for
access. On this occasion we angled down from the summit into the
Allt Mhairc, which was full of deer, to exit round to our camp near
Marble Lodge. The bridge shown on the Diridh–Mhairc river, just up
from the Tilt, looks odd and isolated on the map as well as on the
ground. There is no road.

> "There were mountains, of course, and a stream that leapt
> Rioting under the old stone bridge."
>
> (D. Fraser: Flamenco)

I find it a sad spot: the vivid green, the villages of tumbled stones,
the shivering birch trees — and a sturdy bridge that has not seen
wheels for a century. All this rich limestone area was cleared for

"sport" in the bad old days. A great stir was caused in the 1840s when the Duke of Atholl lost a court case following his attempt to stop access to Glen Tilt, an obvious, historical right-of-way.

Queen Victoria rode through Glen Tilt to Deeside and wrote cheerfully in her journal about the "beautiful scenery", yet just seventy-five years earlier Thomas Pennant thought the pass "the most dangerous and the most horrible" he'd ever travelled. Between these two came the evolution of the general appreciation of scenery to which we are heirs.

Section 7: 6. BEINN BHREAC 912 m OS 43 868821
         Speckled hill (vrek)

This remote summit is one of the more inaccessible Corbetts, and the third highest. It is probably wise to include it with other Munros and/or Corbetts and not find it needing a special expedition later on. Beinn Bhreac is not a very distinguished shape and, being rather crowded by bigger hills, is not much of a viewpoint. There is some Beinn Dearg-like granite on top.

Any time I've visited this Corbett, I've been staying at the Tarf Bothy. Bhreac lies on a natural-enough route from Carn Ealar to Beinn Dearg if doing the Ring of Tarf but is not so convenient for a day expedition. Strong walkers could add it to the round mentioned under Beinn Mheadhonach (7:5) or just combine it with that Corbett, or add it to Beinn Dearg. One possibility would be to take in Leathad an Taobhain (7:7) and Beinn Bhreac (and Beinn Dearg) as a deviation from traversing the Minigaig Pass. There is no quick and easy route to the Speckled Hill.

The least strenuous would be to combine it simply with Beinn Mheadhonach. The flanking valleys of Mheadhonach, in their upper, near-level reaches, are a mass of peat hags; the going is therefore slow and "slaistery". Loch Mhairc nevertheless is a place of character. One could visualise the Tarf catching its waters in a few thousand years. I've seen foxes there on several occasions. I've walked across the loch when it was frozen solid. Late winter is quite a good option, for the frozen bogs then give easier walking than during the months of rain-enriched summer stew. A longer walk, but much on tracks, would be to reach Beinn Bhreac from the Glen Bruar side, over or round Beinn Dearg. The Feshie–Geldie approaches in the north are remote and give wet going, but could be shortened by using a push bike. Beinn Bhreac, one way or another, will demand quite a push.

Section 7: 7. LEATHAD AN TAOBHAIN 912 m OS 43 (and possibly
35/42 822858
Slope of the rafters (Lay-at-an-Tayvin)

This Corbett lies less than a hundred metres above the summit of the
Minigaig Pass and can easily be included on a walk over that famous
old route from Speyside to Atholl. The pass is mentioned in the
sixteenth century and was, until into the nineteenth, a major drovers'
road. It pre-dates Wade's A9 line through Drumochter and was far
more important than the Gaick. Considering that the pass rises to
2,745 feet (*c.* 830 m) and must have been winter- or storm-bound for
months on end, one can only admire the hardiness of its users. From
Tromie Bridge (near Kingussie and Ruthven Barracks) to Blair Atholl
is 41 km (25 miles), a good day's tramp: a classic route. The Corbett is
a bonus.

An estate road runs up Glen Tromie and on to Gaick Lodge but we
take the branch turning left to a small weir on the Allt Bhran and then
on by the path on the north bank (adder country) which is the
Minigaig line. There is an unfortunate junction of rivers and paths
right on the join of map sheets 42 and 43 but, leaving 42 the path keeps
swinging southwards (the fork going northwards to the trees should
be ignored) by the stream and finally flanks up the eastern slopes of
Coire Bhran. In droving days the cattle were often gathered in this
corrie and driven over the pass in a huge herd. The summit of the pass
is just a dip in a rolling wasteland of peat rather than any definite
feature, and as it is just before the county boundary this line on the
map can be usefully copied into compass bearings to reach the Corbett
if the cloud is down, as it often is. Leathad an Taobhain is not strictly
the Corbett but the 902-m western top of two, the higher, 912,
nameless eastern one being the desired objective.

On my one visit to this watershed Corbett, after ascending by the
Minigaig, I headed back northwards to pick up the estate track on
Meall an Uillt. This leads on to Lochan an t-Sluic from whence I
traversed Carn Dearg Mor (6:11) and Meallach Mhor (6:10) back to
Tromie Bridge, a rare 3-Corbetts-in-a-day round, described under
those hills. The Minigaig undulates southwards (quartz cairns on the
upper slopes) to become an estate road again at the Bruar Water. This
is forsaken at Bruar Lodge for the original way on to the Allt
Schiecheachain bothy and then estate road again all the way to Old
Blair, the original hamlet behind Blair Castle. It is one of the great
classic trails and as such highly recommended as the excuse for the
Corbett, or *vice versa*. Adam Watson's *The Cairngorms* (SMC district

guide) has a good summary of this and other mounth passes, as has Robert Smith's book *Grampian Ways*.

Section 7: 8. SGOR MOR (Glen Dee) 813 m OS 43 006914
    The big peak

Sgor Mor was one of several peaks "bagged" in a week of dashing about the wilds hiding food parcels for the journey on foot over all the Munros. I cycled up to White Bridge and then up the new estate road to the west of the Dee as far as the Allt Garbh, where the churned up granite boulders on the road verge made an excellent hiding place for a parcel of food, films, maps and so on. We then climbed Carn Cloichmhuilinn, Beinn Bhrotain and Monadh Mhor and, as a bit of an afterthought, added Sgor Mor. This entailed two paddles across the River Dee and a hillside I described as "messy": not a way I'd really recommend, even for those in a Corbett of a hurry.

Charles, from Sheffield, had been teasing away at the Corbett list on every long weekend, so it was with some diffidence I agreed to join him for the August Bank Holiday on which he intended to do a demolition job on Section Seven. We made a rendezvous at a camping spot on the Cairnwell, and next morning set off on push bikes from the car park near the Linn of Dee, Sgor Mor the objective. The Linn was tame from dry weather but did not appeal as a swimming spot. Menlove Edwards once swam down it. The poet Byron very nearly fell into it, which would have lost the world the chance of Patey's parody on Byron's Black Lochnagar.

This time we pedalled up to Derry Lodge and, as many parts of the road had been newly spread with sand and gravel, this was hard work and not infrequently our wheels sank right in and we'd tumble off our mounts. Storm, on foot, had an easier passage. Derry Lodge is rapidly decaying and the famous bothy at Luibeg had recently burnt down (now rebuilt). Luibeg has never been the same since the late Bob Scott ruled there, a keeper of great character. We used the bikes as far as practical up Glen Luibeg and then dumped them in the heather. Without cycles it is perhaps easiest to start at the Linn of Dee and head uphill when clear of the forest, to reach Sgor Dubh: good walking once the lower levels of clawing heather are passed.

There was a constant stream of walkers on the path for the Lairig Ghru (and one suspects its bordering Munros). We boulder-hopped over the Luibeg Burn easily so did not need to divert upstream to the footbridge. A bit before the pass to the Lairig Ghru we slanted off to the Allt Preas nam Meirleach where we enjoyed a snack by its rush of clear water. Cairngorm water has a clarity and freshness that it is hard to equal. Golden saxifrage was colouring the edge of the stream and the slopes were purple hazed with the heather in bloom — another Deeside speciality.

As we wandered over the easy-angled moor I noticed there was an unusual quantity of dwarf birch among the heather, a pretty tree which grows only a few inches tall. We skirted the knoll of Creagan nan Gabhar and drifted up Sgor Mor's final rise with a keen north wind helping us along, a good approach for the sudden doubling of the view on arrival. We could look up the winding Geldie to Beinn a' Ghlo, and the western Cairngorms were well displayed. Being too chilly to linger we had a snack in lee of one of the rocky outcrops and chuntered down more directly, picking up and following the Allt a' Choire Dhuibh to the Luibeg Burn. The heather became deeper and rougher as we went. There were some big clumps of bluebells (harebells) on the river shingles.

To avoid some bog we shoved our cycles over the burn to Luibeg and picked up the road there. Storm was a bit weary and went in my rucksack for most of the run home; his head stuck out over my shoulder, grinning back at all the surprised looks we received from pedestrians. Charles shot off ahead — it was his turn for producing tea. He then drove off to Braemar and took in Morrone, alone, while I later went up Glen Clunie to meet him on the other side of his second Corbett. We dined and listened to Beethoven under a shock of stars and were snug in bed before the frost glittered the tent.

Section 7:   9. CREAG NAN GABHAR   834 m   OS 43   154841
              Goats crag (gower)

Creag nan Gabhar must be one of the easiest of Corbetts; it therefore tends to be done *en passant*, in a hurry, fleeing to or from Braemar, probably in bad weather. The hill deserves more considerate treatment than that (I have sinned myself) so when a recent "raid" was rewarded I felt I'd gained undeserved merit. I didn't think I was going to be given anything.

My Friday night run up the A93 came to a halt above Bridge of Cally. Weeks of gales and rain had Novembered their way across Scotland and December limped in on metaphorical (meteorological) crutches. When I found I was slithering and scrabbling on black ice under a sheen of stars, I gave in gracefully and spent the night in the next layby. I am much more afraid of driving and cars than I am of walking or climbing on the hills.

I had a miserable night — my sleeping bag was inadequate for such cold. The water in the dixie, ready for tea in bed first thing, froze over. No gritter had gone past, or any other traffic. I had a late departure. During the short drive over the Cairnwell the weather changed four times: the sun shone, freezing mist rolled in, it rained and then snowed higher up.

I parked near the AA telephone box and headed east on the Bealach Buidhe path. There was a dusting of snow and the dog went wild with delight as he always does on the first winter walk: rolling about and racing in circles and finally hurling himself into my arms to give my freezing nose a lick. The main road vanished quickly and the friendly slopes embraced us familiarly. The path goes up a deep heathery gash into the hills with the burn flowing cheerily below. We found a well-chewed antler on the path and, on the flank of the Corbett, above the scree level, a herd of deer sped off, spraying the snow up from the heather.

After we'd crossed the burn we soon left the path (which is a bit overgrown anyway) and made directly up the hill, using the grassy runnels of burns or fire-cleared patches to avoid the deeper heather. The burns were a mass of ice, every dipping grass stem a shining sculpture, and the big bosses wobbling strangely as the water gurgled through below them. The clouds were down and it almost snowed.

Creag nan Gabhar has quite a collection of cairns on top. You can either claim one as the summit or build your own. After an inspection we cringed behind one for a "piece" and the finger-freezing task of inserting new batteries in the camera. The best of the view was across to Morrone. Wandering patches of sunshine in search of a climate were periodically lighting up the hill. The Cairngorms were glossy white but painted over with even whiter clouds. The knobbly hills beyond Glen Callater were much deeper in snow than the bigger hills south of us. These Cairnwell summits were all elephant-grey — a real pachydermatous herd of hills. The sun was glinting on something at Newbigging in Glen Clunie and there were odd colourful shapes which were a puzzle. I was too cold to change the telephoto lens for a spy but curiosity was suddenly satisfied — two hang gliders swung across the corrie below us. Corbett-bagging by hang glider, now that's an idea. The Sgor Mor across Glen Clunie used to be a Corbett, but the re-ascent is not 500 feet and it has been demoted.

We scampered back down more or less as we'd come, Storm taking great delight in discovering and sniffing along our up-track. At one stage he stopped abruptly and when I looked I saw dainty wild cat prints superimposed on my big boot marks. The beast had come on our trail, followed it for twenty yards, then carried on up the glen.

The wind had risen during our brief summit stay and went on rising even at valley level. I had a date in Braemar in the afternoon and I must admit it was pleasant to sit with a dram and look out on the deluge. The storm raged all night and the next day. Miles of upper Deeside flooded, and the Linn o' Dee was a fearsome spectacle of naked power. We had definitely had better than we deserved on our two-hour Corbett.

Section 7:   10. MORRONE   859 m   OS 43   132886
The big nose (Mor-rone)

Morrone (I've never heard it called Morven) is very much Braemar's popular viewpoint, and with good reason: it commands a superlative view. From late August on into October is the best time for a visit which takes in an extravagant range of colours: of heather, green fields, dark woods, glinting rivers, fiery birch tints and the sweeping tint-on-tint of tumbling Cairngorm ridges and summits. I can't think of any other Corbett where you set out from a town, never mind one usefully sprawling at 1,000 feet. If you check the contours, though, you'll see the hill is a Corbett only by the odd foot or two.

Braemar is at a commanding meeting of routes which has ensured it a long and busy history. The first castle was built by Malcolm Canmore in 1059. The Earl of Mar raised the Jacobite standard for the Fifteen in Braemar. Stevenson wrote *Treasure Island* there while recovering from illness in 1881. The Braemar Gathering (first weekend in September) is world famous and always attended by the Royal Family who have their second home just down the road at Balmoral.

For Morrone, walk (or drive) up Chapel Brae to the car park shown on the map above Auchendryne. There is a pond beside it which acts as a reflecting pool — unless the ducks go paddling to wobble away the reflections in their wakes. Carry on along the road past Mountain Cottage, then swing left up through birch woods. Keep right of the fences and house. The road itself bears right (west) and at a fork take the left branch which goes up to the Deeside Field Club view indicator. Skirt the crags above this to the left and the path uphill thereafter is obvious. My favourite viewpoint is on the shoulder, once the angle of ascent has eased slightly, where there are several cairns lined up together. The view over "the waving outline of the distant hills" shows to best advantage from there. The angle continues to ease off up to the summit. The radio mast and buildings are part of an Aberdeen University research station, and the Braemar Mountain Rescue team has a relay station there as the reception is much better than down in Braemar at the Mountain Rescue Post. You can see why the reception is good: the view beams out to the huge panorama of the Cairngorms. The Corbetts north of Braemar can be examined with ulterior motives (Carn na Drochaide, Carn Liath, Culardoch) and with Sgor Mor and others edging the Ring of Tarf to the west and Creag nan Gobhar and Ben Gulabin to the south, Braemar is quite a useful centre for a profitable Corbett-blitz.

The descent can be made by the line of ascent or by going down the track south and then east. This track, built by the Mountain Rescuers, is fairly unobtrusive, unlike so many bulldozed tracks in the Cairngorms. A pleasant walk leads back along the road into Braemar, the main dangers of the day coming where the road passes through the middle of the golf course. Could hitting Corbetteers call for a penalty stroke?

Section 7:   11. CONACHCRAIG   865 m   OS 44   280865
          Jumble of rocks

This is another easy Corbett: most people start to walk at 400 m, at the Spittal of Glenmuick car park, which is reached by a pleasant drive up from Ballater. Conachcraig does not stand out, being a mere outlying spur of mighty Lochnagar but, looking as it does to that mountain on one side and out over Deeside to the other, it gives fair reward for minimal effort. My only regret is the eyesore of Lochnagar path and the bulldozed tracks that circle it, so obvious in a world of granite.

Conachcraig's summit bumps have plenty of granite boulders that probably account for the hill's name which, on the map, is given to the lowest, central bump, 850 m, while north is Caisteal na Caillich 862 m *the castle of the witch*. This northern top has the finest view, worth the little extra walk. Carn na Daimh, which catches the eye when motoring up Glen Muick, is *cairn of the stag*. There are usually some of these creatures living off tourist hand-outs round the Spittal.

Another route is to walk across to Allt na Giubhsaich and follow the big track to the col between the Corbett and the Meikle Pap of Lochnagar from which a very short ascent lands one on Conachcraig. There are alternatives, even if Lochnagar itself has already been done. One suggestion: walk round Loch Muick's south shore to reach the Glas-allt-Shiel (the lodge Queen Victoria built as a hideaway after Prince Albert's death) then go up the path by the Glas Allt waterfall to take the path that branches off right, rounding the Little Pap to gain the Meikle Pap–Conachcraig col. Conachcraig even looks good from this approach, and will reward a good walk rather than just a lack-lustre, list-ticking stroll. The northern approaches lie in the Balmoral estate and are best avoided in summer. Queen Victoria rode up Lochnagar more than once (as well as quite a few other big hills) and I've bumped into various members of the Royal Family up there, once being discovered playing with a wriggle of young adders.

Section 7: 12. BEN TIRRAN 896 m OS 44 373746
    (Derivation unknown)

Ben Tirran is pronounced Ben Turran, which really goes better with Loch Wharral and some of the other guttural names hereabouts. The area is one that rings with splendid names: Burn of Slidderies, Wester Skuiley, Watery Knowe, Wolf Hill, Lair of Aldararie, The Witter, Many Wee, Potty Leadnar, Auld Darkney for starters, and that's on just one small bit of the map I've unfolded to look at Ben Tirran again. Strictly speaking Ben Tirran is the shoulder above Loch Wharral rather than the lonely 896-m trig point — which is the highest point on all this upland of bogs and braes north of Glen Clova.

I first went up Ben Tirran with a party of seven boys (on skis) and Kitchy the dog (who took a dim view of following skiers as they would not progress in straight lines). The hill is rock-free to the south, so a good one for novice skiers; but it was a tired party that finally descended to Rottal in the gloaming. The dog was tired too. A cheeky hare actually chased after him, cut across his bows, and sped ahead in mocking glee.

We were staying in the Carn Dearg Mountaineering Club's hut up at The Doll one March. That night six inches of snow fell and we had fun skiing down forestry tracks, at least till the tail-ender failed to take one corner, shot off the bend into the air and vanished down into the trees. There was a thud, and a tree promptly dropped its heavy burden of snow. The four-letter word that followed set the party hooting with delight. Even better was to come. Round the next bend a pine trunk lay across the road, invisible under the snow; teacher's skis went under it and the rest of me pitched over the top. Score: two bruised shins, one broken thumb, one staved thumb. Life without the use of thumbs is extraordinarily inconvenient. After a thaw, the weather banged off the big guns. We were snowed in with the ploughs taking several days to win through. Skis became a necessity: you couldn't manage on foot. We made the most of it and relished being late back, only the second time over twelve years of school trips.

My next visit to Ben Tirran was during an autumn coast-to-coast trip which took me from Loch Nevis to Montrose, and was one of the few times when I've been bodily heaved about by the wind. I've never experienced such a hurricane as I battled down to the Youth Hostel. A tree had probably fallen for the lights failed and we were issued with candles. The weather was still windy the next day when I was happy to climb up out of the glen to Carn Dearg and be blown along over Boustie Ley, the rim of Loch Brandy, Green Hill (far away?) to reach Ben Tirran's trig point. There are plenty of bogs but the walking is straightforward. Even in mist you can hardly fail to hit targets like the glacial corries of Loch Brandy and Loch Wharral. Coming from up the glen this would always be my choice of route — anything to avoid miles of tarmac.

That day I continued on by the Black Shank to the Shieling of Saughs (scribbled names on the ceiling go back to 1903) and out to Tarfside by Glen Effock. I stayed at the renowned Parsonage, being thoroughly spoiled by Gladys Guthrie who makes her home such a haven to walkers. I mention this because there are some superb backpacking tracks (old whisky-smuggling routes linking the glens) which run north-south rather than east-west and Tarfside is the only convenient B & B in Glen Esk. Several tracks head over to Deeside from Tarfside, and Mount Battock (7:13) is accessible, thus the walk could incorporate some Corbett-picking. Tirran and Battock are worth such a venture.

Ben Tirran was an UC 85 summit for Alison, Ian and myself, a bright and sunny morning to make three out of three good, if contrasting, days for this pleasant Corbett. We wandered up the path from the hotel to Loch Brandy, which was noisy with common gulls, and then traversed across to Loch Wharral. We hit the rim slightly too high so followed the Craigs round to Ben Tirran. With about seventeen others we luxuriated in The Parsonage that night before wandering on to the coast at St Cyrus.

The most recent visit, with Charles, gave good solid cloud on the tops which was a good test of navigation. We took the right-of-way up to pass right of Loch Brandy to Green Hill from where a long bearing led us, successfully, to the lochan just below the Corbett. Sheep loomed like elephants in the mist and vehicle tracks and cairned routes abounded, to mislead rather than help. The right-of-way is in fact cairned. From Green Hill it heads over point 857, White Hill, Muckle Cairn, etc., to descend to Loch Lee by the Shank of Inchgrundle — which is another tasty name.

The hotel at Clova welcomes walkers (there is a bunkhouse for the impecunious) and it is in many ways the best starting point if the best features, Loch Brandy and Loch Wharral, are to be seen. Lochnagar looks well from the summit and Mount Keen, for once, is more than a tiny cone on the Mounth plateau. All the tracks shown on the map exist on the ground. The one up from Weem has been bulldozed which rather spoils that line. The best buy is traversing from Clova to Tarfside.

Section 7:   13. MOUNT BATTOCK   778 m   OS 44/45   550844
             Possibly anglicised from *bad* (chump), *ag* (the diminu-
             tive) and Mount is from *monadh* (hill or moor)

Till recently I'd been up Mount Battock only once and that was with considerable haste as I wanted to visit a Stamp Fair in Dundee on the same day. I made up the Turret not long after six in the morning, near the back end of the year, on a clear but bitterly cold day. The fieldfare were working down as I went up and on the moors the many hares were already into "ermine", as were a belch of ptarmigan that flew past. My route used the bulldozed track up Hill of Turret and the Hill of Saughs but to escape the biting east wind I tumbled down by the White Burn. While brewing in the Dormobile a vicious storm left Mount Battock white, and in Glen Esk I had to shift a huge broken bough off the road. The early start, whatever its motives, had been a blessing.

I've just been up Battock again on a sparkling winter day when the mad March hares were blowing in drifts over the snow. With a night at The Parsonage beforehand, and a vast Indian meal at Forfar on the way back, Mary, Storm and I felt pleased with our 24 hours away from home.

There has been a proliferation of bulldozed tracks on a scale perhaps unequalled anywhere else and if the senses regret them the lazy body is only too glad to use them to dodge the area's peat bogs which are of a type that make Kinder a garden. In the first volume of the *Cairngorm Club Journal*, the January 1894 issue has an article on Mount Battock and Clachnaben which has this: "A fellow-member declares that the worst turn he could do his worst enemy would be to make him cross from Mount Battock to Clachnaben on a wet day." It is "really awful ground", of "abominable moss-haggs". The writer loved every minute of it; I'm sure he would be saddened to find Mount Battock and Clachnaben now largely linked by a bulldozed track. Some of the fun has gone. However, most tracks shy off Mount Battock itself; it still stands as an isolated dome that dominates the rump of the Mounth hills. The summit was one of the major stations used by the Ordnance Survey in mapping Scotland.

Mount Battock stands very much in the centre of radiating rivers which quickly cut deep valleys among the rounded heights. Some of these are short, the Turret and the Tennet flowing to Glen Esk, others are long, the Dye, the Aven, even the Feugh, which all head east and unite before entering the Dee at Banchory. Each of these valleys and each of the ridges between them is a potential route up Mount Battock.

The quickest and easiest ascent is the one I took, driving up to the Mill of Aucheen, then using the estate road up Hill of Turret. Coming back I'd swing south west and descend off Mount Een. Given more time and a tame driver I'd take that once fearsome stravaig eastwards to Clachnaben. It is not *stone of the hill* for nothing, the said "stone" being about 300 paces in girth and 30 m high. It is a famed landmark and a sort of Deeside totem. With no car to meet one, a round could be made from the B974 by going up Glen Dye and north or south of Cock Hill, reaching Mount Battock and returning via Clachnaben. The ruin of Spittal Cottage is the easiest start/finish.

One long, trackless tramp of character is to start at Tarfside (B & B at The Parsonage perhaps) and follow up Glen Tennet and down the Water of Aven to Feughside, with a diversion from the watershed to the Corbett which stands above the pass. Loch Tennet, illogically, is over the watershed and is the source of the Aven. The Aven is a long rocky ravine and the most impressive of all the "waters".

The Water of Feugh valley can be motored up to the Forest of Birse, a quiet forgotten glen with paths and roads going up every other hillside. These peter out on the boggy uplands but if you go on by one Cock Hill or another Cock Hill (and not the Cock Hill already mentioned) you will come to Mount Battock. You will have discovered something about peat country navigation. You will have a fresher appreciation of tracks and paths. Y'll hae clarty bits and be a wiser loon. And hae anither haund of unco names: Hill of Badymicks, Mudlee Bracks, Bonnyfleeces, Hen Hill, Lochnawean, Lamahip, Bogmore. . . .

Section 7:　14. CARN NA DROCHAIDE　818 m　OS 43　127938
Hill of the bridge (Droch-itsh)

The first visit to Carn na Drochaide came as a coda to an ascent of Beinn a' Bhuird and Ben Avon. We had climbed those two giants from the old camp site where the Lui joins the Dee and on the way back I left my gang of school kids to walk down the Quoich and prepare supper, while I "bagged" the Corbett, a game which was fairly new to me then. There was a winter later when Glen Quoich under some feet of snow was a magical place to camp in. Years and visits pass so quickly after each other but the quiet memories of beauty, peace and wholesomeness remain.

Quite the pleasantest day of a rather dreary August gave the most enjoyable ascent of Carn na Drochaide. It was the second day of Charles's August Bank Holiday blitz and we had kept this hill for the Sunday to avoid any clash with possible stalking or shooting activities. We took the familiar road out of Braemar for the Linn of Dee. Two miles on westwards there is the best distant view of the Corbett, nothing spectacular, a heather and scraggy uprising beyond the floodplains of Quoich and Dee, but very typical of the green and mauve bounds of Braemar. After the Linn of Dee the public road runs down the north side of the river and passes above the extravagant Victorian pile of Mar Lodge, hub of feudal upper Deeside, to finish at the Quoich Water. We parked in a quarried moraine where the martins had burrowed under the turf cornice and were swooping about devouring the early morning midges.

The Quoich Glen is made magnificent by a combination of water, trees and hills, and a good round walk is to go up it and through the peculiar Clais Fhearnaig gash (a continuation of the Glen Tilt fault) to Glen Lui where the river can be followed down to the Dee again. We set off up the east bank of the Quoich as the Corbett stands immediately above. The Linn of Quoich is a pretty narrowing of the river between cliffs and just beyond the footbridge above the gorge is the Punch Bowl (the "quoich" or "quaich"), a river-worn hole. Tradition has it that the Earl of Mar filled the bowl for the gathering of his followers at the start of the Fifteen. The river has now pierced a hole through the side of the bowl so its utility is lost.

There are some magnificent old Scots pines by the waterside, and ten minutes on from the Punch Bowl a path leads up and along the river-cut banks to give perhaps the best view of all: a glittering stretch of silver water and a fall, the whole held in the tree-green glen while above and beyond lie the brown and purple hills. We left the river and simply linked together useful deer paths through the heather, crossed the estate track and followed the curve of a shoulder up to Carn na Drochaide, leaving the corrie to our left. The heather grows progressively shorter with height gained and the final plateau is bouldery. Circuit on the edge of this flatness to gain the best of the view; at the cairn much of the view is cut off.

As there had been a snell north wind (a touch of frost even), the sun with that freshness had made the walk up a pleasure for August, a month so often cloudy and midgey and overfed with heat. Lochnagar lay in the eye of the sun but there was a big sweep of hills right round to Beinn a' Ghlo. Schiehallion's shape was a blue hulk beached on the horizon. Bhrotain — Cairn Toul — Derry Cairngorm — Beinn Bhreac — Beinn a' Bhuird — Ben Avon gave a fine sweep of Cairngorms while, forming an outer ring, all the Corbetts from far-west Leathad an Taobhain, to Sgor Mor, Morrone, Creag nan Gobhar, Carn Liath, Culardoch, right on to far-east Morven were visible. It was far too good a day to end there so Charles gathered his Corbett loins about him and set off for Carn Liath and Culardoch. I was delegated to drive round to Invercauld Bridge and have a brew and a beer awaiting his arrival.

Doing these three in a day is perfectly feasible. Invercauld is perhaps the best start/finish point if you have only one car, walking up the Slugain Glen, diverting for Drochaide, circuiting round on the path of Glen Gairn and over the identical heights of Carn Liath, up and down Culardoch, then out by the estate track to Invercauld. If doing Carn na Drochaide on its own, then the western flanks are the most kindly. Storm and I circuited back down them via Carn na Criche and then followed the stream of the western corrie. The breezy day so set the aspens quivering that they sounded like a waterfall. I pigged on the blaeberries growing on the aspen crag overhanging the burn. When we'd set off there had been one other car at the quarry. On our return there were thirty. An early start is an advantage on an August Bank Holiday.

Section 7:   15. CARN LIATH (CREAG AN DAIL BHEAG or CREAGAN
            DAIL BEAG)   862 m   OS 43/36   158981
            Grey cairn (Wee crag of the pasture)

Section 7:   16. CULARDOCH   900 m   OS 43/36   193988
            Big back high place (Cul-*aar*-doch)

These two hills are defended by being remoter than the rest of the Deeside Corbetts but they amply repay any visit, for their remoteness compels one into a corner of sweeping vistas that is typical of the borders of the big Cairngorm mountains. Our local club approached them from the Gairn which allowed Ben Avon and Brown Cow Hill to be enjoyed as well, though enjoyment on Brown Cow was mostly retrospective.

I took everyone tea at 6 a.m. which is one sure way of ensuring people have to climb out of bed, and an hour and a bitty later we were off from the Luibeg camp site for the drive by Braemar, Invercauld, Crathie up to Glen Gairn, well to the east of the range. I had my bike to help with the long tramp in, but a stiff wind had me pushing up any rise. We still gained an hour. Kitchy found no difficulty in keeping up. Every now and then I went skidding on the frozen puddles. There must have been hundreds of crazy April hares jazzing about, some in scruffy cast-off winter garb, others handsome in summer "blue". There were deer and grouse, and the glen rang to the plaintive calling of golden plovers and other waders.

Corndavon Lodge was a ruin except for one big room in the west wing which was gaudily frescoed — it looked like a stage backcloth for *Brigadoon*. A hatstand stood in one corner. Trees and outhouses had all gone to ruin and there was a sad air about the place. A decade later I was to be glad enough of it, as you'll see in the Brown Cow days (7:17).

We were deep in the gleaming snowy mountains and had to deal with drifts on the road but we struggled on by the hidden lochans to Loch Builg. The loch was a brittle blue that soon broke under the wind to turn a surly grey. I pitched my tent in the lee of some ruins by the loch, and had an hour's respite before the foot-plodders arrived. We reached Ben Avon by Carn Dearg, with one heavy blatter of snow on the way and one more on the encrusted summit tor. Some of us had been blasted off Ben Avon back in February when camped up the Quoich; by comparison this was a satisfying success. It left me with just one Munro to go in winter conditions. The others arrived as I was leaving. They had full packs and camped that night at the Sneck, going out the next day to Deeside over Beinn a' Bhuird, while I added some Corbetts and picked them up on the way home.

The miles southwards were hard work and the descent to the upper Gairn a flounder in new snow. A cornice had fallen from the col. Deer in the glen foot were pawing up the vegetation. My log that day said we went "brutally up the slope as the easiest of choices: a thousand feet to the top of the double Corbett. Red outcrops, two cairns and a wall heading for Deeside. Lochnagar a magnificent winter spectacle. On each summit the other, in turn, looked higher. Cursed them both and dropped down the east ridge for a snack in the stable on the Bealach Dearg."

The Bealach Dearg (Red Pass) is the crux of an old right of way from Deeside to Tomintoul, and the easiest route to these Corbetts is up the southern track — which is described below. Now an estate road, it wends up on to the western shoulder of Culardoch (before twisting down to the River Gairn) leaving only the gleaming cone for a weary prod. The old dog curled up at every pause. What a pity I'd not tackled the Corbetts more seriously at an earlier date. He'd done two thirds of them but a heart attack a year later ended his life on the tops. We descended Culardoch's north ridge and at a vantage point stopped to eat the last morsels of food and photograph the silver-shine of Loch Builg below a sweep of curtaining snow. We descended to some old shielings (a superb camp site) and crossed a bridge to wander back to the lonely tent. It was 7.30 p.m. Curlews, a heron, grouse, black-headed gulls and drumming snipe were the last sounds I heard before taking an unbelayed tumble into sleep. For four hours I was unaware of anything, and then only too aware — but that is Brown Cow's story. It was a decade before I made the more usual ascent from the south.

Tony and I crossed south–north by the historic Bealach Dearg during UC 83 when we went from Braemar Youth Hostel by Loch Builg on to Cock Bridge and the Allergue Arms. This southern approach to these two hills is very pleasant. At Invercauld the old military bridge (1752) must be one of the most photographed in the country. Stabs of sunlight were flooding it. Lochnagar was very dark beyond. Pleasant parkland led behind Invercauld House of the Farquharson tribe, and was followed by a couple of miles of forest plantings west of Craig Leek and Meall Gorm where every clearing seemed to have a herd of spectator deer.

One story of the Farquharsons mentions the Bealach Dearg. The first chief attended kindly on the needs of a passing stranger and next day accompanied him a long distance on his way to show him the route over the pass. He later received a letter appointing him Royal Standard Bearer for Scotland, the reward of his visitor who had been the king. It proved a sad reward in the end for the recipient fell at the Battle of Pinkie.

Caulfeild considered the Bealach Dearg as a route north but thought it too difficult — so went round by the Lecht. In 1832 plans were again produced for a road but these too fell through.

We had another brew at the stable on the col after we'd climbed up Culardoch of the short-back-and-sides heather. The cloud chased us down and we sat listening to the grouse chuckling through the murk. A hare actually ran into the stable — but didn't stay for tea! By the time we reached the bridge on the Gairn the wind was raising sheets of spray off the river and by Loch Builg it began to snow hard. May can be like that. Isn't there an old saying "Cast nae cloot till May be oot"? Remember, this is the Arctic side of the Cairngorms: great country but to be treated with respect.

On UC 87 I traversed Beinn a' Bhuird and Ben Avon and descended to the Gairn for lunch before doing an anti-clockwise circuit over the Corbetts again. The north side is rather scarred with bulldozed tracks and paths (not all shown on the map) and the many ruins give the glen a touch of loneliness. One of the lochans by the Builg junction was a nesting site for black-headed gulls, *sturteig* in Gaelic, which is marvellously onomatopoeic. They were making a right sturteig. The three-day crossing took me from Aviemore to Ballater. The variations really are endless.

Section 7:   17. Brown Cow Hill   829 m   OS 36   221044

This links with what I've written on Culardoch, for Brown Cow was climbed from the same camp by Loch Builg after cycling in by the River Gairn track. Having been over Ben Avon, Carn Liath and Culardoch I slept the sleep of weary walkers — for four hours — and then woke up with a sense of unease to find there was a gale blowing, which was the end of peaceful sleep. Can they not invent a tent made of *silent* material?

At about 5 a.m. I started brewing but the cold, frosty night of stars was then swept away when it started snowing heavily. At the back of six I set off, anyway, with the dog in my rucksack and my belongings bundled on the bike's carrier inside a bivvy bag. The bike's gears were frozen solid — fortunately I'd left it in a low gear — and the wind bowled us along. At Corndavon we started up an estate road on foot but this was unpleasantly drifted so we just floundered over the heather in a direct line to the summit. Navigation had to be accurate: the hill is a vast dome with acres of flat ground on top. We hit it off all right and were rewarded with window-views to a dazzling Ben Avon and Lochnagar. Kitchy was complaining at the spindrift and cold which forced us to scamper down, on the same route but cutting corners and setting the hares charging off in all directions. The snow had stopped, the Gairn valley glittered and we bowled along with a tail wind. The only walk was the hill up from Daldownie to where the Dormobile had been left on the A939. Taking our luck we set off on the notorious Cock Bridge to Tomintoul road and added Carn Ealasaid (8:4) to the Corbett list before returning to Deeside to pick up the friends who had shared the camp at Loch Builg and then packed out over Ben Avon and Beinn a' Bhuird — Munro baggers all.

As a child I used to put up with one of those nasty chants kids inflict on each other. "How now Brown cow?" repeated endlessly could usually rouse me. I still don't know the source of this taunt but it gave me a feeling of affinity with the oddly named bump, a name which fascinated Queen Victoria on her treks through the valley surrounding it. Brown Cow Hill has invariably been generous to me.

Brown Cow Hill can equally well be climbed from the north, starting from Cock Bridge. There is a track south from Corgarff Castle which can be followed and the Corbett tackled from the east, or the River Don can be followed up and an approach made from the north. My recommended route for a day expedition would be Corgarff Castle, south to the col, traverse Brown Cow to the Gairn and return by Loch Builg, Inchrory on the Avon, and then east down the infant Don. The Avon at one time flowed eastwards on the course of the Don but another stream flowing northwards "captured" it, causing this peculiar right-angled bend and an empty pass eastwards. Charles Murray's "lythe Strathdon" thus lost most of its water through what is the country's finest example of river-capture.

Corgarff Castle is a stark tower surrounded by a star-shaped curtain wall — added in 1748 when Hanoverian troops were suppressing the last Jacobite hopes. Mar, Montrose and others used it on their campaigns. In 1571 the Gordons burnt it, and everyone inside (27 people) — a bloody history. The castle was garrisoned till 1831 but those last years were a check to whisky smuggling rather than potential rebellion.

Section 7:   18. MORVEN   871 m   OS 37   377040
             The big hill

There are quite a few Morvens in Scotland — and they are all pleasing hills. Best of all perhaps is Morven in Caithness which does not even make Corbett altitude (but then neither do Suilven nor Stac Polly) while another Morven, which is more often seen than climbed, is this one set between the Dee and the Don. Wherever you climb, from the highest Cairngorms down to the eastern sea, Morven seems to be visible, an instantly recognisable cone, standing in bold isolation, on "the edge of cultivation", strangely aloof, strangely neglected, perhaps simply from always "being there", above the Howe o' Cromar.

Morven, my third Corbett, was done as an outing from a schoolboy camp at Ballater in 1957. I can recall the freshness of its windy miles but no topographical details. We found an adder, and when Tony and I traversed Morven on UC 81 we also saw an adder. Our camp site in Ballater was full of them. You could lie in the tent at night and hear them rustling in the hedgerow just outside. Beautiful creatures. Why they occupy some parts of the country and not others is a mystery.

Tony and I set off from the cheery Inn at Cock Bridge with the early sun picking out the newly painted walls of Corgarff Castle, dazzling white against the browns of heather. We took Caulfeild's military road south of the River Don, remembering the old youth hostel which was always so welcome after crossing the strenuous Lecht Road, and wended up to cross the modern road to Deeside at its steepest brae. A track led us to peat workings on Scaulac (741 m), then we walked east along the crest among a typical eastern exhibition of hares, to the huge jubilee cairn of Mona Gowan. Morven, three miles to the south east, was suddenly big and bulky. "Great, spacious walking" was how I described it. We dropped to the col and up to a minor western top where we left our ruckers to climb to the summit unencumbered. Three others arrived simultaneously from the east, the only people we encountered on the thirteen peaks we did on that May's coast-to-coast.

The eastern approach gives only 500 m of ascent from the A97 road which runs through the farmlands of the Howe o' Cromar, an oasis of chequered fields and woods surrounded by hills. The recumbent stone circle of Tomnaverie (488036) or the souterain at Culsh (505055) are two of my favourite viewpoints in the Howe: Morven at its best. Farm roads lead off the A97 and most have continuations up on to the hill, the easiest being by Roar Hill using the old track to the Gairn.

After retrieving our rucksacks we descended round and down Morven's southern slopes (grassy, with blaeberry and cloudberry in flower), crossed the Rashy Burn to pass by Roar Hill and angle down for the Howe. The lower slopes were rough and heathery; we were glad to use one of the farm tracks. I'd just said to Tony it was adder country when we came on a big fellow lying sunbathing at our feet. Morven is generally less heathery than other hills hereabouts but the grass can be tussocky though relieved by paths. A short length of tarred road was enough to make us glad to escape into the birch and water landscape of the Kinord NCC Reserve, passing north of Loch Kinord to see a Celtic cross before a delightful path led us into Dinnet for the night. Waders were noisy, "the scattering of curlew calls like raindrops from the source of spring", and kingcups shone golden in the sun.

Loch Kinord has a *crannog* (lake dwelling). The best feature of all I discovered only later or we certainly would have included it in our traverse of Morven–The Vat, as the OS translates it, an extraordinary rocky gorge carved by a long-diminished river, which drains off Culblean Hill into Loch Kinord. There is nothing else quite like it in the country.

Morven is easily reached by a variety of routes to the south, Ballater being a favourite tourist village. There are paths or estate tracks up the Rashy Burn or the Tullich Burn or by Craig of Prony — Peter's Hill — or from Larg in Glen Gairn up the Morven Burn — another old drovers' road, and also the route taken by Queen Victoria in 1859. She had a burnside picnic on the way, sketched and then continued on a pony which "being so fat, panted dreadfully". The queen knew her

Scotland and had ascended quite a few of the big hills: "such seas of mountains" as she called them. They walked down to the lunch stop, had tea at Morven Lodge and so home to Balmoral.

The Morven Burn valley is a huge basin with an eerie feeling of isolation. An estate road now goes up the Mona Gowan ridge behind the lodge to Glenfenzie and the A939. This is one of the few areas where we have only out-of-date First Series maps. Charles and I recently retraced the route Tony and I took. Charles had been up Brown Cow Hill and Storm had taken me up Earn Ealasaid when the rough miles in hot summer sun left us "gey drouthie". The only high water we found was the stream draining south east off Mona Gowan. An unusual *slochd* (gash) crossed that hill's eastern ridge. A fence runs all the way from Scraulac to the top of Morven. The unusual feature of that day was the silver-plated shine of Loch Muick set in the hills opposite.

The northern (Donside) approaches are less interesting and entail a bit too much forestry for my liking. The poet Byron wrote about "Morven of the snow" and described a temperature inversion on top. The snows will have to wait for next time — on skis perhaps. Mount Keen, Lochnagar, Ben Avon, far Beinn a' Ghlo, Bennachie, the east coast, Donside were all clear on my visits and in the far north, quite plain, was that other remarkable Morven, in Caithness.

SPEYSIDE TO NORTH OF THE DON

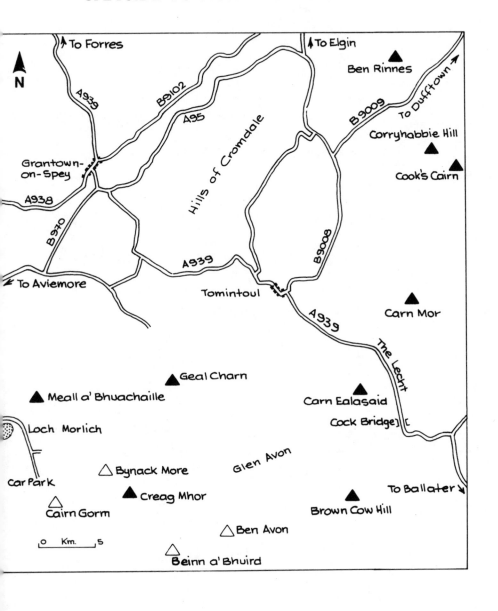

THIS IS A modest Corbett which can easily be combined with other
Cairngorm activities — if one thinks about it at the time. I first
climbed it when a party of us were making our exit from several
days of wandering about the eastern hills, staying at the Shelter
Stone and Faindouran bothy and climbing most hills between. We
set out from Faindouran after a night of wind: gusts of 70 mph the
radio had said.

Three of us headed west up the burn and were right on to the
moors before the wind found us. We sat out one shower, watching
the wavering white mass sweep away down the Caiplach towards
Tomintoul, then had to batter into the blast to Dagrum. From there
to the Corbett we walked with a marked list to starboard as we
leant on the wind. The summit has typical granite outcrops with
weatherworn potholes in them. Across the Lairig an Laoigh the
Barns of Bynack can be seen, perhaps the oddest of all the granite
tors.

Leaving the summit we were caught by a longer period of rain
("showers of a continuous nature" as I once heard the BBC say)
that chilled us to the bone, and we were very glad to pick up the
Lairig an Laoigh track and skirt Bynack More down to the stables
where we could brew before walking out to Glenmore, by which
time we'd been blown dry again. The Corbett can easily be ascended by those walking the classic Lairig an Laoigh.

On the ninth day of UC 81 Tony and I did a circuit of Creag
Mhor and Bynack More before going on to Faindouran. We started
from the Fords of Avon this time (reached from Kingussie via the
Lairig Ghru, Macdhui and Loch Avon) so had only about 600 feet
to climb, which is why I call Creag Mhor a modest Corbett. On
UC 87 my partner managed to take *over four hours* for the easy five
miles from Bynack Stables to the Fords of Avon — so I nipped up
Bynack More and Creag Mhor and still had the tea ready before he
caught up at the Fords. I'd also had a paddle in the chilly Avon,
high with melting snow, for I had to take a boot off to remove a bit
of Creag Mhor grit from inside a stocking. I don't like blisters. My
partner brought up the topic of blisters and said whisky was supposed to be a good prevention — rubbed on the feet that is, rather
than taken internally. One Challenger followed the advice: "I don't

know if the whisky helped my blisters but it made my sleeping bag smell nice."

Section 8:   2. MEALL A' BHUACHAILLE   810 m   OS 36   991115
          The shepherd's hill (boo-*a*-chil)

The big northern corries of the Cairngorms steal the show when looking south from the Rothiemurchus–Glen More area but from anywhere *on* those giants the view to Loch Morlich and Speyside would be much poorer without the undulating sweep of heather-clad hills north of the Queen's forest. The highest, eastmost of these summits is Meall a' Bhuachaille above the Pass of Ryvoan (Rebhoan) — from which it is an easy walk.

Cars can be taken to just past Glenmore Lodge making the pass a quiet walk. Lochan Uaine (which can be all colours in the course of a day) lies in a hidden hollow in the steep vee of the pass among old Scots pines and juniper and blaeberries: Cairngorm scenery at its very best. A path runs up the hill from Ryvoan bothy (which is half a house). Ryvoan is the "Thieves' Pass", which recalls ancient raids by clansmen. Their route on by the Braes of Abernethy to Tomintoul is still a good walk.

I was once staying at Glenmore Lodge observing a rescue course. The day had started with a winter flight in a helicopter, through Ryvoan and up the Nethy to Loch Avon and west to return along the northern corries. (On a subsequent flight I was to be lowered, during a rescue, into an icy, floodlit Coire an Lochain, a magical experience.) Denis, the Youth Hostel warden, rang to say Lorna was staying at the hostel and would like a walk. Thus it was we set off through Ryvoan (still noisy with helicopter games) and went up Meall a' Bhuachaille from the bothy. Ben Rinnes to the north east looked a mirror-image of Schiehallion far to the south. This must be a view to one of the most tree-covered landscapes in Scotland. From the large cairn we dropped to the col westwards and turned down (a marked path) into the forest and out at the Reindeer House near the hostel.

Continuing west from the summit are Creagan Gorm (*blue little crag*) and Craiggowrie (*goat's crag*), which give a marvellous walk with views up and down the Spey and to the Cairngorms and Monadh Liath hills. They are cut off by the pass of An Slugan to the west and from this a forestry road can be taken out to the Coylum Bridge–Nethy Bridge road, or one can return to Glen More by taking the forest road through the Badaguish plantings. This crest traverse is one of the best walks in the area. My old dog did the traverse. Storm simply went up and down from Ryvoan — but that was a moonlight expedition to work off the effects of over-indulgence at the Ossian Hotel in Kincraig.

Section 8: 3. GEAL CHARN 821 m OS 36 090127
       White hill (gyal chaarn)

As part of their Mountaineering Instructors' Certificate candidates being assessed at Glenmore Lodge had a day out on unknown hills where various skills could be quietly watched, navigation tested and, in casual conversation, attitudes and ideas drawn out by the examiner-cum-guinea-pig. Quite a few Corbetts within range of Glenmore Lodge are remote and rough, and were often issued as objectives to victims over the week. I'd name a peak the night before — this Geal Charn was nastily typical — and what we did, how, where and why, was up to the candidate. Geal Charn went to Joe, a lad from an Outdoor Centre in Northern Ireland, which had been bombed not long before.

Considering it was into October, the weather gave us such a grilling that the sweat running down my back was draining down my legs. We had a lift through the Ryvoan Pass to the fork in the road. The rest of the day was an endurance test over moor and bog with most of our energies going on searching for the next water-hole. In that bare, rounded landscape there was no escaping the sun. Deer, and there were scores, simply stood and let us pass rather than make any effort at flight. We went up the Lairig an Laoigh path from the Bynack Stable then angled over to An Lurg then Carn Tarsuinn and Bile Buidhe to reach Geal Charn. A trickle of water on its flank was a life saver. I don't suppose Joe could be held responsible for the conditions and he was new to the Cairngorms. We returned more or less as we'd come, cutting more directly down to Bynack Stable. The only other people we met were on the Lairig path. They were down to underpants and boots.

This route is not very interesting and gives a hard slog in any condition. The water of Caiplich, which moats the Corbett to the south, is notorious for leading people astray from the Lairig an Laoigh, and it is a long way downstream to the nearest touch of civilisation. An approach to Geal Charn from the Braes of Abernethy is preferable, starting either at Dorback Lodge (reached from Nethy Bridge) or even Bridge of Brown (the road to Tomintoul): either of these gives a pleasant walk.

From Dorback Lodge follow the estate road south eastwards to the watershed and then turn up for Geal Charn. Return westwards, skirting Bile Buidhe to pick up another estate road down by the Faesheallach Burn. Turn right at the T-junction and eventually abandon the road to strike through the craggy gap of the Eag Mhor (*big notch*) back down to the Braes of Abernethy. The day can be lengthened by walking over by the Burn of Brown and back by the Allt Iomadaidh. These northern outliers of the Cairngorms receive few visitors. The views north over Abernethy, the Hills of Cromdale and Ben Rinnes are open and the big Cairngorms loom to the south.

Section 8:   4. CARN EALASAID   792 m   OS 36   228118
          Elizabeth's hill

Carn Ealasaid is to Corbetts what the Cairnwell is to Munros: a hill rendered ridiculously easy by the presence of a high road — and also the unsightly presence of ski developments, not that there was much in the way of ski facilities on the Lecht when Sue and I visited Carn Ealasaid.

We had had a great overnight ski tour in the main Cairngorms and had driven west to Laggan hoping to ski up Creag Meagaidh but the weather was all wrong so we turned round and headed east. Of necessity we stopped at Landmark in Carr Bridge to buy maps of Lochnagar, our destination, but, determined to do something on skis, I suggested Carn Ealasaid, for we were taking the notorious Tomintoul–Cock Bridge road over the Lecht. As the top of the pass is 635 m there is not very much of Carn Ealasaid to climb.

A café and three rope tows marked the nascent ski centre. We skied off on skins up the slopes beside the tows, a bit doubtful as to finding the Corbett in the blowing cloud. We had no map beyond what I'd traced from a 20-year-old AA Road Book from the car. We were not too worried because, if we did end up at a loss, a course to the north east could only hit the A939.

A long rising traverse round the head of the glen of Camore Burn led to our hill. If the summer view (tones of brown and blue) had pleased before, the winter scene was as bright and sharp as a Brueghel painting. The skins came off and we made an even longer descending run round that valley. Having lost height we swapped again and skinned back up to the Dormobile. We had been away less than two hours. When Charles and I were Corbett-bagging in summer we camped on the Lecht's roadside verge in an attempt to catch a breeze and keep away the dreaded midges.

There is a pleasant high-level walk from Carn Ealasaid westwards to Craig Veann and the River Avon down to Tomintoul. À lift up to the Lecht to follow this route would be my recommended traverse of the Corbett. The north-south track that passes just west of Carn Ealasaid, from Blairnamarrow to upper Donside, is shown as a road on older maps. Between Blairnamarrow and the Well of the Lecht is a ruined cottage which hit the headlines in 1920, when it was used as a hiding place by Percy Toplis ("The Monocled Mutineer"). The wartime trickster was wanted in connection with a murder near Andover and took off northwards on his bike. When he lit a fire at Blairnamarrow someone saw the smoke and called the Tomintoul bobby. The two of them were shot at, when they approached, and Toplis escaped on his bicycle over the Lecht. (He was killed, some weeks later, in a shoot-out in the Lake District.)

Section 8: 5. CARN MOR 804 m OS 37 265183
       The big cairn

Carn Mor is the rather self-effacing summit of the sprawling Ladder Hills. A mile and a half to the north east of the summit is the top of the Ladder Road, an old right of way from Glen Livet to Donside. The pass is still perhaps better known than the hills which, while dry and easy on the rolling summits, have a deal of peat bog on the cols and in the corries. A walk over the old road, with a diversion to Carn Mor, is highly recommended. The view down into Glen Livet is very attractive, being mixed farmland, still worked: flaunting greens and such a contrast to the brown wastelands of most areas.

The Ladder path splits on the south side of the col with branches going down into Glen Nochty and Glen Buchat, both of which join the Don after a few miles. The former route passes the ruin of Duffdefiance just before the plantations begin. This odd name records a Glen Livet crofter who came over the Ladder and squatted here, in defiance of the proprietor, Duff. The Nochty joins the Don at Bellabeg where there is a striking *motte*, the Doune of Invernochty, which indicates the strategic importance of this junction over many centuries. Glen Buchat Castle guards the Buchat–Don confluence, a Gordon fortified tower of 1590.

Carn Mor can also be climbed very easily from the 638-m summit of the Lecht road, an expedition which is even better if made on skis. Though not giving such a starting-height, the Corbett can also be climbed from the car park at the Well of the Lecht. On the roadside a tablet records that the Cock Bridge to Tomintoul road was built in 1754 by Lord Hay and the 33rd Regiment. (It is not a Wade road as is so often stated.) Looking up the Conglass Burn a trim little building is in view. This is all that is left of an ironstone mine opened by the York Building Company who bought up estates after the Jacobite risings. The ore was carried on pack ponies to Nethy Bridge, the nearest plentiful wood supply, where it was smelted.

I once climbed Carn Mor by following the Conglass on beyond the mine and then tackling the luxuriant heathery slopes up on to the breezy tops, a day of constantly being startled by grouse and hares. There were many black-headed gulls quartering the slopes, snowy with cloudberry flowers, and the upper reaches rang with the plaintive calls of erratic golden plovers. An early summer day of sunshine made it a delightful dander and I wandered back to Carn Liath before descending again. I collected ironstone samples before returning to the car. Drinks were the first priority and I took my tea to the burn and sat with my feet in the water while picking the heather off my stockings.

The Conglass Glen is much easier in descent. Going up is a bit of a heather flog. Charles and I, with two cars available, started on the Lecht and followed the crest then backtracked a bit and charged down into the glen. Several young deer calves went bouncing away as if on springs, a much more efficient way of coping with the heather than our stolid struggling or the dog's tired leaps.

Section 8:   6. COOK'S CAIRN   774 m   OS 37   299275

Section 8:   7. CORRYHABBIE HILL   781 m   OS 37   281289

These two hills gave me a smugly satisfying day. Thunderstorms at Garve camp site led to all night rain. When it stopped at 10 a.m. I departed down a congested A9 (bad old days) to Carr Bridge. A cigarette thrown out a car window had set the moor alight and the forest had burned for several days. Driving through the smoke was like something from a war film. I went on by Granton, Cromdale, Avon Bridge to Glen Livet. Basically I planned to cycle up by the River Livet and tackle the Corbetts from the watershed. The time was 2.30 when I set off in a drizzle, but hoping the forecast of "brighter for early evening" would be true. The drizzle soon ended.

After a stony brae up to Achdregnie farm the track descended again and crossed to the south bank of the River Livet. I sat for a bit and noted some unusual names on the map. What a gift for a novelist they'd be: Shalg, Larryvarry, Urlar, Moniewhit, Crespet, Thunder-slap, Ballintomb, Finnylost, Quirn. . . . The track was stony and grassy in turn and, past Suie, I took one "skite" in a gritty rut. The going became rougher and steeper so I dumped the cycle by the track and walked. From the watershed I followed the burn up (it disappeared occasionally) and arrived at the summit of Cook's Cairn just as the south wind blew away the last of the cloud. South of Cook's Cairn is the old right of way from Glen Livet to Cabrach, passing through Blackwater Forest and Dead Wife's Hillock.

I trundled down the line of some butts and up the other side of the pass for Corryhabbie Hill, preferring the cropped heather to the "road" which, low down, was deeply eroded and useless. The trig point was closely walled in, and there were nettles growing there. The weather looked black. I back-tracked at once. Before retrieving my cycle I found a cairn with a slab that had a crown and V.R. 1867 inscribed on it. Despite a loose cotter-pin the run back to the van was enjoyable. The kettle had just come to the boil when the heavens opened. But I was snug, with my mug, in the fug.

Hares were much in evidence all day. And silly sheep. I saw one fall into the river and another, startled by my approach, dashed off and ran into a hare, which shot off, too, and set a snipe careering up the glen. In all I saw a score of different birds.

These two hills could equally well be approached from the other side of the pass separating them: Glen Fiddich instead of Glen Livet, leaving the Dufftown–Rhynie A941 road at Bridgehaugh. A cycle would still be useful. There are about three miles to the sprawl of Glenfiddich Lodge where there is a choice: an estate road follows the Hill of Glenroads and then takes the long plateau-like NE Ridge up Corryhabbie Hill (this is "Morton's Way" on the map), or there is a footpath along the River Fiddich to the watershed. Up the road and down the burn would be my choice.

Map 36 is worth having for the Livet approaches while Map 28 is needed for the Fiddich route in. Corryhabbie Hill was an important survey station in the 1850 principal triangulation and was occupied for three months. Queen Victoria stayed a few days at Glenfiddich Lodge in 1867 (described in *More Leaves from the Journal of a Life in the Highlands*). She arrived in the early evening but her baggage did not arrive at all. She was not amused and at one o'clock made uncomfy alternative arrangements. One day she visited Auchindoun Castle and on another rode up the glen and over the watershed (hence the memorial). Auchindoun is a stark ruin. This was very unsettled country at one time. The Battle of Glenlivet (1594) and the Battle of Cromdale (1690) top and tail a brutal century.

Now Glen Livet and Glen Fiddich have friendlier associations. And the two Corbetts, not bad wee malts.

While working on this book I had a postcard from Jim Donaldson saying that Cook's Cairn had been "eliminated". The hill, I hasten to add, is still there. It is just no longer a Corbett, the dip to Cook's Cairn being under 500 feet.

Section 8:   8. BEN RINNES   840 m   OS 28   255355
              Headland hill (rinneis)

Ben Rinnes, being the most northerly of the North East's Corbetts, dominates the landscape for many miles around while its isolated position ensures a huge view north over the Laich o' Moray and across the Moray Firth to the hills of Caithness; south and west there is the wide arc of the Cairngorms, the Monadh Liath hills and the glens and bens beyond the Great Glen. Ben Nevis is visible on the western sea, as is Buchan Ness to the east. The River Spey wends below the hill. Dufftown lies only five miles to the north east and Rinnes is encompassed by motor roads yet it still manages to give a feeling of aloofness, rising as a bold cone above the patchwork fields of its lower slopes.

My only visit was a flying one, while travelling from Deeside to Speyside, and I spent longer in "Landmark" (Visitors' Centre) at Carr Bridge that evening than I did on Ben Rinnes. A minor road gains the maximum height possible at the end of the hill's east ridge (Glack Harness) and, with the intervening bump of Roy's Hill, the summit granite tor can be reached in an hour. The summit has the resounding name Scurran of Lochterlandoch and the name scurran (sgoran) is applied to two other tors. I ran most of the way back to the car but would recommend descending by the long, easy-angled NW Ridge to skirt the headstreams and then turn down by Baby's Hill to pick up a peat road to the distillery. Much of the hill peat has in fact been stripped off to fire the whisky stills.

In 1803, a Rev. James Hall bought a pony in Edinburgh and set off to explore Scotland. His account, all 622 pages of it, appeared in 1807. Hidden therein is note of an ascent of Ben Rinnes. He carried a barometer. On the way up he was cold, hungry and lost in the mist. Out of the cloud loomed fearsome beasts: a "phalanx of wedders . . . one in the middle having a pair of tremendous horns". When the mist cleared he recorded "a secret enjoyment, a calm satisfaction and religious fervour which no language can express".

And a good meal when safely down again. This is a very early account of a hill being climbed, for fun, and behind the ageing language there are obviously the same feelings and experiences we enjoy today.

GLEN ROY & THE MONADH LIATH

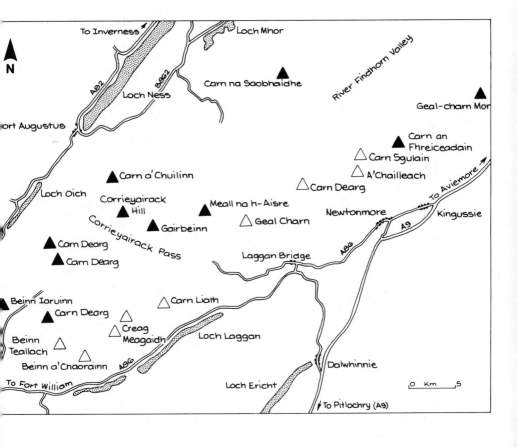

Section 9:   1. BEINN IARUINN   *c.*800 m   OS 34   296900
             Iron hill

ROBERT SOUTHEY, WHO toured Scotland with Thomas Telford in
1819, considered Glen Roy the best glen he had seen in the country.
Happily it has Corbetts but no Munros.

The first time I went up Beinn Iaruinn it rained — after a beguiling
blue sky had lured me upwards. But Kent was being battered by gales
and floods. The second time I went up Beinn Iaruinn it hailed on me at
regular half-hour intervals (ambushing bursts of fire out of the north)
which was quite painful even with a cagoule hood up. Storm did not
like the hail at all and tried to climb under me as I cringed wherever
possible on a rather exposed mountain. "Mountain" is probably a
rather flattering term for this unpronounceable Corbett.

Unlike green Carn Dearg on the other side of Glen Roy the slopes of
Iaruinn are heathery and bouldery as well as steep. There is no
reasonable easy way up so there is something to be said for following a
short, sharp route rather than looking for extra miles and smiles.
Coire nan Eun is my choice, inveterate burn-follower that I am. The
easiest line keeps to the slopes on the north side of the corrie burn, just
wandering up the heather and screes to the rough plateau and along to
the summit — a bit tame and lacking any interest.

I'd parked where the burn crossed the road and set off up the burn
itself. A birch-tree broke the force of the first hailstorm. A spider's
web, spun between a clump of alpine lady's mantle and a fern, was
shredded by the hammering.

One of the pleasures of scrambling up the course of a stream lies in
its wealth of wild flowers. In such gullies lies the greatest concentration and variety of our mountain flora. Often the only trees in miles
are the refugee remnants encamped in the gullies — safe from the
devouring teeth of sheep and deer. The Highlands are a man-made
desert, not a natural wilderness, and only in these secret corners can we
gain a glimpse of the richer heritage we have destroyed. In the gullies,
too, the bedrocks of the mountains are laid bare and our fingers can
feel the rough strata of creation.

The Parallel Roads show up well, as the ledges are greener with
grass while the slopes are deep heather-plum-coloured, but they are
more fully described under the next Corbett, Carn Dearg. We had
scrambled quite far up into the corrie, one carved by a very
mathematically-minded glacier, when the next hail attack hit us.

Entertainment this time was a jet fighter thundering down the glen, below our level, and banking steeply to avoid the south side of Coire nan Eun which juts out in a jagged ridge. This ridge should be avoided in ascent or descent as it is cut right across with crags and foul ground. Having said this, Storm and I, faced with a curtain of scree to the right and a steep headwall, turned left on a rising traverse to escape the corrie on to this very ridge just below where it reached the plateau. We managed to avoid the worst of the loose stuff. Ben Tee, Sron a' Choire Ghairbh and Meall na Teanga at once caught the eye to the west. The view south was a wild mix of storm and sun searchlights. Cloud base was 3,000 feet — which is another advantage Corbetts have over Munros.

Hailstorm number three caught us on the rim to the summit. I just hoped there was no thunder and lightning mixed with the hail. Being close to nature has some limitations. Storm (the dog) was gazing down into the corrie and when I followed his stare it was to see an eagle slowly winging across the crags. Since Coire nan Eun is the *corrie of birds*, a name often given because of eagles or their eyries, this was a good place to see one. The hail did not seem to cause the big bird any concern.

We scampered over the summit and round into a bitter wind, and from the dip beyond turned down on that easiest line, keen to reach the glen before any more thrashings of hail. We just made it. We had one pause and sat with a fine view, both down and up Glen Roy, of the Parallel Roads. Achavady, two miles down, was the site where Montrose rested his army on its march to the Battle of Inverlochy in 1645. He is one of the few heroes to come out of that bloody century. The red Post van passed below and I watched its wanderings till it vanished behind the viewpoint car-park knoll. Three hours after setting off I was back at my Dormobile, enjoying the inevitable brew, while the hail battered on the roof to such an extent I could hardly hear the raucous tape of *Carmina Burana* that I'd put on. Music also has its place in the mountains, with or without the unscored percussion of a hailstorm. It was like trying to have afternoon tea inside a kettle drum!

Section 9:   2. CARN DEARG (South of Glen Roy)   834 m
     OS 34   345887
     The red cairn (Carn Jerrak)

In some ways you have to be ready to grab summits when you can. Carn Dearg was to be one such opportunist's ascent. We were working on the restoration of Brunachan, a cottage east of the river, below Coire Dubh; the Corbett was only a couple of miles away as the fly crows. After several hours of carrying gravel, sand and water for concrete mixing the old back needed a rest. And the sun shone. Whistling on Storm and with only a bar of chocolate in my pocket we set off up the burn.

"Burning up" a hill is a grand way of sneaking footage unnoticed. Gripped up with little technical problems on greasy schist, or hopping from boulder to boulder, so occupies the mind that height is gained almost magically. As I had a bag of cameras, some of the more hairy traverses above deep pools had to be skirted, but most of the ascent was made up the gully. There were good sheep tracks on the banks, too, and the slopes are green and grassy: steep but pleasant going and always, below, down the funnel of the gorge, was Brunachan and our cars parked beyond the river, a view which shrank steadily as we scrambled upwards. Brunachan used to have a quarry where quern stones (Lochaber Stones) were made. These have been found as far away as the Outer Hebrides.

Coire Dubh proper slowed us down as the scree edges were lush with blaeberries. We went up the gully clearly seen from below (quite straightforward), and soon tumbled out on to the edge of the sweeping grasslands above. The burn had vanished for a long time, buried below the slabby screes, but was flowing near the top and helped to quench our thirsts. We caught a chill north wind, too, and we quickly left the downward view for the more horizontal sweep of the grass-moor mile to the summit of Carn Dearg.

Carn Dearg is quite a high hill for this area — we could see over the western rim of Glen Roy to Ben Tee and the Loch Lochy Munros. North lay two other Corbetts named Beinn Dearg. Quite why there is this accumulation of "red hills" in upper Glen Roy I don't know, the area forms an entity and repetition is not really expected.

Carn Dearg's nearest hill-view is south-eastwards to Beinn Teallach (promoted from Corbett to Munro long after the rest which gave it a couple of years of unprecedented activity as all the Munroists had to come out of retirement and top up their collection) to Beinn a' Chaorainn (of the wandering summit) and to Creag Meagaidh's long sweep with the distinctive notch of The Window very clear. That eighteenth-century Munroist, Bonnie Prince Charlie, came through The Window on his long backpacking trip. Carn Dearg's best view is south-westwards to the silver waters of Loch Linnhe and the jagged bastion of Ben Nevis, the Aonachs, Grey Corries and Stob Corries. With the back-lighting of evening these looked fine indeed.

Having come up Coire Dubh we set off to descend Coire na Reinich, keeping well over towards its eastern and northern flanks before descending. The corrie is unusually steep all round but the south-westerly slopes are more broken-up with crags and are not a cheerful prospect approached from above. They are a mass of alpine flowers: the botanist would no doubt cheerfully risk his neck for a view of a vertical acre of *Dryas octopetela*. The northern flank of the glen is marginally easier in descent. We kept on the other and had a couple of deep-cut streams to cross. At the edge of the glen we gained a bonus.

Glen Roy is famous for its "Parallel Roads" and here I was able to photograph the top two in profile, very green in colour, against the browner lines across the hillside at the head of the glen. After centuries of speculation it is generally accepted that these odd level terraces that mark the hillsides of Glen Roy are the levels of ancient reservoirs which were dammed up by glaciers blocking off the mouths of the glens. (Southey and Telford speculated that they were man-made "for a display of barbarous magnificence in hunting".) There are three distinct levels, which can be followed for many miles, at 261 m, 325 m and 350 m. There is a large glacial terrace at the foot of Coire na Reinich and I could also see the bigger one beyond Brae Roy Lodge where Glen Turret and Glen Roy unite. I inspected the "Roads" on site and then followed a path down the River Roy back to Brunachan — arriving just in time to help unload more sacks of gravel from Jim's Land Rover. A concrete floor devours twice the material of any estimate. I then escaped across the river to supper in the Dormobile. By the time I'd reached coffee and the Emperor Concerto it was raining. The opportunist approach had paid off again!

The above route is how I'd suggest climbing Carn Dearg, but starting and finishing at the bridge a mile up from Brunachan. The river is not one that can be forded very often. From the bridge wander down the River Roy and then cut up into Coire Dubh. Make sure it is Coire Dubh. I nearly wandered off up the Allt Feith in my enthusiasm for scrambling up the dry-weather rocks of the burn. If really pushed for time, up and down Coire na Reinich is the way, but a traverse or a circuit is so much more satisfying. Beinn Iaruinn could be done in the same day but I'd advocate doing just Carn Dearg and exploring the upper glen a bit on a first day, doing the other Carn Deargs on the second, and Iaruinn on the day of leaving. Glen Roy is a rather special place after all.

Section 9:   3. BEINN TEALLACH   913 m   OS 41 or 34   361859
              Hill of the forge (tya-lach)

Beinn Teallach is not to be confused with An Teallach. The only thing they have in common is their building material of rock, water, bog and heather — and their pestering summer hordes of flies, ticks, clegs and midges. The builders made An Teallach into The Magnificent. Beinn Teallach was made from the leftovers. The Ordnance Survey, bless it, has raised the hill by two metres, elevating it to Munro status, but as it is still a Corbett in the current *Tables* I've included it here. With the masses going up it now, the Munro could well be worn down into a Corbett again.

Some people regard this elevation as a dirty trick but those Munroists suffering from advanced Corbettitis can afford to grin. It has merely done a quick change from Corbett 913 m to Munro 915 m. All the same scores of people who had sunk into quiet retirement after completing their Munros will now have to dig out the old leather boots, dust off their puttees and sally forth, alpenstock in hand, to add this thrusting newcomer to their bag. My smugness at having been up it several times was shattered by the dog pointing out that he had not.

I was staying at Nancy Smith's renowned hospice (a privately-run hostel) at Fersit, just north of Loch Treig (353783) (see p. 7), when a youth grabbed me and gleefully said he'd discovered a new Munro. As this tends to happen now and then my reaction was not encouraging, but Richard produced a 1:25,000 map bought at Nevisport that morning: Beinn Teallach was blatantly 915 m! (The height was later confirmed by the Ordnance Survey.) Ah well, it should put up Nancy's bednights.

Beinn Teallach is a coy hill that hides away, north of Glen Spean, with little to be seen from the A86 Fort William–Speyside road. Nancy's hostel is the handiest accommodation and Tulloch Station on the Fort William railway line is a convenient starting point, too.

The height is not the only thing to have changed. A vastly increased area has been ploughed and planted with conifers. First find your Beinn Teallach.

Roughburn on the A86 is the easiest starting point and there is plenty of off-road parking. A forestry road on the hillside is shown treeless, but with an extension of trees sweeping west for many miles. Fortunately this makes little difference to the approach. The dog found three young owls roosting in the grass by the track. They were able to fly and fluttered round silently like huge moths. Young trees produce new wildlife like this but the dark adult growth of a plantation is a desert. Oak, willow and other deciduous trees edge the road, and they will improve the scenery eventually — for a rather select type of spectator.

The track suddenly bends sharp right, up the hill (and goes on for miles across the southern flank of Beinn a' Chaorainn), but shortly after there is a branch leading left. Take this to its end and then the rough continuation down to the riverside where a couple of fields sit marooned in the tide of trees. There is a gate and the Allt a' Chaorainn is easily gained. Cross the river and reach the track shown coming over from the A86 at the Inverlair–Fersit road end. This river could be difficult in spate, when the east bank should be followed. The track is good and goes all the way up the glen and crosses the river more than once.

The glen is three miles long, with Beinn Teallach lying west of it and Beinn a' Chaorainn to the right — the latter a green slope of unbelievable uniformity. Both hills have their better aspects to the east, fine indeed on Beinn a' Chaorainn, fairly modest on Beinn Teallach, as can be seen during the walk up. For my first visit in a dozen years I found a white heather growing in the acres of *Calluna vulgaris*. I suspect the path is wet enough normally, but after the months of summer the many streams were welcome indeed, as were the early blaeberries. Only one drink came from a few yards below a long-dead sheep. The dog rolled on the corpse, of course, so was brutally washed — and seemed to enjoy that too. A breeze made the day perfection rather than purgatory.

The east face is named Coireachan Garbh, the *rough little corries*, and here some crag and scree break out to give a bit of character to the new Munro. Garbh, meaning rough, is a good map-Gaelic word to recognise and to heed. It usually describes the landscape well, and trackless routes up a "Coire Garbh" can be rough indeed.

The cairn on the lip of the col can be seen from well down the glen and makes a pleasant picnic spot. The col, or the Chaorainn slopes just above, give the most flattering view of Beinn Teallach. Beyond the col is some desolate country which is drained by the Burn of Agie to upper Glen Roy. Beinn Teallach could be climbed from that direction and is also easily combined with Beinn a' Chaorainn — which itself is easily combined with Creag Meagaidh. This path gives a good start to however many Munros are strung together eastwards. Beinn Teallach could also be combined with Carn Dearg (9:2) east of Glen Roy.

The path seems to amble along but the col tops 600 m and the view back is very much downwards. In the pulsing heat of our ascent the Loch Treig hills and the eastern Grey Corries were cardboard cut-outs, tinted in varying shades of blue. The NE Ridge of Beinn Teallach gives no problems and leads over a few swelling rises to the summit of broken grey stone. The best view is southwards and that is the route I'd suggest for the descent. You are soon off the stone grey and back on to the carpet green and purple of grass and heather. We eventually angled down to pick up the path again at the level of the fence which comes in above the trees and, in ruined state, wanders up the glen as well. (A gate on the col stands like some forlorn modern sculpture.) We reversed the moves through paddock and plantation, cursing the short ascent to the track for we were below breeze level and the heat and midges plagued us. Use the track, however. Short cuts don't pay.

Over the year after Beinn Teallach's promotion I seldom drove past at weekends without noticing a car or cars parked at Roughburn. Locals must have wondered what was going on. A fine winter's day tempted Storm and me back to the hill and we met eight different parties. Several threatened to lynch me for producing the new Munro. I said I'd have been far happier with it left as a Corbett and anyway Richard Webb "discovered" it — I just chose the wrong night to be staying at Nancy's. For the winter ascent we used the only real alternative from the A86, the old path shown on the map. As this is criss-crossed by new forest roads it is not at all easy to find and can be a bit of an obstacle course. On an Ultimate Challenge Tony and I crossed from Luib-chonnal bothy to Nancy's, taking in Beinn Teallach and Beinn a' Chaorainn in passing. We had snow on the tops, even though it was the middle of May.

Section 9:   4. CARN DEARG (South of Glen Eachach)   768 m   OS
     34   357948
     Red cairn

Section 9:   5. CARN DEARG (North of Glen Eachach)   815 m   OS
     34   349967
     Red cairn

The last time I was on these hills was quite a memorable day and one very much in keeping with the conditions of the rest of the UC 86. We had Corbetts both west and east of the Great Glen. The day from Cluanie Inn to Loch Oich is described later. We reached the Great Glen in the rain, which was still pouring down when we set off from Lundie View, just north of Loch Oich, with the objective of reaching Luib Chonnal over the Carn Deargs.

The track up into Glen Buck began right outside the back door, which is one way of testing the gears first thing. The path pulls up hard but normally rewards the toiler with a big view down the Great Glen to Ben Tee and her Munro partners west of Loch Lochy. The view is soon lost as the road twists into the hills but Glen Buck itself is pretty. The birches were in new leaf and the lambs were at the daft follow-my-leader stage. Our path was much less distinctive when we pulled up round into a side glen above the Allt a' Ghlinne, and we held our level till we met this stream at a small meeting of gorges where we crossed and followed the Allt na h-Eilrig, which ran in a deep cleft, woody and active, while all round were the barren moors. As we squelched our way up the bank we had one glimpse through a gap to the line of the Corrieyairack Pass and its indicative pylons. Before going into the cloud at a spot where four burns meet, we had a quick brew, one where the heat-loss waiting and the heat-gain from the tea were about equally balanced. Conditions were obviously going to be nasty.

We decided to outflank the hills ahead in order to leave our ruckers at a col south east of Carn Dearg 815 m before tackling its steep final cone. We followed one burn to its source and then carried on up onto a ridge where we took a bearing along the flank as we were now in driving rain and cloud. Perhaps we should have gone over the intervening bump for in the peaty bogs and runnels navigating was not easy; however, the bulk of Carn Dearg came when expected and we skirted round under its snowy skirts to find the gap with the rocky knoll to the south east. We were pretty certain of our navigation and cut up the snowy drifts towards the col, only we never did seem to arrive and eventually everything was very uncertain; if not lost we were temporarily mislaid. There was only one remedy: upwards. (All points converge on the highest point.) We reached the cairn carrying our rucksacks after all. The cairn could also give us a fixed point from which we set off with meticulous navigation rather than the casual that usually suffices. The cloud then shredded and for a couple of minutes we were able to check everything visually. The symmetrical hulk of Carn Dearg 768 m was straight ahead.

When we reached the Allt Dubh, the burn that rings Carn Dearg on the north, we decided to risk going up this second Corbett. We might manage before the weather really caused havoc. We did, just. First we had a brew again to warm our clammy, chilled bodies and, without sacks, were able to romp up despite the buffeting gale and periods of lashing rain. The hill is really a big convex cone, and I kept looking back across the valley at snowshapes through the clouds as an aid to navigation in descent. The wind made us reel about on the summit plateau: it was a case of "kick the cairn and down again", by compass over the viewless plateau, and then by the noted landmarks, trotting down the grassy steepnesses and odd bogs back to the ruckers by the Allt Dubh.

The rain was on for the day, obviously, and we didn't waste any time in setting off on the three Scots' miles of glen down to Luib Chonnal. Our supplies had previously been buried east of the river and the bothy is on the west bank. It is a big river. Our fears were that the water would soon rise to create an impassable spate. We criss-crossed the upper reaches which steadily became more and more difficult. The burn was sending down plenty of water. As sure as water is wetter than whisky there was an epic looming.

The problem was postponed by my off-loading my sleeping bag, cameras and some dry clothing on to Tony who thereafter would keep to the west bank and reach the bothy, dry and without too much bother, while I'd stay on the east bank and decide what to do once I'd found our food cache. I might have to ascend two or three miles up the burn again to where I could ford the flood, or maybe I could swim across below the Eas Ban junction where the spate eases in the flat valley bottom. There was one big side stream which gave some excitement going down, and there our Allt Dubh became the raging Allt Chonnal, quite unfordable. I picked up a made path and tramped down in a mix of gloom and worry, the likely swim setting the adrenalin to work in anticipation. Why do we do these things? The event was well called the Ultimate Challenge. I suppose Tony and I deserved our troubles for grabbing summits on our high-level route. Someone was to comment that their route was "neither high, nor low, but positively subterranean". The path turned down to the river and there stood a real, safe, solid, wonderful, magic footbridge! What I called the Ordnance Survey is unprintable. The bridge is by no means new but they do not bother to show it on the map.

An hour's work was needed to reach the cache (two parcels of food and two bottles of wine) and return to the bridge and follow Tony to the bothy. Kay, Jeannie, Helen and Martin of my local mountaineering club were already in, as were Ray and George, two old UC friends. As they had variously come via Knoydart and Glen Kingie, while Tony and I had come from Kintail, it was quite pleasing to have kept the rendezvous after such a week of floods and storm. We had a fairly merry night tucked in under the rafters, surrounded by rows of dripping waterproofs ("Berghaus is beautiful"), and the rain tattoo-ing, like shoppers' high heels in a pedestrian precinct, on the old roof. Ours was a tempered conviviality, for relief and worry as well as the wet-heavy miles had taken their toll.

This is one route I'd recommend for the Carn Deargs (a two-day trip with the next day out to Tulloch/Laggan is even better) but to be tackled in settled conditions. Only the quickest and easiest way of gaining these two Corbetts has no danger from spates. For this you'd drive up to the head of Glen Roy (public road to Brae Roy Lodge only), cross Turret Bridge and follow the shepherd's track up Glen Turret to a sheep fank. From there you can puff up to the 350-metre parallel road and follow this round into Gleann Eachach. The Carn Deargs are sited north and south of the Allt Eachach's upper reaches. There are no problems.

If based in Glen Roy a better round is possible. Wander up Glen Roy to the Allt Chonnal, visiting waterfalls and other features, then go up the Allt Chonnal–Allt Dubh (our route in reverse) to the col and, after doing the Corbetts, descend by Glen Eachach and Glen Turret. These secretive glens and the peculiar parallel roads are the best of the day — the hills are unexceptional and the views lacking the sweep usually associated with Corbetts.

Section 9: 6. GAIRBEINN 896 m OS 34 460985
                 Rough hill

Section 9: 7. CORRIEYAIRACK HILL 896 m OS 34 429998
                 Hill of the rising glen

The Monadh Liath inevitably receive a bad press. At best they are described as featureless. This is a pity because comparisons are odious and to blame the Monadh Liath for not being Knoydart is daft. They are different, that is all. The quality of the walking is high. You can stretch your legs and really walk into or across these hills in a way you cannot do on the constant grinding ascents west of the Great Glen. Because they are a vast peaty desert, features become more important. A bothy can seem like an oasis. Because they are seldom visited the wild life is more obvious. There is plenty going for the Monadh Liaths, not least, having their southern bounds the line of the upper Spey and the historic Corrieyairack Pass. These two hills, and Meall na h-Aisre (9:9) are grouped together here for convenience and, with Geal Charn (the Munro), they form the bold edge of the plateau-landscape of the Monadh Liath.

Plenty has been written about the Corrieyairack Pass itself. With our modern road system its use as a main route seems strange and long ago. The use is certainly ancient. James I crossed the pass when making a foray against Alasdair of the Isles, but its great associations are with the eighteenth century when the route was made into a proper road by General Wade after the Fifteen Rising — in good time for Bonnie Prince Charlie and his army to use it in the Forty Five. They say the summit of the pass is haunted by a ghostly piper. As a walk the Corrieyairack is more interesting for its historical associations than for its natural beauty and one "improvement" to a crossing is to make the easy ascent of Corrieyairack Hill from the top of the pass.

The top of the pass had a meteorological building and pylons and fences and is a rather bleak spot. The summit expands the view. Spaciousness is a hallmark of the Monadh Liath landscape. From Laggan a car can be driven as far as Melgarve. Several Wade bridges line the route and Garva Bridge, which is crossed, is one of the General's most artistic creations, built, like many, to suit the site rather than as a symmetrical imposition. These hills would be done from the Great Glen side only if traversing the pass, because that side entails a longer walk and nearly a thousand feet more of ascent.

Since Corrieyairack Hill on the latest mapping is given the same height as Gairbeinn it has been raised to Corbett status as well. The only time I've linked them both was on an assessment outing from Glenmore Lodge when Cathy and Steve were being put through the mill for their Mountaineering Instructors' Certificates. As Cathy was a committed professional and Steve was in charge of RAF Kinloss Mountain Rescue Team we talked rather than walked over the hills. We went up from Melgarve and skipped the vanishing zigzags up out of Corrie Yairack to follow the burn up to the pass. The pylons rather spoil the route. Fences and tracks led us up Corrieyairack Hill, which is not far short of Munro height (2,922 feet). A gate with no fence stands in the middle of nowhere. The walk, with plenty of ups and downs and yet another Geal Charn (876 m) led to Gairbeinn. The going is drier than further into the Monadh Liaths. A "royal" was sheltering in the lee of the cairn so we took the stag's nook for a snack. We seemed to scatter stags all the way down south to the car at Melgarve. The last time I crossed the pass was with Tony on UC 81. Corrieyairack Hill was enough. The weather was not at its best, which is not unusual here. I feel sorry for the poor soldiers under Wade who had to make the "New Road" (Neil Munro's classic story is so called from the Corrieyairack).

If you believe that miles are easier than feet of ascent, then this day's walking can be prolonged eastwards to reach Meall na h-Aisre (9:9). On the map, things like Dubh Lochan (*black loch*) and areas of marsh-symbol hint, quite correctly, that the going is more typical of the range. You are on to the flat palm of plateau rather than the knobbly knuckles of Corrieyairack–Gairbeinn. There is not much to say about the route. A friend called it "a slaistery slog". The descent, down Leathad Gaothach, is firmer underfoot and the path down to Garva Bridge can be picked up. This is the obvious line of ascent if doing just this Corbett on its own. Coire Iain Oig is a bit watery to be a route. I've linked on to Geal Charn, the Munro, and you have another Dubh Loch on that side. There is not much you can do about the *dubhs* of the Monadh Liath — except enjoy them!

Section 9:   8. CARN A' CHUILINN   816 m   OS 34   416034
            Cairn of the holly

The vagaries of the *Tables* (blame the OS) demoted Carn Easgann
Bana to the north east of Carn a'Chuilinn from being a Corbett,
which is a pity for the 6 miles (which feel like 60) linking them are in
a class of their own for roughness. My round of the then brace of
Corbetts took $1\frac{1}{2}$ hours longer than expected, though it included
falling asleep for half an hour at one of the lochs.

This was a walk which emphasised what I'd said earlier about the
richness of Monadh Liath wildlife. Apart from a few stalkers' cairns
and rotting fences there was no sign of man. A fox charged across
our route, there were many parcels of hinds, the flora was varied and
the bird life a constant pleasure with pipits pipitting all day, some
very vocal golden plovers, besides snipe, curlew, dunlin, sandpiper,
lark and wheatear. Some grouse gave the dog a fine distraction
display. Common gulls nested on Loch Tarff where we started and
finished the circuit. I'd still start there to enjoy an aesthetic day rather
than just nobbling the Corbett.

The quickest and easiest way is up the estate road of Glen Doe,
and the pony path onwards, in direct line to Carn a' Chuilinn —
but keep this for the return. Start up the footpath from Loch Tarff
(on the B862 two miles further east) to the Dubh Lochan and on in
the same line to Lochan a' Choire Ghlais, then head along the crest
for the Corbett. This is not easy walking. Even the new map cannot convey the bumpy roughness or the peat hags and tussock
grass. The old One Inch was depressingly inadequate: one lochan
had a contour line across it. This is high-quality wilderness, however, and Carn a' Chuilinn looks its best from this approach: a
moated castle of crag with a sweeping view of the western Highlands from its battlements.

The head of Glen Tarff is a spectacular corner and those crossing
the Corrieyairack Pass for the *n*th time could gain a reward by
diverting over Corrieyairack Hill and Bac nam Fuaran to explore
here, add Carn a' Chuilinn and descend by Glen Doe to Fort
Augustus. Carn a' Chuilinn is the best of all the Monadh Liath
Corbetts, perhaps best of all the summits of whatever height.

Section 9:   9. MEALL NA H-AISRE   862 m   OS 35   515000
            Hill of the defile

To avoid repetition this hill is described in the final paragraph of 9:6 and 7 with which it is sometimes combined on a good day's tramp. All face the upper reaches of the Spey above the Corrieyairack Pass.

Section 9:   10. CARN NA SAOBHAIDHE   811 m   OS 35   600145
            Cairn of the den (fox lair) (suv-eh)

Carn na Saobhaidhe and Carn na Laraiche Maoile (3 miles to the south west) were both Corbetts when I first came this way. They were unusual in being of equal height. The new mapping left Carn na Saobhaidhe higher, so we lost this anomaly though, strangely, it still exists not far away where Corrieyairack Hill was given the same height as Gairbeinn. There are some geo-mathematical quirks in the Corbett game.

This Corbett and Carn an Fhreiceadain (9:11) were done at a weekend. The logistics were complicated but, as Lorna, Mike and I were staying in our vehicles up Strath Dearn, we approached Carn na Saobhaidhe from the upper Findhorn. Mike and I had cycles which the three of us shared to speed us up to Dalbeg. Though it had been a wild night we were determined to visit this hill while in the area. It is not exactly situated for casual access. We had five miles of cycling to Dalbeg and then headed up a stalkers' path by the Allt Creagach which becomes the Allt Odhar. There is a steep-sided glen at the start and some small, whisky-tinted waterfalls. The red deer were very pale in colour. The day before, east of the Findhorn, we'd seen "white" deer, something I've only seen perhaps half a dozen times in my life. We saw a ptarmigan down in the valley and grouse near the summit, which was all wrong. The Allt Odhar runs through some prime bog country, bleak and open as some Andean *altiplano* with rimming snowy *cordilleras*. And as cold. We huddled on top of the Corbett under a bivvy bag for a brief snack. We found it very difficult to pick out features or peaks. As the next lashing of hail came in we tailed southwards for the other (now demoted) Corbett and on to the head of Glen Markie, a remarkable trench. We returned to the bikes down the Eskin River, which completed an enjoyable circular walk. We were back in our homes in Inverness, Nairn and Fife a few hours later.

On the UC 87 several of us shared the cost of a ferry across Loch

Ness, from Drumnadrochit to Inverfarigaig. The day began in dismal fashion but cleared steadily to give a splendid crossing to the Findhorn, via Carn na Saobhaidhe. We walked round the north end of Loch Mhor, cutting corners to gain a new bulldozed track above Farraline Farm. Janet had gone ahead by the farm and was puzzled to find us ahead on the track. We left the track to cut over to Loch Conagleann (trackless, whatever the map says) and had a sunny lunch and paddle in this sheltered nook. The trees had taken a battering, the result of a March gale a keeper informed us. With a car it would have been less effort to come in via Dunmaglass Lodge or from the south end of Loch Mhor by the estate road up the River E (*sic*). With no cars we had the advantage of a long traverse.

A good estate road took us up the Allt Uisg an t-Sidhean and a fork then led to the Aberchalder Burn which was followed to one of its sources on the col east of the Corbett. The track goes on further than shown but the bogs win in the end. Bob, Ray and Cynthia continued more directly for the Findhorn while Janet and Dave (from Philadelphia) sturdily plodded on up the diminishing burn, good 1 mph country, for the Corbett. The view, even with perfect clarity, was still difficult to fit into place. All the west appeared end-on and the big hills southwards seemed to be back-to-front. The Cairngorms glittered along the eastern horizon. As the highest point between the Corrieyairack and the A9, and Affaric and Aviemore, Carn na Saobhaidhe commands a huge panorama, even by Corbett standards.

We made a slow wending descent of the Allt Odhar ("Oh dear" weary Dave suggested) and where it joined the Allt Creagach we found the old stalkers' track had now been harshly bulldozed. The trio had tea and drams waiting at Dalbeg. Janet camped there but we had to walk down to Coignafearn where I'd previously cached some supplies by cycle. The deer grazed across the river from our camp and sandpipers called all night. We went out to Aviemore by the Dulnain and Geall-Charn Mor (9:12). The dreaded Monadh Liath are seldom so kind to visitors.

Section 9: 11. CARN AN FHREICEADAIN 878 m OS 35 726071
             Cairn of the watcher

Carn an Fhreiceadain watches over Kingussie, though I suspect the name may have derived from it being used by human watchers to keep out wanderers in the stalking season. The hill lies just off an old road (on Roy's map of 1755) up the Allt Mor and on by Bruach nan-Imirichean to descend the Allt Glas a' Charbaid to the Findhorn's

The island of Rhum, with its two Corbetts, seen from
Gallanaich on the island of Muck

Talla Reservoir, below the slopes of Broad Law

Beinn a' Chaisteil above Auch, one of a group
of five Corbetts

Beinn na h–Eaglaise and Beinn Sgritheall at Hogmanay;
Storm in front

The Farragons, viewed up Strathtay, Perthshire

A visit to The Cobbler in 1961, with Ben Lomond
in the distance

A Northern Corbett: Ben Loyal in Sutherland,
seen across Loch Hakel

The ridge on the wilder side of Fuar Tholl, a bold peak
above Achnashellach

Meall a' Bhuachaille, a Speyside Corbett, a few miles
east of Aviemore

Right: Beinn Airidh Charr across the Fionn Loch, from the remote summit of A'Mhaighdean

Below: Hamish and Storm at Invermallie with Beinn Bhan behind

Left: The Sgurr a' Mhuillin hills over Strath Bran, from near Achnasheen

Below: Arkle, above Loch Stack, with the waters torn into the air by the wind

Ben Gulabin above the Spittal of Glenshee

Cul Mor in the North, seen from the hamlet of Elphin

upper reaches — quite populated at one time. Now I suspect a few walkers and stalkers are the only visitors. Note how cairns on the Corbett and Beinn Bhreac are positioned on the edge of the flat summits where they are well seen from lower down. This Corbett gives a mere stroll and the two estate roads (by Meall Unaig and Bad Each) can be linked by a traverse of Fhreiceadain and Beinn Bhreac.

One Friday in May, Lorna came from Nairn, Mike from Inverness and I arrived from Fife. We went up and left their two cars by the golf course above Kingussie, then drove round to Tomatin and the road up Strathdearn, the valley of the forgotten Findhorn River, to spend the night in my Dormobile. In the morning we drove on up to Coignafearn Old Lodge and, despite the attentions of curious garrons, set off early to walk on to the smart modern lodge. (Post bus runs to here, weekdays.) We crossed the Findhorn to follow a good path up the Elrick Burn, which ran down a deep glen and was the first of endless pleasing places we were to find that weekend. The burns were always a delight.

At a bothy we had a brew then zigzagged up to a vague watershed and down to another bothy at the head of the Dulnain River. It was a desolate pass with bog and snow booby-traps for the unwary. We lunched by the stream, enjoying brief sunny shafts that broke through the scudding clouds. After climbing out of the burn, a long, boggy moor led to the Corbett. Sleet showers had been swiping at the summits all day, so we carried on down Meall Unaig to pick up the track to Kingussie. Sunny and windless, the Allt Mor seemed a different world from the high hinterland. Carn an Fhreiceadain had proved a typical Monadh Liath hill.

We piled into Mike's Mini and drove back up the Findhorn, hoping for Carn na Saobhaidhe as well, but the cheery day went sulking to bed and a storm left us pessimistic for the Sunday that has already been described (9:10). It only remained for me to drop Lorna off at Kingussie on my way back down the A9.

Section 9:   12. GEAL-CHARN MOR   824 m   OS 35   837124
              Big white cairn

This is a very easy ascent which is nearly always made by walking up the estate road that crosses the Corbett's NE shoulder as it heads for the River Dulnain. Lynwilg, the start, has plenty of parking places and a pleasant hotel.

Having gone that way before with Kitchy, this time Storm and I set out from Aviemore after lunch one February day, first wending up Craigellachie by the Nature Trail. This gives a good view (over the mess of Aviemore) to the Loch Morlich basin and the wave-crest ridge of Meall a' Bhuachaille. I'd brought overnight gear and planned to stay at a bothy near the Corbett and then walk out down the River Dulnain back to the A9. These empty hills have an atmosphere all of their own, a crying sort of beauty and a sad desolation, as if abandoned by both man and God.

We met roe deer, red deer, hares and grouse in plenty as we skirted (rather a boggy route) along by Lochan Dubh and on by Creag na h-Iolaire (no eagles) to Carn Dearg Mor which greeted us with a salvo of hail.

I left my rucksack at the highest point on the road, itself about 660 m, with the summit just a kilometre away. Being above the level of deep heather the ascent is a pleasant stroll and no more, though in a rising wind there was a touch more effort required. As I wandered back and forwards the view changed from the array of the Glen Feshie side of the Cairngorms, across Speyside, to the nearer brooding Monadh Liaths across the Dulnain. Too cold to linger I circuited the trig point, an aberrant acolyte at an altar to strange gods, and romped back to the road in a blatter of horizontal snow and down northwards to the bothy — only there wasn't a bothy or, rather, the bothy wasn't.

My informant obviously had not been there for a long time and his "perfectly usable shelter" was now a doorless, windowless wreck, with parts of walls, floor and roof missing. Being dusk I decided that this inadequate shelter would have to do and we cringed over the stove in a corner to make a meal and then spread the sleeping bag on a drier area of creaky boards. The wind (which kept blowing out the candle) had been slowly rising all the while, and before midnight it became a considerable gale. Big winds like that almost invariably end in big "wets" and if a deluge caught me there I'd be soaked. There was also the possibility of the tin shack disintegrating in the storm. A section of wall blew out just at the time I was playing my torch-beam over the interior in a pessimistic survey. Somehow you feel singularly vulnerable lying in a sleeping bag. Hiding my panic I lit the stove for a brew, packed everything up, downed the warming tea — and fled. (On UC 87 we found the bothy looking exactly as it had done a decade earlier — and there must have been a few gales in that time.)

There was a half moon which lit the sky enough to see the splendid turmoil of clouds and I had a torch. Walking out was therefore no problem. The wind bullied me up the short distance to the top of the road, and then I had it downhill all the way to Lynwilg. There is an exhilaration at being out in a wild night and I was let off lightly with a few snow showers. The rain came rattling down just two hundred yards short of the welcoming Dormobile.

THE WEST, SOUTH OF LOCH ARKAIG

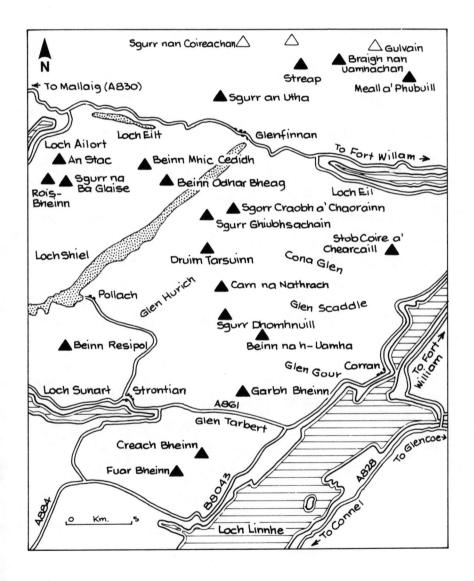

Section 10:   1. FUAR BHEINN   766 m   OS 49   853564
Cold hill (foor)

Section 10:   2. CREACH BHEINN   853 m   OS 49   871577
Mountain of spoil

THE CORBETTS OF Ardgour and Morven, climbed on one extended visit, gave days of ever-increasing heat. They are detailed later; but, briefly, I traversed from Strontian northwards with one camp, then cycled down Loch Shiel, traversed Resipol, added Garbh Bheinn and had a chilly night of frost in the Dormobile in Glen Tarbert. A meeting at Bridge of Orchy the next evening left me with the chance of adding these peaks only if I did "a quickie" ascent rather than the obviously classic circuit of Glen Galmadale.

To avoid the grilling I was up at a frosty 4 a.m. and off an hour later so, by the time the sun had glared up the sky, we were high enough to have a salvation breeze. There was no problem crossing the Carnoch River in Glen Tarbert. We cut up Coire Frithalt on to the bulging ridge of Meall a' Bhainaiche, for once avoiding all opportunities of "burning up" or scrambling on exposed rock. (My finger-tips were already worn smooth and rather sensitive.) The going was rough enough, anyway, and this, a rather scrappy ascent line, led almost on to Maol Odhar before suddenly producing the view down Glen Galmadale, a view like the proverbial gun-barrel with the sprawl of Lismore the target. Could the upper recess of Glen Galmadale (a hybrid Gaelic–Viking name) be where the *creach* spoils were hidden? On the way up the good ridge to Creach Bheinn there is an enclosure which looks a bit like an old fort but is reputedly a watch post dating to Napoleonic times. We had the only rest of the day on top, and devoured a tin of fruit salad with enjoyment. The Glen Coe hills lay in the dazzle of sun.

The west side of Glen Galmadale rather reminded me of the hills along from the Grey Mare's Tail: a succession of bold buttresses and deep-cut burns overlooking a fine valley. Here the rock is granite, which weathers into rounded shapes, while the burns have cut down in to the softer basalt dykes. There was a mile down to the col, the Cul Mham, before Fuar Bheinn, rather dull from that side. I left everything on the pass and pushed on in pants alone. Fuar Bheinn was hardly living up to its name.

South of Fuar Bheinn is Beinn na Cille, hill of the cell, which indicates a long gone religious settlement. Perhaps it was those Vikings again. *Gall* is stranger (Gaelic), *dal* or *dale* is valley (Norse).

The finest day on these hills is to walk anticlockwise round the rim of all the peaks surrounding Glen Galmadale. The morning sun will be at its best for the steep slopes above Loch Linnhe; you look across at the pap of Fuar Bheinn above the ranks of buttresses, you can dine on Creach Bheinn, and descend with the sun, off Fuar Bheinn or Beinn na Cille. One bonus for this route is the drive down Loch Linnhe on the B8043 under that riven chaos of red rock and green gullies. I can't think of anything like it except west of Dingle in Kerry.

I, perforce, returned to the Cul Mham (*the pass of the recess*) from where I contoured round and down. The cliffs of Choire Dhuibh are not as dramatic as the map suggests and I cut down them to follow the stream back to the valley. The heat and the heather increased with the loss of height. The conditions made me agree with one of my pupils who once declared, on top of Schiehallion, "If there's one thing I don't like about climbing hills it's going down again." A cuckoo belted along the hillside, making for the woods to the west, chased by several irate pipits, flying, you might say, hell for feather.

This half day brought to an end a May week of Corbetts and fine trekking which I thought would never be equalled. With only 40 Corbetts to go, the following summer brought eleven days of even hotter weather, which is why, when I think of Ardgour (or Arkle) the memories are such sunny ones. Just occasionally you are spoilt, and go spoiling. Ardgour had given a good *creach* of Corbetts.

Section 10: 3. GARBH BHEINN 885 m OS 40 904622
    Rough hill (garven)

From the Ballachulish crossing the sunset hills across Loch Linnhe often look dramatic and, like a Victorian silhouette, the features of a head lying back among pillows can be made out. This is "the sleeping giant" which, on checking, proves to be Garbh Beinn of Ardgour, an eminently suitable peak to bear that title.

Everyone who writes of Garbh Bheinn goes into raptures about the hill and its setting. After two viewless ascents and a score of times refusing to add a third disappointment I'm prepared to go along with the roughness and the drama; the "astonishing views" and "the best mainland rock for climbing in the west" I'll take on trust. Some day, instead of planning Garbh Bheinn, and calling off at Corran Ferry as another depression sweeps the west, I'll go off proclaiming quite different intentions and, when the sun shines, I'll quickly sneak into Ardgour instead.

Donald Bennet's *Scottish Mountain Climbs* has a chapter on Garbh Bheinn which, in text and photographs, shows the nature of the hill. It very much lives up to its name. Bell and Brown, who made the first mountaineering approach to the hill in 1897, took the still popular route up Coire an Iubhair (yoo-ir, *yew*), probably a less muddy track then, and commented, as generations have done since, how "bit by bit Garbh Bheinn creeps into view, forming by the gradual addition of ridge to corrie and crag to buttress one of the boldest pictures of mountain grandeur to be seen on mainland Scotland". They climbed to the summit by the Great Ridge, the great tongue of rock facing east below the top, well demarcated to the right by Great Gully. Haskett Smith and Hastings tried the gully — unsuccessfully — just two days later. The first ascent was made by W. H. Murray and D. Scott in 1946. The attraction of the peak is mirrored in the long list of notables who have made new routes but, though that story deserves telling, I'd better stick to the easier lines for walkers. The hill relents in places.

Probably the easiest way up Garbh Bheinn is by Coire a' Chothruim, which drains the western flanks of the hill southwards to the Glen Tarbert road. This is an almighty slog as the whole height is gained in little over a mile. There are better ways. Coire an Iubhair is the favourite route, and deservedly so.

Inglis Clark in 1904 described the glen as being "swampy ground alternating with bog", and the thousands of tramping feet since have hardly improved the path. The walk starts through a landscape with the soft greens of an old kilt or the dun sett of last year's grass but the slopes are soon pleated with rocks and water. Boiler-plate slabs break through the thin texture of vegetation and after a couple of miles the stream junction below the summit corrie is reached. The old dog and I sat there with the clouds masking everything above. Up in the mists a lark was unwrapping a parcel of song and the burns were cheery company, vigorous with April showers. We went up into the corrie and swung right to puff and scramble to the crest of the mountain. There are crags on crags and summits on summits. We visited all the bumps to make sure of claiming the Corbett.

The best route up keeps more to the burn draining the corrie, and then moves left to the obvious col south of and below the summit mass. The long ridge of Sron a' Gharbh Choire Bhig is the alternative skyline approach and these two routes combined, in one direction or the other, are what I'd recommend for normal walkers. Those who are fit, fast and at home on the Cuillin crests could "make a day of it" and traverse Druim an Iubhair, Sgorr Mhic Eacharna and Beinn Beag to the pass at the head of the glen. This route gives a magnificent circuit; some day I still hope to claim its reward — the most impressive of all views of Garbh Bheinn. From Lochan Coire an Iubhair in the Bealach Feith n' Amean the northern bastions of Garbh Bheinn have to be tackled. This needs some competence in route finding and scrambling so "caw canny" as they say.

Garbh Bheinn being, in Donald's view, one of the half dozen grandest mountains in the West Highlands and, for rock-climbers, the finest, the investment in the 1:25,000 map is recommended. (Sheet NM 86/96 Strontian and Ardgour.) The starting point for all the recommended routes begins near the bridges (old and new, plenty of parking space) over the river of Coire an Iubhair, one kilometre past Inversanda the estate hamlet with the buildings seen after the road turns inland from Loch Linnhe. I give this description of the start, for the 1:50,000 Sheet 40 ends just north of these features; they are on Sheet 49. Coire an Iubhair is stalking country so check at Inversanda for access during late summer–autumn days. In winter conditions Garbh Bheinn becomes a peak for the experts only.

Section 10:   4. BEINN RESIPOL   845 m   OS 40   766655
Horse stead (ON *hross-bolstatr*; from the farm)

Beinn Resipol commands the heart of Sunart and as it rises in rough isolation it has a panoramic view which is hard to equal. An ascent just has to be kept for a clear day. I've had two such days and certainly endorse all the praise Resipol is given. Ardgour and Moidart are unusually wild areas, with a great jumble of peaks and ridges filling much of the near view but allowing distant views of ranges from Skye to Ben Nevis while, south, lies the graceful sprawl of Mull and, west, the magical margin of the island-studded sea.

My first visit was in a May 1975 Corbett blitz — the only such spell I've had, my excuse being that completing the list lay not so far ahead and some impatience was intruding into a game which had been going on for 22 years. I see a certain analytical note in my log which I'm sure others will recognise: "Only once 4 Corbetts in a day (Auch), 3 just a few times (Ardgour and Glenfinnan in the last few days, Moidart, Arkle, Merrick) and the rest in ones or twos. You have to work harder for the Corbetts than you do for the Munros."

I'd abandoned the car to walk over Ardgour's hills to Glenfinnan where I'd left my folding cycle, and I used it down Loch Shiel (forestry road) to camp at Polloch from whence, on a frost-crisp morning, I set off for Resipol by the old miners' track across its east ridge. The path was hard to find — a quarry had bitten into it — then it was very wet and heavy going up into Coire an t-Suidhe. After looking about the site of an old lead mine I angled up to reach Meall an t-Slugain, the saddle east of Beinn Resipol. The path bears off and drops down to Strontian and is quite often used as an approach to the hill. Strontian, an attractive village, gave its name to Strontium and up near the top of the public motor road to Polloch there has been some recent working again of the old mines. Having descended off Resipol, more or less by the same route, I had to cycle over that pass — a 342-m "pech" up and a wrist-straining braking down to Strontian. The dog had no difficulty keeping up but went in the rucksack for the A861 run along to Garbh Bheinn and then back to the Dormobile at Corran — a logistical exercise in itself.

The second ascent was exercise of another sort for I took in Resipol on a day's tramp from Acharacle to Corran Ferry, part of my UC from Ardnamurchan Point to Buchan Ness. (Once across Corran Ferry it rained every single day.) I didn't want to walk along the tarred A861 road so cut off at the end of the hamlet hoping to make an approach between the dreaded Claish Moss and the heathery lower hills. We ran into new plantings which were not on the map and wasted hours teasing a way through to the Allt Mhic Chiarain which is probably the most used line of ascent — but coming up it, sensibly, from Resipole Farm on Loch Sunart. The woods along the loch are oak and the walk up from Resipole uses a track on the Chiarain's south/left bank. The burn has quite a deep-set gorge, even above the tree line, but such a gorge usually ensures traces of deer or sheep tracks on its banks. I followed the pleasing stream up to Lochan Bac an Lochain (which would have been a scenic camp site) and left the rucker there to wander up the craggy slopes of Resipol carrying nothing but my cameras.

The view was as sweeping as ever and I scribbled down a few of the places I recognised: "Mull, Jura, Scarba, Arran, Cobbler hills, Argyll's Buidhe, Cruachan, Chocuill, Lui, Staravs, Clachlet, Sgulaird, Bidean, Vair pair, Aonach Eagach, Loch Leven's Corbetts bracketing far Schiehallion, Mamores, Nevis, Creag Mheagaidh ranges, Corbetts on both flanks of the Great Glen, Gulvain, Streaps, Thuilm, Gleouraich, Cluanie Ridge, Sgurr Mor, Ciche, all Knoydart, Sgriol, Applecross, Torridon, the Cuillin, Rhum, Eigg, Muck, the Outer Hebrides and then the great jumble from Moidart through to Loch Linnhe; a score of Corbetts and I'm sitting on the best perhaps."

John Leyden, that extraordinary genius from the Borders, who died young in the Orient where he collected languages quicker than most of us acquire Corbetts, made an ascent of Resipol in 1800, both to enjoy the setting and to search for good samples of garnets which can spot some of the rocks in great numbers. He so enjoyed cataloguing the view that he failed to notice darkness approaching and then tried to take a short cut down off the rocky peak, thereby landing in all sorts of trouble, scaring himself thoroughly and reaching Polloch in pitch dark where everyone had given him up for lost.

After lunching back at the loch I made a flanking traverse to the Meall an t-Slugain col and followed the crest eastwards to pick up a path down through all the mining sites to Bellsgrove Loch and so through to Glen Gour and eventually out to Corran Ferry and a good night at the Ardgour Hotel. Any benefit of using a car to the top of the road is lost by the heavy going thereafter. The best route is up from Resipole and down to Strontian — and a very good best it is.

Section 10:   5. BEINN NA H-UAMHA   762 m   OS 40   918665
              Hill of the cave (na hoo-ah)

Section 10:   6. SGURR DHOMHNUILL   888 m   OS 40   889679
              Donald's peak

Section 10:   7. CARN NA NATHRACH   786 m   OS 40   887699
              Cairn of the adders/serpents

There is the feel of an island to Ardgour: it is *nearly* surrounded by water and reached, as like as not, by ferry. Ardgour, ruggedly hilly, reminds me of Mull or Rhum or even Skye, except it is more complex and wooded than any of those genuine islands.

As well as the array of demanding peaks and ridges, Ardgour offers some of the best glens in the west for tramping through on back-packing trips. Willy nilly the glens will be explored in garnering the Corbetts. Glen Gour is the natural approach for Beinn na h-Uamha and Glen Scaddle for the other two. Uamha was discovered only with the metric revisions. I did it after the others.

Fortuitously I had been lecturing at Loch Ailort one January and next day drove round the Ardgour side of Loch Eil and Loch Linnhe to Sallachan at the foot of Glen Gour. Conditions were doubtful with a strong east wind, which I made full use of, but a dank, black thaw held some menace. The path up the glen was wet, with ice underneath; wellies with skates would have been useful. On the May Ardna-murchan to Buchan Ness walk, the day from Acharacle to Corran Ferry over Resipol took in a descent of lonely Glen Gour. The loch then was noisy with stonechats, wheatears, redshanks and a bedlam of curlews, today it was noisy with wind and waves, the only birds being a pair of communicative whoopers out in the middle of the loch. The path more or less disappears after a pleasant two miles, leaving one on bare tawny levels with Beinn na h-Uamha wrinkling down north of the strath. The river could be difficult in spate conditions but we crossed with no problems. Deer splashed over ahead of us. The dog found a very dead deer and I just caught him in time to prevent him rolling on the carcase.

We went up the SE Ridge of the Corbett, which was rather an infuriating route for someone in a hurry as there are endless bumps and crags entailing descents and diversions. The hurry was to try and beat the big bang promised by the black sky. The wind gave a good push, sometimes erratically, and the snow became sugary firm, perfect for making steps without needing crampons. We were soon up, cringed on top for a moment only, and we baled off more directly into Glen Gour, an easier, quicker but less interesting line.

The peak could as easily be climbed from Glen Scaddle, if based there for the other Corbetts, but linking it with Sgurr Dhomhnuill and Carn na Nathrach would be a real marathon of rough-stuff ridge-walking. I just managed across Corran and Ballachulish ferries before the rain began but, as everyone knows, all Scotland's weather is first distilled in Glen Coe.

Sgurr Dhomhnuill, highest of Ardgour's summits (just), and Carn na Nathrach, by the east-west nature of the glens, can be tackled from either east or west, or done in the course of a tramp through the glens. I'll describe both briefly for these hills merit exploration.

From Strontian I drove up the narrow road that crosses east of Resipol to reach the shores of Loch Shiel and parked near the old mine-workings above Bellsgrove. The hills are such a jumble that I took some time with the map to work out what was what. We then cut down by Bellsgrove Loch to the end of the Strontian woods (the attractive natural forest of the Ariundle Reserve) and on to a further area of old mine-workings. The Strontian River curves east and leads through a splendid pass to Glen Gour while a higher offset stream, the Feith Dhomhnuill, drains the Sgurr Dhomhnuill *cirque*. The last shaft at the mines was dry enough to enter but I had no torch so soon came out, to the relief of the dog who was rushing about trying to find me. This day in May was icy with a blasting wind and my Berghaus Goretex jacket earned its keep. My shoulder, increasingly in agony from cold like that, became bad enough to seek medical advice. Our local village GP tried acupuncture — and it worked. He retired not long afterwards and our new doctor, of Chinese descent, has never tried acupuncture. It's an ill wind . . .

We cut up the valley to gain the col south of the big peak which lies not far above, with just one bump on the way. The extra height of Sgurr Dhomhnuill ensured the summit kept a cloud streamer all day, but it was too like being in a wind tunnel to stay by the trig point, the only one on any of the Ardgour Corbetts, which is perhaps indicative of the general roughness and of this peak's dominance. Druim Garbh, the equally steep twin, which completes the western-facing horseshoe, has been demoted as a Corbett (the cols don't have a 500 foot drop) but would be worth climbing, anyway, and will be by those traversing to Carn na Nathrach. The name Druim Garbh (*rough ridge*) applies strictly to the contorted ridge leading west to the summit of the Strontian–Loch Shiel road with its scores of lochans, a good way back if just circuiting Dhomhnuill.

While sheltering out of the wind on Druim Garbh the cloud lifted and the sun shone a shaft of light on Resipol. Rhum and Skye were sun-touched too, but Mull and the south stayed grey. The grim east was not studied at all; my eyes were streaming with the wind's assault. We started our descent on the west flank to keep out of the wind, but this was steep and craggy and we crept back on to the crest which still had plenty of rocky slabs and domes. For variety, the col had a peat bog. We went up a rib and then allowed the wind to bustle us up a rake on to the west ridge of Carn na Nathrach where I was thankful to leave my rucksack before wending up to the summit, a fine perch of a cairn following some scrambling on slabs and walls. The huge length of Glen Scaddle showed well from the top.

Having picked up my rucksack (ballast) we turned down the north flank, easy going if steep, to pitch the tent on the Mam Beathaig. The leeside of the hill was sunny and warm though there was a sharp enough frost overnight to form a skin of ice on my dixie of water. I'd envisaged being blasted off the col and needing to shelter among the trees of Glen Hurich. Resourie, just a mile away, was not yet a bothy but when the building was about to be restored I took the chance of doing the big traverse without having to carry a tent.

Two of us with our vehicles crossed the Corran Ferry on Saturday morning and, after leaving my Dormobile at the foot of Glen Scaddle, we drove in Sandy's car to Strontian and the familiar hill road over to Loch Doilet where we parked and walked up Glen Hurich to Resourie which the MBA had just adopted. The rest of the day was spent clearing back the brash, boulders, brambles and junk from the bothy walls, opening the back ditch and damming the burn for a spout of water, a much harder day than climbing Corbetts. The surrounding area had been felled and was smothered in foxglove spires, mostly pink but with a few white flowers as well.

The Mam Beathaig is rather like Knoydart's Mam na Cloiche

Airde. Sandy, Storm and I crossed the pass early, descending to a "Lost Valley" where the path ended. Round a corner we suddenly came on Loch Dubh and a two mile tramp beyond led to the great junction area, the classic pass behind, open Glen Scaddle ahead. We'd come down Gleann an Lochain Duibh and now went up Gleann na Cloiche Sgoilte, traversed Druim Garbh to Sgurr Dhomhnuill, and descended Gleann Mhic Phail — thus exploring all three of the triple glens. The walk down Glen Scaddle was most enjoyable: we had one long brew stop, and one delectable swim in a big pool. On reaching the Dormobile I found I'd left my watch at the pool so, while Sandy cooked supper, I took the dog up the glen again, making a 20-mile day.

We slept the night in the Dormobile with the intention of driving along to Loch Sunart and traversing Resipol back to Sandy's car but the weather changed for the worse. We merely collected Sandy's car and drove home. I was luckier on the camping trip. From the Mam Beathaig pitch I was to traverse northwards to Glenfinnan over the even tougher trio of 10:13, 14 and 15, where the day is described.

Section 10:   8. ROIS-BHEINN   882 m   OS 40   756778
                         Hill of showers (= Froisbheinn)

Section 10:   9. SGURR NA BA GLAISE   874 m   OS 40   770777
                         Peak of the grey cow

Section 10:   10. AN STAC   814 m   OS 40   763793
                         The stack

Section 10:   11. BEINN MHIC CEDIDH   783 m   OS 40   829788

Section 10:   12. BEINN ODHAR BHEAG   882 m   OS 40   846778
                         The small tawny hill

Munroists acquainted with the sandpapered landscape of Knoydart will find a similar set of hills in the Corbetts of Moidart. Comparisons are arduous but the Corbetts are in no way inferior to the Munros and both areas have a parcelled completeness, a geographical and historical individuality. They are of the west, however, and take all that the Atlantic cares to throw at them. They are worth a visit in clear, settled conditions, even if you have to stalk them for weeks or months.

The Corbetts of Moidart are unique in offering a clutch of Corbetts all laid out along a single high-level walk. Only on the other side of Loch Shiel or north of Tyndrum might you cull five Corbetts on a single walk, and they are jumbles of peaks rather than anything else.

So make the most of Moidart. Not for nothing does Richard Gilbert include this traverse in his book *The Big Walks*. Had these hills been just a bit higher (i.e. Munros) or sited above Windermere they would be swarming with walkers. As it is they are "magnificent but unfashionable".

Before the road through Glenuig was opened Moidart could not be circled by car and even now there is a feeling of extraordinary remoteness to the area. That perimeter is worth careful exploration: from Castle Tiorim to Glenfinnan it offers varied scenery and a history still marked by the Forty Five. The mountainous interior is unpeopled and untracked, with some of the steepest corries and mountain flanks in Scotland. The going is tough and one advantage of the long traverse is that it minimises the physical demands. The day gives a long, hard traverse, certainly, but that is easier than the alternative of several medium-long, equally hard expeditions. I say this with feeling, having been blasted off several efforts at a complete traverse. Nor was I helped by the table revisions which added Beinn Mhic Cedidh, demoted Druim Fiaclach and promoted Sgurr na Ba Glaise. These map alterations are themselves an indication of the rough terrain and, as for certain Munro sections, only modern surveying methods finally covered the area adequately.

With my parents I'd sailed down from Kyle to Mallaig on the *Iona* and while they stayed at Morar I left the train at Glenfinnan with the plan that we all meet again on the homeward train two days later. "Just time for the Moidart Hills."

I had a Zarsky bivvy and minimal food. The normal direct assault from Glenfinnan to the Beinn Odhar peaks had always struck me as being an unduly complex and rough line so I backtracked westwards (sitting out a deluge under a railway bridge) and headed up Doire Dhamh. As I climbed, the weather leaked down, and a day of showers simply turned into sweaty clag. I took most of my clothes off in order to have them dry at the end of the day, and puffed up in my own steam tent of waterproofs. Moidart wetness has the touch of long practice. The ground was sodden and there was plenty of tussocky grass.

I gained the north ridge of Coire Odhar just as the cloud blotted out the view but a rising rim of steps led easily enough round and up to the trig point on Beinn Odhar Mhor (870 m). "Big" here presumably was the overall impression when viewed from below as Beinn Odhar Bheag is higher (882 m) — now equal highest, with Rois-Bheinn, of all the Moidart summits. The ridge between is corrie-bitten and complex but by careful compass work and dead reckoning I teased away at it. Well washed slabs gave the last pull to the Corbett. "Very windy, very wet, and no visibility" my log complained. I followed a dogged compass line down to the Bealach a' Choire Bhuidhe and baled off into *the yellow corrie*. (*A yellow corrie* is often so because the ground is grassy and will give a reasonable route — though Moidart grass is sometimes unreasonable. *Garbh choire*, rough corrie, would, conversely, be a warning of potentially bad walking conditions.)

Richard Gilbert had an almost identical experience when wind and rain lashed his party. They beat a hasty retreat by this same route. I cut through the gap behind Sgurr na Paite, the viewpoint bump above Loch Eilt, in a scattering of deer and a scattering of cloud. I felt relief in seeing the landscape was where it should have been after the hours of groping blindfold in the clouds. Bluebell banks and tumbling waters led me down to Essan which I'd spotted from the train as a possible emergency shelter. Since restored, at that time it had long been open to sheep and cows. Deluge or not, I passed by and spent the night in a wooden shack further on. Two pints of tea was the first priority for I was dehydrated. The last of my Martigny-brought *Reddy* (muesli) was all I had to eat. I was in bed before nine, coffee in hands, eyes closed, listening to the sounds of solitude. My waterproofs dripped like a ticking clock (to form puddles on the floor), the rain rattled on the roof and those bright summer-birds of the Highlands, the sandpipers, reeled and flitted along the margin of the loch. If sunset on top of the hills had been ruled out I was perfectly content with my low-level substitute.

The next day I set off up the Allt Easain. There were plenty of deer then and throughout the day. I gave myself some fun to gain wild Coire nan Gall. I had to skirt crags and then found the Allt Easain had cut a deep gorge, crossing which would mean quite a downward detour; however, I managed to fight down a rake in the corner with the hope of climbing up to the right of the waterfall. This line was dangerously loose, so after a good look at the fall I climbed straight up it in waterproofs only. Midsummer or not my fingers were frozen. Coire nan Gall was crossed regardless of surface water and I went for Druim Fiaclach *en face* only to find another small corrie tucked in its side. "Chinese boxes of corries" I noted at the time.

Before gaining the ridge I had a meal stop and the day's third long shower went over, but as soon as I gained the ridge the grim quality vanished: the rain stopped, the clouds broke and the sun shone. My yell of glee on the summit might have raised Corbett himself. I grudge having had Druim Fiaclach, *the toothed ridge*, demoted.

The toothed ridge runs eastwards but my way on, south and west, also gave ridge-traversing of great character. Coire Reidhe, which is circled, is ferociously steep and rimmed with precipice, and the bumpy crest of Slat-Bheinn leading to Sgurr na Ba Glaise is a delightful ridge between vast corries: Glen Moidart to the south and Coire a' Bhuiridh to the north. The col, Bealach an Fhiona, beyond Sgurr na Ba Glaise, is an old right of way linking the heads of Loch Moidart and Loch Ailort, a worthwhile walk.

At that time Sgurr na Ba Glaise had a special mention in the introduction to the Corbetts Table, suggesting it should be in the list. Now it is, but Fiaclach has gone. Always do everything is a good plan though, hopefully, the OS will leave things alone for the forseeable future. The biggest crags of the area flank *the peak of the grey cow*. (How did it come by that name?) Life seemed too good to be true as I lay in the lee of the cairn in warm sunshine. Plans to hitch along to join the parental comforts at Morar evaporated with the clouds. We could surely squeeze in Sgurr an Utha the next day and still catch the train, which is what happened (see 10:16).

I trotted down to the Bealach an Fhiona and was blown up beside the dyke that leads to and along double-headed Rois-Bheinn. From a distance the trig pillar had looked like a figure. The heads of thrift were dancing in the wind. The pillar is on the higher, eastern summit but the west top has the greater view, one even finer than Resipol's for Rhum and Skye are nearer and Sgurr na Ciche and other giants straddle the north view. Who needs a peak in Darien? Tir nan Og is just over yonder!

An Stac still remained, a Stob Ban to Rois-Bheinn's Claurigh, and was reached by returning almost to the Bealach Fhiona and then off to a lower col from which An Stac rose sharply. An Stac's clear shape is instantly recognisable from many directions. As the weather looked like changing for the worse I juddered directly down to Alisary on the Lochailort road rather than making for Inverailort by the crest or the Allt a' Bhuiridh. After sheltering for half an hour among birch trees I walked and read my way up to Lochailort. Too late for the train I read and thumbed and eventually had a lift up and over the watershed for a night in a bothy, another which has long disappeared.

Naturally, having omitted Beinn Mhic Cedidh, it was later promoted to Corbett status. A lecture tour one mid-January gave the chance of climbing this isolated peak, though I was lucky to win west as the A9 was blocked by snow soon afterwards. I had a night in the van near Glenfinnan, where a full moon hung like a Chinese lantern over the Beinn Odhar peaks, a view seen through the dark, bonsai-shaped pines clinging to the crags above Loch Shiel. At first light the mountain tops glowed pink. The weather was obviously settled and an unhurried start was pleasant. I drove along to the watershed and, with the dog, set off for the sneck behind the bump above the east end of Loch Eilt, leaving a tawny trail across the white-washed slopes. A long traverse led us into Coire Buidhe and the col where I had abandoned our traverse a decade earlier.

The east ridge up to the new Corbett required crampons as the ground was sheeted with ice, probably from rain which had then frozen. Every boulder and pebble and blade of grass was sheathed in ice. Storm had a difficult time slithering along at my heels. In the blaze of golden January sun the hill was a superlative viewpoint. Ben Nevis lay between the two Odhars; Ardgour, normally so dark, gleamed silver; Loch Shiel glittered; the Streaps pass and Knoydart were familiar shapes and, up Coire Reidh, the heart of Moidart was a bold, steep jumble of white mountains. The Cuillin Hills, rising from a plum-coloured haze, were an array of bright fangs.

We went down the narrow north ridge and I carried the dog till we were on snow again. I had quite a flounder thereafter. Storm found a blood track from a wounded deer and, later, appeared carrying the hoof of another beast. (The culling of hinds by estate keepers after the autumn stalking is over can go on into January or even February.) We drove fast to Lochailortside but were just too late to watch the sunset beyond the Sgurr of Eigg. My lecture at Lochailort Castle (on Morocco) was delayed a bit as the sky was full of the "northern dancers", one of the best displays of northern lights I've seen in Scotland. If all new Corbetts could give days like that, the OS are welcome to keep adding them indefinitely!

Section 10:   13. DRUIM TARSUINN   770 m   OS 40   875727
                   The transverse ridge

Section 10:   14. SGURR GHIUBHSACHAIN   849 m   OS 40   876751
                   Peak of the fir wood (goosachan)

Section 10:   15. SGORR CRAOBH A' CHAORAINN   775 m
                   OS 40   895758
                   Rowantree peak (cruv-a-*chae*ran)

"The Callop Corbetts" has long been the collective name I've used for these three scabrous summits. They catch the eye as one motors west from Loch Eil, and Callop gives the easiest access. They are a clan of steep, craggy and tough hills.

They are worth more than just a quick visit from Callop, however, and besides the day described below, another fine expedition is to make a two-day through trip using the Cona Glen, from Glenfinnan to Corran Ferry, doing these three on the first day, camping in Cona Glen, walking down it, adding Stob Coire a' Chearcaill (10:19) and so on to Corran. This grand walk gives varied scenery of the highest order.

As described in 10:6, 7 I'd started at Strontian and traversed the Sgurr Dhomhnuill hills to camp on the Mam Beathaig between Glen Hurich and Glen Scaddle. The site was also between Carn na Nathrach and Druim Tarsuinn so there wasn't far to go to begin the day's effort. I was off at 6 a.m. for, frosty or not, the sun was going to smite later in the day. Right opposite, a long buttress led upwards, and this gave 1,000 feet of scrambling on rough, solid rock which was quite exposed on the flank. (The rock could all be avoided by going up Coire an t-Searraich.) There was a bump or two and a tiny lochan before we could traverse across to the Bealach an Sgriodain below the shapely summit of the Corbett, called Druim Tarsuinn in sloppy *Tables* fashion, though Druim Tarsuinn is clearly shown as the knobbly ridge running away from the other side of the bealach. The Corbett name is perhaps Sgriodain. That so much is named is indicative of past use. Loch Shiel, now so quiet, probably had quite a population dwelling on its shores.

A derelict gate on the col was useful to hang the tent on and while it was drying we scrambled up the Corbett. Some deer were on top when we arrived. There was a sudden view downwards, and out along the silver-glittering Loch Dubh and Glen Scaddle to big Ben Nevis. Druim Tarsuinn, the ridge, dropped down to a boggy col from where a long, slowly ascending traverse led towards Sgurr Ghiubhsachain. A rocky buttress proved irresistible; I left the sack and had a 400-foot climb. This led nowhere near the summit as I'd hoped, so, after going over to look down the forsaken Loch Shiel corries, I returned to my burden. After another long traverse, with one nasty quartz band, I tried again. The best climb of the day ended right at the big cairn of the day's biggest peak, a fine rocky perch overlooking Loch Shiel.

We tend sometimes to think we are being original or doing something special but the Scottish hills have a long tradition of unconventional enjoyment. Back in 1893 the artist Colin Phillip set out to climb Ghiubhsachain at midnight, to avoid the oppressive heat of summer. He came up from Callop (then a watcher's cottage) to the head of the glen and made a rising traverse across the grassy slopes to the Corbett, scrambling up the rock to the top just in time for dawn breaking. He returned over the second Corbett and was back at base in time for breakfast.

When did you last make a night expedition?

I was loath to leave that splendid summit but the heat was oppressive and the day would become hotter yet. We dandered down to the gentle col to the east and set off a large herd of very dark-coloured deer. They trotted along the flank of Glac Gharbh; we followed, catching them up on the rough ridge that dropped to the head of the Callop glen. They turned downhill and, after leaving the rucksack again, we turned uphill, almost immediately startling a fox into flight up a rake. The rock was slabbier but we kept to it as much as possible, to the top of Sgor Craobh a' Chaorainn, which can look even rockier than Ghiubhsachain; and while there is plenty of rock on these hills it is not continuous enough for real climbing, but can give a day with constant scrambling options, which I was ready to take up.

The views had vanished in haze and I was glad to zigzag down the rakes and, at the first burn, after collecting the rucksack, have a longer stop. Nothing quite beats fresh tea under such circumstances. The time was only 2 p.m. but felt like evening. On reaching the col we put up our herd of deer for the third time. Colin Phillip saw some feral goats on his descent.

The glen down to Callop is wild but, in places, gives a superb mix of old forest: Scots pines, birch, hazel, alder and so on. I walked down with my mind away in daydreams, with the dog panting after. At the foot of the glen, a few days before, I'd left my folding bike which I bolted together for the long run down Loch Shiel. The bonus for the day was discovering the lochside forestry road was tarred all the way. A locked gate keeps the public out, of course, even though public money built the road, but as an old right of way they can't stop you walking, or cycling, and a push bike is often a useful "aid to pedestrianism".

The run down the loch gave a hot eleven miles but we had a delectable camp to end the day. Dog-tired would well describe my companion — even if he had journeyed down the loch in my rucksack. I'm glad he is not a St Bernard. The next day we traversed Resipol to the car, returned for the bike, and also went up Garbh Bheinn. You don't waste sunny days in Ardgour.

Section 10:   16. SGURR AN UTHA   796 m   OS 40   885839
                Peak of the udder

A bothy, no longer in existence, allowed a 7 o'clock departure for Sgurr an Utha. I was back at the Mallaig–Glenfinnan road by 10.30 and had time for coffee in the Stage House before catching the afternoon train home.

The start from the A830 is obvious, a path leaving the road just east of the "cross" shown on the map. The path crosses the Allt an Utha by a bridge (not shown) but is in a poor state thereafter. I simply followed the riverbank, the clear water racing down through a succession of pools and deep guts beside me, and then took a north fork, direct to the summit: "a pile of toast-filled racks of mica schist like some Lewis Carroll creation." The burns and pools I'd passed would have given any number of fine camp sites — I begrudged my night under a roof. The arrival on top is dramatic or perhaps instamatic, certainly photographic.

I came up and, bang, there, straight ahead, was the great pass to Loch Arkaig between Sgurr Thuilm and the Streaps. Below Utha, to the north, was another grassy trench of a pass (with a zip of path up the slope beyond) leading the eye westwards to the dark, spilt-ink length of Loch Beoraid. The Moidart hills lay to the south, northwards I looked over Carn Mor and Sgurr na h-Aide into Knoydart. The looking took half an hour, till I grew chilled and had to move. I cut all the corners running back down to the path. A shepherd and his dogs found me brewing at a pool above the road. One of the dogs cocked a leg over my rucksack. My yell of "Hey! Piss off you!" struck the shepherd as hilarious and he went on his way chuckling. I only noticed the choice of words later. By then I was in the hotel at Glenfinnan with the rain playing Gilbert and Sullivan on the west window-panes.

With a pack left below the hill my route was more or less dictated by necessity, better would have been to follow the path up and traversed everything from Sidhean Mor to Fraoch-bheinn and then down direct to Glenfinnan. "Next time", I promise, for this is one of the very best Corbett viewpoints — or any kind of viewpoint. At the west end of Loch Beoraid is a cave used by Prince Charlie on his post-Culloden wanderings, and he finally sailed away from Loch nan Uamh, a few miles beyond. On a Clan Map I noticed the name "Corbett" printed across the landscape between Sgurr an Utha and Loch Nevis. It seemed both symbolic and appropriate.

Section 10: 17. STREAP 909 m OS 40 946863
             Climbing hill

Section 10: 18. BRAIGH NAN UAMHACHAN 765 m
             OS 40 975867
             The slope of the caves (brae-nan-oo-achan)

The Streaps were such a lure that Joe and I traversed them long before Corbetts became an interest. They have an eye-smacking boldness that provokes response. The pass between Streap and Sgurr Thuilm must have some of the steepest flanks of any in Scotland. Seen from Strathan at the west end of Loch Arkaig, or from Sgurr an Utha, or the hills west of Loch Shiel the pass is a much photographed feature, classic U-shaped, honed in glacial times and guarded by jagged, rough mountains. On Sgurr Thuilm Bonnie Prince Charlie skulked for a day before breaking through the redcoat cordon to the safety of the north. That pass is still a vital link to all sorts of mountain treks, climbs, Munros and Corbetts.

Joe and I traversed the Streaps (which are nearly Munros) on Christmas Eve 1961, the coldest Christmas for 40 years the radio reported. We believed it. Prunes left soaking overnight were encased in a cylinder of ice and our eggs froze solid inside the tent. On Boxing Day we took a lift to the Fort on the back of a lorry and ended up closer to hypothermia than ever I have been on a mountain.

Glenfinnan was unplanted then and very lonely. We wandered up to Corryhully and up on to point 844, Meall an Uillt Chaoil, to traverse all the ridge of many bumps to Streap. Stob Coire nan Ceare, *the peak of the hen's comb*, is a fine summit in its own right and gave a good view of Thuilm–Coireachan, the major objective of the day and the completion of a circuit that is the best for doing those Munros. Streap is no easy addition. I called it "a most impressive peak of narrow ridges and shattered corries, with unremittingly steep slopes". A glissade on firm snow shot us down to the pass.

Streap has an eastern Top, Streap Comhlaidh, reached by a fine ridge, this pair forming corries facing both north and south, a big H of ridges, all dropping down to give practical ascent or descent routes to the good access at lower levels. The crest between Streap Comhlaidh and its own SE toplet is a narrow crest, with steep grass precipices on the flanks.

Over the years I've tried most routes. The best of Streap is the ragged crest Joe and I followed. Beinn an Tuim is worth adding and can be approached by a forestry road on the east of Glenfinnan which has a branch ascending on the north side of the big gully draining Beinn an Tuim to the south west. Having travelled to Glenfinnan by train Joe and I spent the rest of the day cutting steps up this gully. Tuim, a Corbett, though we knew it not, was recently demoted as not having quite 500 feet of re-ascent on all sides.

Beinn an Tuim is a good climb from the east, too; from the Gleann Dubh Lighe I'd recommend finishing the traverse of Streap and Streap Comhlaidh by dropping down the green and gentle south ridge of the latter to take this forgotten glen out to the Glenfinnan–Fort William road. An even grander circuit is to do the complete skyline of the Gleann Dubh Lighe peaks. There are two Corbetts available, after all.

I've not actually done that, for, always being in Munro-dominated parties, Braigh nan Uamhachan has usually had to be combined with Gulvain, its neighbour to the east. So it is the circuit of Gleann

Fionnlighe I've more often done, often enough ending on my own, abandoned by Munros-only companions. As there is a long walk to this Corbett, the circuit of Streap and Uamhachan has much to recommend it. If the Gleann Dubh Lighe skyline walk was situated in the Lake District it would be a famous day's darg. I first did Braigh nan Uamhachan by its northern approaches. These are neither so illogical nor so rough as they look on the map. It was a route Tony and I repeated on UC 80, on a day that took us from Glen Pean bothy to the Loch Eil Centre near Corpach.

Gleann a' Chaorainn is the Strathan approach, a glen dominated by the Streaps, and we followed this till well past the lowest col on the ridge linking Leac na Carnaich to the Streaps before doubling back up to reach this col. You lose only a few hundred feet in angling down to near the head of Gleann Camgharaidh, and the Braigh is there on the other side of the valley. Usually, having heavy packs, we've made a rising round of its north end to dump things on the Gualann nan Osna col before tackling the Corbett and/or the Munro of Gulvain. It is a novel route out from expeditions into the Rough Bounds of Knoydart. Tony and I had a hot day and on UC 84 Claudia and Sandy, the two young nurses new to walking and to Scotland, had a full scale roasting. Having walked Loch Morar to Glen Pean the day before, we cut out the Braigh for an hour by (or in) Lochan a' Chomhlain (the deer were doing the same) and a dander down pretty Gleann Dubh Lighe where we spent a relaxing day and night. I don't recall much about the Corbett, in fact, but the fester hours with Tony or the girls are unforgettable. There are days when the best is *not* climbing hills! The traverse of Braigh nan Uamhachan, while not as spectacular as the Streaps–Tuim outing, is, as Donald Bennet writes, "a very interesting traverse which would undoubtedly be better known if the Braigh had the extra height to bring it to Munro status."

Needless to say the views from these hills are of the best. What a pity we have lost Beinn an Tuim, the best of all, with views out along, down along Loch Eil and Loch Shiel! Beinn an Tuim is more accurately Beinn an Tom, *hillocky hill*, which is a good general description of everything in the area.

Section 10:   19. STOB COIRE A' CHEARCAILL   771 m
                  OS 41   017727
                  The spike of the circular corrie

This hill is more often observed than climbed. It is a Corbetteer's Corbett and few other walkers make the ascent. Like many isolated

Corbetts there is a panoramic view, with the big bad Ben bold in the east. The circle of corrie facing east is well seen from Fort William. Fort William, alas, is well seen from Stob Coire a' Chearcaill. Most spectacular is the sweep of country from Ardgour to Glenfinnan: as wild and dramatic as anything in Scotland — and not a Munro mugging that magnificence.

I feel a bit guilty about this Corbett as it was one which I did in that frantic period when suddenly completing the Corbetts became important. It was bagged, it was raided, it was raped. It was barely enjoyed. Some day I will make amends, wandering up Gleann Sron a' Chreagain and descending off Sgurr an Iubhair to the Cona Glen, the best combination. That will be in early summer, the trees will be in new leaf, the flowers at their best, the moors tangy with myrtle scent and the Ben a snowy glitter in the eye of the sun. There will be swims in the rivers and brews in solitary places. That landscape south of the Mallaig line and west of Loch Linnhe is one of the most varied and rewarding in Scotland. The hills are all malts. Drink slow and deep, my friends.

My ascent was made at the end of a long drive from Fife with several calls on the way. Coming out of the Locheil Centre I looked across the loch at the Corbett, looked at my watch, and quickly drove round the loch, past the Doire na Muice plantings to park by the Blaich crofts. I took to the hill with no great enthusiasm: the afternoon was too stuffily hot, I was too tired and a left calf muscle ached from rock climbing the day before. I took a book and read as I walked up the long, featureless slope. By Braigh Bhlaich the surface was too stony to read and walk. The view was disappointing as grey haze was overtaken by greyer dusk. Being April I was at least spared midges. Gaston Rebuffat once wrote of such a day, "the human animal was not happy". We all have off-days, I suppose, so, in this case, don't do as I did but do as I suggest.

Section 10:   20. MEALL A' PHUBUILL   774 m   OS 41   029854
         Hill of the tent

Poubelle is the French word for a dustbin and, perhaps justifiably, Meall a' Phubuill, to me, became linked with that word for, on my first visit, the hill treated me with the respect given to used tea leaves. I've had happy ascents since.

The normal route to Meall a' Phubuill is up Gleann Suileag from Fassfern, on the loop of old road by Loch Eil. An estate track runs up through the attractive forest to Glensulaig with a good path, not on the map, angling up to the Allt Fionn Diore col, above which stands the dumpling bulk of the Corbett. A poorer path also continues up the glen beyond Glensulaig and descends Glen Loy, becoming a seldom-used minor road, to reach the Great Glen. Beinn Bhan (12:1) above Glen Loy is a Corbett which could be linked on a pleasant two-day expedition. Meall a' Phubuill can also be reached via Glen Mallie, making a splendid high-level circuit, Monadh Beag–the Corbett–Druim Gleann Laoigh. The views *from* Phubuill make it memorable. The hill itself is less interesting.

Another good route to the Corbett is to combine Phubuill with the Munro Gulvain (Gaor Bheinn) by tramping up Gleann Fionnlighe, which is what led to my misadventures. I'd been trying to find the sailing schooner *Captain Scott* and eventually saw her anchored up Loch Eil and managed to get on board to meet her redoubtable skipper, Commander Victor Clark, a character in the Tilman class. The meeting was to lead to regular autumn months' instructing on the *Captain Scott* until financial necessity saw her sold to the Arabs where she now sails the Gulf as *Youth of Oman*. Nobody in Britain would pay the price of half a mile of motorway to save her. The trainees did a sort of sea and hills Outward Bound Course and when I was told they were off up Gleann Fionnlighe for a couple of nights with instructor David Osselton I decided to combine a visit to a wanted Munro and a wanted Corbett with seeing them operate in the field. I drove to the head of Loch Eil, packed and prepared, had supper and slept in the Dormobile.

I woke to that strange hush that means snow has fallen. The weight of snow nearly closed the roof down on to my bunk. I rose in self defence. Being a fair morning there would soon be a thaw so I made a dash west and back for photographs and only then set off, bare to the waist (in early March!) to try to track the others, a task which could be made difficult — or easy — by the new snow. Their first camp was spotted because of the beaten bracken where they'd commuted between tents and burn, and a good furrow of track in the new snow led on into the hills. We finally found their new site at 1,600 feet in Coire a' Chaorainn on the SE flank of Gulvain. One cripple was in a tent and he said the rest were up the hill. I'd just pitched and brewed when they returned. Soon there was a bustle of pitching tents and cooking, with the voices sinking into a murmur and finally silence. A slice of moon shone down on the pass under Meall a' Phubuill opposite. I read for a while by candle light and snuggled down in the new tent I'd just bought.

An hour later a howling gale and lashing rain were battering the camp. The new nylon tent rattled noisily and I had little sleep. Nearing dawn I realised the tent also leaked badly and my duvet, which I'd been lying on, was sodden, and much of the floor an inch deep in water. The sewn-in groundsheet was doing a fine job at not letting water out. The dog perched on top of me to keep out of the wet.

This was not one of my more cheerful camping experiences but I think the trainees (suffering a bit, too) rather enjoyed seeing one of the "experts" in the toils. David quoted bits of Gerard Manley Hopkins's "Inversnaid" to me as we retreated off the monsoon mountain.

A couple of days later I came back and cycled up the glen as far as possible then traversed Gulvain, an icy ridge and sodden flanks, before crossing, feet saturated, to climb Meall a' Phubuill. Such an effort for such a tame hill. The irony of its name was not lost on me.

Bonnie Prince Charlie, on his confident march from raising the standard at Glenfinnan, came by Fassfern, marching up Glen Suileag and through by Glen Loy to reach Invergarry. Sir John Cope retreated, and the rebel army went over the Corrieyairack to Edinburgh and the Battle of Prestonpans. Meall a' Phubuill had its moment of history. Since the killing times that followed that rebellion it has remained a forgotten, silent corner.

> "Where essential silence cheers and blesses
> And forever in the hill recesses
> Her more lovely music broods and dies."
> (Robert Louis Stevenson)

LOCH MORAR–LOCH ARKAIG TO GLEN SHIEL

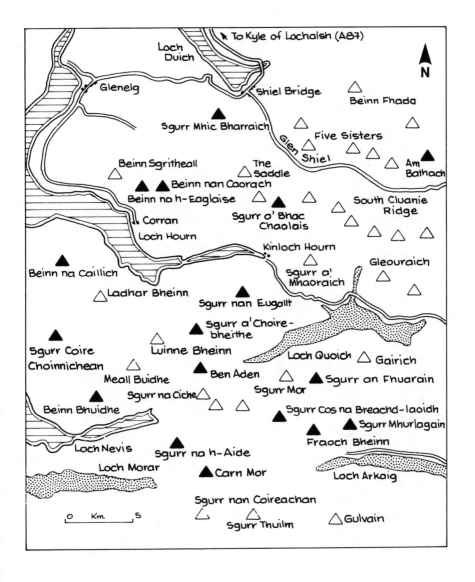

Section 11:   1. CARN MOR   829 m   OS 40   903910
Big cairn

Section 11:   2. SGURR NA H-AIDE   867 m   OS 40   889931
Peak of the hat (sgoar na h'Atch)

USING A CAR these peaks can be reached from the west end of Loch Arkaig, remote by motoring standards, yet only the starting place for the walking to come. The fang of Sgurr na h-Aide so dominates the view up Glen Dessarry that walkers have been known to begin climbing it thinking they were heading up Sgurr na Ciche. It is a Hobson's choice which side of Glen Dessary one walks up. The glen is heavily planted. A' Chuil can make a good base, as can a tent pitched west of the massed forestry. The southern slopes of Sgurr na h-Aide have a straight trench of valley draining them; a fascinating through route, only tracked beyond Lochan Eanaiche, but worth using for interest as well as probably giving the easiest route to the Corbett.

Go along (very little *down*) to near the lochan and then turn up for the heartbreak steepness of the ascent. This toil cannot be avoided. The east ridge to Meall na Sroine is very rough and gives plenty of extra footage but so wild is the setting that the effort is repaid by the views. If adding Carn Mor, descend by the ascent line and follow the burn opposite more or less to the top of the second Corbett, then descend by Meall nan Spardan, or its flanking corries, back to the head of Glen Dessarry. This is a long day if done from a car. If done over two days, the alternative approach to Carn Mor by Glen Pean could be taken. Do not underestimate these Corbetts. They are as rough as anything in Knoydart and their flanks are among the steepest slopes in Scotland.

Beware of Lochan Leum an t-Sagairt. There is no path on the north side as shown, so pass by the south shore. (Note again the unusual feature of a contour line wandering through the loch.) Newcomers to Glen Pean should walk on over the watershed for the view down to Loch Morar then backtrack almost to Lochan Leum again before heading up the Corbett. If Glen Pean is a favourite western pass, Carn Mor is not one of my favourite ascents from this side. There are some unusual landslip fissures on the slopes above the loch, dangerous as crevasses in winter. The walk back along the crest to Monadh Gorm is grassier and easier than h-Aide's equivalent. The view stays fierce and rugged.

Two other access routes are used frequently. A train (or car) can be taken to Glenfinnan, and the pass between Sgurr Thuilm and the Streaps followed to Strathan at the west end of Loch Arkaig. Bothies in either Glen Pean or Glen Dessarry are alternatives to camping, and Sourlies, at the head of Loch Nevis, provides the same choice. Sailing in is perhaps the most satisfying approach to these hills. The mail boat from Mallaig will land you at Inverie with the Mam Meadail to be crossed to Sourlies (more Corbetts in Knoydart, or en route, if so desired) but a seldom-used alternative is to land at Tarbet and walk the south side of Loch Nevis to Sourlies. This is much more straight-forward than most books would suggest. They put me off trying this route for years but I now regard it as the easy way in; easy in Knoydart terms of course! There is nothing easy about Sgurr na h-Aide from Sourlies, or Finiskaig where I pitched camp on one occasion. (Sometimes, in summer, or if you book and pay for it, the boat will go up to land you at the head of Loch Nevis. Check the times etc. with Bruce Watt Cruises, the Pier, Mallaig, tel. 0687–2233.)

The dog and I had first called in to Camusrory, then an Outdoor Centre, before coming over to camp at Finiskaig. On a previous occasion there was a bitch on heat at the centre and Kitchy took off in the night. There was no bridge over the Carnoch at that time, which gave me several paddles to collect him. This time he was tied to the tent pole overnight.

We left Finiskaig in warm summer rain, I'd minimal clothing on under waterproofs and put my boots on over bare feet to keep my stockings dry. A Berghaus cover for my rucksack was pressed into service. On the way up Coire Dubh I made a point of inspecting the unusual feature of a burn shown as splitting into two but, sadly, it had stopped flowing off in two directions. A steady plod took us up to the so-called "pass" of the Bealach nan Daoine (680 m). Most of my gear was left there while I groped up Sgurr na h-Aide which has two tops, nearly a kilometre apart — and on a bit to make sure it really was the top. The cloud was thick as toffee, the air still — a grand evening for midges unless a salvation breeze could find us. The cloud peeled away as we descended the Leac Bhuidhe slopes and I was pleased to see we were actually descending to the right place.

Plans were altered in faith and, instead of aiming for the head of Loch Morar, we angled down to Gleann an Lochain Eanaiche, a descent which was hard on the knees. Gullies rather than crags drove us to the path below, which we followed up to Lochan Eanaiche, passed along its south shore and sweated up Carn Mor. We descended more directly and put both feet in the burn crossing back to the path. The walk to Loch Morar was like the River Carnach in character. We watched, with mixed feelings, as the clouds blew off our tops. (On h-Aide the wind had been southerly, on Carn Mor it was northerly.) At Kinlochmorar we met a cyclist heading from Glen Pean to Swordland. "Would you be Dave Norgate?" I asked. He was — and how had I guessed? "There are only half a dozen folks daft enough to take a bike along Loch Morar side, so it seemed likely." There is a certain satisfaction in meeting someone undoubtedly crazier than oneself! Rounding the head of the loch I gathered the accumulated driftwood before going on for a comfy night in the bothy. The wet tent was hung up to dry and five cups of tea began a well-earned binge. Our exit was made by Gleann Taodhail to Loch Beoraid and the train at Lochailort, a magnificently wild and lonely route out. This exploratory element is the greatest reward of Section 11 of the Corbetts.

It is interesting to see how things change — or don't change. A. E. Robertson (who, in 1901, was the first to complete a round of the Munros) visited this area in 1895. His party caught the morning mail-coach from Fort William as far as Glenfinnan and crossed to Loch Arkaig as I've mentioned (climbing Sgurr Thuilm) then, "at Glendessarry, a farmhouse, we asked for and obtained accommodation. Next morning a very high hill in front, Sgurr na h-Aide, so attracted our attention by its sharp and narrow summit that we determined to set foot on it. Its appearance led us to expect some scrambling, and we were not disappointed. A very rugged descent brought us to the pass, the Mam na Cloich Airde . . . the keeper at Carnach put us up and his kindness will not be forgotten." They continued on over Sgurr na Ciche to a keeper's at Kinlochquoich (now *under* Loch Quoich) and out by Altbeithe and the Bealach Dubh Leac to Kintail.

Section 11: 3. SGURR COS NA BREACHD-LAOIDH 835 m
OS 33 948947
Peak of the cave of the bonny calf

Section 11: 4. FRAOCH BHEINN 858 m OS 33 986940
Heather hill

Section 11: 5. SGURR MHURLAGAIN 880 m OS 33 012944
Peak of the bag-shaped sea inlet

These three Corbetts are all lined up next to each other so are described together to avoid some repetition of practical information. Just how many are done in a day is up to the individual. I personally found each of them a useful half-day sortie going into or back from Knoydart or

Glen Kingie. They are all reached from the end of the tortuous public road along to the west end of Loch Arkaig. A private road, unsurfaced, continues up Glen Dessarry; they therefore have, for such a distant place, surprisingly easy access.

Sgurr Cos na Breachd-laoidh is rather meaningless. The *Tables* suggest the last word should be -laoigh (*cow*) but it is hardly the sort of place one would associate with cows. The erudite Rev. A. R. G. Burn (Munroist No. 2) in a 1917 *SMC Journal* suggests it is Sgurr Chois Breacaich, *the peak whose foot is speckled with stones*, which seems more reasonable. The whole peak is usually referred to as Druim a' Chuirn *the ridge of stones* rather than just its eastern summit, which is not a *druim*. This is the best of the three Corbetts but received scant attention until its promotion in the "Big Bang" changes of 1981. A party from our local club went up the hill a year earlier during a Western meet. We started with the Glen Kingie track from Glen Dessarry House and then moved on to the long SE Ridge up to the eastern top, Druim a' Chuirn. There is a mile-long crest along to the Corbett and this gives some scrambling. Half-way along a large flaky pinnacle sticks up, a feature which immediately distinguishes this hill when seen from other summits. Everyone scrambled up — even the dog — but an icy wind threatened to blow us off. The Glen Kingie flank is very craggy. The normal descent would be to the south but we dropped steeply down to the col to reach An Eag and traversed everything along to Sgurr Gairich, quite a long day, but midsummer encouraged a 10 p.m. return to Strathan. This Corbett could be combined with Sgurr nan Coireachan in a traverse of the crest of Coire nan Uth.

Fraoch Bheinn I took in on a March day after having gone through, by that same path to Glen Kingie, to climb Sgurr Mor. Deep snow and over-warm weather made a tiring day: Fraoch Bheinn was enough, rather than with Sgurr Mhurlagain as planned. There is very little heather on *heather hill* and the craggy buttresses can easily be bypassed. Using one or other of the flanking paths to gain as much height as possible before heading for the summits is a good plan. Kinbreack bothy in Glen Kingie is a good base for tackling these Corbetts by their more interesting NE Ridges. Fraoch Bheinn from the bothy looks like the Buachaille Etive Beag from Lagangarbh.

Sgurr Mhurlagain I took in while walking out from Kinbreack on another occasion. I tried to go up the gorge of the bothy burn but a big pool blocked the way so I just zigzagged up on to the Corbett's north ridge: walking with few clothes on and my umbrella up: one way with sweaty condensation in pre-Goretex days. All too soon I was into clouds, but the summit can hardly be missed as the cairn perches on the edge of a cliff-bitten corrie headwall. We descended the "interminable" SW Ridge as the car was parked by the Dearg Allt, but anywhere on the southern flank can be chosen if a quick and easy ascent is wanted. There is no telephone at Murlaggan — don't break a leg on running down those grassy slopes! The best of the descent is the view across to the Streaps and the scrum of peaks westwards.

> "Passing through,
> Stop for brew;
> Feel like new —
> Thanking you."
> (Entry in Kinbreack Bothy Book)

Section 11:   6. Sgurr an Fhuarain   901 m   OS 33   987980
              Oran's peak(?) (*ooaran*)

This hill, being twinned with Sgurr Mor, should have been done at the same time as "the big yin". If not, there is a long journey to penalise the original slackness. Even Rev. A. E. Robertson noted Sgurr Mor as being one of the remotest Munros and advocated, as have many writers since, taking in the peak as part of a cross-country tramp.

My most recent tramp was on an Ultimate Challenge: a long day that took us from A' Chuil bothy to Tomdoun Hotel; before that it was on a BFMC Meet based at Strathan when we traversed from Sgurr Cos na Breachd-laoidh to Sgurr an Fhuarain with one diehard adding Gairich; on my Munro marathon I'd camped above Loch Quoich, north of Sgurr Mor, and followed the ridge eastwards to the dam; earlier still my brother David had dropped Jim, Andrew, Kitchy and me off at Glenfinnan on a Friday night and picked us up at the Loch Quoich dam on Sunday — quite a weekend trip from the Lowlands. That was my first visit to this Corbett and the most memorable.

Saturday was spent traversing the hills south of Glen Pean and heading to A' Chuil for the night. On Sunday, we were off at six o'clock, grabbing the chance of shade for the steep haul up the Allt Coire nan Uth. Frogs were rather pathetically scrabbling about in the dried-out landscape while an eagle swung lazily overhead — even the thermals were up early. We thankfully left our packs on the col to go up Sgurr nan Coireachan. A clammy mist was fingering over the ridge and kept us cool but the signs were all of a scorcher to come. An Eag, with packs, set us on the start of the grand highway between tawny Glen Kingie and the out-of-bounds of Loch Quoich.

There is an abandoned stalkers' path of some character along the crest. High on Sgurr Mor it breaks into steps and swanks through the crags. We sat on Sgurr Beag, to brew, in an attempt to try and reduce the height of the tent-topped giant of Sgurr Mor. Our perch site was dotted with some freshly-made mole hills. I've never seen them so high. There were scores of deer, all high in search of some coolness, and we charged on over the Munro behind a herd of stags. Sgurr Mor is well named.

The heat was intense for the steep "down" and the long easy sweep up to Sgurr an Fhuarain. The landscape shimmered. After a few minutes by the trig point we set off down the east ridge to find water as soon as possible. The crags shown on the map are not so fierce as one would expect and the north ridge is equally easy for a continuation eastwards. (An ascent from the south is easy anywhere, just a matter of working up long grassy slopes.)

We found a delectable pool, drank half of it, swam in the rest and drip-dried over an hour-long lunch break. I'd draped all my clothes round me but the others had on only pants, and, by the day's end, they were glowing red. You could have fried eggs on their shoulders.

The stalkers' path up on to Gairich Beag is the steepest I've ever met, which made hard work for us, but we crossed the deer-busy "mountain of yelping" (Gairich) in good heart. The way off to the dam was well known and a "yoo-hoo" across the loch ensured there was tea ready for our arrival, 13½ hours from our A' Chuil departure. There was an element of unreality about work the next day and the glow was not just sunburn. We had experienced a majestic day; "smitten and addicted". I'm sure A.E.R. would have approved, even though it had been the sabbath. The sun shines on the just and the unjust — just like the rain.

Section 11:   7. BEN ADEN   887 m   OS 33   899986
          The hill of the face

Ben Aden is the forgotten peak of Knoydart. Being wedged between three of the roughest Munros in Scotland probably accounts for it being overlooked or ignored. The Carnach valley is dominated by Ben Aden and the peak stands over Lochan nam Breac, the secretive heart of the country of Knoydart. Be warned, though: the heaviest rainfall in Scotland is recorded at the west end of Loch Quoich.

The last time on these hills I canoed in along Loch Quoich with the loch wasted by summer drought and giving reflections of a clarity I've never seen equalled. You could turn slides upside down and nobody noticed. A camp by Lochan nam Breac is one of the classic experiences of the Scottish Highlands (like climbing the Inaccessible Pinnacle or traversing the Aonach Eagach by moonlight or seeing sunrise over the stacks of St Kilda) but Ben Aden is not the easiest of places to reach. The raising of Loch Quoich's waters destroyed some useful paths while almost all the rivers in these hills can quickly become impassable after heavy rain. Rain falls often and with lively exuberance and Lochan nam Breac can feel a long way from anywhere. Ben Aden and Druim Chosaidh which hem in the lochan are some of the least-climbed Corbetts. Corbettitis is usually well advanced before they are taken. Strong medicine.

There are no ambling routes up Ben Aden for the peak is one of the steepest, rockiest and roughest in Scotland. The rock is good — I am surprised climbs have not been recorded on the bolder cliff faces. Ben Aden doesn't hide its challenges, but is a peak best ascended on a clear day. Work out your line of ascent from the Carnach valley *before* rushing up into its complexities. I preach all this from the experience of having done none of these things.

Finiskaig used to be my original Knoydart base. This old building is a complete ruin now and Sourlies across the river is often over-crowded. In July 1973 a party of us sailed up Loch Nevis, landed at Camusrory and set up our tents at Finiskaig for several days before making an exit to Glenfinnan. We decided to combine Ben Aden with Sgurr na Ciche and do the Garbh Chiochs–Coireachan hills on the way out. I wonder if anyone has ever gone all the way from Ben Aden to Gairich in a day? It would give an incomparable traverse.

Some people complain that "Knoydart" should be used only of the country west of the Carnach but historically this was not so. The Cameron–Macdonnell march is at the head of Glen Dessarry, and Sgurr na Ciche and Ben Aden have always been part of the Knoydart Estate, centred on Inverie, at least until recent exercises in asset-stripping. Geologically these hills are Knoydart and Ben Aden is the roughest of all the Rough Bounds.

The path up the River Carnach is often more imaginary than accurate and you may not cross easily to reach the foot of Ben Aden. The tide was out when we set off on our grey summer morning, which enabled us to walk along the sands, wend through the saltings and on up the glen, keeping to the east bank. We resisted some fine pools at a rocky step. There were old walls and ruins where the Allt Achadh a' Ghlinne joined the Carnach. A solitary rowan had sprouted: a poignant memorial to the long-departed families who once lived in that lonely spot. We couldn't see much so tackled the hill *en face* (more or less what one does anyway). "Warm and muggy. Soon in a disgusting lather of sweat", I wrote later of that toil up into the mist. We ran against some crags which pushed us along into a gully. This required the use of our emergency abseil line and gave two pitches, first a backing-up exercise followed by a slabby wall and then a dank, black flue, down which a burn was pouring. The gloom was brightened by great clumps of roseroot and globeflower. Two hours were needed to land eight people, one dog and all our rucksacks at the top of the difficulties. The mist was really thick and we had some casting about among all the many rocky bumps to make sure of the summit.

The navigation after that was a complex business. We were aided by the line of lochans (something actually recognisable!) and a clearance on Meall a' Choire Dhuibh, where the general direction changes completely, was a welcome help. The clearance ended with rain sweeping in but by then all we had to do was to go upwards and, when there was no more up, that would be the top. Sgurr na Ciche's summit can always be recognised by its collection of shattered trig pillars. We weren't back at Finiskaig till 8 p.m.

The SW face of Aden is generally recognised as the easiest, but if you can't see a route up from below the best course would be to follow the Allt Achadh a' Ghlinne to where the map rather vaguely gives the name Bealach na h-Eangair. Head up the side stream which cuts the word "Bealach". This leads up to a gap, which is drained, on the NE side, by the Allt Coire na Cruaiche. This gap is a very definite pass (Bealach a' Chairn Deirg on 1:25,000), and as such could be found in mist, with not too difficult a ridge on up to the summit. The Allt Achadh a' Ghlinne descends from a wild corrie crowded with crags. The dip with the lochans is Bealach a' Choire Cruaidh (1:25,000), probably another old pass. From the north side, the Allt Coire na Cruaiche is the one relatively easy route. The rest of the north face is more suitable for climbing, rather than walking, not that the granite pegmatite has received much, if any, attention, from climbers. Ben Aden is worth an investment in a 1:25,000 map. (Sheet "NM89/99 Glen Dessarry")

I've just been reading some 1905 notes by the Rev. A. E. Robertson: "The best way to explore this region is probably to traverse it in several directions, carrying a rucksack with a few necessities, obtaining a night's shelter at some of the outlying shepherds' or keepers' houses in Glen Dessarry or Glen Kingie or by the shores of Loch Quoich. In fact this is the only way one can really see it, the distances from hotels being too great. A few days spent in this fashion will be a unique and charming experience; for this is one of the few districts not yet corrupted by the moneyed Sassenach, and the people in the glens are kind, courteous and hospitable." What would he make of today's desolation I wonder?

Section 11:   8. BEINN BHUIDHE   855 m   OS 33   822967
                  Yellow hill (boo-ee)

Section 11:   9. SGURR COIRE CHOINNICHEAN   796 m
                  OS 33   791011
                  Peak of the mossy corrie

Section 11:   10. BEINN NA CAILLICH   785 m   OS 33   796067
                  Old woman's hill

Section 11:   11. SGURR A' CHOIRE-BHEITHE   914 m
                  OS 33   895015
                  Peak of the birch corrie (corrie vey)

These are the Corbetts of Knoydart, an area renowned for its tough landscape, as the term "Rough Bounds" indicates. The Corbetts are up to expectation and are listed together here for descriptive convenience rather than with any idea of climbing them all at once. For that you would need several days. For Knoydart you will want many more days than you ever have available. Knoydart is a far country as well as a rough one.

The convenient ways in are few. Easiest is the mailboat from Mallaig to Inverie, the only hamlet in the area (farm bunkhouse/B & B accommodation) and the boat may also be chartered to take a party to the head of Loch Nevis. Sometimes it is possible to hire a boat from Corran to Barrisdale across Loch Hourn. I've also sailed and used a canoe to reach the near-island of Knoydart. There are no public roads reaching it, and only two, long, dead-end minor roads, by Loch Quoich to Kinloch Hourn and by Loch Arkaig to Glen Dessarry, come anywhere near.

At one time there were no bothies or bridges and Knoydart had a deserved reputation as a difficult and potentially dangerous place. Alas, it has been thoroughly tamed, and has lost greatly thereby. There is a constant, vociferous public demand to make things easier or safer which nibbles away at the glorious wildness of our mountains. Knoydart has suffered this aesthetical erosion and should be a lesson to all of us. We must learn, somehow, to leave things alone as much as possible. The safety arguments are fallacious for, however much you level the rough, there will always be someone who will stumble and hurt himself. Taken to its logical conclusion these people should bridge every single stream and level every mountain. It is time we stopped catering for the lowest human denominator and gave consideration to the landscape itself.

The Corbetts look as if they could be linked on to Munros easily enough, but such is the roughness of the ridges in Knoydart that this is often harder work than making two ascents from sea level. Sgurr a' Choire-bheithe (914 the OS now say) and Luinne Bheinn face each other across a high pass, Meall Buidhe and Beinn Bhuidhe do so as well, but less easily. As like as not, a first visit to Knoydart has been a Munro-bagging raid so linking Corbetts to Munros is not of particular interest. Time is what is most needed in Knoydart.

Even back in the bad old days when visitors were not welcomed to Knoydart we used to have school parties camping and trekking there, usually sailing in from Inverie and trekking out to Glenfinnan. As the kids were all hooked on Munros I had few chances of adding Corbetts. They had to be dealt with on later visits, but gave an excuse for making the most of Knoydart's best feature, the remarkable high-level traverses available.

The dog and I sailed from Mallaig in the familiar *Western Isles* and, as they were having to take a policeman up to Camusrory, I scrounged a lift as well. When a tiny inflatable came out to meet the *Western Isles* it could take only one other person, leaving me stranded on board till the bobby could finish his work (a tramp had broken into the outdoor centre there) and I could land with the Warden on his return trip. There is no good anchorage off Camusrory, and the skipper offered to put me ashore further along. The *Western Isles* was edged into the cliffs near Rubha Dubh a' Bhata and, from the bow, I placed the dog on a ledge and quickly stepped across myself. My rucksack was passed over and the boat drifted back. The landing took a few seconds: quite an impressive bit of seamanship.

I was tempted to go straight up Beinn Bhuidhe but I'd promised to call in at Camusrory. I set off along the coast, with stunning views of Ben Aden and Sgurr na Ciche at the head of the loch. The Warden had the kettle boiling when we arrived. This was a sad visit in some ways for the centre was on its penultimate course. Camusrory was just too remote and expensive to compete with the subsidised centres in the south. Tony Montgomery, the Warden, moved his ponies to Moray where he still offers real trekking rather than the gentle amble that passes for pony trekking. I miss meeting his ponies in the wild glens of Knoydart. The paths are drier, though!

The dog and I went up Glen Carnach and pitched our small tent a thousand feet up in Coire na Gaoithe, with Ben Aden just across the valley and a bold view up the Carnach River to the castellated wall of

Druim Chosaidh. There was plenty of dead wood. I lit a fire after supper and was relaxing in the delight of a pre-midge, perfect evening when two people descended on us — with mutual astonishment. The two students were camping at Carnoch and had traversed the Munros and our site was on their natural route back, but in those crags and folds and gullies to come upon the tent was quite a coincidence. They apologised! We sat and blethered over tea: they had a week and were wandering from Lochailort to Arnisdale.

We were up at five o'clock and carried the rucksack up to the loch before setting off on a long, intricate traverse for the Mam Unndalain and Sgurr a' Choire-bheithe. The gear had to be left in a spot with the utter certainty of finding it again. Aden and Ciche were damming back an eastern cloud sea. Stray streamers of cloud broke round to ebb and flow along Druim Chosaidh, the long, craggy, five mile ridge which runs from Sgurr a' Choire-bheithe to Loch Quoich. The shores of Loch Quoich offer another, difficult, approach walk in to Knoydart, one to be attempted only in reasonable weather as the Abhainn Chosaidh is impassable in spate.

Sgurr a' Choire-bheithe juts out as a bold, craggy step above the Mam Unndalain but this was easily outflanked to the right and the final bump gained. The whole east was under a starched cloud sheet but the ragged array of Ladhar Bheinn lay under a smiting sun. There are two superb big Corbett days to be had from Barrisdale. One is this hill, from the Mam Unndalain, followed by the scrambly traverse of Druim Chosaidh and back by the Gleann Cosaidh–Glen Barrisdale path, the other links this Corbett with Sgurr nan Eugallt over Slat-Bheinn. Barrisdale, green and with some remnants of natural woodland, is a delightful base. An estate bothy is available for walkers.

The Druim Chosaidh ridge.was used by the Prince's party in escaping the Redcoat cordon strung up the western glens. The party came down Coire nan Gall having made a night escape from Glen Dessarry. From Druim Chosaidh they spied out the troops camped in the glen below and made another escape, over Eugallt's long crest, presumably to reach Coire Sgoireadail above Kinloch Hourn.

Luinne Bheinn, across the pass, felt an easier ascent. Though a Munro, it is not much higher than the Corbett which had enjoyed some months of prominence when there was speculation that it could be a new Munro — which would really have put the stoat among the widgeon. The Munro is double-headed, as were the two Bhuidhes to come. The cloud drifted on to us so I had to use map and compass back to the loch where my rucksack was waiting.

The traverse between the Munros is a complex one and I made slow progress carrying a pack and having to navigate. The cloud slowly began to break up and suddenly vanished as we neared the top to give a day of blazing sunshine thereafter. Meall Buidhe is a grand peak of ridges, crags and corries, and a central position gives it a panoramic view. Sgurr na Ciche and Garbh Chioch Mor jagged up dramatically in rough symmetry above the cloud sea.

We picked a careful way down to the Mam Meadail and lunched beyond its draughty cleft, continuing on in the same line to bypass Meall Bhasiter. Left leg muscles ached on the descent, right leg muscles felt the strain on the pull-up. We more or less ended on Meall Bhasiter, anyway. There was a big cairn beyond and, above the Mam Uchd, a tiny lochan acted as a reflecting pool for Sgurr na Ciche, now clear of cloud and soaring in all its glory. The rucksack was left on the Mam Uchd and, tired legs or not, I felt I was floating up the ridge. The summit looks well-defined on the map but the trig point, sticking up like a pinhead, lay on a second bump. Beinn Bhuidhe gave a more spacious panorama than Meall Buidhe, the Munro being a worthy addition to the scene.

Back at the rucksack I had a brew and sunbathed for an hour in a nook out of the chill east breeze. That breeze, blowing our scent ahead, had ensured we had seen very few deer during the traverse. When we descended north to Gleann Meadail we saw dozens. Twelve hours out and with over 6,000 feet of ascent (Knoydart miles and feet), I was glad to pitch the tent near the Dubh Lochan. The dog curled up in the bracken and only woke, briefly, for supper. Primroses, wild hyacinth, celandine and violets created a garden site. There was a perpetual cuckoo but I wrote in my log, "Even a crazy cuckoo won't keep me awake tonight."

We set off early again and, if the day before had steadily improved, this one did the opposite. A bright morning all too often means a wet afternoon. We left the tent standing and wended up the corrie above. This is a favourite deer calving site in June and best avoided then. Sgurr Coire Choinnichean is brutal by any standards — I was glad to be carrying only a day pack. This is the hill which so dominates the view as one sails in to Inverie but, as that aspect is craggy and planted low down, the Corbett is usually approached from the flanks: steep, craggy, demanding work. We aimed for the col east of the peak and then followed the crests up into gathering cloud. There was a top but, being suspicious, I continued — and found a higher. We came out of the cloud beyond that and could see all the way down to Inverie: no more summits.

After back-tracking to the col we descended to the north east, a knee-jarring descent which called for a laze by the pleasant Eas an

Fholaich before contouring round to some more waterfalls on the Abhain Bheag. While resting on the path up the burn a lizard ran over the dog's back and for the next half hour he kept twitching in reaction. On the way down I had a swim in a pool in the Abhain Bheag and took the chance of tick-hunting. I found a brace, in the usual place.

Beinn na Caillich was tackled from where all the burns join up, and it proved a disappointment. The wind had gone and the humid heat was very exhausting, besides which the hill was "a heap of rubbish, like the Sgriol Corbetts, greasy and loose, full of scree and boulders". The north side is fine, but seldom visited. Obviously a hill to go back to some day, perhaps by canoe across Loch Hourn as I've done twice for Ladhar Bheinn. An Arnisdale boatman once ferried A. E. Robertson across to Knoydart and was fascinated by his long ice-axe. He reported, once home, that the minister travelled "armed with a tomahawk".

The return trip was made round the flanks of Ladhar Bheinn and over the Mam Suidheig down to the Dubh Lochan. With only two sweets left I then had to cross the Mam Meadail in the rain to reach Camusrory where I'd left a stock of food. It rained all night (Sourlies Bothy did not exist) and I just wished I'd taken the boat out from Inverie. Knoydart rain is super rain.

That was a typical Knoydart Corbett-hunt, but you can take them a bit less frantically. I've been up some of the Corbetts again and still look forward to future visits while, on the periphery of Knoydart there are the equally tough Corbetts, Sgurr nan Eugallt, Ben Aden, Carn Mor and Sgurr na h-Aide. My escape from Knoydart after this assault was over Sgurr na h-Aide, already described in 11:2. Knoydart will never, ever, be other than a demanding proposition, an irresistible lure.

Section 11:   12. SGURR NAN EUGALLT   894 m   OS 33   931045
        Peak of death streams

"Dormobile dripping with condensation and drying clothes. Bloody rain. What a miserable April." So I wrote at my chosen spot by Loch Coire Shubh (*the loch of the raspberry corrie*) just above the steep descent to Kinloch Hourn. My frustration was that of a shopper finding so many goods on a shopping list "out of stock". Petrol costs the same whether one has days on the hill or not — so one tends to go regardless. I can laugh a bit, now, for my effort had gone into climbing Buidhe Bheinn, which has since been demoted as a Corbett. I'd rather given up Sgurr nan Eugallt (with a name like that!) when there was a wobbling shimmer of light on the book I was reading. The sun was shining through the puddle on the skylight.

At 3 p.m. we crossed the road and headed up bulbous crags to gain the stalkers' path which runs up a long slot and then to a ridge joining Sgurr Dubh. We lost the traverse line of the path under the snow but just continued up Sgurr Dubh and along the ridge leading to Sgurr nan Eugallt. There was more to the ridge than the map showed and we had plenty of fun on small crags, finally reaching the summit up "a gem of a chimney". Most of the time there was a dribbly, vertical rain, and, when not using my hands, I used my umbrella — I am a confirmed brolly boy, I loathe wearing waterproofs, even my luxury Berghaus Goretex set.

Like The Saddle to the north, the trig point is not on the highest point of the ridge. We arrived with a clearance in the weather. The country to the south (the outer peaks of Knoydart) was very impressive and I noted it then as "an area to explore valleys and ridges, once the silly Corbetts are done", a promise I have kept. The bigger hills stayed in the cloud and a Corbett was just right for the occasion. Time, alas, forced me back down, but this is really a hill to be traversed, end to end, or taken in with Sgurr a' Choire-bheithe. The path up from Coire Shubh is a temptation to slackness.

Coire Shubh (*corrie hoo*) gave a long bumslide, after I'd put on my waterproof trousers to reduce the coefficient of friction. The dog sat on my lap and greatly enjoyed his ride. At the foot of the slope I found a badly-mangled deer which I'm sure had been the victim of an avalanche. The ground below the snowline was deeply frozen, hard and also difficult to traverse back to the path. The lone monkey-puzzle tree welcomed me home to the now hoar-covered Dormobile — back to my book over a warming curry supper.

The bulbous, scoured nature of the *montagnes moutonnées* hereabouts was noted by the early geologists, Geikie and Murchison, who considered the pass from Glenquoich to Loch Hourn to be one of the best examples of ice action to be found in Britain. Landseer also spent many days here, drawing and painting.

Glenquoich Lodge is now under the waters of the raised Loch Quoich. One of the proprietors, E. C. Ellice, last century wrote a book, *Place Names of Glengarry and Glenquoich*, which is full of interesting associations. This lonely road where I camped was once the scene of a race from Loch Hourn to Invergarry. The chief, Glengarry, one day drove home from Loch Hourn in four hours and later rather boasted of this to Mr Green, the family tutor, who in turn suggested he could do the journey as fast on foot. Glengarry bet £20 he could not. A Glengarry man, Somerled Macdonell, was backed against the Sassenach and Glenquoich wagered he could get "an old wife" off his farm to beat them both. Macdonell spurted ahead at the start but the ascent from Loch Hourn brought on a nose bleed and, while he was washing in a burn, the tutor went ahead. The highlander won, however, doing the 27 miles in 3 hours 40 minutes, but Mr Green won his wager by beating the 4 hours. The old wife lasted 7 miles but that was still up the brae from Loch Hourn and on to Glenquoich. Glengarry's wife received the successful pair with "bizzed porter on meal".

Section 11:   13. SGURR A' BHAC CHAOLAIS   885 m   OS 33   958110
Peak of the hollow of the kyle (narrows)

This is one of the Corbetts which came in with the revisions of the 1981 *Tables*. As I had not been on it before, I had a good excuse for a Hogmanay visit when it could also lead on to Sgurr na Sgine by its seldom-climbed east face which had long been on my "wants" list. Seven Munros are arranged along the Cluanie ridge south of Glen Shiel; this Corbett, being tacked on at the west end of the seven, can be added to them at the cost of 500 feet of ascent rather than 2,500 feet if done later from the valley. There is some reward in careful planning — though few of us treat the game as tidily as we later wish we had. This Corbett has replaced Buidhe Bheinn which lies just over a mile to the south. Buidhe Bheinn, *the yellow hill*, towers above the head of Loch Hourn and is a superb hill which hardly deserved demotion. Good paths lead up it, and linking in with Chaolais and Sgine gives a magnificent "horseshoe" circuit from Kinloch Hourn.

Under a corona of frosty stars we set off from the roadside in Glen Shiel, heading up the path to the Bealach Duibh Leac, a pass which was used by Bonnie Prince Charlie after he'd escaped from the Rough Bounds further south. Largely due to his successful escape after Culloden, we now have Ordnance Survey maps. The locals who guided the prince knew the landscape, the government forces didn't, making a good case for producing proper maps.

We had a warm dawn plod up to the Allt Coire Toiteil, a good way of dealing with an overindulgence of seasonal fare. We paused there, to recover a bit and to admire Sgurr na Sgine at the head of the valley; it looked as grand as The Saddle in a rosy sunrise flush. We donned crampons, for the path was often icy or filled with hard snow. The surface promptly changed to granular snow — the crampons were not really needed. Ben's kept giving trouble. Ernst and I were on top of

Sgurr a' Bhac Chaolais an hour before him. Storm has built-in crampons and with twice the number of legs covers twice the ground.

In summer the path can be difficult to follow after crossing the Allt Coire Toiteil. Time and vegetation have largely obliterated the historic route's delineation. With everything covered in snow we angled up more directly for the summit, missing the small "mauvais pas" on the ridge up from the Bealach Duibh Leac. (Only on the descent does it really cause any delay.)

The summit is a large dome rather than a sharp point. Our view along the Cluanie Ridge was made dramatic by clearing clouds which spilled over the ridge in ever-changing shapes and colours: instant Henry Moore shapes which formed and melted in minutes before disappearing completely to give a day of pristine primary colours. The Glen Shiel ridges swept along like huge breakers caught as they prepared to topple over into surf. The best of the view however was westwards to the east face of Sgurr na Sgine, that secretive Munro which only looks its true best when seen from Knoydart. Quite a few casual plans to traverse from The Saddle to Sgurr na Sgine and on eastwards end with the aspirant peering down these eastern cliffs in surprise.

We went on to climb the face and, one way or another, having taken three different solo routes (with varied fortunes) lost most of the day before everyone was re-united on top. I'd left sandwiches on the main cairn for the others before going on to the West Top to drink in the view of The Saddle, and they failed to see them. A present for the ravens! Black clouds, shot with lurid red, rimmed the western view to the islands. We descended into Coire Toiteil fast and managed to reach our upward tracks before it became really dark. Two other walkers caught us up and, as so often, the number of torches present or working was less than the number of people. I pushed on ahead, following the white flag of Storm's tail, and when we all gathered at the Dormobile a hot brew and a glass of *Jura* was waiting to round off the day. Sgurr a' Bhac Chaolais is worth a winter visit.

There is no real hope of adding another summit to the Cluanie Ridge "seven" in midwinter; Sgurr a' Bhac Chaolais can conveniently be added to Sgurr na Sgine to make a fuller day. A descent can be made to Coire Toiteil from the col between Chaolais and Sgine, if a modest traverse of the Corbett alone is called for, or it can be taken in while following the old pass route between Loch Duich and Loch Quoich, a route which has royal precedents after all.

Section 11: 14. BEINN NA H-EAGLAISE 804 m OS 33 854120
The hill of the church (eglish)

Section 11: 15. BEINN NAN CAORACH 773 m OS 33 871122
The hill of the rowan berries (curuch)

One way to ensure good conditions in a period of doubtful weather is to forget, or decide not to take, a camera on the hill. Or you forget to carry a spare film. Under these circumstances the weather always clears up. When Charles and I set off for these hills on the penultimate day of 1986 there was no call for the camera, I thought. A couple of hours later I was cursing my laziness. Beinn Sgritheall (Sgriol), perhaps my favourite mainland Munro, was arrayed in all its winter glory.

We made our approach from Glen More, passing under the prehistoric fort of Torr Beag (splendid viewpoint) and Loch Iain Mhic Aonghais to the many junctions of Strath a' Chomair. Here we crossed a ford to a gate and a bad jeep track that swings round up the Allt Gleann Aoidhdailean, a route now milestoned with ugly pylons. This is a fine old right of way to Kinloch Hourn and was the route followed by the cattle which had swum across Kyle Rhea on the way to southern markets. We found the going messy, so crossed the stream to follow up the burn that drained the corrie between the northern spurs of the Corbetts. "Waterfall" on the map proved to be a whole series of little falls rather than any one leap, which made for an attractive line. The corner between the stream junctions has been planted; we cut into the corrie by walking along above the plantation fence.

The snow-line was half way up the corrie and rather wet — we were glad of our wellies. When the snow began to harden I walked up actually *in* the water, at one stage going through a tunnel of old snow which arched over the gash. Sgurr Dearg was a prominent tor to the east and we hit the ridge from it to Beinn nan Caorach after the angle eased, pleasant walking on the bands of old hard snow which were only slippery where clear of newer snow. The peaks of Sgriol and Eaglaise were dramatically arrayed.

On the ridge a knifing wind stabbed us. The east wind is always the executioner. We battered up the ridge to the summit for a brief visit. Knoydart was hidden in a black pall of cloud as was every Munro bar Sgriol but, away to the north west, Applecross was clear and the sky and sea shivered a lurid glow that promised nothing good.

A fence links the summits of the two Corbetts, which is worth knowing if caught by mist, but after following it for a while on the north ridge off Beinn nan Caorach we cut more directly down to the wide grassy saddle of the Bealach nam Bo. This seems a strange area to have so many *cow* names. The wind, whistling up Coire nam Bo to the south, had driven the grazing deer almost up to the pass. They were unconcerned at our presence. The wide saddle really leads to the Druim nan Bo, *the ridge of the cattle*, and this has quite a distinctive dip to a "sneck" before rearing up to Beinn na h-Eaglaise as a fine fin. We were lucky enough to find a wind-free spot on the Rosdail side and there changed out of our wellies into boots and gaiters.

The change was well judged for the route was iced up. In the end we banged our way along a swooping series of drifting crests to reach the summit as snow began to fall. Sgritheall had now vanished under the black blanket. We did not linger on Eaglaise in case there was any lightning about. It is a finer peak than Caorach. I've linked Eaglaise to Sgritheall, but the descent to the Bealach Arnisdail is steep, a mix of loose gullies and crags. The Corbett summit is only a mile back from Loch Hourn, and is really steep everywhere, but what an erne's viewpoint we have because of that! Sgritheall and these Corbetts form an overspill to the Rough Bounds of Knoydart.

My first visit linked the Corbetts to Sgritheall, from a camp at Corran where the public road to Arnisdale finally admits defeat at the roughness of the Loch Hourn slopes. We went up by the Allt Utha and Coire Dhruim nam Bo for Caorach first. There is now a bulldozed track up the east bank of the Allt Utha. The fall is an impressive one. While perhaps shorter in miles the approaches on the Loch Hourn side require a long drive in and then give brutally steep ascents. I'd recommend the approaches from either Glen More or Gleann Beag. The latter has the best-preserved brochs on the mainland (and other antiquities) so should be visited whatever one is doing in this magic area beyond Mam Ratagan.

Charles and I picked our careful way back to the gap on the ridge. The fence posts were icy pennants. Just before the dip the fence off Eaglaise makes a sharp turn right, downhill, but from the gap a line of smaller, more widely-spaced posts crosses the broad saddle and so up Caorach. After changing back into wellies we walked up to follow Druim nan Bo homewards rather than go down by wet Rosdail. The ridge is a long series of bumps and we wended along them in torrential rain. The burns were rising and we were very glad to reach our Glen More base. Friends who had been on Sgritheall came in several hours later.

Section 11:   16. Sgurr Mhic Bharraich   781 m   OS 33   917174
Peak of the son of Maurice (Varrich)

With Beinn Sgritheall to the west, Sgurr Fhuarain to the east and The
Saddle to the south, Mhic Bharraich is perhaps rather junior in such a
family of brothers and sisters but the astute would recognise that the
hill must be a prime viewpoint. I'm biased for, on the first of January
1980, we were given one of the most magnificent days of deep
winter I've ever known in Scotland.

On my first visit I'd wandered up the Corbett with Kitchy from
Shiel Bridge via the Loch Coire nan Crogachan path on a manky day
when my friends nevertheless went off for The Saddle. The
Corbett's lesser height gave me some view, The Saddle yielded
none. On the last day of 1977 the hill was a bad-forecast alternative
and four of us went up the Allt Grannda to its lochan source, giving
ourselves fun on the snow-slobbery rocks of the gorge, then scrambling, where possible, to the summit and back by Loch Coire nan
Crogachan. The path down the Allt a' Ghleannain is not easy to
follow, now. Bealachasan is a ruin and the easiest line makes for the
Glenmore River forestry track. The whole hill is knobbly and rocky
but doesn't yield proper rock climbing. Part of its neglect is that the
side facing Loch Duich is intimidatingly steep and barred by forestry, but the Allt Undalain gives an easy-enough approach. Being
based in Glen More at Hogmanay we always went up from the west.

On the first of January 1979 two inches of new snow were lying
on the bothy when Martin, Anne, Ben, Storm and I set out.
Bealachasan we noted was rotting away fast. I found a newspaper
from 1950 which was full of rationing problems and gave an
obituary of Lord Wavell. Fashions and prices were a bit different
then, too. This time we scrambled up by visiting every lochan. We
had some good slides on them, whooping like schoolkids at play-
time. It was snowing on top and we were glad enough to escape
to the south *voie normal* and drop below the powder snow which was
all too often hiding ambushing ice. We put up a woodcock on the
pass, and a chatter of snow buntings had gone through while we
nibbled in lee of the cairn.

The Hallelujah start of the following year is the one that really
sings in the memory. I've never seen the west so white. We had
problems motoring over Mam Ratagan, and Glen More was choked
with snow. The bothy was snug enough and we'd carried in plenty
of logs, coal, festive food and appropriate libations. Some went to
bed, some were put to bed, but six of us and the dog made Mhic

Bharraich on the first day of 1980. Ben, Anne, Storm and I had been up exactly a year before. Ernst, Harry and Peter believed our good reports.

From Bealachasan we went straight up to break through the crags at the first gully. We sidled into the gully on thigh-deep drifts and the whole ascent was a furrow-ploughing slog, for all the world like fighting up some big peak in the Himalayas, but without the avalanche danger there. We used all the rock we could find but the climb was hard work in the blaze of sun. The day was bitterly cold. The snow on the flatter top levels had worked into glittering Lux flakes or Rice Krispie grains. The view to Sgritheall was Arctic rather than Himalayan, and the white went down to the sea waters of Loch Duich. Applecross and Torridon hardly showed any of their dark banding in this extravagance of whitewash. The Five Sisters were arrayed in a simplified geometry of triangles: sun-white on one side, plum-shadowy on the other.

The weather on the summit was Arctic too. We set off down at 2 p.m. Away on Sgritheall we could make out figures on one ridge: Donald and Charles, Munro-rivals, starting their final year of that game together. It was long after dark before they were back to the bothy fug. We collected and sawed wood and were just in before dark, having had a day as near perfection as we may ever know.

Browsing through the bothy book I noted one entry which said the bothy "was worked as a croft by my great uncle Donald Campbell, at the turn of this century before moving to Glenelg. Donald, a close relation of Sir Malcolm Campbell, lived until his 95th year." I'm sure Donald Campbell would have thoroughly approved of our gathering of the clans.

There were 24 of us (and 3 dogs) in his old house, which the Braes o' Fife had steadily renovated for several years to turn into a cosy bothy. Buildings as well as mountains can be much-loved places. Suardalan, *and* Mhic Bharraich, *and* Sgritheall; with such a combination our Hogmanay cup was filled to the brim and running over.

Section 11:   17. AM BATHACH   789 m   OS 33   073144
                  The byre

"All very sleepy including the driver so we have a break before Loch Cluanie dam. Jim was feeling unwell. Andrew and I set off from the inn at about 9.30 a.m. Back at 6.30 p.m. after a lazy, blazing, marvellous day. Rather than go up either flanking glen with the views shut in we went straight up Am Bathach, seeking out the odd scramble, and with the cloud rolling up ahead of us, a prelude to all the hills from Ciste Dhubh to Saileag. Our route up gave a grassy crest and fine views back along the loch, over to A' Chralaig and across to the old road snaking down from Tomdoun way."

That was the first paragraph of my log note of a day on the Cluanie Hills which gave a first visit to Am Bathach. Most guidebooks suggest approaching an east-west walk along the north Cluanie ridge by either the Caorann Mor or the Caorann Beag valleys but, for the reason given above, the Corbett is the better way. I was unaware of its Corbett status on that occasion. It just happened to be in the right place for an approach to some Munros — and that is a bonus which is paid all too rarely. (The Cluanie Inn is another.) Ascended on its own I'd be tempted to go up one of the valleys and traverse back along the crest for the sake of being ambushed by the views. The southern panorama is a good excuse for resting on the descent of what is a steep nose of a hill.

The road coming over from the south is an old military road (but not built by Wade) which continues down Glen Shiel and over Mam Ratagan to Glenelg's Bernera Barracks and Skye. It was fifteen years in the making (1770–84) and Johnson and Boswell saw the work in 1773. They saw soldiers working on the road and called it a "dreariness of solitude".

LOCH LOCHY & LOCH CLUANIE TO GLEN AFFRIC

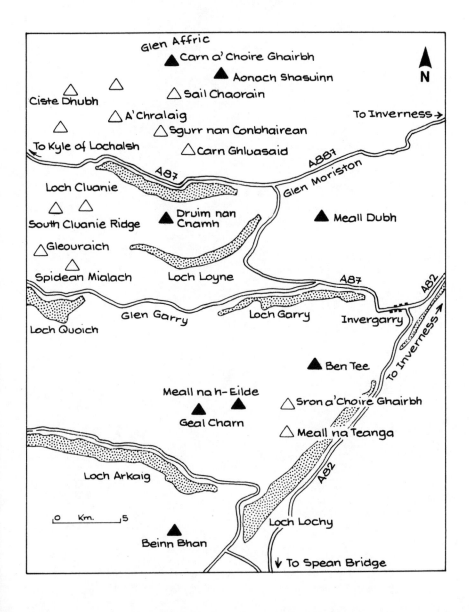

Section 12: 1. BEINN BHAN 796 m OS 34/41 141857
White hill (van)

THERE IS A perfectly easy way up Beinn Bhan from the south, but as nephew Colin, his mate Roddie and I were, ostensibly, canoeing up the Great Glen and just happened to be staying at Invermallie on Loch Arkaig, we climbed Beinn Bhan from the north. West of the Great Glen, northern slopes are often wickedly heathery low down — and this was no exception. A sticky hot day at the end of July was another drawback. The midges loved us.

To escape the swamping forestry we "burned up" into Coire Dubh right from the bothy, a long haul, indeed, but there was little water in the burn and we left its course only occasionally. Fallen tree-trunks frequently made good bridges and, as we sweated and puffed up, one of the lads commented that he felt like a cross between Tarzan and Richard Attenborough. We took the eastern stream in the corrie, which curved up to the summit edge, very welcome water. That was one benefit from our northern approach.

The best of Beinn Bhan's view is towards Ben Nevis and the Lochaber giants, and it was suddenly "opened to us" as we made our exit from corries almost at the trig point. We looked down on the Caledonian canal where we'd paddled up from Banavie the day before, a brilliant day which had turned on us after the portage from Clunes to Loch Arkaig, and gave the boys in their Canadian canoe "a new dimension of roughness" for the miles to Invermallie.

There was a breeze to chill our sweaty garments so we strode along over the two 771-m Tops to descend west of Coire Bhotrais. Horizontal deer tracks and red scars of "wash-outs" were frequent. Eventually the slope steepened for a midge infested, scrag and heather descent. Breaks in the trees were choked with bracken — and luscious clumps of blaeberry. I walked down the road stripping berries off their stems.

The normal approach which I'd used years before (and can remember very little about) is from Glen Loy. This has a minor motor-road up from the Banavie–Gairlochy B8004 which wiggles along linking Loch Linnhe and Loch Lochy. A couple of miles up the glen the road crosses the River Loy to its north bank. Walk up a side track to deserted Inverskilavulin and wander up the slopes above, east of Coire Mhuilinn, to the flat summit area. The circuit of Coire Mhuilinn would make an enjoyable high-level scenic promenade and vary the route as well. The ascent is still quite a slog.

If private transport can be arranged a good two day west–east tramp could be made from Fassfern on Loch Eil: day one being up to Glensulaig bothy and climbing Meall a' Phubuill and day two the long descent of Glen Loy and climbing Beinn Bhan on the way.

Section 12: 2. GEAL CHARN 804 m OS 34 156943
White hill

Section 12: 3. MEALL NA H-EILDE 838 m OS 34 185946
Hill of the hinds (eilid)

Maybe those who complain to me about changes in the *Tables* of Munros or Corbetts, as if it was my fault, will feel better if they knew that such changes can be as inconvenient to me as they are to them. These hills are a case in point.

With Kitchy, I traversed the then Corbett Meall Coire Saobhaidh and Geal Charn, our planned longer day over these hills being shortened by heavy snow conditions underfoot. I was not pleased when the first of these hills was struck off the register and replaced by Meall na h-Eilde next door, forcing a return, and yielding yet another dreich sort of day for the ascent, along with the newly acquired Storm.

Meall an Tagraidh, the hill east of Meall na h-Eilde, saw Bonnie Prince Charlie seeking refuge on it for several days and nights. Cameron of Clunes managed to take up some whisky and bread and cheese, and a fire was lit for half an hour. By day they lay on the summit, wrapped in plaids in the rain.

The first visit gave some views, at least, with only the Ben staying cloud-covered. The sun turned the considerable snow cover into porridge, however, and long before the path (now a bulldozed track) up the Allt Dubh ran out we abandoned all idea of circling everything up there with a descent by Gleann Cia-aig. That still waits for "next time" and there is also the temptation of Glas Bheimn which must be an even better viewpoint than Geal Charn for looking along Loch Arkaig, one of the west's most pleasing lochs.

Meall na h-Eilde was squeezed in with a work party visit to our local club's bothy near Glenelg. With several hundredweight of cement, tools and furniture in the Dormobile there was no way I could sleep in it, so I decided to spend the night at Invermallie Bothy on the south shore of Loch Arkaig. As I hadn't checked on the bothy I made a couple of mistakes: the first was cycling in — the road is a big dipper of wickedly sharp stones; the second was not checking Invermallie's exact location — I pedalled all the way up the glen to discover the bothy was a ruin. Dark by then, Storm and I survived a night tucked in under the rafters on the few feet of loft flooring that remained. I took the dog up Gulvain the next day and then we dropped down to the real Invermallie Bothy, superb in every way. A bird cherry hangs over the house, and seed from that tree has yielded me several small trees now flourishing in friends' gardens from Leicester to Aviemore. Howard Ashton, maintenance organiser of Invermallie, had a gang of us there to celebrate his last Munro, which was one way of acquiring a work party. I've a grand photo of Howard and Jim Cosgrove on top of Meall na Teanga in the rain.

As I still had to deliver my load to Suardalan Bothy I could only afford the morning for Meall na h-Eilde. I'm not really complaining but next time I want those hills by their northern approaches. I've had enough of the Allt Dubh. Perhaps they would make a good traverse at the start of a future Ultimate Challenge. Some of the routes put in for that event seem quite illogical and devious (days heading west, for instance), until you realise the motive is the linking of Munros and/or Corbetts.

There are some excellent stalkers' paths on the northern side, and wooded Loch Garry is as fine as Loch Arkaig while, westwards, the view into the country of Streap and the Rough Bounds is very grand indeed. These hills teem with deer and I've seen blackcock at their *lek*, others in the snow, and ospreys in their fastness. Perhaps the wildlife and emptiness are the special treats of this area but at what a price: a list of "vermin" destroyed in Glengarry early last century included "198 wild cats, 246 pine martins, 67 badgers, 48 otters, 78 merlins, 63 harriers, 27 white-tailed sea eagles, 18 ospreys, 63 goshawks, 371 rough-legged buzzards, 275 kites, 38 owls . . .'

Section 12:   4. BEN TEE   901 m   OS 34   241972
              The fairy hillock

Just what Ben Tee means is lost in the garbling of the original Gaelic. I've seen it given as coming from *tighe*, meaning "house" as well as *sidhean* meaning "fairy hillock". Both occur frequently in place names. I wonder if skiers rushing off up Glen *Shee* realise they're away with the fairies? The derivation has also been given as *di*, "the mountain of God". Whatever the name means, Ben Tee is one of the best of Corbetts, perhaps not to be bagged so much as potted.

In the sixties, when I used to have school parties climbing and canoeing from Loch Lochy Youth Hostel, we came to know the area quite well. Ben Tee's symmetrical cone became one of those instantly-recognisable summits, the Great Glen's answer to Schiehallion — which is another "fairy hill", of course, and backs up that derivation for Ben Tee. Because of the kids' endless Munro-bagging Meall na Teanga and Sron a' Choire Ghairbh received the brunt of youthful excursions. The only time the kids did Ben Tee I was laid low with flu so, while kindly Mrs Fraser nursed me, the boys went off on their own. The responsibility made a memorable day for them and I was regaled with their stories for months afterwards.

They'd made what is probably the standard approach, starting from Laggan Locks and rounding to the Kilfinnan Burn, seeing the falls, and then making a gradual rising line to reach the east ridge. There is some rough going on the lower moorland. Tidy-minded Munroists can also add the Corbett to their pair, continuing along Meall a' Choire Ghlais, down its north ridge, and straight up Ben Tee (a steep haul) to descend by this easiest-of-all route. A decade after our regular hostel parties I was rewarded by an ascent of the hill.

I escaped from Fife after a frustrating morning in the office and drove up to the Great Glen and set off at 5 p.m. This was on 20 June, one day off the longest day. I wanted to see the Kilfinnan Falls (a small bridal veil) so didn't keep high above the east bank which is the easiest line; but then I was lured on to follow up the gorge above the falls. Forcing the gorge took extra hours, was good fun, and I had a couple of intentional dips and one which was not planned. Luckily I was scrambling along wearing only shorts. It was 7.30 before I emerged at the top of the wood. I steamed up Ben Tee, keeping my eyes firmly on the ground until the summit was reached and then drinking deep of the 360-degree panorama.

The view was tonal rather than colourful, my perch utterly restful and quiet, after the uphill labour, a visual, spiritual counterpart to Beethoven's 6th symphony after the thunderstorm. Sgurr na Ciche was the most eye-catching of the sprawl of peaks to the west. Ben Nevis was a familiar cut-out shape, only in mirror-image, being more often seen from the south. Ben Tee is a particularly fine viewpoint as there is such a mighty outlook to the west. The converse also holds true, and from peaks like the Streaps, or those round Glen Kingie or Loch Quoich, the cone of Ben Tee is always a notable feature. From Faichem, or from along the shores of Loch Garry, Ben Tee rises in bold symmetry. Its colourful woodland must have attracted thousands of photographers without the viewer knowing what he is looking at. The name, for once, is easy to remember, Ben Tee being easier on the tongue of memory than Meallan Liath Coire Mhic Dhughaill or Sgurr Cos na Breachd-laoidh. The summit of Ben Tee was, anciently, known as Glengarry's Bowling Green. A local belief had it that Glengarry Castle was built of stone from the brow of Ben Tee, the rocks being passed, man to man, the seven miles down the hill. Pochin Mould in *Roads from the Isles* (the best book on old drove roads and tracks) singles out Ben Tee as being an exceptional viewpoint.

I descended by reedy Lochan Diota with the hills to the east of the Great Glen putting on nightcap clouds and the view up to lonely Coire Glas streaked with shafts of primrose light from the setting sun, calling to mind the primroses which had been flowering right up to the 2,000-foot level. The evening walk was rich in flora, from creeping azalea on high, through cloudberry moors with lousewort, cudweed, tormentil, milkwort, ladies' mantles, to the hyacinth-scented woods below. I squelched across the moor and down to the locks in the gloaming.

The other obvious approach to Ben Tee I took in May 1977 when walking from Sgurr na Banachdich to Mount Keen. The day was so appallingly hot that the two Munros were left well alone. I'd slept out in the heather the night before and started brewing at four o'clock in the first tweek of day, amid the hubbub of a blackcock *lek*, so had to watch that weird dance for a bit before wandering off along to Greenfield and the right-of-way up the Allt Ladaidh. By eight o'clock I was sweltering up to the Bealach Easan. The most notable object seen from the summit was a cloud. The OS is a bit over-generous with the marsh symbols. There are some peat hags but nothing very unusual. I cut corners to drop down to the locks quickly. The tearoom produced three Cokes and a pot of tea while I sat outside watching the idyllic *Wind in the Willows* life on the canal. I then crawled into the shade and slept for three hours till hostel-opening time.

Section 12   5. MEALL DUBH   788 m   OS 34   245078
         Black hill (myowl-doo)

Just how slavishly we are held by the bigger hills is shown by the fact that this hill and the next, Druim nan Cnamh, do not receive even a passing mention in the latest SMC district guide. Apparently there is nothing of note from Cluanie to the Great Glen, which is ridiculous: these two Corbetts have given me memorable days, and Meall Dubh has one of the country's finest summit views.

These two and Ben Tee, equally fine, were done one June when my real activity was canoeing in the west, a month of broiling heat and periodic storms. Some rams bumping the Dormobile woke me and we set off from the car park near the dam of Loch Loyne, back of eight.

Garbh Dhoire (*rough wood*) was all too apt but, by a mix of fresh track, a burn, and crawling under a deer fence, old Kitchy and I reached the moors. The cairn has a double view: through Garry–Kingie way and through to Cluanie. The Streaps, Gairich, Sgurr-Mor, Sgurr na Ciche, Spidean-Gleouraich, the South Shiel Ridge, the North Shiel Ridge, the Conbhairean hills, Affric, Farrar hills were all displayed. Meallfuarvonie, the impossible country east of Loch Ness, the pylons of the Corrieyairack, Glen Spean hills, Grey Corries, Ben Nevis, Ben Tee and its Munros, the Arkaig Corbetts, Gulvain, far Ardgour complete the circle. Wyvis was the most distant recognisable peak. That is not a bad selection.

We lingered by the cairn for an hour and then ambled west through a scattering of lochans before regretfully turning down to the car. There was some lively Scottish dance music on the radio and my delight obviously had the better of me. I performed a sword dance over imaginary weapons beside the car. When I collapsed, out of breath, there was polite applause. I looked up the bank to see two car-loads of German tourists.

That rough western approach is the obvious one but I was determined to revisit "Dubh of the View", as I'll always think of the hill, as soon as possible and to traverse it "properly". ASAP turned out to be a wait from 1973 to 1986, when I linked it to Druim nan Cnamh, the next Corbett. They were both traversed in one day, from Cluanie Inn to Loch Oich.

Section 12:   6. Druim nan Cnamh   790 m   OS 34   131077
              Bony ridge (krav)

This hill was earmarked for a possible canoe-assault long before I had the motivation of Corbetting. When a gang of us were based on a Lundie camp for a few days I was able to make my "raid". There was only a mile to paddle across and I climbed up Coire Beithe, reduced to boots and pants, to keep near water. I came down the corrie's western arm and then cut in to enjoy a long swim in a pool I'd passed going up. A squall on the way back churned the loch to foam and this proved the start of another weather tantrum. A canoe was a most useful aid for this Corbett for, otherwise, access yields a certain frustration.

Thirteen years passed before I returned to Cnamh. I had started in Glenelg and had a very flexible first few days as we hoped to go high and stay high all the way from Sgurr Mhic Bharraich to the Great Glen (after all, several people had suffered heat stroke on the Cluanie Ridge the year before). The rain belted down, all day and for days on end.

We sneaked over Mam Ratagan and plodded up to the Cluanie Inn, that ancient haven of drovers' days, which took in Challengers like boat-people. As Tony and I had booked a B & B by Loch Oich for the next night, and were meeting friends in Glen Roy the day after (see 9:4, 5), we were concerned in case we could not proceed — there are limits. The next day, however, was "only raining" so, well fed, we set off for Cnamh on what is probably the easiest pedestrian route.

After an hour of steady plodding we reached the top of the old Road to the Isles. In very dry summers the old bridge over the River Loyne rises out of the water of the loch in a weird resurrection. Not today, though. At the pass we were able to take off our waterproofs and, after honey sandwiches, we plunged into the peat bog and river braes that defend the mountain.

Druim means ridge and Druim nan Cnamh strictly speaking is misappropriated as a name for the summit. As we toiled up the slopes we set off deer, golden plovers, a hare and then ptarmigan, the last whirred away with rude noises into the gathering clouds. We cringed below the stark, round, trig point only long enough to force in some food and check the compass bearing, then we fled as fast as the rough going would allow.

On a half-decent day it would be best to stay high and traverse Beinn Loinne, the real centre of these hills between Loch Cluanie and Loch Loyne, but we were glad to slither down poggy snow beneath the peak and skirt round to descend the Allt Coire na Creadha. This took us below the level of cloud and rain. We crossed the river high up (in case it was impassable lower down) and just linked odd deer tracks in a long, gradually descending traverse line to reach the Loch Loyne dam. We saw only one stag — which cantered off in a great splashy run across the sodden slopes.

Given helpful transport this traverse, in either direction, would make a good walk. Perhaps east-west would be better as the craggy eastern end of the ridge is then taken in ascent. The day gives ten rough miles. The rain was following us down. We therefore passed below the dam and took shelter *under* the A87 which crosses the Allt Garbh-dhoire on high stilts, a dry but draughty howff. We brewed, had hot apple flakes, Alpen and other goodies and at 2.30 p.m. set off on another day's walking, for Meall Dubh (12:5). After five minutes we had to stop and don all our waterproofs. I had my brolly which, with a back wind, allowed me to walk with my top half open. Once the clawing heather level was passed the going was quite good, though with sopping feet we were not very fussy. We made a steady rising line all the way. The last bit was on that "dead" ground which had just lost its winter snow covering. There is a second big cairn along from the highest one. The summit area is all rather knobbly and, as soon as we arrived, the weather really let rip.

My fingers holding the compass went numb as we navigated over a succession of mist-exaggerated bumps, and there was a certain relief in finding that an ancient fence and a boundary on the map were in agreement. We scurried down the rocky eastern ridge to a col. The cloud cleared a bit and we could see the Great Glen at last, with the distinctive shape of Ben Tee thrusting up out of boiling blackness. We descended, waterproofs off again, on another gentle traverse which took us to the Allt Lundie. This was another feature which had caught the eye years before. In about a mile of river the map has nine strokes and three verbal indications of waterfall. Ours was an excellent day for visiting waterfalls.

After the roar and clamour of the impressive riverside descent, mirror-still Loch Lundie was quite a contrast. The trees and green verges were reflected in its *dubh* waters. There were two possible tracks down to the Great Glen; we took the northern sweep by the Invervigar Burn to avoid any A82 walking and in just over an hour we reached the northern end of Loch Oich. It was 9 p.m. We'd been out for 13 hours. Before the UC walk I'd left an evening meal there as I was not sure just what accommodation we'd be using, or if an evening meal would be possible for our late arrival. We ate before doing the last mile to the B & B. The brolly proved quite useful again as we huddled underneath it waiting for our haggis to heat on a slowly-dying gaz stove . . .

Section 12: 7. CARN A' CHOIRE GHAIRBH   863 m
OS 34 & 25   137189
The cairn of the rough corrie (garve)

Section 12: 8. AONACH SHASUINN   889 m   OS 34 & 25   173180
The height of the Englishman (onach sassun)

I've linked these two together because they can be done in combination quite reasonably from the Glen Affric side, a walk giving varied and majestic scenery. The public motor road ends at the car park by Loch Beinn a' Mheadhoin (Benevian) as shown on Sheet 25. Walk west, then cross to the south side of the glen to take the path up the Allt Garbh, which rises about 450 m to a junction, joining what is now a Land Rover track for the continuation up the glen. Aonach Shasuinn can be climbed thereafter and the ridge followed over An Elric and Carn a' Choire Ghuirm to Carn a' Choire Ghairbh. Descend by the stalkers' path west of Coire Crom to the end of Loch Affric or the one off Cnapain back to the Allt Garbh.

Carn a' Choire Ghairbh was one of the Corbetts that was netted with my Munros-in-one haul. I was staying at Glen Affric Youth Hostel (Alltbeithe) and made the strenuous round of the Mullach–A' Chralaig–Conbhairean Munros, five of them, with Tigh Mor na Seilge then still the Munro before Sail Chaorainn superseded it. Carn a' Choire Ghairbh was simply a continuation of the circuit. I'd been on Aonach Shasuinn the year before so omitted it on this occasion. Little Loch a' Choinich had dried out into a black smudge with the heat. Looking up to Carn a' Choire Ghairbh from below there was a big cairn visible, but this is not the summit which is further on, on the more northerly of the two bumps. The lie of the land led me down westwards — into plantings which were not on the map. They are, now; and a line can be made to the gap which leads to the estate road down Gleann na Ciche to Loch Affric. With the bogs so dry I cut all the corners to gain the hostel track as soon as possible. If based on the hostel I'd prefer to climb up by the path at the west end of Loch Affric and, after linking the Corbetts, drop directly into Gleann na Ciche from Loch a' Choinich to avoid the plantings altogether.

Aonach Shasuinn had also been climbed on a hot day, with a party of friends from Inverness, Aberfeldy, Edinburgh and Adelaide! This was a round of the Conbhairean Munros for some and a Prince Charlie's Cave hunt as well. We left Mike's car at the Ceannacroc road-end and drove along to Lundie for the good track that twists up on to Ghluasaid. Even at the end of May there were big rims of snow along from Conbhairean to Tigh Mor. The Munroists went Top-bagging while three of us went down to look for the cave — which is really a boulder-shelter. By plugging the gap and laying heather on the floor we made quite a snug howff. Historically the Prince stayed for a week in a cave or caves in this area, but there are several contenders for the site besides the one shown on the map.

The next day the Munroists set off for A' Chralaig and the Mullach, to be met at Cluanie Inn, while the rest of us wandered up to Beinn an Iomaire to study the corrie for other cave possibilities and then skirted in and out to the top of Gleann Fada. From the col at its head easy walking led up Aonach Shasuinn. We had a noble view of all the big Affric hills, and Ben Nevis stood boldly to the south. The day was hot with blue skies and blue hills. We went on over Carn a' Choire Bhuidhe and down into Coire Dho. Conbhairean opposite was a snow-flanked cone, the centre of a big, balanced panorama. We had the first swim of the year before walking down to the car on the Glen Moriston road.

APPLECROSS & TORRIDON

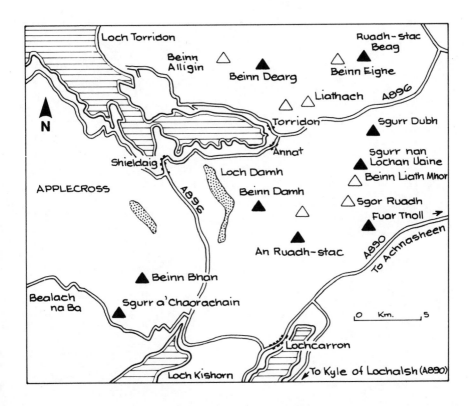

Section 13:   1. SGURR A' CHAORACHAIN   792 m   OS 24   797417
           Peak of the little field of berries

Section 13:   2. BEINN BHAN   896 m   OS 24   804450
           White hill

"IT HAS EVERY attribute of hell except its warmth", was one climber's first reaction to seeing Beinn Bhan on a wild winter's day.

More than one "off day" from Gerry's hostel in Glen Carron (see p. 7) has seen a group of us motoring round Applecross. This secretive western corner often stays dry or showery while the Atlantic weather pours in overhead to let loose on the big Applecross hills or the Torridons. Good rainbow country is Applecross.

When we had climbed all the local Munros or Corbetts, Dave, Jim and I, regulars at Gerry's towards the end of the year, were more or less forced to head for Applecross. The weather was unsettled but we went nevertheless. And we went early — no mean feat on 31 December.

We drove round by Kishorn to park at Tornapress at the head of the loch, usually noisy with oystercatchers and covered with nodding heads of thrift, rather forlorn this grey dawn. From Kishorn on up the road past the Rassal oakwood there are spectacular views of the stratified cliff-faces and corries that make Applecross special. The cliffs are so ferocious that there are still only a few winter climbs recorded. Even the Torridons don't produce such vertical walls. Being salvationists we had no intention of climbing anything serious but we still wanted to nose about the corries of Beinn Bhan. We set off from the head of the loch up the stalkers' path shown on Sheet 24.

There is a whole array of corries: Coire Each, *horse corrie*; Coire na Feola, *corrie of blood*; Coire na Poite (with its twin lochans), *corrie of the pot*; Coire an Fhamhair, *the giants' corrie*; Coire Toll a' Bhein, *corrie of the hole in the skin*; Coire Gorm Beag, *little blue corrie*. Corrie na Feola is the first steep, deep one, with the prow of Beinn Bhan's A' Chioch (*nose*) jutting out as its north arm. We cut round under it (looking down on Lochan Coire na Poite) after investigating a bifurcation of streams low on the burn from Coire Each. This split in the stream is shown accurately on the map, unlike others I've checked. The most accessible of such features is on the northern slopes of Chno Dearg by Loch Treig and there's another at the west end of Loch Quoich — anything but accessible.

Coire na Poite is a deep rock cauldron. Oddly one of its lochans was completely frozen over while the other remained clear. Could there be warm springs or was it some freak chance? The head of the corrie soared up, featureless and ice-draped, into cloud while the sweep out to A' Chioch presented a series of buttresses and gullies: routes galore. On the other (north) side the lower prow of A' Poite had a level ridge connecting with a stepped ridge vanishing towards the plateau above. We continued on steep but firm snow, half hoping it would allow us up easily. Being a grade IV climb we did not go further. We also went to the A' Chioch col. The ridge from there to the top was first climbed in winter by Tom Patey and Joe Brown. We crept round to Coire an Fhamhair.

The NW corner of this corrie is free of cliffs and, apart from some icy slabs, we ascended quickly. The upper part of the A' Poite ridge drops in bold perpendicular fashion, a superwall with no chinks in its armour. (One can appreciate such features fully when there is no risk of having to try to climb them.) Before exiting on to the plateau we ate and muffled up in extra layers. We could just see the corniced edge so followed this rim along to Beinn Bhan, the highest summit in Applecross.

We carefully took bearings, counted steps, recorded time, etc., to steer accurately down to the Bealach nan Arr, the fine pass which separates the sprawling Corbetts. Coire Attadale to the north is a deer sanctuary: loch-splattered and defended by miles of cliff. Coire nan Arr to the south runs down to the sea at the oil-rig construction yard, now closed, but the site still waiting to be returned to the original state as agreed when it was opened.

Applecross was a human sanctuary in pre-Reformation times and was the site of one of the earliest Christian settlements, founded by St Maelrubha in 672. The crofts on the coast and the empty hinterland are the result of more modern Clearances. The link road along the north coast has done something to alleviate the isolation. As we'd discovered often enough, the Bealach na Ba can frequently be closed in winter, being over 2,000 feet in height. The road was originally planned to reach Toscaig by the coast but the elderly ladies who owned the land refused to allow this easy route.

Corbett, writing of a winter visit in the Thirties, commented that Applecross was an easy place to reach but not so easy to escape from. A boat from Kyle to Stornoway dropped him off into a rowing boat in the afternoon and he was told the exit was the same boat, same schedule, i.e., Kyle via Stornoway! Or he "rode St Francis' pony" over the Bealach na Ba. There were only Gaelic services held in the church. His first hill had a name he could not pronounce and the locals could not write, so it goes unrecorded. Sgurr a' Chaorachain became *Scoor a Hurricane*. Even Corbett had to work for his Corbetts.

We were tempted just to turn down Coire nan Arr, but there was also a certain pleasure in the navigational challenge, and there was a Corbett to be claimed. Both hills have long plateaux of very broken sandstone, sometimes detached blocks from areas of paving, but always unusually rough and reducing our speed. Why a *white hill* is made of *red* sandstone is a puzzle. Cairns led down to the col but we preferred to trust our own navigation (the cairns could go anywhere). The white flat area marking the lochan before the final pull up Sgurr a' Chaorachain gave us one certain position and from it a careful bearing led to the North Summit. A piece of linoleum sticking out the snow was an oddity — and then we found the top had some communications structures on top. They rather spoilt the polar exploration atmosphere.

Chaorachain (the OS spelling is a printing error) has a deep cauldron corrie facing east, with a minute tarn embedded in it, but the best-known feature is the terminal prow of its northern arm, A' Chioch. Norman Collie was the first to climb it, followed by Slingsby, Ling and Glover, J. H. B. Bell and others, but it is the "Cioch Nose" (Patey and Bonington, 1961) which has become one of the great sandstone classics. The southern spur of the corrie bulges out as a huge, obese buttress and has the Corbett on top of it, reached by a crest full of ups and downs which we found very tiring in the mixture of softening snow and the ambushing ice under it. Dave slipped and nearly knocked himself out and Jim left a blood spoor from a nose bleed, quite a useful help in backtracking from the summit cairn. We saw nothing and were still on compass bearings when we hit the Bealach na Ba road. "God help the poor cows", someone muttered.

The time was 4.15 and we quickly cut the corners of the 1-in-3 hairpin bends to tramp down in the cloudy gloom. Deer, like shadows, crossed the road, and the dark edge of Meall Gorm was stark against the satiny shimmer of Loch Kishorn. We were sitting round the fire, well fed, malts in hand, dreaming the year away when Dave looked up from the MacInnes walks guide to quote: "It should be noted that in the event of snow, or high winds, these high routes should be avoided."

Section 13:   3. BEINN DAMH   902m   OS 24/25   893502
             Hill of the stag (dav)

After a fairly cheerless day on Beinn Dearg (Just a few miles away) Beinn Damh gave me "a day among thousands" which I almost missed by sleeping-in at our comfy base at Glen Cottage under Liathach. I set off alone from the Beinn Damh Hotel by Loch Torridon.

A gate just west of the Allt Coire Roill bridge led to a path up through some splendid Torridonian forest. The track was well constructed for the tramp right up Coire Roill to the tiny lochan on the Drochaid Coire Roill, the col at the head of the valley.

Most guidebooks suggest ascending Beinn Damh by a branch path not far above the tree-line, and so along the ridge, but this then presents some awkward choices for the descent, assuming one is going to make a traverse and not just backtrack.

It is much more practical to go the other way round. The walk up Coire Roill gives a grand view of the tiered Torridonian cliffs of the east face, there is a sudden opening of the view from the col, and the route up to the summit can be studied from below a great deal more easily than trying to wiggle a route down such a maze of ledges, walls and screes. The way up looks impressive, too, especially once up the first spur above the col, for this spur leads to a corrie, not a ridge as one would expect. The two arms of the corrie are rocky prows, the northern angled across the spur down to the col. My log recorded: "Nice easy scrambling compared to yesterday [Beinn Dearg (13:4)] but equally a 'summer' ascent even if early January. Sandstone gave way to quartzite on the summit crag."

Being aware of what was happening weather-wise I carefully refrained from looking at the view. Picking a scrambling line up made that fairly easy, of course. At the summit I lifted my eyes to the hills. Fantastic! Beinn Damh was the bastion holding back a white, surging sea of cloud which stretched away over the eastern horizon and onto which a sun of molten magnificence set the blaze of white into spectrum brilliance. I sat on the cairn for over an hour, spellbound. All the hills to the east rose like dark islands out of the cloud-sea. Strangely, Torridon was clear and its giant hills stood pale and flat. Even as I watched the cliffs of Applecross were attacked by waves of vapour and slowly these overwhelmed the bluffs like a rising tide.

If driving round from Lochcarron village, have a look from Loch an Loin and you'll see why the map names the "Stirrup Mark" just below the summit. Loch an Loin is a pleasant alternative start/finish to a traverse of the Corbett, using the path up Strath a' Bhathaich, while a low-level-bad-weather-alternative of interest is to circumnavigate the hill: hotel, Coire Roill, Strath a' Bhathaich, Doire Damh, hotel — naturally ending back at the hotel. Thoughts of refreshment *in* the Beinn Damh stirred me from my sun-smitten perch *on* Beinn Damh.

I took some pleasure in kicking down a line of fatuous cairns along the perfectly obvious ridge. (Cairnomaniacs are leaving their mark all over Torridon.) Two figures were coming up the steep ascent and gave good scale to the clouds behind, already licking over the double col to Sgurr na Bana Mhoraire, the end top of Beinn Damh above Loch Torridon. On the col there was a flitting glimpse of a brocken spectre before the milky coldness of the inversion obliterated the magic. After picking up the path I danced back down to the Dormobile, quickly re-loaded the cameras, and drove round till dark, making the most of the glory given. Sunset lit Slioch like a torch and then plunged the peak into the black waters of night.

Section 13:   4. BEINN DEARG   914 m   OS 19/24   895608
The red hill (jarrak)

Beinn Dearg had the misfortune, in prehistoric measurements, to be 2,998 feet and, in the change over to the sloppier metres, there was a great searching of decimals before it was finally allowed to rest as a Corbett. Quite a few Munroists climb it "just in case". As Beinn Teallach showed, promotion to Munro status has the same effect as throwing a bone to a pack of hounds. Beinn Dearg had a near escape so can now, hopefully, return to its shadowy "fourth man" position, hidden behind the big bad boys of Beinn Eighe, Liathach and Beinn Alligin. The SMC will — eventually — tidy the awkwardnesses and anomalies in the Corbett list.

The peak is split awkwardly between 1:50,000 sheets numbers 19 and 24 but because of its complex and serious nature it would be worth obtaining the 1:25,000 Outdoor Leisure Map "The Cuillin and Torridon Hills", which will also be useful for the other local Corbetts (see 15:1–4) and also for the Skye pair. For no obvious reason the *Tables* separate Beinn Dearg from other nearby Corbetts and, as some points will apply "equally to all", the following notes could be helpful.

A traverse of Beinn Dearg has something of the feel of traversing the two Munros of Liathach except Dearg has rough red sandstone rather than cold grey quartzite. The Corbett, too, is a peak demanding a head for heights. It is most easily approached by the Coire Mhic Nobuil path, and from that route the peak fills the view ahead, its many-tiered defences giving the more sedate walker some concern. This comes out in all accounts I've read of the peak. Even the restrained SMC district guide states, "The south and west sides rise in a continuous precipitous escarpment which at first glance seems impregnable", but quickly adds, "Fortunately, the walls are breached in several places by rock gullies and, while these offer a way on to the summit ridge with varying degrees of difficulty, caution should be exercised at all times . . . in adverse weather (or winter) this is not a hill for an inexperienced party." My one and only ascent was made one January through thick cloud when I was occasionally quite glad not to be seeing too much.

Like most of these hills of Torridonian sandstone a view uphill makes the slope appear all rock, while the view down appears all grass or heather — the basic cause of many troubles, especially in descent when only the horizontal terraces show and the vertical bands of rock are hidden. Worked into this horizontal world of wall and terrace are plenty of vertical lines of weakness caused by the eroding streams. A route will usually "go" by using a gully for much of the time but period-ically moving out on to the terraces. Safety lies in choosing a line suitable for one's capabilities. On both sides of the barrel-shaped bulk facing Coire Mhic Nobuil there are plenty of gullies to choose from, but I'd use the bridge and go up the Bealach a' Chomhla path to where it crosses the Allt a' Bhealaich and then continue on the *east* bank, taking any one of the tributaries to its gully source on Beinn Dearg. The steep teasing-up of a route then follows, the angle eventually falling back on to a relatively bare summit area. There is a big cairn, as if someone were determined the hill must pass the 3,000-foot barrier.

During the walk in, have a good look at the possibilities and also note the rocky prow that juts out to the right below the summit dome. This is the hang gliders' route off. Plenty of walkers stray on to it but the real way crosses a pinnacle more to the north — the line is shown on the map by the NTS boundary — and this is the only scrambly bit on the traverse eastwards. Stuc Loch na Cabhaig and Carn na Feola are both worth a visit for they are great prows thrusting into the Empty Quarter northwards. Oddly, I've met no descriptions of ascents from the north, and if a cross-country Corbett expedition is being made on that side, as suggested in 15:1–4, then that is the time and place to add Beinn Dearg. The Stuc is far more accessible on its eastern flank, and a south–north line down into Coire Beag from the lowest point on the ridge would be a simple descent by Torridon standards. To descend to the south, return to this lowest point and head just south of east, and the dip of the rocks will lead you down quite naturally. The gullies falling south from the main summit are sometimes suggested as descent routes but they are better left for the more experienced, being steep and tricky at times. Glen Torridon can be gained by finishing off the "circumnavigation" of Liathach by the Coire Dubh path.

Brenda Macrow, who lived in Torridon for some years, wrote a book *Torridon Highlands* which perfectly captures the feel of the area in the early 1950s, when corned beef and "Pom" in Inveralligin Hostel, reached after a sail from Shieldaig, would be the prelude to a good going sing-song round the fire. She and some friends climbed Beinn Dearg and their story is worth reading both for some practical information and to capture the special atmosphere of this mountain. They gained the summit from the east and commented how, glancing back, they were amazed at the wild beauty and seeming difficulty of the ridge they had traversed. This mix of threat and treat really sets Beinn Dearg aside as a Corbett for the more experienced walker. The Macrow day ended with a typical Torridon escapade: descending to the Bealach a' Chomhla.

"The gully was thick with wet grass, and we slid for a while beside the course of a stream. Then outcrops of rock appeared — the stream cascaded through a deepening chasm, and we ran into a little difficulty which was increased by the unbalancing tendency displayed by our rucksacks. A loose stone started a landslide just in front of us. It went with a terrific roar down the gully, drowning the rush of the waterfall. With one accord, we forsook our chimney and scrambled on to the left-hand spur, where we rested and 'recovered' before completing the last, and easiest, stage of the descent. Looking up from the bottom, we could hardly believe that we had managed it without mishap, for it looked almost perpendicular."

LOCH DUICH–GLEN AFFRIC NORTH TO STRATH BRAN

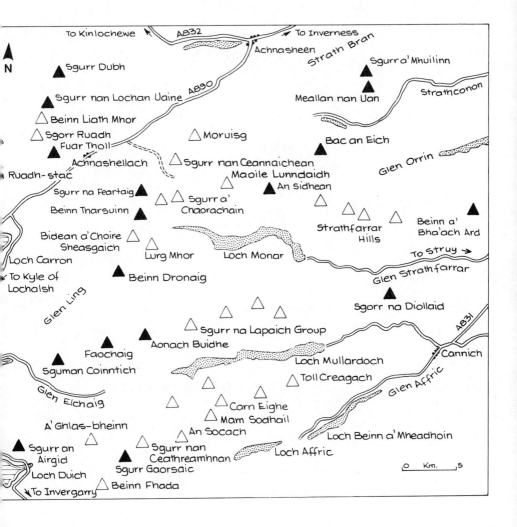

Section 14: 1. SGURR GAORSAIC *c*.838 m OS 33 036219
Peak of the thrill or horror (goresac)

SEVERAL TIMES I'VE approached, or descended from, Sgurr nan Ceathreamhnan without going up Sgurr Gaorsaic. I always meant to, even before this dome became a Corbett in the new listings, but either I'd run out of time, or steam, or the weather would pack in. When I finally climbed Sgurr Gaorsaic it was on a foul day, from Loch Duich, and the rewards were few. I missed out Gaorsaic again, even as I was compiling these Corbett accounts. In mid–May 1987, during the Ultimate Challenge, I had a grand solo day over An Socach, Mullach na Dheiragain and Sgurr nan Ceathreamhnan and had every intention of adding Sgurr Gaorsaic but, perched on the Alpamayo-like snow peak of Ceathreamhnan, one look at the West Top ruled out any hope of the Corbett beyond. Cornices and big snow sweeps made it far too risky without an ice-axe.

At the Alltbeithe hostel that night I raved about the view and then, just a few minutes later, someone else, quite independently, praised the view from Sgurr Gaorsaic. Everyone expects mighty Ceathreamhnan to have a view. Only those who ken the Corbetts know they always, well nearly always, are good viewpoints as well. I was pleased to have such a confirmation. The current SMC guidebook only mentions the Corbett in suggesting the best way round it to reach Ceathreamhnan.

My favourite way to Gaorsaic is an evening "descent" to it from the big Munro, which an earlier SMC guide highly recommends. The view then is quite something with Skye and Sgriol and all manner of good things showing boldly in the golden west. Some day, *Insh 'Allah*, I'd like to camp — or bivvy — by the summit tarn and see the sun go down from that high place. And the flat summit would be the perfect spot for a hockey match.

This Corbett is a strangely symmetrical bump, tacked on to a big neighbour, and jutting out into the furthest west end of Glen Affaric, as Glen Affric is known locally. At one time you could obtain permission to drive up Glen Elchaig to the A. E. Robertson memorial bridge and approach via the Falls of Glomach and the Abhainn Gaorsaic, but the foreign owners have forbidden this of late. There is still a good alternative expedition from Dorusduain, situated in from the head of Loch Duich. The Belach an Sgairne (Gates of Affric) is fine in its own right as well as for what it leads to. One winter I was greatly assisted by having Loch a' Bhealaich frozen and I walked over the ice as an easy option to floundering round. Gleann Gaorsaic tends to be peaty. The Corbett can be ascended from any direction, really. After traversing Sgurr Gaorsaic, the Falls of Glomach can be visited and a return made over the Bealach na Sroine. Good paths in and out make up for Gleann Gaorsaic. The Corbett could also be combined with as many local Munros as heroes care to add or it could be taken in on the way to, or from, Alltbeithe, the "iron lodge" that is one of Scotland's genuine, old-fashioned, primitive hostels (the hostel is left open out of season). As only those who have walked will be staying there, good company is normal.

Section 14:   2. SGURR AN AIRGID   841 m   OS 25/33   940227
              The silver peak

This is a quick and easy Corbett, but that does not make the hill any less of a "good thing". Airgid is another of my Hogmanay hills and the last time I climbed it was typical of the chancy nature of the Hogmanay mountain game. We set off from our Glenelg bothy base to climb Ciste Dhubh north of the Cluanie Inn and, instead, went up this hill above Loch Duich. No doubt many other gangs moderated their plans that day, at least those in a condition to be summit-bound on the first of January. As Byron said:

> "Let us have wine and women, mirth and laughter,
> Sermons and soda-water the day after."

It was our day after!

We had had rain on top of rain for days and days. The ground was sodden and we were weary of splashing about in our wellies. Kintail doesn't have a climate so much as a roulette wheel of various weathers. The tail-end of the 7.55 a.m. forecast told of blizzards sweeping in from the east — which was the end of plans for the bigger hills. They were too far away, too high, and bad in east winds. The neglected cars (and dogs), however, needed some exercise. We decided to chance Mam Ratagan and nip up Sgurr an Airgid, the near but neglected cousin of Kintail.

A pause on top of the Mam showed the peak well, but the Five Sisters were smothered in cloud and the glower of snow shone down the glens under the mantle of the dark. There was no time to waste. From a road verge in Glen Croe we set off up the hill direct, soon joining the pony track that wends back and forth on the steep south side before eventually leading off to the next hill to the east. The path was a good aid for gaining height fast.

The Professor, Martin and Alice had come up from London, Dave, Tim and I were more local, which perhaps accounted for our being three Munroists, as was my dog Storm, while Tim's Zoë (named after Joe Brown's daughter) was just starting her youthful career. Sgritheall two days earlier had been Alice's first Munro, a wild and wintry one. Three of the party had poor eyesight (contact lenses or essential spectacles) and I'd just recovered from several stitches in an eyeball. No recruiting officer would have looked at this mix of the halt, lame and half-blind but it was a cheery-enough platoon that plodded up into the rising wind. The days of wet had filled a bellyfold of hill with crystal-clear water and Zoë danced along its rim trying to catch the splashes from the stones we threw in. The pool was grassy right to the bottom so was obviously a temporary feature. It reminded me of Loch a' Chuirn Deirg on the steep flank of Ben Attow above Glen Lichd where I'd once had a winter camp. It is held by a similar slip of the slope. You also find this on the Five Sisters, the Grey Corries and other schisty areas.

Our only pause was at the gate in the deer fence which girdles the hill. Above, we were on to snow which had the dogs dashing back and forth in excitement. Zoë climbed the hill six times over as she chased every kicked-up piece of snow. Storm is more sedate, his chief joys being olfactory (he sniffs out mice with all the enthusiasm of a truffle hunter). He kept wrinkling his nose into the east wind, which usually indicated deer. We saw none as the icy blast made looking for them too unpleasant.

When the path veered off we had a last pause to don our full protective panoply of winter clothing. I changed from light wellies into boots and Yeti gaiters. Pockets were stuffed with food. Ice-axes in hand we angled up to the col. The clouds came down on us and the spindrift hungrily hunted over the frozen drifts. The change from a casual walk up a path to a serious fight on an Arctic mountain took only a few minutes. It was what we wanted, of course, the fun of the fight to hansel in the year, but it was treading, Agag-like, with a respect frosted with awe. A Scottish mountain can be a fearsome place.

The east ridge was a double one and the hollow between was a white road of hard snow which gave easy walking, if walking is the word to describe our wind-buffeted, drunken course. A bank of steep snow tempted us to cut steps up its wall — only a few metres but retrieving rusty rhythms and techniques. Sometimes we had to cut steps on almost level ground for the wind had planed the old snow hard as glass. Tim managed to cut a step in his dog's tail making a brief blood spoor for the laggards to follow. (Zoë constantly dived at one's feet trying to catch flying bits of snow.) Storm donned an additional pullover of white, his eyes staring out from a balaclava of snow.

Alice enjoyed her second winter-battering. She was a robust young lass who went home from Kintail to face trials for a place in the English rugby team. Often guile, not brute strength, counts most in these situations. Being aware of cause and effect, or sensing dangers (like rocks being suddenly coated in invisible ice) is something that comes from imagination as much as from direct instruction. I enjoyed seeing someone so at home, at once, in such a savage environment. Those with poor eyesight had the greatest problems. Long before the summit I realised we would not be able to retrace our upward route: the gravel-sharp searing of the storm on any bare skin would see to that.

Battling *into* storms or refusing to modify plans has led to some sad tragedies in the hills. I remember hearing a keeper commenting on the Cairngorm school kids' disaster with, "Aye, they should hae gone *with the wind*. It widna matter where as long as it wis doon. You can aye win roon when you canna gang ower."

After a scrum-down at the ice-sheathed trig point we blew on westwards. A first attempt at flanking off landed me thigh deep in drift — Tim had to yank me out on to the rocks again. The rock strata dipped conveniently to the south east and we angled down-along, out-along these gentle ramps in turn, to come out suddenly below the clouds. Through the thickly falling snow we could see the dark waters of the loch with the A87 curving across on its causeway. The storm had lowered the snow line by several hundred feet and it was with regret we came down below the dry (if wild) freezing level. I changed back into my wellies, and we made a fast contouring descent to the cars to escape this ambushing, lower wetness. A wild and rainy day followed at bothy level — once we'd slithered over the snow carpeting the Mam.

Next day the radio reported one climber killed in Torridon and one air-lifted from the Nevis cliffs. Now, I don't know the details, but I do wonder why they risked such big brutes of hills with such a forecast. Maybe they did not listen to a forecast. All I know is that we cowards had a grand day when we exchanged the big devil of Ciste Dhuibh (the black chest or coffin) for the safer stimulation of Sgurr na Airgid (the silver peak). Happiness is a hill successfully climbed at Hogmanay.

"Only a hill: earth set a little higher
above the face of the earth . . .

Only a hill; but all of life to me,
up there between the sunset and the sea."
(Geoffrey Winthrop Young)

Section 14:   3. SGUMAN COINNTICH   879 m   OS 25   977304
              Mossy peak

Section 14:   4. FAOCHAIG   868 m   OS 25   022317
              The whelk

Section 14:   5. AONACH BUIDHE   899 m   OS 25   058324
              Yellow ridge or height (oenach boo-ee)

These three hills stand in a remarkably moated block of wild country, circled by the waters of the River Ling and the River Elchaig. Loch Mhoicean, however, does not have a river flowing from its NE end even though the loch sits on a sprawling watershed whose escaping waters soon flow off to encircle this hilly area. The hills are bulky rather than beautiful and their rather chaotic nature is reflected in the summit panoramas which offer a confused view of other summits near and far. With Glen Shiel and Affaric on one side and Torridon on the other the scenery is a bit overwhelming.

Beinn Dronaig (see 14:7) had been climbed on a New Year raid that whetted the appetite for a return visit, which came the following Boxing Day, motoring to Killilan (where we were set on by a pack of enthusiastic dogs — Yorkshire terriers luckily), visiting the Falls of Glomach and, after a social call at Iron Lodge (a lot of the buildings were originally clad in corrugated iron), taking the good path up the Crom-Allt. Above Iron Lodge the steep path east has been bulldozed. Our route, however, lay northwards. A steeper pull led to a ruin topping the pass and, suddenly, we were looking to Beinn Dronaig, Bidean and Lurg Mhor. We sang down to Maol-bhuidhe where a cheery fire led to a pleasant bothy evening. Bright moonlight illuminated the deer meadows.

An early look out was discouraging but we set off later, six of us, back on the path to the watershed. We went up by the waterfall into the inner recesses of the hill in a vain hope of finding good snow for practising winter techniques. In the end we climbed the crags on to the stepped ridge and crossed the plateau to the summit of Faochaig. Unlike the peak next to The Saddle in Glen Shiel this *whelk* hill gave no hint as to why it should be so named. Carn nan Searrach, the west top above Coire Dubh, looked as high so we went over to climb it just in case the OS, aided and abetted by Jim Donaldson, should ever change the order of precedence. Sguman Coinntich appears as a huge, corrie-edged sprawl from here. The clouds had been building up and we were glad to take the path down to the col again and head for the car at Iron Lodge. We reached it just in time.

Aonach Buidhe had also been on the programme for that day, but our "winter" course was keener on avoiding a soaking than staying on the tops, a pity as the members were beginning to go well. I'd long ago learnt that the average hillman from the south is often content with a low level of challenge and achievement. If I'd paid for a course I'd want to be out 25 hours each day! I was back there in April with a younger group of three, two friends, and the dog. We returned to Maol-bhuidhe as before. This time there was a clear winter tideline on the hills and the sky was spilling over with frosty stars.

We wandered south up the river that passes the bothy. This came down over swelling slopes of bog, north of the ridges and corries of Aonach Buidhe. Our stream descended in a thin fall from the west corrie. We had been practising techniques, which took us up to the western spur, but the crisp morning had been slipping away as the temperature rose and the clouds fell. Helen had not been feeling too well. Later I read a long account of hers which was amusing in its innocence. She thought the Falls of Glomach visit was the end of the previous day's activities so was horrified to be faced with the night walk to the bothy. "Hamish did this deliberately," she had to explain. "I expected a meal ready, as in the huts in Austria, but the place was cold and dark and we had to do our own cooking. Hamish cheered me up by telling me there were mice, the reason for hanging up our food." And on the hill (ice-axe work): "I was extremely frightened. Hamish just threw himself down this slope, talking as he did, to demonstrate, then told us to do it. . . . Worse was to come, we had to fall head-first on our tums. On the summit it began to snow heavily."

My log doesn't even mention snow falling. We traversed the fine corrie to An Creacha Beag before baling off down the middle of the three northern spurs. After lunch by the river Dave took Helen down to the bothy. "I just went into my sleeping bag while Dave filled all the dixies and even got a lovely fire going." We were not far behind as the ice, for climbing practice, was simply peeling off with the rise in temperature. We shared our bedtime brew with a couple, Roger and Anne, who had come through from Glen Affaric. By then it was a wild, wet night and our exit next day, put off till noon, was into the face of a blizzard.

On the col we found some sheep in trouble, we saw an eagle (huge in the mist), and snow buntings went cheepering past. Helen wrote quite enthusiastically of the plod out. One adjusts surprisingly quickly. The car radio reported someone missing in the Cairngorms. "It was too wild to camp so we went to a hostel at Achnashellach run by a nice guy called Gerry. There was a bath and a real loo." A couple of days were spent at Gerry's, then we tramped and climbed in Glen Affaric before everyone departed from Kyle by train, "a glorious day just when I have to go back home. Please can I stay, Hamish?" Having seen Helen and the others off I felt a bit guilty at driving straight along to Ardelve and Killilan again. I had a dry but dreich day for Sguman Coinntich.

Just as Aonach Buidhe thrusts ridges and corries northwards this hill does so to the west, a whole fistful of ridges slanting off from the long crest that links Sguman Coinntich with Faochaig. Nearly every glen has a stalkers' path but the Allt a' Choire Mhoir, descending to Killilan, is the longest and most direct for the Corbett. Kitchy and I sweated up this path till it vanished under the poggy remains of snow under the Bealach Mhic Bheathain. Bidean a' Choire Sheasgaich appeared again, a sharp cone from this angle, framed by an arch of white clouds against the well-washed blue sky. This is the best viewpoint of the three Corbetts and, having gained them one by one, with a certain amount of struggle, I looked east and promised myself a return one day, a kindly day of early summer when "the dew is on the season", to traverse them all in a single walk. But that is another story. . . .

Most recently Charlie, on a trip north, and Storm the dog outvoted me and another raid was made on these hills. I'd been in Morven, Charlie on Jura, but we met up at a roadside rendezvous at the head of Loch Long.

Loch Long is the *loch of the longboat*, the boat being a galley which brought home the body of St Fillan for burial. This is probably not the more famous St Fillan but a local saint. In fact some of the legends here go back far beyond Christianity. When St Fillan was travelling in France he always carried a hazel-staff from Kintail. One day he met an alchemist who asked him to go back and catch the white serpent which had its hole under the root of the tree on which the staff had grown, at the north-east end of Loch Long. St Fillan went back and put out a pail of honey. Out came the serpent, and crawled into it. St Fillan had to cross seven streams with the pail before he was safe from all the other serpents. The Elchaig was one of these. When he had returned to France the alchemist put the pail on a fire to boil and told the saint not to touch any bubbles which rose to the surface. Unthinkingly, St Fillan burst the first bubble, put his scalded finger in his mouth, and was thereafter possessed of magical powers of healing. He then returned to Kintail, where he became renowned as a great physician.

Killilan is named after the saint and so is Ben Killilan which, with
Sguman Coinntich, dominates the estate hamlet. Charles had done
Sguman Coinntich. We cycled the eight miles up to Iron Lodge (now
empty), quite an effort as I could not raise my saddle enough to pedal
with any power and Charles's rucksack weight caused his carrier to
disintegrate and the metal to dig huge chunks out of the tyre. We
walked over the familiar path to Maol-bhuidhe. I made one diversion
to check on the stream bifurcation shown on a stream descending to
the col. This was more a braiding of trickles (like an estuary) being set
in an alluvial fan. We did Beinn Dronaig that afternoon.

The next day, in rather sad conditions we squelched up to the pass
and, free of rucksacks, did Faochaig (by the splendid, if steep path) and
Aonach Buidhe (up *in* the big burn, a mix of climbing and botanising).
The range of flowers was greater than usual in the west. Even the ruin
on the col hosted six different fern species. I was collecting frogs for
the bog-garden pond at home and Charles commented on the odd
sight of myself on Aonach Buidhe, striding through the mist in shorts,
brolly in one hand, a bag of frogs in the other.

Tea was brewed before cycling down the glen. Charles was lucky
and did not have a blow out. Storm was lucky — he did most of the
journey in a rucker on my back. After soup at the car Charles departed
to try and make the Corran Ferry into Morven for the night and the
first ferry to Mull for its Corbetts the next day. Even Storm drew a
line at such fanaticism. We stayed where we were and did Sguman
Coinntich the next morning, curving up out of the corrie to miss the
crags in the mist, rain and wind. A few days later at home I unpacked
Sheet 25 of the trip and from it came a tingling smell of wood smoke
and wetness.

Section 14:   6. SGORR NA DIOLLAID   818 m   OS 25   282363
			Peak of the saddle (sgoor na jee ulij)

Sgorr na Diollaid has a hook-shaped summit which makes it easily
recognisable from other hills. A knobbly crest rising to the highest
point at the NW end is responsible for this individuality and a bit
of (optional) fun can be had scrambling up the rocks. As there is the
inconvenience of obtaining clearance to drive up Strathfarrar most
people climb Sgurr na Diollaid from Glen Cannich to the south,
which is probably the easier way anyway. Northern slopes in the
western glens tend to be much more heathery (low down) and craggy
(high up) compared to their gentler southern aspects. Dave, Kitchy
and I went up from Glen Cannich one Boxing Day.

We started at Loch Carrie and wandered up in a chilled cocktail of weathers. We sat out some blatters in the recesses of the hill, or just contoured with the blast on our backs and then worked upwards in the dry spells. The slopes were a rich ochrous colour; apart from some bog, heather and crag, we had a very casual ascent. There were plenty of deer and as we approached the last bumps thirteen ptarmigan whirred off. We climbed the peaklets but had our snack in the lee of the crest.

A decade later (on 1 January) with Charles, Belinda, Ernst and Storm, we set off up the Allt Charaich again. This was entirely Charles's fault. The day before we had been grounded by amazing rain, some of the deluge that washed away roads all down the west. We were staying at Cozac Lodge beside the original outflow of Loch Mullardoch (now raised 110 feet by the big dam) and, simply to experience the wetness, we walked along the loch a bit. The waves were crashing and spraying over the dam and the Allt Mullardoch was a fearsome sight, full to the brim, roaring in spate, and grumbling its boulders down into the brim-full loch. Salmon, venison and Danish specialities made a memorable dinner that night. The year was well and truly washed away.

Corbett-bagging Charles demanded the scalp of Sgorr na Diollaid before we headed south the next day. We had reached the level area (630 m) just below the last bulk of hill when a ferocious blizzard swept in. Ernst and Storm found this sufficiently unfriendly to opt for a retreat. Charles and Belinda battled on up to the summit. A mere blizzard was not going to deprive Charles of the pleasure of the first new Corbett of the year. A dedicated lad is our Charles.

Section 14:   7. BEINN DRONAIG   797 m   OS 25   037382
            Hill of the knoll or *Ragged hill*

Dave, the two Jims and I set off early from Strathcarron, taking the path from Achintee over the moors (fine views to the dawn-flushed Applecross Corbetts) and on up to the Bealach Alltan Ruairidh. Once down from the pass we briefly used the estate road to Bendronaig Lodge, as far as the bridge over the Uisge Dubh, an arch of iron fretwork with stone supports at the ends, a real period piece. We followed downstream and then began to cut round to join the eastern branch of the remote River Ling. Deer moved ahead of us and a buzzard circled above. Dave compared the country to Norway, where we'd been the summer before.

The scene was certainly as wild and the going was as difficult:

waterfalls, an awkward crag, some steep bits, then endless bogs and braes as we followed the many wendings of the river. In two hours of effort we passed only two places which had names on the map, *the speckled plain* and *the crooked bend*. The river was unusually low (for 2 January) so we could swap banks periodically. Dry feet were also a welcome change in that part of the world. An Cruachan, a 706-m cone north of An Socach, dominated our view along the valley. The peak never seemed to come any nearer; there was almost a feeling of surprise when we came on Loch Cruoshie and the bothy. We paddled across and a herd of deer grudgingly moved aside for us. Few bothies have such a setting of wide open spaciousness, an emptiness that made our haven feel snug and friendly. We had a brew and, at 1.30 p.m., set off again for the hill.

In normal — wet — conditions the river of that whole valley, from An Cruachan away down to the River Ling, can be difficult to cross. East of Loch Cruoshie the waters run slow, but deep; west of the loch they rush off down the glen in potentially dangerous spate. Over the years that moat has given us plenty of river-crossing experience. There is sometimes a reasonable crossing a mile east of the bothy but the easiest place, which we used on this occasion, is on the reach between the exit from the loch and the Allt na Sean-luibe junction. The river can change in character but we have nearly always managed across here. In real spate it would be safer crossing east of the loch — or even *in* it — as all one's belongings can go in a bivvy bag which can then act as a buoyancy aid for swimming over. A brief swim is a safer option (assuming you can swim) than perhaps being swept away downstream.

All my log recorded after we'd paddled over was "a gentle amble up Beinn Dronaig, another Corbett of smart views. Bidean was an angular pap and Lurg Mhor a bulk beached on Loch Monar. The barrier hills west [which we'd crossed] were overtopped by the paired pyramids of Maol Chean-dearg and An Ruadh Stac. The Corbetts in the south [14:3–5] deserve some attention soon." Beinn Dronaig is a plain, lumpy hill and easy enough, once you reach it. Loch Calavie and the pass to the north give the only features.

Just how remote this area is we saw from the entries in the bothy book or, rather, the absence of entries. The last party had been there in September, and the year before the first visitor of the year had been John Hinde on 27 January.

We had walked barefoot up the grassy meadow after our return paddle, then sat outside for a cup of tea. The mildness disappeared with the light and our paddle at dawn the next day was distinctly chilly. We made our exit over Lurg Mhor and Bidean a' Choire

Sheasgaich. Beinn Dronaig, I felt, had rather been a sop for my Corbetting hopes. Interestingly, though, Dave (Munros done) is now ticking off the Corbetts. I'd hazard he is glad to have Beinn Dronaig safely gathered in — and no more rivers to cross.

The bothy book had a note on previous residents. At the turn of the century there was a family of ten Renwicks, descended from Covenanting stock. One son, Alexander, went on to become a Professor of Divinity and Moderator of the Free Church. The last family there were the Burnetts who left in 1916. They shared a teacher with the children at Pait Lodge, seven miles along the glen. Pait is still occupied, perhaps the loneliest house in the Highlands, served only by the chancy miles of Loch Monar, which is the end of long, lonely Glen Strathfarrar.

On the recent July raid from Glen Elchaig with Charles there was no difficulty crossing the river at the loch's outflow. We went right up the Allt a' Choire Odhar which rises on the east ridge only five minutes off the summit. With a stiff wind in our faces we kept coming on browsing deer. One stag was even "doing a Landseer" by the tall trig-pillar. Charles raved about the view — the only one in a very wet week — and told me this was a marked feature of Corbetts!

We had walked in with the cloud down on the tops but, as we climbed, so did the cloud. We had our views then, as we descended, again with the cloud. That night gave one moment of magic. I went out in the dark, and in the midnight range of blacks, greys and silvers there was a window in the clouds, and there, right over Beinn Dronaig, was the friendly outline of the Plough.

Section 14: 8. BEINN THARSUINN 863 m OS 25 055433
            Transverse hill (tarshin)

This is certainly a Corbett which should have been done (or should be done) with the Munros Bidean a' Choire Sheasgaich and Lurg Mhor. If still "outstanding" you can easily combine it with the next peak in the list, Sgurr na Feartaig (14:9), as they both rise from the unusual *triple* col of the Bealach Bhearnais.

The usual, and most practical, approach is from Craig in Glen Carron. I'd like to hazard that Gerry Howkins' private hostel (always open) is likely to be the base from which most people set off into these remote parts. At Craig an estate road crosses the railway at a level-crossing, then bridges the River Carron and pulls up through the forest to end eventually at Glenuaig Lodge. Before the levels of Pollan Buidhe a pony track crosses the Allt a' Chonnais and makes a wet way up to the Bealach Bhearnais. If the river is in spate there is a footbridge downstream a bit (not immediately obvious on the ground). From the triple col Beinn Tharsuinn rises in a series of knobbly bumps, the summit giving a grand view to the sharp peak of Bidean a' Choire Sheasgaich. This Corbett, which acts as a stepping stone to that Munro and its very different twin, Lurg Mhor, is often the one Corbett a Munroist will have done, knowingly or otherwise.

Unless adding the Munros, or going on into the uninhabited hinterland, the easy option is to return to the Bealach Bhearnais. From the col a path, not on the map, makes a rising traverse on to the Sgurr na Feartaig ridge above Coire nan Each, which makes Feartaig an easy addition. The paths off Feartaig to Lair, or to the Allt a' Chonnais, are pleasant alternatives for the homeward journey.

Beinn Tharsuinn the Corbett, like Beinn Tarsuinn the Munro, is a slightly irritating hill in being positioned in the way of more desirable objectives. All Tarsuinns seem to have this habit, living up to their name, and invariably being long, rough, craggy, lumpy hills which are better traversed than flanked.

Section 14:   9. SGURR NA FEARTAIG   862 m   OS 25   055454
             The peak of thrift (i.e. sea pink, *Armeria maritima*)

Strange, how thrift (*feartaig*) thrives in the wilds only on the inhospitable summits or on the edges of the sea. Sgurr Fhuar-thuill, one of the Strathfarrar Munros, has a Top with the same name. Thrift can be found on most of the hills east of Glen Carron. The Corbett is the long skyline above Achnashellach, a cliff-topped array of corries rising above the massed forests. Gerry's hostel at Craig looks up to Feartaig and, not surprisingly, the Corbett is a popular easy day's walk from there. It is also a useful Corbett to take in while going into (or coming out from) the remote country further east.

During several Christmas holiday periods I used to run winter courses based on Gerry's and I always had a day beforehand laying out markers for a big map and compass exercise. Feartaig was first traversed and studied between laying markers in Golden Valley and at Pollan Buidhe under Ceannaichean. The obvious path traversing between these spots gives the best of walks on Feartaig, one that I never grow tired of repeating.

If the River Carron is low, paddle across the shallows and shingles opposite Lair. The bridge shown is simply two wires suspended over the river, and most people find it as off-putting as a high wire act in a circus, with the River Carron substituting for a safety net. Golden

Valley has some mature trees and once gave us a green-glowing, secretive camp site which felt like being in the foothills of the Himalayas. On that first visit I left my orienteering-type marker at the burn junction and walked on up the hills to the deer fence. The gate somehow managed to slam into my face and I was left sprawled on the path half unconscious!

The path flanks up Coire Leiridh (which has some good winter gullies in the headwall) and then wiggles successfully up to a wide plateau-like mossy col. Bidean a' Choire Sheasgaich is an impressive spike and Fuar Tholl, with its "white spider", dominates the jostle of Coulin and Torridon hills. There was hardly any snow, even with Christmas three days off, but at least there was no rain. I gave up "winter" courses eventually — they probably contravened the Trade Descriptions Act.

This sweeping saddle with its confusion of lochans and a path junction can be a tricky place in poor visibility. One path drops southwards to Bearnais and the uninhabited wilderness beyond, but a left fork zigzags up a flank to the offset western top of Sgurr nan Feartaig before wending along above the cliffs to the large cairn of the eastern, highest top, at 862 m. Deer down in Coire nan Each were grunting, sounding just like guinea pigs. Liathach and Beinn Eighe towered over the nearer hills while Skye and Sgriol and other favourite spots were all blowing out streamers of cloud. Sgurr nan Ceannaichean across the valley was long ago promoted to a Munro, to the chagrin of those who had "bagged" only Moruisg. This is poetic justice (as with most of the additions), in that, if the aesthetic *traverse* had been followed, the "new" would already have been done.

The path skirts the final bump to descend over several more bumps (grand walking) down to the Allt a' Chonais where there is an interesting bridge just above the tree line and a bit of spectacular gorge. Another path (not shown on the map) breaks off, right, before the final bump and angles down to the Bealach Bhearnais. Beinn Tharsuinn, if not climbed on a Bidean–Lurg Mhor traverse, can easily be done from here, and the rather wet path taken down to Pollan Buidhe. The path fords the river, but in spate the footbridge downstream (not easily seen) should be used. This day can be extended by starting further down Strathcarron at Arineckaig (south of Loch Dughaill). A path (not shown) breaks off the main one to head up towards Loch nan Gobhar.

Section 14:   10. An Ruadh-stac   892 m   OS 25   922481
    The red peak (roo-ah stac)

Dawn was just yawning when we parked at the foot of the Coulags Glen and set off up the footpath northwards. Long-tailed tits were busy in the riverside trees and the puddles on the path crackled their ice-plates underfoot. The year 1969 had two days left.

After a steeper pull the path crosses to the west bank, by a good bridge, mercifully, for the yellow water was high and the exposed boulders were bosses of ice. Half a mile further on we came to a lonely cottage (shut up and sad then, the building has now been restored as a bothy). We had our first pause at the isolated stone, Clach nan Con-Fionn, *the stone of Fingal's hound* Bran, traditionally tethered there during a stag-hunt.

Ten minutes up the glen the path forks and we took the steeper track left which heads to the col between Meall nan Ceapairean and Maol Chean-dearg. Andy opted out of proceedings as his boots were torturing him. Before reaching the windy col David, Jim, Kitchy and I traversed along to the line of crags on the east side of the long SE Ridge of the Munro. We took the left-most of the two biggest buttresses and enjoyed a modest 400-foot climb: a series of small quartz walls between which we rushed to restore life to freezing fingers till, higher, we were able to move together. The dog was patiently waiting at the top so we called our climb Ketchil Buttress (pronounced Kitchy). There was a cairn on top of the right buttress.

Maol Chean-dearg gave quite a tussle in the gale and we fought our way down again to bale off the ridge to the frozen lochan at the start of An Ruadh-stac's east ridge. The path from Coulags Glen is shown crossing the col but in fact ends on the col while the one from Torridon, skirting below the Munro, goes on a bit further than shown, to the Ceapairean spur leading to the col with An Ruadh-stac. Meall nan Ceapairean, 2,150 feet in old money, is worth climbing for its view — not that we had much today. An Ruadh-stac is worth seeing, however mis-named.

Ruadh is *red*, but An Ruadh-stac is a *grey* hill, sometimes touched white by the sun, but never red like its ruddy, bald-headed neighbour. We were at once struck by the grim north face looking down on Loch Coire an Ruadh-stac: two steep tiers and a broken one below them; and were not surprised to see that Patey and Bonington had put up a 600-foot route in 1960. Why such neglect since? Our delight was to find not quartz scree, but acres of ice-polished slabs on the south-east flank. David compared them to the Dubhs, even if the coefficient of friction is a bit different. We took to the slabs and romped about on them as we gained height. The route higher up became scraggy (crag/scree mixed) but soon landed us by the big cairn, and a big, if brief, view. Skye was wedged between silver sea-glitter and black, fingering clouds.

We had discovered An Ruadh-stac to be one of the roughest hills in an area of rugged hills; the paths are godsends. The east ridge is probably the most ascended route up and, whether coming from the Coulags Glen and Strath Carron, or by the path from Annat at the head of Loch Torridon, there is, successively, a good first view of the peak, the rousing scramble up and then the wide view from the summit. You cannot really ask for more of any mountain.

On one of the many Christmas days on the hills round here we climbed An Ruadh-stac from the Kishorn–Sheildaig road (sheet 24: 853445), skirting Loch an Loin to Glasnock and following up the secretive Allt a' Ghiubhais and the Allt Eisg which has a succession of small falls on its sandstone steps. This is a variation I'd recommend if two cars can be organised in the party.

Just to be different we descended the south ridge. This was rough, too, but the main memory is the desperate effort required to make headway into the gale. We were glad to turn off across the moors to pick up the burn draining Loch Moin a' Chriathar, the loch that keeps wicket below the An Ruadh-stac slabs. The burn sidled along the sandstone strata to drop into the gorge below. We cut across to the bridge and reached the car at dusk, yawning our heads off from a day of windy walking.

Section 14:   11. FUAR THOLL   907 m   OS 25   975489
            The cold hole

There is some lack of clarity as to which corrie of this grand hill is responsible for the name but my money would go on that grim, cliff-held eastern hollow which is *the* feature of the peak seen from Glen Carron. Names were usually given from below, of the most obvious characteristics, and that shadowy corrie certainly can be gruey even in summer and an icy cauldron in winter. Fuar Tholl, to me, is a winter mountain. I am past the age of being tempted by its considerable cliffs and being there at the back end of the year anyway, means my many visits have all been snowy ones. I've climbed the hill on Christmas Day, on Boxing Day and on the first of January, besides less-noted days.

Almost invariably we've been staying at Gerry's hostel at Craig (see

p. 7) for we like our comforts and freedom and good company, and Gerry's is the right accommodation in the right place for a good number of fine hills and as a link in some f the best trekking available in Britain. Fuar Tholl is the nearest notable peak on the western side of Glen Carron, very visible as it scowls down on Craig.

My attachment to the glen pre-dates the hostel: for several Christmas holidays we camped there, always in conditions of massive snowfall. On one occasion we bivouacked in the shelter at the old Glencarron Halt (built to serve the Lodge above) and, to ensure the morning train stopped, we climbed up to bring down the signal lantern which we filled with paraffin from our stoves and then set at red. This worked, but the following year lantern, signal and station had gone, and even Achnashellach Station was reduced to a pathetic hut lit by time switch, which assumed the train would always be on time. As it seldom is, arriving at Achnashellach can be fun. One friend I was meeting assumed the platform was as long as the train and stepped down with his heavy rucksack. Long after the train had proceeded we found him down the bank, on his back, caught in the rhododendron bushes, thrashing about like a stricken stag.

Achnashellach Station is the starting point for Fuar Tholl and the other hills surrounding Coire Lair. Fuar Tholl should have been done when traversing the Munros, Beinn Liath Mhor and Sgorr Ruadh. However, in winter Fuar Tholl is sometimes quite enough by itself. The path starts on the north side of the railway line near a cottage enclosed in high fencing. The fence has kept the devouring deer out and allowed the creation of a beautiful Highland garden — well worth a look. The estate road heads off on a long traverse to the Coulin (Cow-lin) Pass while the footpath wends up through fine woodlands and massive old pines beside the River Lair. This river flows in a deep ravine and is virtually impassable, while any approach to Fuar Tholl across it, or up its west bank, will be hampered by deep heather and rock. The path is an aid not to be scorned. Follow it up to Coire Lair.

On gaining the corrie the path splits into three and the left branch is taken to ford the river. You won't manage across in really wet weather. The path goes up and over the col, "the big pass", that separates Fuar Tholl from Sgorr Ruadh, the highest peak of the area, rising under several buttresses which give some of the longest, hardest and best sandstone climbs in the country. In 1870 the Prince of Wales (later Edward VII), a crack shot and fanatic sportsman, took part in a deer drive up here and nearly lost his life in a big rockfall.

You can pick a way up between the cliffs or follow the ridge up from the highest point of the path, keeping on the Coulags Glen side. The Coulags Glen flank is recommended by one guide as an easy way up but my wording of that line would be "purgatorial", which is being polite. The col itself holds an array of bumps and hollows and lochans which on one occasion gave me a very frustrating time.

Being a rather unpleasant winter day, and being alone, I followed this *voie normale*, perfectly straightforward even in the cloud and falling snow. Back at the col, and set on adding Sgorr Ruadh, I found my compass was missing, thanks to a hole in my pocket. (It turned up in Gerry's garden.) Now, on the map, Sgorr Ruadh looks a big enough target and is definite enough in shape that, once on its slopes, going uphill would inevitably lead to the summit while my track in the snow could be followed down again. I set off. After a while, following along one of the elongated bumps, I came on other footprints, which of course were not other footprints but my own footprints, all too recognisable by a distinctive tread. I'd gone in a circle, not the imagined straight line.

A long wait did not produce any clearance so I tried again. I ended making a second circle! In the mist, snow hollows and snow-covered lochans could not be told apart. I went through into water once. I tried every dodge. In the end a clearance allowed me to see down into Coire Lair and I quickly marked the snow in the assumed direction of Sgorr Ruadh. By carefully looking back, I made a slow but straighter line, which almost landed me in a bigger loch. It could only be the one immediately under the desired peak. Ironically, I'd traversed the Ben in mist the week previously and never used a compass though I found I'd accumulated *three* in my pockets and rucksack.

Perhaps my best-ever climb of Fuar Tholl was the Boxing Day one. Over the years I'd steadily been trying routes up and down all round the peak and had already come to regard the east ridge as favourite. This is the right boundary of the Cold Hole as you look up from the glen. There is one spot, high up, where the ridge becomes narrow, steep and exposed. On this day the route was very snowy and corniced, but compressed drift snow gave us a good climb and, at the neck, I was able to throw the rope down for each of the party to follow. That spot was like something in the Alps, for the cliffs of the corrie were draped in snow and ice and rimmed with cornices, a world of startling white that contrasted with the black depths of the forested glen. Two ropes' lengths were used as a hand-rail to gain easier ground and we edged round to the cairn. (One of the illustrations shows this route.)

There a vicious storm hit us, so we stomped and slid down the gully under the 500-foot Mainreachan Buttress and followed a burn down to Loch Coire Lair. We tracked wildcat prints across its frozen surface and had a memorable tussle through the pass to the Ling Hut in Glen Torridon: a ten hour expedition. We returned to Gerry's the next day over the classic Coulin Pass, using the old footpath that can still be traced down from the elbow on the road (at 024496) to reach the A890 just west of Craig.

There's a special warm spot in my affections for the Cold Hole, tenth highest in the Corbett hierarchy.

Section 14: 12. SGURR NAN LOCHAN UAINE 873 m
　　　　　　　OS 25 969531
　　　　　　　The peak of the green loch

Section 14: 13. SGURR DUBH 782 m OS 25 979558
　　　　　　　The black peak

This is a pair of surprisingly neglected peaks; or maybe not so surprising as they look across Glen Torridon to Beinn Eighe and Liathach and for most visitors the giants will claim precedence. I know I'd been up the Big Three many times before I realised there were other good hills nearby, sometimes climbing them for the views of the big ones, sometimes to escape bad weather on high and sometimes, dare I confess, to avoid "yet another slog" up Liathach's 3,456 feet.

For a quarter of a century I've usually had a week in Strathcarron or Torridon during the Christmas break and this has equally given fabulous days and dreadful days out on the hill. On Christmas Days we always tried to climb something worthy. Christmas Day 1979 gave us two crackers: Sgurr nan Lochan Uaine and Sgurr Dubh.

We drove round to Glen Torridon in Dave's car and set off up the track past the Ling Hut, which sits below an extraordinary area of hundreds of small moraine bumps — a good start to a day of considerable geological interest. In Torridon you feel very close to the raw beginnings of life. The bare hills are scoured by glacial Brillopads. Some of the hills have even been stood on their heads — literally. Such forces are mercifully subdued now, but the evidence remains stark and clear. Torridon is not a tame part of the country.

The path goes on to join the one through to Coire Lair and Achnashellach, though the map shows it stopping. There was a south gale blowing so we followed the path into the wind to gain the maximum useful altitude with the least effort, then cut up to scramble on the sandstone chaos to the summit of Sgurr nan Lochan Uaine. We had a picnic before the top where we were partly sheltered and could look down on the lochans that give the peak its name. They were frozen over but patterned with cracks. A raven croaked through the pass. Dave and I recalled our camp there on a Christmas Day/Night seven years before. We'd carried up to camp below the lochans and climbed Beinn Liath Mhor; quite a worthy day. The wind blew big guns on that occasion as well, and the camp, on snow at dusk, was clear of snow by dawn. Our tent doors looked out to the high battlements of Liathach. While Dave and Stephen circuited Beinn Liath Mhor on the east to descend Coire Lair to Gerry's, I nipped up Sgurr nan Lochan Uaine being, by then, keen on Corbetts, and descended to collect my car in Glen Torridon. Today was Dave's turn for the Corbetts. Stephen, sadly, had been killed in a motoring accident not long after that Christmas visit.

When we set off to descend the NE Ridge I was at once in trouble. I'd worn Bogtrotters, seeing it was a "soft" day, but that exposed side of the peak was iced-up and I ended chipping steps to link every rock that managed to break through the glassy surface: nervy work that had the adrenalin going. On An Teallach once we had something similar and I cheerfully warned a friend, as we crept up from pebble to pebble, "Don't slip or you're dead." That was his first winter Munro — and his last.

The ice slope eased off eventually and on the col I put my boots on for Sgurr Dubh, which then presented nothing but soft snow. (In winter I keep my boots for use above the freezing level so that they never become wet, and last indefinitely, while, below that level, I use Bogtrotters or wellies so that my feet never become wet.) Fionn Bheinn was an impressive cone and the "Conon Corbetts" looked good. Slioch and the Fannichs and the near giants of Torridon were all arrayed in plain monochrome, from blackest rocks to brightest snow. Sgurr Dubh, like its namesake between Loch Garry and Glen Moriston, is a "Dubh with a view". (On the last day of 1987, we wandered on to the lower summit overlooking Glen Torridon to find the ground ruptured, and boulders tossed aside, by a recent lightning strike.)

Dave and I descended by the array of lochans shown on the map. They had decided the line of my first ascent, with Stephen, those seven years before, and on subsequent occasions. They were as interesting as expected and the burn flowing from them breaks down by a fine ravine up which we had climbed by rock or ice till its fierceness always forced us out. That is the way up I'd recommend, for the ground features will keep the interest going and on the final cone you can play the old game of not lifting eyes until the summit is reached. There is a similar landscape of knolls and lochans on the col between Fuar Tholl and Sgorr Ruadh. The Dubh of Sgurr Dubh is probably from the summit cone being grey quartz rather than the warm-coloured Torridonian sandstone.

We made some fun out of the descent, at one stage penguin-sliding on our bellies down a snow gully while a parcel of stags stood landseering at us. Sgurr Dubh is high enough for ptarmigan to mock one on top, while the heathery lower slopes have go-backing grouse. Nature is very conservative. We cut some holly berries to take back to the hostel.

Fourteen of us sat down for Christmas dinner that night in Gerry's, a royal feast. I'd saved some exotic wine for the occasion (and a box of Turkish Delight bought in Bodrum). I doubt if Torridon hills have been toasted very often in Turkish wine, but we'd had a worthy day so earned the treat. *Sliante!* — to the Green and the Black.

Section 14:   14. AN SIDHEAN   814 m   OS 25   171454
              Fairy hill (shee)

Section 14:   15. BAC AN EICH   849 m   OS 25   222489
              Bank/ridge of the horse

Strathconon gives the easiest access to these hills, though An Sidhean is also within reasonable range of the Monar dam at the head of Glen Strathfarrar. Strathconon can be motored up as far as the west end of Loch Beannacharain where there is a small car-parking area. This route, also applicable to 14:16, 17, is on Sheet 26.

The A832 Muir of Ord–Achnasheen road is left at Marybank for the 11 miles up to Scardroy. If one has crossed the bridge avoiding Inverness and on across the Black Isle, turn off at Moy Bridge, a mile across from Marybank. The road from beyond Contin via Loch Achilty is private after some miles so is not a motoring route into Strathconon.

One or both these Corbetts can be done from Scardroy with little difficulty, the area being liberally supplied with pony tracks. Gleann Fhiodhaig with its dominant Creag na h-Iolair is followed for about five miles, then the path up the Allt an Amise. The River Meig can be impassable in wet conditions, so plan accordingly. From near the watershed a stalkers' path wends high up on to An Sidhean. On the other side, note the unusual feature, below Loch a' Chlaidheim (*loch of the sword*), of a burn which splits and later rejoins.

An Sidhean is too hemmed-in to be a great viewpoint but at least it is not an over-populated summit. I'd several times walked through the glens round the Corbett before actually going to the summit — an expedition made from the less convenient starting point of the Loch Monar dam. Glen Strathfarrar has a locked gate at its foot, and a key has to be obtained (from the gatehouse) to drive up for the day, which can rather inhibit lengthy walks or multi-day visits unless one makes appropriate logistical plans or has a helpful driver. Information is on the gate, so check at the time as arrangements change periodically (tel: 046–376260).

Fortunately I was staying up the glen and was able to squeeze An Sidhean into a winter day from the Loch Monar side. The only problems, driving up, were the stags lying on the tarmac. The path along the north shore of Loch Monar is a fine one but we caught the westerly wind and had a foul day on top. I abandoned the poorer path up the hill to ascend the south ridge (Mullach a' Gharbh-leathaid) but came down by the burn so as not to need to use the compass — hands were warmer in pockets.

A high-level route over Sgurr Coire nan Eun can lead one to Bac an Eich or down by Coire Mhoraigein, which is also the best wet-weather approach to An Sidhean. Alternatively, descend An Sidhean east of south to the watershed to pick up the poor path on the infant River Orrin and out to Inverchoran. This is a more interesting approach if just doing An Sidhean. Gleann Chorainn or Coire Mhoraigein are equally easy ways to gain height for climbing Bac an Eich. I wandered on to Meall Buidhe for the view down to the loch and then descended the west ridge to Corriefeol — quite a pleasant way off, if steep.

Gleann Fhiodhaig is an old track through to Glen Carron, and another old way linked Scardroy westwards to Achnasheen, both useful routes if using trains and then backpacking into the area. A Post bus operates up Glen Conon from Muir of Ord.

Section 14:   16. MEALLAN NAN UAN   840 m   OS 25   264545
                Little hill of the lambs

Section 14:   17. SGURR A' MHUILINN   879 m   OS 25   265558
                Peak of the mill (voo-lin)

These are extraordinarily shy hills which manage to stay hidden from most directions. Even from the A832 Dingwall to Achnasheen road along Strath Bran what we see are strictly speaking their outliers. Nor are the approaches from Strath Bran worth contemplating unless one has a fetish for flogging over miles of peaty moorland. Admire from Strath Bran and approach up Strath Conon — as for 14:14, 15.

Strathanmore is the obvious starting point but I have preferred to go on slightly to the church shown (292538) which is one of the thirty or so built by Thomas Telford, a side of his work not as well known as the

Caledonian Canal, for instance. His churches are instantly recognisable: all have four door or window settings along the side of their
simple design and a small belfry atop one gable. (There is a Telford
church by Loch Luichart on the A832 at 334634.) Visit the Telford
church, anyway, wherever you start.

Simply angle up the slopes behind Strathanmore or the church to
gain the NE Ridge up to Creag Ruadh. These have some bracken in
the summer, and heather higher up, which can give the group a rather
dark appearance. Meallan nan Uan sticks out as a sharp cone, and a
grand highway leads along to its double top with unusual views of
many ranges. I've only once made the circuit and was nearly blasted
off this traverse by batterings of hail and sleet. The Torridons to the
west had begun the day as black spikes. By the time I'd wended down
and up Sgurr a' Mhuilinn they glittered like white teeth. I've seldom
been so cold on a hill. Some wheatears looked as if they wished they'd
stayed in Africa.

On another occasion I cycled up Gleann Meinich, an easy-angled
forestry track, on a spanking January day (for which there had been a
dismal forecast). Creag Ghlas is a very rocky top and the whole north
side of the glen is steep and rough. I went up by the burn just beyond
the ruin (254537). There was a cheery fall and an awkward fence. It
was a joy to leave the heather for firm snow. There seemed to be snow
buntings about all day — a day among millions — and on Sgurr
a' Ghlas Leathaid of the two peaks I sat and wrote out a catalogue of
the view. As it is a page long I won't repeat it. "As fine a view as
possible", I summed up. (The second peak, not named on the map, is
Sgurr a' Choire Rainich.)

Sgurr a' Mhuilinn was very snow-plastered on the day of my late-
April circuit. I came down the SE Ridge then bore over, eastwards, to
avoid the great bog-hollow below, not that the bare moor was much
easier with the paring wind out of the east. I crossed the Allt an t-
Strathain Mhoir high up to make my way back down to Strathconon
church.

Given time it is well worth adding Sgurr a' Ghlas Leathaid to the
round. (The Gleann Meinich approach is best.) This is the peak that
dominates the view from Strath Bran and is, itself, the finest
viewpoint of this juggle of peaks. Watching sunset over Torridon
from up there is a breathtaking experience, and to north and south
there is a great huddle of hills which can be difficult to recognise from
this angle. Loch Coire a' Mhuilinn is a lonely spot (frozen, and
cracked all over like a jigsaw, on the January trip). What a place for a
camp! The *mill* is probably a reference to the racing river rather than to
any building, just as the similar brawling burn from the CIC Hut on

Nevis is the Allt a' Mhuillin. This round gives enough rough walking throughout to ensure you will grind slowly.

Section 14:   18. BEINN A' BHA'ACH ARD   862 m   OS 26   361435
             Hill of the high byre(?) (Vaichart)

This hill, at the eastern end of Glen Strathfarrar, is not a very striking summit but its isolated height ensures good views to the Lapaichs, Sgurr a' Mhuilinn, Ben Wyvis and even the far Cairngorms. Motoring up the glen is restricted so a cycle might be worth taking for the odd mile of road along to the power station, as it is for the Munros further up the glen. (Munro himself took a day off stalking to cycle up for these hills.) For the initial approach the 1:50,000 First Edition map leaves much to be desired.

Last winter, returning from the north, I turned aside to let the dog have a shot at the Corbett, but we had only just reached the locked gate at Leishmore when the snow began to fall. I'd half thought of trying the road to Dunmaglass on the south of the Farrar River, but the bridge shown at the Culligram Falls does not exist. You could not cross the gorge. On the north bank are various Hydro works and the estate road (not path) up the Neaty Burn starts beside an underground power station. By the time I'd had a look at these changes the snow was pillowing down and there was no hope of going high. The dog arrived back at the car with a saddle of new snow on his back. Cars were slewed all over the road on the Aigas Brae and we had a hairy crossing of the Slochd before giving up the battle against the snow at Aviemore.

On the only other visit I'd been up seeing the keeper at Loch Monar and had also hidden a parcel for the Munro trip which started a few weeks later. Because of this latter, my One Inch maps were not available (all being packed for picking up along the way) and my Half-Inch Bartholomews were with my brother who was to keep tabs on my progress. All I could muster was a Six Inch to One Mile map. I therefore set off too soon and had a bit of wood-and-crag thrashing on a direct assault up the Corbett, whereas there was a helpful path up the Neaty Burn which gives easy access to the Corbett's west ridge. I used the snowier east corrie for starting off down (a good slide) and came out to Culligran. The lower slopes have pine and birch forests which make for attractive scenery compared to what lies at the head of Glen Strathfarrar. With views out to the Black Isle this Corbett has a strange feeling of being perched between "the desert and the sown".

WESTER & EASTER ROSS

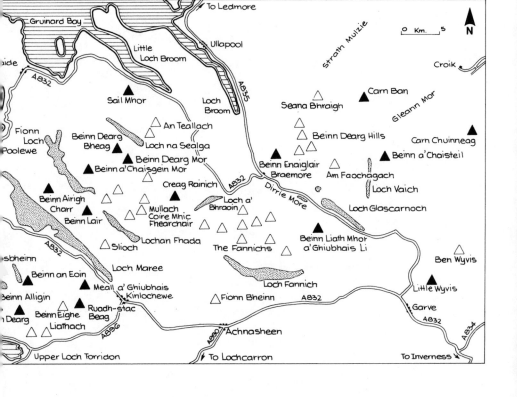

Section 15:   1. BAOSBHEINN   875 m   OS 19/24   871654
              The wizard's hill (bus-ven)

Section 15:   2. BEINN AN EOIN   855 m   OS 19   905646
              The hill of the bird (bin-in-eeon)

Section 15:   3. RUADH-STAC BEAG   896 m   OS 19   973614
              The small red spike

Section 15:   4. MEALL A' GHIUBHAIS   *c.*880 m   OS 19   976634
              Fir tree hill (meyoul a huish)

FOR THIS CLUSTER of Corbetts I'd advise using the 1:25,000 Map "The Cuillin and Torridon Hills" as they are set in an unusually rugged bit of country for which increased detail will be needed when trying to walk through the wilder parts.

Baosbheinn occupies a unique place in my affections, being my last Corbett back in 1976. You can never have another last Corbett, though there has been a sort of altitude musical chairs over the years since. If Munroists thought they had grievances with the 1981 map revisions theirs was a mild inconvenience compared to the poor Corbetteers who had to ride forth for up to nineteen more scalps, scattered at a maximum range and sited in the most inconvenient places. I still regard Baosbheinn as my last.

Flowerdale and Torridon (as in the SMC district guide) form an entity, and a glorious multi-day trek can take in these Corbetts in several possible combinations. You could start at Kinlochewe and take the path west from near the Anancaun NCC Centre over the col between Ruadh-stac and Meall a' Ghiubhais, from where those Corbetts can be tackled, before going on to camp further west. Similarly, on the second day, Beinn an Eoin may be added and, on the third day, Baosbheinn, exiting thereafter on the same or the following day. The pass between Beinn Alligin and Beinn Dearg is the easiest way out. The path shown coming through the Bealach a' Chomhla continues right on under Alligin's east face to end in Toll nam Biast. A bridge links to the Coire Mhic Nobuil track. Check, beforehand, the time of the Post bus for the return up Glen Torridon to Kinlochewe. Beinn Dearg, of course, could also be included in this quality Corbett-bagging. An alternative entry could be made up Glen Grudie and alternative exits could lead out, north west to the Gair Loch or, west, to the lonely walkers' hostel at Craig; neither being an easy option.

While I've criss-crossed this area in all sorts of combinations I've not actually made the long Corbett-traverse I've advocated; for my Corbetts, like my Munros, and like most people's peaks, were never done with any tidy planning or execution. Ruadh-stac Beag was reached with three friends on a full traverse of all Beinn Eighe's ridges; Beinn Dearg on the fourth day of January was quite sufficient unto that day on its own; Beinn an Eoin was grabbed during a course, after a thrashing while camped by Loch na Cabhaig; Meall a' Ghiubhais was chosen to fill a half-day in early January, and Baosbheinn was an autumn sortie that saw camps in Coire Mhic Fhearchair and by Loch Toll nam Biast with several Munros and Corbetts culled in between.

Those were just the first visits. This is an area of such tough character that one has to keep returning. It is so tough and remote that few people other than dedicated Corbetteers stray far from the paths shown — and these should be fully utilised, for vast areas are a mix of scoured sandstone and endless bog and water holes or, as nowhere else in the country, a spreading of chaotic boulders. One mile an hour is good going, out in its centre, an area I once described as a "Piccadilly of peaks and passes". Rather than retell too many tales, I'll give a brief practical summary of the Corbetts in turn, then finish with the story of our wanderings that led to Baosbheinn as the last Corbett.

Ruadh-stac Beag is not usually included in the traverse of Beinn Eighe, but as the Corbett is hardly more "out on a limb" than the Munro of Ruadh-Stac Mor it would be logical to add it to such a day. The traverse is a major undertaking and therefore a recommendation for the fit and experienced. In winter all these hills, Munros and Corbetts, are demanding climbs rather than walks and should only be attempted by those qualified to tackle winter challenges. A rescue on Baosbheinn hardly bears thinking about!

Lochain Uaine, *the green loch*, on the col between the Corbett and the rest of Beinn Eighe is at about 710 m. If Beinn Eighe has not caused problems the descent to the lochan will "go" quite easily. Coming up from Anancaun leave the track on the col to head south and then south west to reach the Corbett without losing precious height. There is pleasant walking up to the lochan; then the ridge should be tackled from there, turning crags on the right. The Corbett's north side is not advisable and the worst of the screes should be avoided. There is no problem dropping down into Coire Ruadh-staca and by traversing under Ruadh-stac Mor the Maol Cheannan shambles can be circumvented. Meall a' Ghiubhais presents no real problems from the top of the Anancaun track. Note the

Corbett is the south-westerly of the two summit bumps (not given a height on the 1:50,000; 886 m on the 1:25,000) but the *lower* 878 m bump is indicated. There is a fine aerial view over Loch Maree to Slioch from the lower top.

The 1:50,000 cannot hope to indicate the complexities of the central "Concordia" that lies surrounded by these Corbetts and Munros, while what the 1:25,000 shows is probably discouraging. On my first venture we had just reached Loch na Cabhaig (over the western watershed) when a storm hit us. We had a wild pitching of tents, and cringed inside for the rest of the day as an endless succession of blasts battered the site. At dusk a watery sunshine lit Loch a' Bhealaich, our view down along, out along, west, while Carn an Feola and Sail Mhor were like the bows of big liners churning through bow-waves of cloud. Torrents were pouring off Beinn Dearg. After survival camping that night the weather cleared up in the morning. Our shocked systems needed some time to return to Corbett tuning.

"Lumpy" was someone's description of the landscape over to Loch na h-Oidhche (*loch of night*, often meaning good night fishing), and from Pocca Buidhe we wandered up to arrive right at the trig point on top of Beinn an Eoin (*the hill of the bird*, usually meaning eagle, of which this area has several). The track along the loch is now an estate road rather than a pony path. Given the choice of walking along the crest or exploring down the rockier southern prow of the hill we chose the latter — and had the fun we wanted, finally traversing off on some exposed sandstone slabs. Two people were fishing in "our" loch and fourteen orange dots could be seen descending from Beinn Dearg — probably innocent trainees off the *Captain Scott* which we'd seen anchored in Loch Torridon. We packed tents and Naismith and began wandering east. Some hours later we pitched our tents on the promontory in Loch nan Cabar (*antler loch*), an apron stage, with Liathach a surrealist backcloth.

Both Beinn an Eoin and Baosbheinn can be climbed, fairly unadventurously, from Loch na h-Oidhche, which can be reached by the estate road that breaks off the A832 Loch Maree–Gairloch road near Loch Bad an Sgalaig (857720) but this approach removes the special quality of the southern approaches. The Talladale–Strath Lungard glen is tracked on the west bank to the end of the trees but gives easier walking than might be expected.

The best tramp of all was the one that led to Baosbheinn. We started by going up to camp in Coire Mhic Fhearchair which is one of those special things one should do at least once in a lifetime. The landscape was lapped in the ochres, purples and silvers of early autumn. What an idyllic site! We could hardly tear ourselves away to make a traverse of the corrie top from Sail Mhor to Ruadh-stac Mor, then we could hardly bear to leave that seat in the gods to return to the tents: Ian and Mary in one, dog and myself in the other. A local stag serenaded us to sleep.

All next day the rutting of the stags echoed on the crags ("very Walter Scottish") and frequently the beasts would be charging about, so involved with themselves that they paid little heed to us. The end peaks of Beinn Dearg took on bold shapes, in turn, as we slowly wended west over the watershed, passing Loch na Cabhaig, as every journey seems to do, and eventually ascending by a brawling burn and through a slotted rock gateway into Toll nam Biast (*the hollow of the beast*). A snooker table of grass among the sandstone pavements made a comfy site — as long as the river did not rise more than two feet. The rest of the day was spent on a traverse of Beinn Alligin and the Horns and we returned to camp as the rain came on for the day/week/month/ for ever. . . . Our earlier jokes about the river rising sounded a bit misplaced as we listened to the increasing roar. My log of the day ended, "The world reduced to a mad wetness. Sealed into the tent like a hornbill in its hole. A small tunnel of security a mere skin of nylon in thickness. What about Baosbheinn now?"

The barometer rather than the cloudy view gave us the faith to move for mountains the next day. We skirted the corrie below Loch na Cabhaig (an area of black gabbro rocks) to reach the ridge leading to Baosbheinn, flanked Ceanna Beag, the 707-m top, and finally used deer tracks along to go directly up on to the highest top, Sgorr Dubh. As we arrived the clouds symbolically rolled back and we had a succession of brilliant brocken spectres — a magical way to finish the Corbett.

Section 15:   5. BEINN AIRIGH CHARR   791 m   OS 19   930762
              The hill of the rough shieling (bin arry har)

Section 15:   6. BEINN LAIR   860 m   OS 19   982732
              Hill of the mare

Beinn Lair is a long flat but broken ridge presenting on its south or Loch Maree side no outstanding features. To the north, however, for a distance of some $2\frac{1}{2}$ miles it throws down what is possibly the grandest inland line of cliffs to be found in Scotland.

                                                            (H. T. Munro)

Ben Lair: graceful, solid, and broad.

                                                      (John Maccullough)

We spent a little time on the summit of Beinn Airigh Charr and agreed that hills do not rank by height alone.

(G. T. Clover)

Mountaineers were long in discovering the spectacular nature of these Corbetts, for their grandest faces point northwards to one of Scotland's wildest empty quarters. Loch Maree did not have efficient roads till recent times. The post went on foot along the north shore, which sounds impossible, and boats were the main means of travel till well into the nineteenth century. Maccullough, writing in 1824, enthuses both about Loch Maree and the surrounding hills, at a time when hills were still generally regarded with horror. He is worth quoting in part for he was far ahead of his time. A cart and twelve men helped haul his ship's boat from the sea into Loch Maree, along which they rowed on a fair summer day.

Loch Maree's mountains present a greater diversity of form and character than any of the Scottish lakes. Ben Lair is the principal feature. The middle ground is splendid and wild: rock and wood, silvery clouds and the sun shedding a flood of light over the lake. Even the dark firs and the cold grey cliffs of Ben Lair seemed to rejoice in the bright sunshine, while the warm brown and purple of the heath tinged the nearer hills with that richness of colour known only to these mountainous regions. Every summit assumed a bluer tone till the last peaks emulated the misty azure of the sky into which they melted. It was a scene, as the Emperor Charles said of Florence, too beautiful to be looked at except on holidays. But such days are indeed the holidays of the Highlands, rare and precious and compensating for many previous ones of mist and rain, of weariness and disappointment.

It is not only that nature gives us a keener enjoyment of those gleams of happiness which break through the dreary atmosphere of life but, as if in compensation for the savage aspect of the mountains derived from bad weather, its hours of sunshine are hours which can be found nowhere else. No one can know the full value of summer who has not known it in a land of mountains, no one can feel, who has not felt it among the hills, the joy which can fill the mind, the sense of beauty, the bounding, exuberant happiness . . .

An even earlier traveller, James Hogg, the Ettrick Shepherd, came this way in 1803. Two locals "who, perceiving that my attention was much taken by the scenery, promised to lead me through some which I should not see equalled, and I believe they were as good as their

word. Some parts are grand beyond measure, parts were named after
Fingalian heroes, the chief being the Fion Loch."

Ling and Glover in 1909 made the first serious climbing sortie to
these northern cliffs and half their account is taken up telling of their
travel to reach the hills. As Ling said, "It is a far cry to Poolewe." The
Munro quote at the head of this section, made in 1905, was the spur
that sent them this way. They hired a charabanc at Achnasheen,
somewhat taken aback at the fifteen-seater just for the two of them.
Their "modest weight" was insufficient to keep the vehicle from
bouncing into the loch so they "were obliged to carry some ballast in
the shape of bags of corn". They walked along the north shore and up
and across to the Bealach Rheinnidh (a route I too followed, in reverse)
to come on "the appalling overhangs" of Beinn Lair's north face. They
climbed a gully to reach the summit, had a snack where they could
look down on Isle Maree and then returned to Poolewe. That would
still be a long day's walk today.

The next day a keeper led them round to the north side of Beinn
Airigh Charr. The great tower, north of the summit, is locally known
as Martha's Peak. Martha was a legendary heroine who took her goats
to pasture on the mountain and was reputed to have made the first and
only traverse of the tower. Unfortunately she dropped her distaff and,
in endeavouring to recover it, fell and was killed. Ling and Glover's
day on Martha's Peak was sufficiently interesting for them to return
the following year with some other climbers. Several new routes were
climbed. This sort of chance discovery and enthusiastic follow up has
marked climbing on these two mountains ever since. Often on a first
visit people had not been equipped for climbing such unexpectedly
huge cliffs so felt compelled to return. Students, with longer holidays,
have often been the winners in this game. If today's colourful
ballerinas could manage the walk they'd find rock beyond their
dreams. Thankfully this is not country for psychedelic egos so much
as for those with a touch of the Maccullough enthusiasm.

Having read about the area, and made some long tramps through it,
when I came seeking the Corbetts I did so across Loch Maree — as did
Ling, Glover *et al* in 1910 — as did Maccullough before them in 1824. I
was to enjoy Maccullough's weather, too, the start of a long summer
heatwave such as I have never met before or since while actively
seeking Corbetts. I'd been canoeing further down the west coast and
when I drove north I felt I was blundering into the Sahara. I did not
launch on Loch Maree until 7.30 in the evening and the day was still
monstrous hot. I paddled out on an oily swell to the choke of islands
and had some interesting navigation through their jungly, chunky
sandstone chaos as my maps disagreed with each other and with the

reality. A startled deer on one island careered off along the shore and right round to come back almost on top of me again. The number of islands on Loch Maree varies according to the level of the water but Eilean Subhainn is the biggest, and has a loch in it, obviously higher than Loch Maree, yet 64 feet deep, 30 feet deeper than Loch Maree. On the original bathymetrical survey, no boat could be carried to the loch; soundings were taken by a member of the team swimming about in the water. I rounded Eilean Subhainn and, accompanied by a noisy diver, moved on towards Isle Maree, where I landed.

The old walled graveyard on Isle Maree had all but vanished and the carvings on the few old stones were weathered beyond reading. St Maelrubha's well, scene of ancient bull sacrifices and many hoped-for cures for insanity, had also disappeared but I found the penny tree, a real oddity. The original tree has died (copper poisoning?) and bits and pieces, embedded with a scaling of coins, lay about among the deep litter of pennies going back over generations. Queen Victoria visited this older tree but now a new oak has taken over and already its trunk has the scaly appearance of an armadillo hide. Pure superstition sees modern man enact this custom of hammering a penny into the tree, for the allied hope of a cure from the well has long gone. The well supposedly went dry after someone dipped a mad dog into it. (The book *Sacred Waters*, by Janet and Colin Bord, is a good introduction to the topic of wells in Britain.)

The midges rather curtailed my explorations and I paddled across to the north shore. Maccullough again: "The northern margin presents rocky, wooded bays and creeks rising into noble overhanging cliffs and mountains. The effect of Sleugach [Slioch, *a spear*] is perhaps more striking than of any mountain in Scotland. Where the skirts of Ben Lair descend into water the remains of a forest are almost incredible, producing a landscape that might be expected in the Alps rather than the tamer arrangements of Scottish mountains.

"The long shadows of evening gave a repose to the scene so that even the liquid sound which followed the dip of the oars seemed an intrusion on the hush of nature. The last crimson at length vanished from the summits and all became alike wrapped in one gentle hue of tranquil grey marking the summer twilight of a northern July."

Maccullough had fun navigating the islands, in the gloaming, back to the western end of the loch. Even at midnight he recorded the temperature was up over 70°F. I pulled my canoe on to a slope of bracken and camped on a knoll 200 feet up among the oak, birch, alder and holly: a world of grey verticalities and vegetative advance, the hornblende schists and the most northerly outposts of the old wood of Caledonia. "Camping" was lying stickily inside a sheet bag on top of my rucksack in the heather. There were a lot of wee beasties making scratchy noises and a roding woodcock went round and round on his clockwork flight.

"Ben Lair will well repay the toil to its summit. The height exceeds 3,000 feet [mercifully, it is only 2,817 feet] and though it produces few alpine plants there is perhaps the greatest variety of quartz in the world, ranging from jet black to snow white. The great attraction is the view, and chiefly to the north over the wildest mountains of Ross. It is usual to speak of rocks and precipices, whether present or not, but here they exist with no need of exaggeration. Here are mountains which show the very skeleton of the earth. Everything is gigantic and fearsome, wild and strange and new." (Maccullough)

Hogg was equally impressed. Of the Black Rock (the East Top of Beinn Lair is still Sgurr Dubh) he considered its spectacle far out of reach of comparison with anything else he'd ever seen: "It extends a whole English mile, along which nothing may pass, and is so appropriately termed black that it appears stained with ink, its face everywhere distorted by dark slits, gaping chasms and a most awful deformity."

At 6.30 a.m. I was teasing my way up the steep mix of crag and forest which is so typical of this shore of Loch Maree. Slioch had an edging of sunrise brightness and the day soon pulsed and shimmered in heat haze. The Torridons stood on their heads in the loch below, the reflection and the reality identical. I was not lucky enough to see a sea eagle as did Maccullough. (Next time maybe, for, since his day, they have become extinct, and reintroduced.) The gorge of the Allt na Cloich-bheith led to grassier slopes and my devil's halo of flies slowly faded. The flora was quite rich and varied with quiet banks of avens and campion and louder shouts of tormentil and thyme. A wild rose had glowed a ghostly exuberance against the dark trees when I'd landed the night before. The day was too hot to botanise properly. I didn't perspire so much as run with salt water. Long before the top my swimming shorts were as wet as if I'd been in the Loch.

Approaching Meall a' Choire Ghlais I set off some goats (the descendants of Martha's flock perhaps?), but all the deer just lay and let me past. The view all round had largely vanished into haze so when I finally stepped on to the summit of Beinn Airigh Charr the view *downwards* came as a shock. A knoll beyond made a fine perch. A score of goats were lying on the ridge out to Martha's Peak. A tiny tent, obtrusively orange, down by one of the lochans, gave scale to that lonely country, surely one without equal in Scotland for sheer wildness.

Eventually I went on, down to the Strathan Buidhe pass and up *the*

Middle Hill, Meall Mheinnidh (where a rabbit scampered off on the summit), and down again to the Bealach Mheinnidh where a short traverse led to welcome water and two pints of tea. I angled up — for ever, it felt — to a notch above the cliffs and then wended to a cairn on the edge of the summit dome. Gleann Tulacha, between the cliffs of Beinn Lair and those of A' Mhaighdean, can have no rivals for dramatic grandeur. Superlatives falter here. They are superfluous in such elemental simplicity.

The summit cairn was reached at 11 a.m. When a small breeze blew, the heat was like the opening of an oven door. I descended on a long, falling traverse line that bisected both the paths over the hills (Ling and Glover reached Beinn Lair doing the opposite) and having collected my buzz of flies, launched the canoe at once. I passed Isle Maree again and, the circumnavigation of Eilean Subhainn completed, landed below the main road at 3 p.m.

I've never sweated so while canoeing, and before driving off I waded out into Loch Maree with a bar of soap for a tepid bath, to the amusement of some tourists. The canoe was left that night at Garve and the next day I was off for the Lewisian gneiss of the far north: Hee, Arkle, Quinag — all in beating sunshine — described later on.

With hindsight, I'm amazed at my dedication but then, given our normal weather conditions, who would not push things a bit? After Beinn Airigh Charr and Beinn Lair I tended to call such heat "Maccullough conditions" — then I read further and found him complaining because his champagne was skimmed with ice by the freezing blast on top of Ben More in Mull. We were both just lucky on these singeing summits above Loch Maree.

A boat might be hired at the Loch Maree Hotel, popular with fishermen, otherwise the approaches to these Corbetts are long tramps from either end of the loch. The paths shown are all good pony tracks. With permission a car can be taken to Inveran or Kernsary but the road is a rough one. Carnmore has limited bothy accommodation, otherwise the country to the north offers no shelter. This utter remoteness, which has not changed at all since the days of Maccullough, or of Ling and Glover, combined with the sheer scale and drama of the landscape, makes it altogether a special place. Walk gently in this wilderness.

Section 15: 7. CREAG RAINICH 807 m OS 19/20 097751
            Bracken crag

Wanderings in the Fannichs and through between Loch Maree and Dundonnell had kept showing me new, good prospective expeditions, for this is tremendous country for trekking — and the hills are not so bad either!

Creag Rainich became a summit which was long-intended but somehow never ascended. Eventually I made a special trip to the Corbett at the tail end of the scorching days which began on Loch Maree and marked ascents of Arkle and Quinag in the north. I found a quiet spot off Destitution Road (A832) for the Dormobile and, by burning smoke coils, I could sleep with the door open. Big green-eyed flies were the main pest. The only car that pulled in, briefly, disturbed a pair of common gulls who were putting on a fascinating courtship display outside my mobile hide. I was away by 6.30 a.m. A rolling mass of clouds was being held back on the Dirrie More by a cordon of Fannichs. A streamer broke forth every now and then only to evaporate into nothingness.

I'd walked a mile up Destitution Road (built in the 19th century to provide work for the hard-hit local population) towards Fain, the now derelict inn/staging post of those days and crossed to a nettle-covered ruin to utilise a path up on to the moors. Though only about four miles from road to summit, I needed three hours to tease a way over the bogs and braes. On the broad saddle below the Corbett I left my heavy rucksack, a line of fence poles clearly marking the place. (Losing a rucksack is rather embarrassing.)

The NE Ridge gave an enjoyable ascent but I was beginning to long for water. Even the Allt na Faine, draining the big eastern corrie, had nearly dried out. There were 200 noisy deer on the slope across the burn: plenty of grunting, the odd bellow and the bubble and squeak of the calves. The clegs were making life miserable for the sheep — but at least they seemed to prefer the sheep rather than the stray human. The view round the ring of Fannichs, Deargs, An Teallach and Torridon was a mighty one (as expected) but conditions were hazy, a milky haze which I did not like the look of at all. I was not long on the summit.

The lochan in the first dip, as I retraced the route up, was bubbling with tadpoles and the water felt tepid. The air reeked of drying bogs, sheep and deer, for the big herd had crossed the corrie and the deer were streaming down and along, past where my rucker lay, to wallow in any small pools they could find. They were not keen to move when I, with rucker again, began to descend westwards off the saddle but I was not very keen to move either when at last I found some clear, flowing water. Down, nearer the Eas Ban, I peeled off my clingfilm clothing for a delicious dook and a brew.

The gash of a side burn forced a detour to the west bank of the river which tumbled lethargically from pool to pool then fell, as the Eas Ban (White Falls), into another big gash. I couldn't really see the fall from above but the view over the strath to the many spires of An Teallach was rewarding. The woods were strangely silent. The fall must be one of the country's most impressive. Only the top half shows from the valley below and, even with the severe drought, was spraying up daintily. I crossed below the fall but was forced on to the bed rocks by another side gorge. Out into the valley, golden with sweet gale, the clegs decided I was worthy prey after all. Perhaps I hadn't cooked enough till then.

I followed the strath past Achneigie to Shenavall where I had a couple of nights and climbed the Deargs (15:9, 10) before heading out. My armful of firewood had to be abandoned as I needed my hands to slaughter the pernicious clegs. I cleared seven sacks of rubbish (mostly empty whisky bottles) out of the bothy and was brewing when a lady, with a posse of terriers, arrived from a boat on the loch. We chatted and it turned out that she and her brothers owned Camusunary in Skye. They were wondering what to do with the old Celtic Lodge by the shore there, so I suggested the MBA might be interested. Who knows, that cup of tea for the visitor could have been a crucial influence?

The barometer had been falling all day and the stifling heat finally exploded into a (for once) welcome deluge. I felt like going out to dance in it — then I remembered I'd left the skylights of the Dormobile wide open! I went out from Shenavall over the moors to the A832 at the head of the Dundonnell River's steep setting. In dry conditions reaching Shenavall this way is less toilsome than the tramp up the stony road from Corrie Hallie.

This was quite an interesting round-route for Creag Rainich (if having to return to a parked vehicle) but, if a kindly driver could help, it is easier to walk along the path north of Loch a' Bhraoin, *the loch of the showers*, and start the traverse from there. The hill is also perfectly possible in a day from Corrie Hallie. By whatever route the Eas Ban should not be missed: not every good Corbett is twinned with a splendid waterfall.

Section 15: 8. BEINN A' CHAISGEIN MOR   857 m   OS 19   983785
       The big forbidding hill

Being neighbour to A' Mhaighdean, this hill is a contender for the title, "remotest Corbett". We had dealt with the remoteness problem by basing ourselves at Shenavall for several days. At that time Corbetts were not specifically being chased, just "good things", so this hill was done for its own sake, as was Beinn a' Chlaidheim which later escaped to Munro status, and we went out via Loch a' Bhraoin, unaware of Corbett Creag Rainich above. Since then Shenavall has become so busy that I tend to camp in order to keep the element of solitude which this magnificent area demands.

Beinn a' Chaisgein Mor is a two-faced hill: to north and east a big dome, utterly unpretentious, but from south and west every bit the big, forbidding hill. Above Carnmore rise blocks of cliff with some of the longest and best rock-climbing routes in the north. Carnmore has a barn howff which could be a useful overnight stop if Beinn Lair and Beinn Airigh Charr are also planned. They are a little too distant from a base at Shenavall.

There was quite a gang of us: Dave and Stuart (local friends), and newcomers David, Louise and Glyn. A first look through the skylight showed misty tops but nothing to delay setting out. "Just another ordinary sort of day", someone suggested. Soft-boiled eggs were an interesting breakfast game. We walked down to the river in bare feet, paddled across and edged the bogs to Larachantivore. There was a bridge then, one which tended to come and go (now definitely gone), which enabled us to keep moving, essential with a clout of clegs giving us their undivided attention. We scurried up Gleann na Muice and Gleann na Muice Beag until the path, curling over the head of the glen, brought our pace down. At the scattering of lochs on the watershed we had a coffee break and were caught up by a keeper with five terriers, a bag of fish and a pony. He was returning to Letterewe but was happy to pause for a chat and a drink.

A long grassy brae took us up to the top of the Corbett. We found the remains of a meteorological balloon and also the remains of a stag. Dave wanted to collect the antlers but they were attached to the skull, not being cast, and were full of putrified goo with the most revolting smell. Dave had to walk downwind from us for the rest of the day. We found one of our daintiest mountain flowers, dwarf cornel, whose white "petals" are bracts and the dark centre is the real flower.

We sat for a long time on top, with the Fionn Loch below, and all the southern hills wrapped in a fur of cloud (ermine round their shoulders, like a duchess) then slowly followed the cliffs round before returning to the path where we'd left our rucksacks. We pitched tents by the Fuar Loch Mor, then headed off for A' Mhaighdean which was reflected in the black waters: a world of reds and greys, sandstone and gneiss. We went up the NW Ridge, and the evening became one of sheer splendour.

The clouds largely vanished and a lit pathway of watery brilliance led the eye west over lochs and sea to the Outer Hebrides. The thirty buttresses of Beinn Lair faced us, with Slioch and the Torridon giants beyond. The Mullach group looked like snow-capped active volcanoes, and northwards lay the mighty Deargs and mightier An Teallach. Between good scrambling on sandstone towers and gazing at this incomparable view sunset was near when we reached the summit. We raced down to the Fuar Loch which burned red as the sun was setting beyond the Carn Mor crags of Beinn a' Chaisgein Mor. One could almost hear the frost sliding off the stars, and the breathy silence was broken only by one tingling, echoing cry from a loon. In the ghostly moonlight the cloud re-formed and rose up the face of those crags, churning and towering high into the sky above the Corbett. We may have started on an ordinary sort of day. We ended on one with awe, an almost mystical splendour.

Section 15:   9. BEINN DEARG MOR   908 m   OS 19   032799
      Big red hill

Section 15:   10. BEINN DEARG BHEAG   818 m   OS 19   020811
      Small red hill

Sir Hugh Munro described Beinn Dearg Mor as being "a long way from anywhere", a base at Shenavall was therefore a help in making the first sortie to these Corbetts. They are well worth the effort but I suspect they are more often admired (from An Teallach opposite or from the Fannichs to the east) than they are climbed. I'd reached Shenavall over Craig Rainich (see 15:7) on a day that saw a long heatwave finally crash out with rain and storm. An early visit outside next morning showed that it was still raining, but later the barometer rose and so did the cloud.

When I set off, the red peaks of Beinn Dearg Mor were lancing the clouds and the strath glittered as if newly painted in silver and green. The rain had been refreshing and the hot world had drunk deep of it: all was crisp, sharp and wondrous clear again. Even the pestilential clegs had vanished.

I criss-crossed the plenteous rivers and bogs of Strath na Sealga and eventually pulled up into the NE Corrie, the mountain's great feature, via a gurgly underground burn. Asphodel spears and heather bells were colourful and the first blaeberries of the year (in July) an unexpected bonus. From the corrie lip I went up a sizeable split-rock deposit and then took to the rocks: odd wee steps that became quite good walls which were skirted or climbed and, as so often, gave more sport than was envisaged. I was experimenting with a pack frame and it proved a great inconvenience. At one stage I had to lower it before being able to climb down a crack and then I was forced right under chimneys and ribs till these were more climbable. In a good old sweat I reached a subsidiary peaklet (*c.*810 m) and was glad to rest awhile for the view was perhaps one of the Top Ten, as befits one of the top ten Corbetts for height.

After a small gap a short pull led to the grassy top with its substantial cairn. The NE Corrie (Corrie nan Clach), seamed with gullies and jutting prows of rock, looked very wild. One gully framed An Teallach. I ran out of film — and discovered the spare I'd brought was the used one I thought I'd left in the bothy. Ah well, the sky was steadily clouding over, so the loss was not too annoying. Beinn Dearg Bheag looked very small in the scale of that wild landscape. Strath Beinn Dearg and the water rushing down from the worn plateau of Lochan na Bearta reminded me vividly of Norway, a country which is in many ways a sort of super-Scotland. In either country one keeps making comparisons. It is quite different in my other stamping ground of Morocco; there it is the contrasts that startle and attract.

Two ptarmigan burped off as I descended to the col for the narrow ridge to the second Corbett. Loch Toll an Lochain, down to the right, was a text-book corrie lochan. Beinn Dearg Bheag I noted in my diary as being "about the easiest second Corbett ever" and, for all its startling appearance, Beinn Dearg Mor is easy enough if approached from the top of Gleann na Muice Beag and Loch Beinn Dearg or even the NE Ridge. I'd just been looking for fun by going into the corrie.

The second Corbett had a tiny cairn on its grassy summit. I went on along the broken crest for a while but, with rain threatening, I chose to turn down steeply on to an indeterminate east ridge. There were a few crags to avoid and on one the mossy surface had peeled away taking a rowan tree with it. I shoved the tree in my pack and it is now growing and flourishing outside the bothy. The strath had plenty of long-leaved sundew in flower and the lochside produced plenty of clean bogwood.

Two Glasgow lads had arrived and one yarned and drank with me (he drank Grouse and I drank tea) until he keeled over off the end of the bench. A while later they went off to "fish" and four Aberdonians arrived. After the two returned, a girl staggered in, wearing town shoes, and rather exhausted. She was given tea *with* whisky to drink, and became loquacious. With lack of discretion she asked the lads what they were up to. One quickly said, "Oh us, we're frae the department", and when pressed about which department added, "Oh, tourism an aw that. See you, we canna have the likes of you hirplin in here. We'll hae a proper motorway. An we'll hae a five star hotel an no this dump o a place. An you see yon [pointing to Beinn Dearg Mor], we're gonna shift yon bing."

My most memorable day on Beinn Dearg Mor was on a New Year's Day. We ploughed into the bothy through deep snow on the last day of the year and with song and drams saw it away in pleasant ease. John, on a last fling before going off to be a doctor in Bhutan, led Dave and Jim off for a likely line on the corrie face of the East Top. He gave them an unforgettable Hogmanay. Dave said he'd never been so scared for so long, ever! The other Dave, Duncan, Margaret, Stuart and Tommy and I went along the moraine, then had a flounder in deep snow before going over the gouged centre to the East Ridge. Its successive steps gave plenty of fun and I sent plenty of wind-compressed snow tumbling on their heads. We kept very much to the rock crests as the big snow slopes on the flanks had a slabby feel that threatened avalanches. We zigzagged up some ledges, climbed a corner, revelled in an icy gully and soon reached the East Top. The view was unbelievably white, blazing white, and the sun glittered the powder we kicked up into the freezing air. You could go a lifetime and not equal that view.

Young Duncan was pushed ahead to flog a trail from Top to Summit. We photographed him, with the drift blowing off against the blue sky, then plodded along behind. Cameras clicked madly. In that pristine winter array the scene was so intensely beautiful that I, for one, found it deeply moving. What a way to start a year!

After an almost ritualistic naming-off of every hill in sight we went on down to the col to Beinn Dearg Bheag, but it was already 1.30 p.m. so we cannily said "Enough!" and floundered off downwards, on the Loch Beinn Dearg side as it was still in the sun, to reach the Carnmore track. At Larachantivore a storm ambushed us out of nowhere and the bogs and the paddles across to the bothy reverted to their usual interesting state. You can never take liberties in that wild country. If they ever shift "yon bing" they can happily put it in my back garden.

Section 15:   11. SAIL MHOR   767 m   OS 19   033887
         The big heel

The last time I went up this superb hill was with a frisky octogenarian, Ivan, a borrowed black labrador, Widge, and my own Sheltie, Storm. If I thought I could gain a leisurely ascent I was soon disillusioned. Most of the time I seemed to be chasing Ivan (with Widge climbing the hill six times over as he dashed to and fro), for Ivan just never stopped while I took photos, ate lunch, plastered heels and enjoyed standing to stare. Beware energetic octogenarians!

Sail Mhor forms a sort of coda to the symphonic sprawl of An Teallach. While the eastern corries of *The Forge* are famous there is a huge complex of circling ridges facing north west, and one arm ends in Sail Mhor, a tiered sandstone upthrust of grand character. All that secretive land drains down by the Allt Airdessaidh; even in rare dry conditions there is a brawling burn, which cuts down in a series of falls, among the best in the country, to Ardessie, about $2\frac{1}{2}$ miles along Little Loch Broom from the Dundonnell Hotel where we were staying. We set off up the east bank path on a morning of golden spring sunshine.

There are waterfalls all the way. After several smaller shoots there is a wide one falling into a pool with Sail Mhor as backcloth. The gorge runs deep and straight, as you notice looking down, but the four main cascades are out of sight, and need to be seen from the west bank. There is no crossing the river, however. Even after we'd breasted the slopes overlooking the sea loch and could see away up a high valley with the jagged top of Sgurr Ruadh at its head (the westmost top of An Teallach's west ridge) the river was just too deep to boulder-hop across. The tributary draining from Sail Mhor was passed before we managed to pick a way over. We then followed this side stream up towards the col between Sail Mhor and Ruigh Mheallain, a bump on the ridge leading to Sgurr Ruadh. Deer tiptoed over the skyline ahead of us.

We turned to zigzag up to the prow above. The glory had gone from the day and an icy wind made the jagged crags on the skyline a first objective. There I found a lee to plaster feet and to eat. Ivan stormed on. Widge commuted between us. We walked an erratic arc round the south-facing hollow of Sail Mhor to the summit cairn. The stone cairn-shelter, earlier, is the cairn visible from the A832 road to Gruinard Bay, from which angle Sail Mhor is an inverted pudding-bowl shape.

The view from the upper slopes is tremendous. An Teallach's great circuit is near and bold and the Beinn Deargs — Mhor and Bheag — thrust up in jagged array with all the jumbled country of rock and water sprawled to the south giving perhaps the most dramatic landscape in mainland Scotland. The Summer Isles, Coigach, Beinn Ghobhlach make the north as interesting. Sail Mhor is a viewpoint high even in the Corbett ratings.

We arrived at the summit with a touch of rain. Ivan was for going on. He completed the ridge round and down to the col to Ruigh Mheallain, to retrace his upward route (the only straightforward one), but I lay out of the blatter hoping the sun would reappear for photographs. After a cold and fruitless wait I returned to the lowest point on the summit rim and made a direct descent to Ardessie, sneaking past a snow edge and down a steep gully to reach the moorland and on down the west bank of the stream.

My combination of routes would be possible in either direction, but the direct route is brutally steep on the upper slopes of the mountain. Most people, I think, would prefer Ivan's gentler return route. There is no recommended route off along to Sail Bheag and the only attractive addition needs a tame driver — descending south to the col, as Ivan did, but then going down west to Lochan Gaineamhaich for the path which leads down to Gruinard Bay; wild and lonely country.

Section 15: 12. BEINN LIATH MHOR A' GHIUBHAIS LI 766 m OS
           20 281713
           Big grey hill of the colourful pines (bin lee-ah vor
           a goo-vus lee)

This is one of the less memorable of Corbetts and, having been brought in with the metric revisions, my memories are perhaps enhanced by doing the hill on my birthday (mid-August), a day which completed my topping-up of all the new Corbetts. Sadly, I had a dull grey day: the ascent was redeemed neither by the view nor by much in the way of wildlife or topographical interest. The Abhainn a' Ghiubhais Li probably preconditions Munroists against Beinn Liath Mhor. A big grey hill above big black bogs.

The Corbett can be climbed from anywhere along the A835 Dirrie More road. As my Dormobile was parked overnight towards the west end of Loch Glascarnoch I crossed the heathery moors to pick up the stream running down from Meall Daimh. This is *the hill of the hinds*, which was fair description, as the corrie was crowded with them. They were surprisingly vocal, their grunting and groaning being a sound the dog immediately recognises. I returned over Meall Daimh. The one place I would not go is that peat-riven valley west of the Corbett. Those who have approached the eastern Fannichs by that route will know why.

The view is restricted but varied: Fannichs close, Deargs with their Coire Lair trench *en face*, Am Faochagach (another unfavourite hill with many), and Wyvis away to the spacious east. I keep meaning to go back. Objectively, this must be a good hill on the right day. A stuffy, viewless, midsummer plod affected my judgment — but at least there were no midges.

Section 15:   13. BEINN ENAIGLAIR   889 m   OS 20   225805
              The hill of the timid birds

If anyone asked me for a typical Corbett I might suggest Beinn
Enaiglair. The hill has the sturdy individuality and superb view of so
many. The Beinn Dearg hills are sternly impressive yet, after a long
tramp in their fastness, the six of us who puffed up Beinn Enaiglair
agreed it was the best place we'd found on our ten-hour day.

We had started out early from Loch Droma on the Dirrie More and
taken the path over to the ruins near Loch a' Gharbhrain (not shown on
the map) to walk up the Long Corrie, then up through the Princess
Corrie to the scoured world of lonely Loch nan Eilean. After wending
along to Loch a' Choire Ghranda we had a good climb up to traverse
Cona Mheall, a very fine ridge indeed. By the time we were off the
boulders hunger cried lunchtime and we sat in the lee of the wall by the
tiny lochan on the col to Beinn Dearg. Though midsummer there were
still large snow patches on this big hill. We toiled up Dearg and followed
the wall which swooped along above deep Gleann na Sguaib. We then
went up the cone of Iorguill (*battle hill*) which gave a nasty descent until
we found ourselves on a path down to the col and up to join the one
(shown on the map) which circuits Beinn Enaiglair. We turned along it
and, by the stream of the Corbett's eastern corrie, found another non-
map path which took us up to the summit.

What a viewpoint we found! From the bouldery dome we looked at
near Fannichs and far Torridons and all the giants from there to
An Teallach to Beinn Ghobhlach between the Loch Brooms, where
we'd been the day before (it only just makes 2,000 feet but lacks nothing
else), to cloud-streaming Coigach, to distant Assynt and the big, bold
Deargs. The last two to arrive were given the bonus of seeing an eagle
gliding past.

A descent by the SE Ridge led us to the path which wanders on and on
along the heights before turning down to Lochdrum at the west end of
Loch Droma. The Allt Leachachain did not present an alternative,
being full of peat bogs; its waterfalls were later explored from below. In
this rough country everyone is only too happy to use paths when they
exist. Beinn Enaiglair is ringed by paths — take your pick — but finish
up the eastern corrie: the unmapped path goes up the burn's north bank
and then turns to zigzag up to the SE Ridge not far from the top.

If starting from Braemore (the lodge has gone but the path goes up by
the Home Loch) don't omit to visit the Corrieshalloch Gorge and its
falls (NTS). Lael Forest is full of hidden surprises and the views are on a
grand scale. The Cuileag Gorge is an interesting place too.

Section 15: 14. BEINN A' CHAISTEIL 787 m OS 20 370801
    Castle hill

The six of us who had been on Beinn Enaiglair (15:13) the day before went our various ways this day: some left from Braemore to Ullapool for Lairg and the rest were dropped at Aultguish Inn to wait for the Ullapool–Inverness bus. That evening I was meeting three other friends off the Inverness–Ullapool bus at Braemore — the day was mine and Beinn a' Chaisteil beckoned.

Beinn a' Chaisteil and Meall a' Ghrianain are the two rolling summits east of Loch Vaich. They face that most massive of Munros, Am Faochagach, which sprawls from west of Loch Vaich to the Allt Lair boundary of the Beinn Dearg hills. Strath Vaich, a pretty strath, drains to the south and is served by a private estate road leaving the A835 two kilometres east of Aultguish Inn. I cycled up the road with the dog trotting along, sometimes ahead, sometimes behind. He was a bit puzzled at a black sheep with a black lamb. Being midsummer the strath rang with the voices of oystercatchers, peewits, curlews and sandpipers — and the ubiquitous cuckoo.

The good road goes up to Strathvaich Lodge but we were left with a rough old road which put in a stiff brae above the dam of Loch Vaich. The view is very much dominated by the hogsback of Meall a' Ghrianain above and by the Tollomuick Forest crags and corries across the water. Most hollows held dirty remnants of the winter snows, even on hot midsummer's day.

At Lubachlaggan I was quite glad to dump the cycle. By going up beside the burn (or in it) I was able to enjoy a breezy shade, and also avoid some of the heather. It seemed a long haul up on to the sprawling dome of a summit plateau. The view from the trig point was very different from yesterday's on Enaiglair: that being of the stark west, this the rolling, bovine bumps of the east. Wyvis rose large and blue beyond Inchbae and Rannoch Forest, and Carn Chuinneag was a very visible Corbett to the east. This is vast uninhabited deer-forest country with long valley approaches. The track by Loch Vaich goes through to Gleann Mor and Alladale: great country for bike and hike, for bens and bothies and solitary exploration. All the water drains out to Ardgay/Bonar Bridge and buses and trains make long tramps through (even coast-to-coast) perfectly feasible — and more rewarding.

The bike dictated my return route, but if I'd *walked* up by the loch I'd have returned along the heights, over Meall a' Ghrianain. *Grianan* is a sunny spot, or a peat-drying place or a lovers' meeting place. The hill's long south ridge is eventually cut by an estate road that leads back down to Strath Vaich. An interesting variant would be to drop down the other side to Strath Rannoch which exits to the A835 a couple of kilometres nearer Garve, at Inchbae Lodge. I juddered down directly, west, to the head of the loch and back along the road, wheeled the bike over the dried-out bogs to the dam, crossed it, and so enjoyed the good road down by the lodge. Chickweed wintergreen grew near the wood and a hoodie crow was noisily objecting to the presence of a kestrel.

Shoving the bike into the Dormobile I gave my head such a crack I nearly passed out and by the time I'd recovered the Inverness–Ullapool bus, followed by a long tail of cars, had gone by. I drove all the way to Braemore Junction before overtaking everything, and a minute later Tony and Mike stepped off the bus. Tony, on his first visit to Scotland, was astonished at the emptiness. He had expected Braemore Junction to be a town at least, not just a junction of roads. But what roads and what Corbett country they led us to!

Section 15:   15. CARN BAN   845 m   OS 20   339876
               White cairn

This must be a claimant for the remotest Corbett, being equidistant from nowhere. Tackling the hill on the last day of the year was perhaps unconventional, but Dave was Munro-bagging and keen to visit Seana Bhraigh, etc., so I managed to do a trade: a chance of Carn Ban for joining his Munro foray. (As he is now climbing Corbetts he is pleased not to need another expedition into the area.)

We went in over Am Faochagach from the Dirrie More and, abandoning camping ideas as the weather deteriorated, stayed in the private bothy at Glenbeg, next to an "iron lodge". Neither looks much used, being a long way from Inverlael, whose deer-forest extends down to here. We sealed ourselves in, made a fire of bogwood and cooked a festive meal, trying not to think of the weather — a wild night, with a violent wind eventually giving way to hours of torrential rain. The alarm clock was ignored.

At dawn we looked out on rushing torrents where the day before there had been minor streams. Most of the snow cover had been washed away. We set out only at ten o'clock when the floods had subsided a bit and managed to cross the river without difficulty. Some big crags overlook the glen; among the tumbled boulders below them there are several likely howffs. The stream down from Loch Sruban Mora was a dashing waterslide. We picked up a good stalkers' path which wiggled up to the loch. Water was sheeting off the surface and as the outflow was a deep torrent we, perforce, rounded the boggy west side to cross the inflow. A long rising line led us to the corner of Coire Mhor, a plunging glen, cliff-lined and wild. The clouds were down on the bigger hills but somehow we stayed just on the dry side of wet. We had a snack before sidling up and along a bump or two in the gale to the debatable top of Carn Ban.

I called the summit "debatable" in my log because we were not at all convinced that the highest point was as shown in relation to other features. We thought the summit somewhat further north. I dragged Dave over every possible claimant rise, before allowing him to hobble off down Coire Mhor. He'd collected as many blisters as Munros and/or Corbetts. The Corriemulzie shepherd was at the bothy and I had a crack with him till Dave limped in. We collected driftwood from the loch. Two whooper swans were bouncing on the waves.

The bothy was fairly primitive, with a concrete floor. After we'd dined we took to our sleeping bags for comfort, setting the alarm for 11.30 to hansel in the new year (1975). When the alarm went off the fire was out, the night was raw-cold, Dave was snoring, I turned over and went back to sleep; an eleven hour kip was a novel Hogmanay. The swans called on the loch and we went out to a golden crisp morning with a faint half flush along the jagged cliffs above. We had a grand two-day exit over all the Dearg Munros back to the Dirrie More. "Exit swimming", I wrote. Dave ended with more Munros than blisters so felt satisfied. And I'd collared Carn Ban.

If Carn Ban is tackled as a day walk many of the approach miles can be cycled. From the south the hydro road along Loch Vaich reaches into Gleann Beag and the path which we followed. From the east a car can be taken from Ardgay/Bonar Bridge to The Craigs in Strath Carron, then a cycle by Glencalvie Lodge, Alladale Lodge, along Gleann Mor to near Deanish Lodge, before rounding Meall Dionach to walk up the Allt Bheargais to Carn Ban.

From the north there is an estate road up Strath Mulzie to Loch a' Choire Mhoir which makes cycling possible from Oykell Bridge. This loch could also be reached from the west by Glen Achall and the Allt an Caorach (which now has an estate road too). Cycling to Loch an Daimh and making a long walking circuit up Glen Douchary of the many falls, Seana Bhraigh, Carn Ban, Coire Mor, Allt na Caorach would be my aesthetic recommendation.

Inverlael is also a possible — pedestrian — starting point. Enquire about using Glenbeg bothy from the keeper at Inverlael before leaving and reach it up Gleann na Squaib and exit over Coire an Lochain Sgeirich. Several Munros can be added *en route* on what is a three-day jaunt. The obvious southern trench of Loch Coire Lair–Loch Prille gives very heavy going and walking is easier over the pudding of Am Faochagach. Munroists will need little urging to make another foray into these hills for they are among the finest in the land.

Section 15: 16. CARN CHUINNEAG 838 m OS 20 484833
Cairn of the churn/buckets

This is the highest hill in the empty country north of Wyvis. The twin summits are often visible from a long way off and their identity can be puzzling. Carn Chuinneag is almost invariably climbed from Glen Calvie in the north.

I motored up Strath Carron one July from Ardgay/Bonar Bridge partly to climb this hill but also to see Croik church, remembered from the 1845 evictions. The people of Glen Calvie took shelter in the churchyard and scratched messages on the window panes. I remember the shock when I read of their being scratched *on the outside*. The church was barred to them in their need. "Glen Calvie. A wicked generation," they wrote. Having motored to Glencalvie Lodge, the end of the tarmac, I walked up Glen Calvie. There were no buildings visible, the bracken invades the in-fields and the heather creeps down. The silent emptiness was like Munch's "The Scream".

After an hour's walk up Glen Calvie the glen suddenly becomes Glen Diebidale, with Diebidale Lodge in Diebidale Deer Forest. The glen swings away west as a steep-flanked valley, and dominating this bend is Carn Chuinneag. A stalkers' path contorts a route up the western ridge of the Coire Cas-like corrie that runs down from between the two summits. As I set off up this path I was enveloped in a cloud of small whitish moths, which rose out of the deep heather. On the ridge the heather was closer cropped. Down in Glen Diebidale there were many deer grazing. I turned east at a junction of paths, using all the uphill help possible. All these tracks and paths make the Corbett a very easy ascent. The top path leads almost to the col between the summits.

The summit is a granite cone. Three stags were nearby and I managed to stalk them to about three feet. They were so stunned at finding me that they took a while to react and gallop off. Wheatears were active and ptarmigan flew round and round. Wyvis was the nearest big hill in view but black clouds on the Deargs sent me packing: down by Carn Maire and Loch Chuinneag to descend by estate road rather than the path I'd used in ascent: a modest expedition but an enjoyable one.

Section 15:   17. LITTLE WYVIS   764 m   OS 20   430645
The little noble or high mountain (wi'vis)

Wyvis the Munro rather hides its nobility, the normal approach from
Garbat showing rather bald features on top and a beard of forest
below. Little Wyvis is even more surrounded by spruce but has plenty
of interesting routes. Both hills, Munro and Corbett, have noble
views. Seen from Inverness or the coast they certainly impress with
their height. Little Wyvis looks tiny compared to the Munro.

I'd managed to park my Dormobile near the Black Water Bridge
(22 December). The snow fell quite heavily that night. The scenery
looked very Christmassy when I woke. (Bridge and road have since
been re-aligned but adequate parking places are available.) Several
tracks are shown on the map on the lower slopes of Wyvis and in
reality there are more of these than indicated while the NW flank has
substantial additions to the forest shown. The best track is the one that
wanders up towards the Bealach Beag and then swings south west
under Beinn a' Ghuilbein where it forks, one branch going on to
Meall Ruighe an Fhirich and the other angling down into the forest.
Before crossing the Bealach Beag stream, another branch turns left
(north) for a bit and then zigzags to the top of the Corbett. There are
not many Corbetts with a road to the top!

Not that the road was very useful in the deep powder snow. The
view from the top was relished: ice cream Fannichs and Wyvis cassata,
with a dark peppermint-cream tablecloth of forest below the panorama. The summit cairn was small (with an iron post stuck in it) so is
probably seldom visited. Coming back down, a clump of rushes held
the new snow on its seed heads, the cluster gleaming like a diamond
tiara. Little Wyvis rose as a shapely cone behind. I cut all the corners
descending this grassy hill and at the sheep fanks saw a group of
strange beasts which later research showed to have been Andean
guanacos (related to llamas). There were plenty of red deer, too, and
hyperactive coal-tits and long-tailed tits.

This is the easiest way up Little Wyvis, but the hill could also be
reached from the Bealach Mor in combination with Wyvis the
Munro. A path continues up the Allt a' Bhealaich Mhoir to the col east
of Tom na Caillich. They are hills worth saving for a fine winter's day
and, if small is beautiful, then little is noble.

COIGACH & ASSYNT

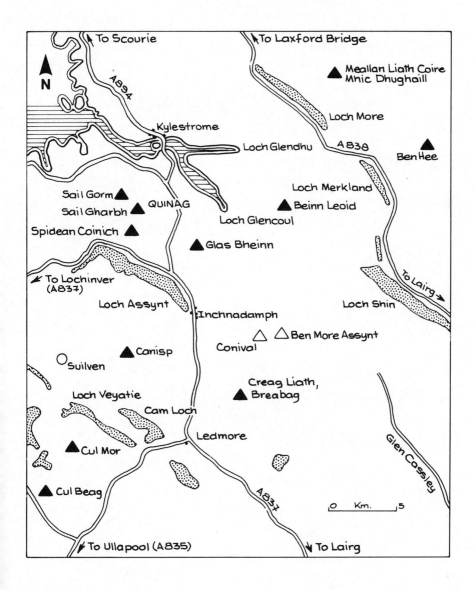

Section 16:   1. CUL BEAG   769 m   OS 15   140088
             Small back

Section 16:   2. CUL MOR   849 m   OS 15   162119
             Big back

"A LAND FOR young and eager and active" was how Inglis Clark
described the North West in 1907, but, if good roads and cars have
reduced the distances and isolation, it is still possible for us, as for the
Clark family, to be "excited by tales of the ridges and precipices of Cul
Beag and Cul Mor". These peaks now stand in and dominate the
Inverpolly National Nature Reserve. They are thus officially des-
ignated as worthy by man as well as God.

Both peaks have surprisingly easy access for such grand-looking
mountains, but their wilder, remoter corners deserve exploration. A
tramp through the area, looking at these peaks, is as rewarding as
climbing them. Every view seems to have a loch in the foreground
and, as if these two were not sufficient, there is the bonus of little Stac
Polly. I was a gangly schoolboy on a bike when I first came this way:
young, eager and active, indeed. The lure has lasted and, when I
wandered from Duncansby Head to Cape Wrath and southwards to
Land's End, I stravaiged by Canisp and Suilven and out again by
charming Gleann Laoigh between Cul Mor and Cul Beag. Several
people reading the account in *Hamish's Groats End Walk* have
commented, "It is easy to see which part of Britain you love best."

On another occasion we boldly attacked Cul Beag from Loch
Lurgain, setting off in thick mist; perhaps we did not know what lay
above, but then we wanted some sport, not a plod. As loch to summit
is only a mile the hill is steep and we had the fun we wanted, following
up gullies and tackling trim crags and heather ledges to break out
eventually on the upper grassier slopes. Danni and Kathy had never
scrambled before and Dave and Alex were no tigers. The dog chose
his own line and was usually grinning down at our escapades. There
were some adventurous frogs, and a wren family which churred
loudly at our intrusion. Our clothes were silvered by the mist on the
summit and after half an hour we gave up hoping for a view and found
another exciting route down the cliffs. Saner walkers will not scale
Cul Beag by these western cliffs. Both hills are normally approached
from the east.

Oddly enough, the same off-beat approach occurred on Cul Mor.

My Watch from the *Captain Scott* was camping between Suilven and Cul Mor so, perforce, our approach was from the north, thereby discovering the grandeur of Coire Gorm. This is so deeply gouged out that one would expect there to be a lochan. The corrie is crowned with a circle of crags, and it teemed with deer (new to most of the English trainees). We swung up, right, to the Pinnacled Ridge, and steep scrambling among weird shapes led to Cul Mor's NW Top and a sudden revelation of Suilven, Stac Polly, Cul Beag and Coigach above an extravagant water world. One pinnacle looks exactly like the knight from a set of chessmen. There is a sudden change from Torridonian sandstone to the capping quartzite: purply-red to stark grey in a few strides. Our half-hour on top had heaven itself in the view. We descended north eastwards until able to cut down into Coire Gorm again. After a brew, camp was struck and we packed round Suilven ready for Canisp the next day. Ah yes, they were young and active. I'm not so sure about the eager.

The same year I ascended Cul Mor from the east, with Tony, Mike and Peter, setting out along the path heading north from, near the Knockan centre and then on by Meallan Diomhain and the final cone —a route with unnecessary cairning. The reward of the North is that so many peaks stand clear in the view. Suilven, Canisp, Quinag, Assynt, Arkle, Hope, Klibreck, Seana Bhraigh, Beinn Dearg, The Fannichs, An Teallach, Coigach is quite a roll call. We made the circuit over Creag nan Calman, which can look the highest point from some angles, putting up a family of ptarmigan, the young only just able to fly and scattering in a great flurry. "How do they find each other again?" Tony asked.

Cul Beag has the same sort of feel from the east, setting out on a path from just south of the Knockan centre before wandering up the long, easy-angled Creag Dhubh Ridge to Meall Dearg and then the steep, boulder-capped cone of Cul Beag itself. Both hills are double-headed, prows to west, cliff-ringed and with long, gentle angles to the east. Cul Beag can equally well be approached from the Drumrunie–Loch Lurgain road or, for burn-followers, by the stream that drains the eastern corrie. The eastern approaches keep views hidden, then yield summit revelations. Ah well, I may not be so young, nor so active, now, but I'm as eager as ever to return to these Tweedle Dum and Tweedle Dee Corbetts. Norman MacCaig who knows the area well referred to the peaks here as his "mountains of mountains".

Section 16:   3. CANISP   846 m   OS 15   203187
         White mountain

Canisp exemplifies that big is not necessarily best. In most minds Canisp is completely overshadowed by neighbouring Suilven, which does not even make the Corbett altitude. Canisp's great merit, however, is as a viewpoint — it stands in the centre of the huge rock-and-water wildness that is so typically "North West" and out of which rise the starkest and most dramatic peaks in Britain: Cul Mor, Stac Polly, Suilven, Quinag, Conival, to name the nearest and clearest. These are names that can whistle a fresh wind into Southern hearts. Nowhere else is height so unimportant, but Canisp is a Corbett, for all that, built on some of the oldest rocks in the world.

One June day in 1967 saw my first visit to Canisp. Ann and two boys, both Davids, went Munro-ing east of the A837 while James (aged 15) and I set off to traverse Canisp and Suilven, Ann to collect us from Lochinver in the evening. The A837 (Ledmore Junction–Inchnadamph) is the obvious start and, unless the river is in spate, you can leave the road at any point. (There are bridges over the River Loanan at the Loch Awe outflow and near Stronchrubie.) There is little in the way of vegetation and the grey skeleton of the world surfaces in shattered layers of Lewisian gneiss, pleasantly dry underfoot. Following up the Allt Mhic Mhurchaidh Gheir to the lochan below Meall Diamhain is pleasant, the stream is a succession of stepped falls and pools. The lochan made a good reflecting pool (two Canisps for the price of one). A circling uphill sweep leads to the final cone and the summit cairn which perches on the edge of a bite of corrie. We may have looked down on Suilven but it was still big, black and monumental — and gave us the exciting traverse we'd expected. In the pub I ordered a Guinness and a Coke. James had the Guinness and I had the Coke. He was a hefty farmer's son, a talented mechanic, theatrical stage manager and climber; when he was killed in a tractor accident a year later, he was much missed.

Our walk through to Lochinver hit off the right way to visit Canisp. The peak, and the crying wilderness from which Canisp soars, are an indivisible whole, giving a rounded experience; merely to nip up and down Canisp from the A837 would be an unworthy effort. I've been back many times since, and always spending a night or two in that fastness. All the paths shown are well-made pony tracks, allowing easy if long approaches. Even the widest river-crossings seldom give problems. The heartland is too flat to create ferocious spates (those are on the perimeter), and the quality of tramping is hard to beat anywhere.

Canisp was an introduction to the wilds for one group of trainees from the schooner *Captain Scott* and they had two overnight camps, and three days of hill exploration in riotous October colouring. We climbed Canisp via the path that rises from Loch na Gainimh to its NW Ridge, perhaps the most pleasing way up the Corbett. The view down from Canisp has a map-like quality which is peculiar to the far North. Canisp means *white* mountain, which is accurate enough when sunshine beats off the grey rock. Suilven (*the pillar*) is always dark in contrast.

An even more memorable camp was during a May visit on my *Groats End Walk*. I had camped above the salmon hatchery on the Allt nan Uamh so made a fairly standard ascent from the east (two hours from the road). I had snow on top of Canisp and next morning the snow was down to my camp by Loch nan Rac under Suilven. The SW flank of Canisp is craggy and/or scree but there is no difficulty descending to Lochan Fada from the foot of the SE Ridge as I'd done. I came up to the SE Ridge at the start of a 1985 trek from Lochinver to Berriedale — my "most impressive ever" coast-to-coast tramp.

From half way along Loch Fada we made a rising line to a waterfall spouting off the lower band of crag. Once we'd tiptoed up to the lip of the fall we entered a more spacious world. Suilven's fangs dominated the backward view. The layered hollows led on for Canisp. Storm was led off by a grouse doing a broken wing act, several deer trickled over the skyline and a fleeting shadow on the crags suddenly resolved itself into a swooping golden eagle, just a hundred yards off.

Section 16: 4. CREAG LIATH, BREABAG   814 m   OS 15   287158
          The grey crag

My last visit to Creag Liath's summit was on 20 December 1975 when hill, sky and human were all pretty *liath*. I had a streaming cold with a strangling sore throat and even the completion of a fifth round of the Munros on Ben More Assynt did not cheer me. There weren't even decent winter conditions.

Kitchy and I had travelled north in foul conditions and had spent the previous day cooped up in the Dormobile, so desperation as much as anything else drove us out. We set off up the Allt nan Uamh, three miles south of Inchnadamph (where the salmony hatchery has been built since), a river with plenty of surprises. There was a charming fall to start with, then a gush of water spouted out of the left bank while the main stream disappeared. Up on the right there were caves, with green aprons below them, like overgrown shearwater burrows, which once yielded the archaeologist stacks of bones of long-extinct animals. This whole area is riddled with vanishing rivers, resurgences, caves and a rich flora, for here the Moine thrust is at work with limestone, rare in Scotland, providing the material for centuries of work by aquatic Henry Moores — a unique area. Walking routes should be planned so as to explore some of the peculiar sites.

We took to a side burn to avoid the heather and as we climbed the view back down began to open up, allowing us to see Canisp and Suilven to the west. We went up into the clouds by a small waterfall just north of the slabby barrier. The landscape resembled nothing so much as an open-cast coal-mine with broken rocky pavements and banks of dirty snow. I needed a cast or two before catching the Corbett's summit. There were two cairns with a shelter where we cringed out of the icy blast.

Creag Liath is strictly speaking the crag at the 650 contour and Breabag on the map is strictly speaking the slope up to the 715 top to the north, but I don't believe the summit is nameless, only that the OS haven't found or given us a name. Most books compromise with Creag Liath, Breabag as did the *Tables* until now. Mind you, Breabag is not accurate. The name is probably *brae* and *beg*, meaning the *little slope*.

The walk along Breabag is very rough in places and on the eastern, Glen Oykel, side, a line of ragged cliffs should provide climbing routes, though I know of none. There are odd little pools perched above the Glas Choire Mor headwall and on Breabag there is a deep slot across the ridge. As a lad I had thought it would make a grand murder hole, or perhaps one worth abseiling into to see what had fallen in over the ages — maybe a Victorian mountaineer with a pocket full of sovereigns! (There are something like 60 cases of unaccounted-for disappearances in the Highlands.)

Kitchy and I went along and down over Breabag Tarsuinn to the well-defined pass under Conival and then traversed the Munros. Oddly, Ben More had also been my last Munro of round four. Sgurr na Ciche had happily been that of the first, Sgurr Gairich of the second, A' Chralaig of the third, Ben Lomond of the sixth and new Beinn Teallach of the seventh. This was the least enjoyed of endings for the weather became pernicious and I was creaky with a cold. Adding the Munros certainly makes for a good testing day, and with Glas Bheinn, another Corbett, away north of them, a very big, very demanding and quite magnificent traverse is possible.

For simply climbing the Corbett I'd come up as described, traverse to the col under Conival (the Bealach Traligill) to enjoy the contrasting geology and the allied flora and wander down the Allt a' Bhealaich for half a mile before swinging round and down into Cuil Dhuibh, the well-named *black hollow*. Several burns join to wiggle across the boggy flat as a juvenile river which then suddenly runs up against a clasp of crag — and vanishes. Perhaps it is the source of the gush of stream into the Allt nan Uamh, perhaps it heads to one of the resurgences in Gleann Dubh. If transport can be arranged, or an hour's tramp up the road does not appeal, take the path from Loch Mhaolach-coire down into Gleann Dubh to Inchnadamph, otherwise beat across the moors back to the salmon hatchery. On this day of mine I had to tackle these miles in the dark. As the moor is amply supplied with sink holes it was a nervy crossing, even with a torch. Ducks taking off from one lochan nearly gave me a heart attack.

Altnacealgach Hotel is sometimes suggested as a starting point, but this merely gives many more moorland miles for much less interest. Cycling up Glen Oykel would be interesting, and the whole horseshoe of Creag Liath, Breabag, Conival, Ben More and Carn nan Conbhairean is another traverse of northern austerity, grandeur, and rewarding exertion, though not a circuit for novices. Easy miles don't exist in Assynt.

Section 16:   5. GLAS BHEINN   776 m   OS 15   255265
             The grey hill (glashven)

Glas Bheinn lies just a couple of miles east of the Inchnadamph– Kylesku road. Despite its rough gneiss defences it is an easy Corbett by northern standards. There was logic, however, in our climb of the hill from the east — which cannot occur very often.

Dave, Danni, Kath, Alec, Kitchy and I had been on a short camping visit to that good Badlands country east of the Assynt barrier, making the most of two cars to wander effectively. We made our exit over Glas Bheinn from a camp by Loch Beag, as the head of Loch Glencoul is called, and walked out to Alec's car at Inchnadamph, from where I'd be run up to my own vehicle at our entry point at Loch na Gainmhich (*sandy loch*). The others would no doubt replace sweat with something from the Inchnadamph bar.

We had come out from the wilds on the first of August and close, muggy weather made uphill effort a drip-drag affair, the only real spur being the need to keep moving to avoid the midges. We had departed sometime after 8 a.m. "Pack and off up the wet, dripping, infested jungle", was my logbook description. Lower slopes in the North often give the harder walking, the going being pleasanter once the clawing heather is left behind. We worked our way up to the lochan above the Leitir Dhubh and quickly erected a flysheet when heavy rain started. By the time we'd scoffed a brew the shower had gone past. There is quite a maze of paths in this complex world of bumps and gashes but all we did was take the one that runs south east towards Gorm Loch Mor and then branched off it to double back on another which led up to the col between Glas Bheinn and Beinn Uidhe, quite a bonus as the pass is 2,000 feet. The summit stands on a wide, flat, mossy green, but the ridge up is quite narrow. Glas Bheinn gives a full-frontal view across to Quinag, and Suilven is splendidly arrayed. We returned to our rucksacks on the col when the warm cloud closed in.

The favourite ways up Glas Bheinn are, I suspect, from the north, using the maximum height-gain possible on the Kylesku road. Make for either the NW or the NE ridge of the Corbett, but which burn and/ or corrie you follow from Loch na Gainmhich is a matter of personal choice. Up one ridge and down the other is a good circuit. The long western flank is not recommended. If two cars can be arranged the path down to Inchnadamph completes a fine traverse. In fact traversing can be taken to almost any length; what about Glas Bheinn to Creag Liath (as suggested in 16:4)?

We followed the path down under the barren slopes to Loch Fleodach Coire and an hour later reached the road and Alec's car at Inchnadamph. There we found a great clutter of vehicles: the RAF Kinloss team, police, and press vultures. Folk camping on Conival reported hearing shouts in the night and an enthusiastic local rescue lad put two and two together with Alec's car and made a wrong number. They were looking for us!

We found it embarrassing to be "rescued" unexpectedly but the police were very nice and we soon tumbled into the hotel with the Kinloss lads for some "area familiarisation". I had to climb into the police car to be able to speak with those in charge free of harassment from the photographers. They were most upset at the complete lack of blood and drama but made such ridiculous copy of the non-event that some of our party wondered whether they should sue one paper.

As Dave and I had recently been involved in a horrific rescue following a gaz-stove explosion, when a photographer had barged into the rescue helicopter to get a picture of a schoolboy with his face melted (which the paper actually used!) we had a job not to let rip and give them real copy. The police had been aware of both cars and were not concerned. They agreed that leaving notes in cars is more an invitation to robbery than any help.

We had a midgey camp by Loch Assynt and I wrote in my log that here was country for exploring on a through-expedition; but thirteen years passed before I made the walk through from Lochinver to

Berriedale, a story told in my book *Travels*. That gave Storm new Corbetts: Canisp, Beinn Leoid and Ben Hee.

Section 16:   6. QUINAG: SPIDEAN COINICH   764 m   OS 15
              205278
              Mossy peak

Section 16:   7. QUINAG: SAIL GHARBH   808 m   OS 15   209292
              Rough heel

Section 16:   8. QUINAG: SAIL GORM   776 m   OS 15   198304
              Blue heel (Quinag is *Cuinneag* (coon-yag), Gaelic for
              a *bucket* or perhaps, *water stoup*)

Unlike the Munros, it is not easy to scale three Corbetts in a day, so three Corbetts sited on one mountain, or mountain group, is quite a cause for rejoicing. Quinag, being the sum of its superb parts, rather defeats glib description. This is a mountain among mountains, even in the north of Scotland where superlatives are scattered as liberally as the lochs. "There is no mountain to equal it in Sutherland, not even Suilven", declares Gwen Moffat, writing of Quinag.

From below, Quinag can look quite intimidating, its gully-riven, barrel buttresses and jutting prows of bare rock hopelessly steep, yet my memory is of greenness, which photographs confirm. The horizontal lines of crag support green terraces and there is a majestic openness to the walking. The only complaint is that "Quinag is all ups and downs", not only on the three Corbetts but over the intervening lesser heights. The group takes the form of a rather squashed E; the three Corbetts at the ends of the prongs add a certain amount of out-and-back to the ups-and-downs.

Quinag owes its features to the familiar north western pattern of Torridonian sandstone cake on a gneiss platter with an icing of quartzite. It is worth circumnavigating the group by car so that the peak can be seen over a diversity of foregrounds. The road from Lochinver to Loch Assynt gives a view of the hill's backbone (with all the ups-and-downs linked like vertebrae), while from Kylesku there is the dramatic view of the prows and buttresses. These prows and buttresses are every bit as fierce as they look but most of the saddles and corrie slopes are relatively easy, however steep. The path over the Bealach Leireag from Loch Assynt to Loch Nedd is a recommended extra. Sail Gorm is a new Corbett, following recent map revisions — those who failed to traverse everything previously will have to make a return visit.

I set off from near the top of the Kylesku–Loch Assynt road early one summer morning. The stalkers' path, which goes off in the wrong direction, was abandoned for the East Ridge. The quartzite strata makes for easy walking and the ridge, being well edged on the right with crags, is an easy line so I was a bit disappointed to find cairns all the way up. There must be some quirk, some lack in *homo sapiens* that he cannot let the natural world be; he has to leave his mark — figurative or literal turds in the wilderness. There is a long steady rise, a small dip and then the castle-edged, table-top summit of Spidean Coinich is reached. Suilven, which is akin to Quinag, sits boldly out on the moor to the south, westwards lies country as much water as land, leading the eye to the Minch and the Hebrides, north is the queue of good things to come. I sat there for an hour while ravens dived and called in the corrie below: black birds that glittered silver as they spun in the morning sunlight.

The biggest descent of the day followed with the drop down to the Bealach a' Chornaidh. From above I could spot deer, the young ones just sprawling on the ground, and by using the ledges made several successful stalks to within mere yards. The camera clicking usually frightened them more than the human presence. I watched other deer tip-toe through the shallows by the sand spit of Lochan Bealach Cornaidh and envied them their cool water. I had to traverse along under the 745 m Centre Top to find a trickle of water. A gentle-angled walk led out to Sail Gharbh, the highest point of the group. Thyme, alpine lady's-mantle and bedstraw made attractive carpets. Sail Gharbh, strictly speaking, applies to the gully-divided prow with the climbers' Barrel Buttress on it, but the name has been hijacked for convenience for the Corbett.

There were more towers and rises along to Sail Gorm (not yet a Corbett) where I had "lunch". The view had become hazy with the heat and, as on Arkle the day before, I was down to boots and pants. (On the next visit I was blasted off Quinag before even reaching the crest.) My car being at the pass, I threaded my way back and dropped down into the corrie to join the deer in the loch. They promptly fled. The corrie between the two *Sails* can be descended equally easily. It is deeper and narrow but lacks a loch. Bhatchaich is *barn*. Cairns marked my route down to the loch and across to the stalkers' path — quite uncalled-for. There were cars parked along from mine and tiny dots on the long ridge up to the Spidean. Being midday, with the day just warming up, I did not envy them their grilling ahead. Most of the afternoon I spent near Ardvreck Castle — in and out the loch — before going on to the charming Achiltibuie hostel with its sea view — and no clegs or midges. Heat and insects came up a great deal in conversation. An early start *always* pays off. I don't really want to do Quinag again. How can you improve on the perfect day?

Quinag is covered in W. A. Poucher's *The Scottish Peaks*. This idiosyncratic book provides plenty of illustrations, not only of Quinag but of Foinaven 17:1, 3, Ben Loyal 17:6, Cul Mor and Cul Beag 16:1, 2, Applecross 13:1, 2, Garbh Behinn 10:3, The Cobbler 2:4, and the Arran hills 18:9–12.

Section 16: 9. BEINN LEOID   792 m   OS 15   320295
          The sloping hill

Even without Beinn Leoid as bait, the "behind the ranges" area of Assynt is one which draws again and again. This is really wild and spectacular country with a feeling of remoteness seldom known anywhere else. The area's problems are more imagined than real. Beinn Leoid can be reached from several directions as a day outing, but it is worth combining several good things in Assynt and making a through-trek over several days. A mountain takes on a special quality when you sleep on it.

Though I've followed every coastline and track shown in the area, I've been to the summit only twice and both times were on multi-day adventuring. Once was on the Lochinver to Berriedale coast-to-coast. After crossing Conival and Ben More we (Storm and I) descended into the cloudy, wet wilderness of the upper Cassley and were delighted to find the waters low enough to cross between Gorm Loch Mor and Fionn Loch Mor. We camped finally a mile up, on a stream-side sward by the Fionn Allt which drains the southern slopes of Beinn Leoid. While that approach is really the least practicable, the descent and exit took what could be termed "the line of least resistance", yet I have not seen that line suggested anywhere.

If you take the A838 from Lairg to Laxford Bridge you pass a watershed just beyond Loch Merkland and then, shortly after, there is a good path which heads up south from the road through a gap in the trees. This is right on the edge of sheet 15 (356333) which is convenient. The track is good and the initial steep slog up is rewarded by a big view over Loch More to the Reay Forest (Arkle mountains) and other giants. Ben Hee is well seen, too. The path ends on the Meall na Leitreach saddle from which one angles down to pick up the Strath nan Aisinnin track, from Lochmore, that leads past Loch Dubh to the col east of Beinn Leoid, a very easy ascent up grassy slopes with a few rockier bands. The summit would make a pleasing bivvy spot. There was a vivid clump of white moss-campion by the stone circle round the cairn. With neighbours such as Quinag, Ben Stack, Arkle and Ben More Assynt, the view is first-class. That route is the simplest, but is just one of many variations. The most satisfying approaches are from the west, from the sea.

Loch Glendhu and Loch Glencoul are arms of a *fjord*, their joint exit narrow and blocked by islands and reefs, and now spanned by the bridge which replaced the old Kylesku Ferry. At Kylestrome or, better, Unapool one can usually arrange to hire a boat up Loch Glencoul, to the landing at Glencoul, where a good track leads up under the Stack to Loch an Eircill and the soft, southern underbelly of Beinn Leoid. A return could be made northwards to descend Gleann Dubh, which has a large waterslide, and out along the north shore of Loch Glendhu to Kylestrome or, from Glencoul, round the peninsula of Aird da Loch (*point between the lochs*) for the same exit. There is a path gradually descending to Loch Glendhu along the top of the crags from near the 205 spot height.

On our first visit we wanted to see the Eas a' Chual Aluinn, Britain's highest waterfall, so we went in over the gneiss-knobbly miles from Loch na Gainmhich on the Loch Assynt–Loch Glencoul watershed and managed to break down the steep Leitir Dhubh slopes to camp near the head of the loch, a day of calling divers, as I remember it. The river at some time has completely altered its course down the valley. We strolled up to see the fall. As it plunges and splatters down the crags in full view it can be wholly appreciated. The evening was spent huddled round a seaweed-driftwood bonfire trying to smoke some sanity into midsummer midge madness.

We climbed steeply up to the Stack of Glencoul, wending under its prow of cliffs and setting off a ptarmigan family and an eagle which rose just twenty yards away and drifted south along Loch nan Caorach. The natural rock sequence has been upended, the gneiss lying on top of the Cambrian layer. The whole area is one of knobbles and hollows, of naked bulges and loch-filled navels. Looking south from Leoid later we could see that the strata of the hill north of Conival were so contorted that it looked like a petrified jam roll. Loch Shin was so big that it gave the impression of cutting the North in half. Our summit picnic on Leoid was spoilt by a persistent drizzle but after we'd wandered back down Glen Coul we enjoyed a swim and sunbathe at the camp. The tide was out. When the flow started, some areas bubbled furiously. We decided the shore must be porous and that the ebb-made air pockets were being recaptured by the sea. Our exit, and what befell us, is told under Glas Bheinn (16:5) but do, when it comes to visiting this area, make an expedition worthy of a landscape rich in serendipity.

Section 16:   10. MEALLAN LIATH COIRE MHIC DHUGHAILL
                  801 m   OS 15   357392
                  The grey hill of Macdougall's corrie

The Reay (Ray) Forest, with such spectacular summits as Arkle and
Foinaven and with an abundance of climbable rock and long cross-
country tracks, still has neglected corners. Even graceful Ben Stack is
more often admired than ascended while Meallan Liath Coire Mhic
Dhughaill might as well not exist for all the notice the hill receives in
the books I've consulted.

Combining this peak with Ben Hee on a hot summer's day left me
with no great impression of either and my approach by the Allt Beithe
was mostly enjoyed for a prolonged swim in one of the pools on the
way down. The sensible route is from the Kinloch–Aultanrynie estate
road using one — or both — of the stalking paths shown on the map.
This is deer-forest country. The hill is to be avoided from mid August
to mid October, no great sacrifice as that is also the midges' open
season for humans, and the midges of Reay are man-eaters.

I'd be inclined to slant up the track above Loch More and curve
round to take the Corbett by its bold western ridge (no real problems)
and then descend the south ridge on to the Meall Reinidh plateau,
cross the Allt an Reinidh and pick up the other path down to
Aultanrynie. The walking is rough off the tracks (everywhere in the
far north, not just here) so where paths exist they are worth using.
They are there to allow pony access to retrieve the stags or hinds
which have been shot, rather than for the convenience of hill-walkers
or Corbett poachers — so be grateful.

Being the Cinderella of the Reay country this Corbett is worth
doing *before* its northern neighbours. It will make quite an impression
then, but if you do Arkle and Foinaven first, well, you may consider
you've gone from the sublime to the ridiculous. And Meallan Liath
Coire Mhic Dhughaill is not ridiculous. An eagle soared above the
summit, I saw plenty of deer on knobbly Meallan Liath Beag and the
long pull up was made amid a constant crying of golden plovers — a
sound that suits the savage nature of the northern wilderness. Past sins
have made this perhaps the emptiest landscape in the country. No
wonder the plovers' voices are so sad.

Section 16: 11. BEN HEE 873 m OS 16 426339
The fairy hill (from *Shidh*)

This hill was climbed right after its mouthful of a neighbour during a 1976 summer blitz of Corbetts in the far north, with the result that I can recall little of the day except the heat which boiled over into a storm on Ben Hee, interrupting the prolonged heatwave. Near the summit I had to duck fast to avoid being hit by a cuckoo which was being chased by an irate pipit. I had gone up and down the Allt Coir' a' Chruiter stalking path, which is the quickest and easiest route, but was determined to revisit the area for a more protracted stay. This came during the 1985 crossing of Sutherland and Caithness which gave a rich haul of Corbetts.

The day began camping west of Bein Leoid and ended camping to the north east of Ben Hee. The whole crossing is described in *Travels* and I'm now sure the most enjoyable Munroing and/or Corbetting experiences are those done as part of a big journey. The travelling is the thing, the ascents are just the plums in the pudding. My entrance to Ben Hee was still from the north end of Loch Merkland, that lonely loch left between huge Loch Shin and the lochs which are backed by the shining peaks of Arkle and his kin. The Bealach nam Meirleach which separates the Reay Forest from Ben Hee is an old drovers' route, leading through to Loch Hope and the north coast. The name means *the pass of the robbers* but if these are specific, the story is lost. The right-of-way track is also a private estate road, useful, but hard on the feet. The atmosphere is rather bleak.

The footpath shown cutting across the neck between the lochs was my point of leaving the road. The path led up on to the hillside, and from there I made a circuiting traverse to drop down to Loch Coire na Saidhe Duibhe, *the loch of the corrie of the black hay*, which sounds daft. Probably the word is Saidh which is a *bitch* or the *prow* of a ship. The loch was rough, and for shelter I pitched in the lee of a peat bank, a strip so narrow that my port guylines were anchored to boulders in the loch. I hoped the wind would not change direction! It was a superbly empty spot — I'd walked for four days without speaking to another person. I looked out from the end of the loch over a huge moorland (the OS goes daft with bog symbols) to the sprawling bulk of Ben Klibreck and the distant Griams, still three days of walking away. The hills of the north rise from such a vast lower platform that they are unusually visible from each other. Later, on Morven, the last peak of the crossing (not even of Corbett height), I could see all my hills right back to Suilven. Ben Hee may be a schisty dome compared to some of the other giants but it shares this special, spacious splendour.

The path coming in from the Altnahara–Loch Hope road shies off at the loch and heads up towards a bold buttress. I took it, and then angled up across the crags looking down on the loch, to end eventually on the secondary, NE peak, Ben Hee being double-headed. Coire Gorm was living up to its name as we rounded to the trig point of Ben Hee proper. Gorm is *blue* and the shadowy depths were a deep violet-blue with a jutting crag which might yield some sporting climbing lines in winter. I would have liked to have descended southwards to return under that wild eastern profile with its lonely lochs, but I had a long way to travel (to and over Klibreck that same day) so returned more or less as I'd ascended.

The path out to the Altnahara–Loch Hope road was my continuation, and that is the route of approach I'd recommend for Ben Hee, a long route but one leading to all the good things of the mountain. Walk in, traverse Ben Hee from north to south, and exit by the lochans again. The only comparable route would be the same way to the summit and then out to Loch Merkland by the easy route first mentioned.

THE FAR NORTH

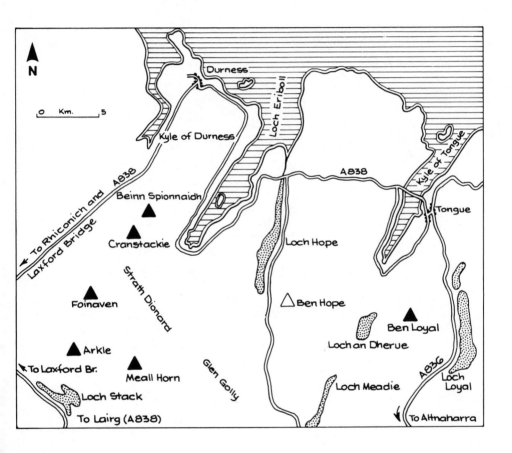

Section 17: 1. ARKLE (ARCUIL)   787 m   OS 9   303462
Ark-fjell from the Norse?

Section 17: 2. MEALL HORN   777 m   OS 9   353449
Hill of the cairn

Section 17: 3. FOINAVEN   908 m   OS 9   317507
The white hill

THE REVEREND A. E. ROBERTSON, writing in 1907, suggested that Arkle (Arcuil) "may be somewhat profanely likened to a vast shale heap, and the individual who essays to scale 'the ghastly cheek of Arkle' will have an experience in rough walking he will not easily forget". You have been warned. If it is as bad as that it must be good.

Foinaven and Arkle are jagged heaps of Cambrian quartzite rather than douce shale. Meall Horn is into an area of schistose rocks, gentler in appearance. Appearance is the one thing all these hills enjoy — the drive along Loch Stack would surely tempt anyone into Corbett-bagging. Ben Stack (718 m) may fail to reach even Corbett status but should not be omitted. Every step yields a view and the summit panorama is one of the best in Scotland. I've enjoyed several visits to the area, either climbing on cliffs, wandering the rough ridges or criss-crossing the fine glens and passes that define it. The stalkers' paths are vital for access and any day's plan should utilise them. All Reay is prime deer forest. The estate office is at the hamlet of Achfarry at the head of Loch More.

Anciently the Lords of Reay were chiefs of clan Mackay but they sold out in 1829 to the Sutherland-gobbling Lord Stafford, later Duke of Sutherland, the man responsible for the "improvements" that have left Sutherland the desert we see today. The hills are now part of the Westminster Estates, one of Britain's largest land conglomerates. Contrary to what I've heard suggested more than once, the famous racehorses were named after the hills and not vice versa. On the radio I once heard a sports commentator say, "Lochnagar is a fine horse too. Like Foinaven and Arkle, this is another peak found in the north of Scotland."

In fact, A. E. Robertson's warning should be heeded. The going is rough and the quartz crests can be precipitous and tricky in poor visibility. It is not country for the inexperienced. Assuming visitors will be competent I can perhaps give less detail. Really wild country gains by not being over-described. Part of the experience should be exploratory. In big, bold country like this more than one visit is desirable and, once visited, is desired. Sometime, one has to walk through by Glen Golly and Strath Dionard or reach Arkle-foot by that loch-scattered region cutting south from Rhiconich or traverse the Bealach na Feithe, the southern boundary of these peaks. Some of this is described in my *Hamish's Groats End Walk*; musing over the map of the area makes me want to go off and do this circuit. There is quite good access, too, from the head of Loch Eriboll over the Bealach a' Chonnaidh to Loch Dionard, and a path, not on the map, runs up the west bank of the Allt an Easain Ghil to join the Glen Golly–Lone path. Strath Dionard, even with its track, is infamously boggy and is having a vehicle road built along its length. Those climbers willing to walk have found bold routes on remote cliffs here. Ling — Weir — Tranter — Patey — Nisbet were, or are, some of the pioneers.

I've only once done all three Corbetts in one day. It was 12½ hours, car to car; with 10½ hours on the hill. At 5.30 a.m. larks, divers and greenshanks were calling as I cut across from the Rhiconich–Durness A838 road to reach the northern battlements of Foinaven. This was easier going than guidebooks had suggested. It was such a broiling day that when I began the steep assault I soon took to going in my birthday suit, sneaking up by the burn in the cleft of the northern corrie, dipping in every wee fall and hugging all the shade possible. The Ceann Garbh (*rough head*) summit was reached at 8.30 and a salvation breeze dried the sweat. Perched on a block on the cliff edge I found I was looking down on seven tents in upper Coire Duail — probably one of John Ridgway's gangs, I thought, his centre at Ardmore being not so far away.

A narrow crest led along to Ganu Mor (*big head*), Foinaven's highest point, 2,980 feet in the old currency, and a mere 600 feet more would have allowed it to overtop Ben Hope as higher than anything else in the far north. The grass (and thrift) ceased on the crest and for much of the day naked rock would give rugged going. Sadly, there were no more layers I could take off for the hot march along the cliffs and screes. Such blinding screes. They would look quite at home in the Jbel Sahro. The A' Cheir Ghorm ridge is worth a diversion. Coire na Lice with its tiny lochan is impressive. At the head of the corrie is Lord Reay's Seat, not quite up to Lord Berkeley's; the next rise gave me some scrambling. Meall Horn and the Corbetts to the south were inverted pudding-bowl shapes. There was a good earthy smell from the rocky crest. Eventually I skirted round Coir a' Chruiteir, one of the many corries-off-the-corrie holding Loch an Easain Uaine. (The 778-m trig point is Creag Dionard.) A grassy rake, and then grassy slopes, led down to the col with the bliss of water at the first burn available. Dwarf cornel, cow-wheat and thrift adorned its banks.

My rucksack was left by the path and, clad only with a camera, I tackled the scrag up on to Creagan Meall Horn then, after a banded saddle, Meall Horn, the Corbett. Deer were grunting and I could see them just down a bit on the northern flanks. They were finding little coolness even on the heights. Back at my rucker a spotty calf ambled past twenty yards away. The prospect of a dip had me romping off and I left a precious knife behind. The topmost lochan (count them down to Loch Inchard) gave a fabulous swim, and I kept going in again and again. The tadpoles in the shallows were, I'm sure, slowly cooking. A tin of chicken I'd brought smelt foul and my bar of chocolate had run over everything else in the lunch bag. I didn't even put on my boots after eating, and had a prickly walk up to Lochan na Faoileige for another swim: diving in off the east corner crags and swimming right round the lochan. While drying off I realised how pink I was becoming and (too late) covered up flesh rather than exposing it any further. That night I suffered.

Foinaven looked very grand from Meall Aonghais. I went over to the white blaze of the dried-up burn which led to the plateau-like south top of Arkle. The highest summit lies a mile on round a scalloped corrie, facetiously called The Barn (*Am Bathaich*). Scree led down to a col and there was one intermediate bump. The Corbett was reached at 3 p.m. I'd had a good look at the western flanks the day before when motoring north so was able to make a fairly direct descent to where the stalkers' path bends at right angles to pass between two lochs. I swam in only one of them.

The easier and safer descent is down to the north west (Sail Mhor) to pick up this track. From then onwards the day produced a few nasty experiences. The sun was butchering me but I had to rush off down the path to evade some of the clegs, and in the two miles down to Lochstack Lodge and the A838 I killed over 100 of the devils. There was also a multicoloured fly of an unknown species whose bite became all too well known. The road was reached at 4.30. I'd left my folding cycle in the heather and raced off to escape these insect attacks. The sea at Laxford Bridge stank and the brae beyond nearly killed me. The tired tyres made a zipping sound in the melted tar. At Rhiconich the shop was on the point of closing. I drank two cans and ate two ice-creams, which made the run up to the car just bearable. Its locked oven interior was registering 120°F. Most of my food had gone bad. At 8 p.m. the thermometer still registered over 90°F, even with windows open — but netted to keep out the clegs. At 10 p.m. it felt quite cool: down to 70°F. My thighs looked like well grilled gammon.

Lone–Arkle via Meall Aonghais–Meall Horn–Foinaven and out by Lochstack Lodge is probably the easiest round if having to start/finish at one place, but you can make all sorts of different routes. Arkle and Meall Horn from Lone and Foinaven via Strath Dionard would be a better two-day accumulation. You don't have to be a glutton for punishment, not that such a day of heat as I've described will stalk these hills very often. Do keep these hills for clear days. The views are spectacular, in every direction, westwards they are both spectacular and unusual, the eye being led over a landscape of scoured gneiss and scores of lochans to the shimmer of the western seaboard. This is eagle country and, if you believe one seventeenth-century writer (Sir Robert Gordon), the Reay deer can be told from all others because they have forked tails.

Section 17:   4. CRANSTACKIE   800 m   OS 9   351556
              The rugged hill

Section 17:   5. BEINN SPIONNAIDH   772 m   OS 9   362573
              Mountain of strength

There is a certain end-of-the-world feeling to walking the crests of these, the most northerly Corbetts. The sea lies near and visible both to the west and to the north. After the day over the Foinaven hills, already described, they gave a kindly walk, even if the heatwave continued.

The car was parked at Carbreck on the Rhiconich–Durness A838 road at 6.30 a.m. and the pebbly track taken over to Rhigolter. The bogs were dry and I filled two water-bottles low down in case there was none higher up; a wise move as it proved. The early start allowed me to zigzag up the steep western side in shade. This led to the marked NW spur of Beinn Spionnaidh and was followed to the summit trig point, bouldery in the end after being grassy nearly all the way. Unusually the lower of the two Corbetts has the trig point on it. These hills were obviously sheep country yet there were no sheep. Later I could hear a great bleating, but still no sheep visible. Eventually, from Cranstackie, I saw big flocks down near the A838. They were being gathered by the Gualin shepherd.

Cranstackie was reached by pleasant grassy walking, though I diverted at the band of crags to get some scrambling on the rather tottery rock. This led to the summit boulder-field with its cairn perched on the west. The haze was too thick for views and the descent was made directly to Rhigolter. It was interesting to see the vegetation change several times in the course of the descent. There were some brilliant patches of tormentil, the burn was edged with starry

saxifrages; ring ouzel and dipper were resident and the air was loud
with skylark song — becoming all too rare these days.

I was back at the car at 11.15 — under five hours was a very gentle
day compared to that on Fionaven. Making Corbetts while the sun
shone I drove south for a day on Quinag.

Section 17: 6. BEN LOYAL (LAOGHAL) 764 m OS 10 578489

A long weekend beguiled us north of Inverness, quite a crowd in
Ann's wee car, two adults and three lads. On the Sunday night we
camped by lonely Loch Naver, a site made noisy with oystercatchers
and sandpipers calling. The boys rescued some curlew chicks from the
road. June is the best month for the north: at 4 a.m. there was
sufficient light to read, and the early sun soon danced the dewdrops off
the grasses. We sunbathed over breakfast tea and omelettes. This was
almost too perfect a day to be spent on mountains and I only escaped
being dragged off for Ben Hope by pleading a case for Ben Loyal. The
Munroists still went to Ben Hope and I was dropped off on the tangy
moors by Loch Hakel. "See you this evening," Ann grinned as she
drove off with her crew of fanatics.

The normal route up Ben Loyal is from Tongue (the northern end)
via Ribigill and Cunside, then sneaking up east of the rock prow of
Sgor Chaonasaid to gain the weird heights. I was dropped off two
miles further along the Kyle of Tongue road and was rewarded with
the classic view of the long reach of mountain mirrored in Loch Hakel.
The gorse was in flower and the blue loch complemented its golden
extravagance. Ben Loyal has a succession of bold towers above lower
slopes, which can be intimidating, and exaggerate the height. The
highest tower scrapes over Corbett height by less than two metres. My
choice of starting place allowed me to see the cup-and-ring marked
stones by the southern corner of the loch. There is a prehistoric islet
fort as well. It is a spot well worth a visit and, with the moor dry, there
was no problem ambling on towards the black triangle of Sgor
Chaonasaid, nor would there have been any problem angling up by
the trees to gain the tops by the corrie between Sgor Chaonasaid and
Sgor a' Bhatain. In fact I'd recommend this route, especially with
hindsight. The way I went I would wish only on my best enemies.
Ben Loyal, like Ben More and others, can have a distorting effect on a
compass, the rock being magnetic in places.

Since that visit I've read several accounts of attempted and actual
climbs on Ben Loyal's rocky towers and all indicate the decayed nature
of the rock, the unadhesive quality of the vertical vegetation and the

botanical bounty of the more aquatic flora. All this I can verify from the direct assault I made up Sgor Chaonasaid. I'd gone to the white scar of a stream hoping for a drink but there was no water and even the globe flowers were looking drouthy. I set off to scramble up the burn. My log account barely conceals my panic. "Slabs led to a corner which led to a 50-foot groove with a beast of a pull over a heather cornice . . . vegetation can't be so steep . . . the only handholds were into gravelly granite under the rolls of dusty moss . . . I stopped throwing down the loose rock for there soon wouldn't be anything left to climb up on . . . the sting in the tail left me lying gasping like a dying trout. Never again!" Aye, Sgor Chaonasaid is best outflanked. My only reward was finding a 60-year-old lemonade bottle after scrambling through a cave pitch — a Riley's patent screw-stoppered bottle with the beaver symbol of Walter Forbes and Co., Edinburgh.

On the top I was suddenly savaged by a fierce wind. Having climbed up in boots and Y-fronts I quickly dug out some clothes before wandering on to Sgor a' Bhatain by a scattering of tors, two quite big and many with completely round holes weathered into them. The same thing occurs on the summit tor of Ben Avon in the Cairngorms. (Wind and water erosion is the cause.) I noticed a dead ptarmigan that had its innards completely full of granite grit. On An Caisteal (the Castle — which it looks like from some angles) I overtook another walker. He had come up the proper route from Tongue. After a brief summit snack and a chat we descended a rift southwards and on to the 741 m top (Heddle's Top), where we separated, he to visit Sgor a' Chleirich and descend its corrie and so back along under the battlements to his starting point. I continued to Carn an Tionail, with its views of the moors to the south west, moors which are more water than land, before losing height over cloudberry slopes to Loch na Beiste (a low sun striking silver off the high waves) and a final top, Cnoc nan Cuilean, where I put up an eagle. A breast feather floated down as the bird flew off — and now adorns the pelmet over my bedroom window.

There is a curious legend attached to Ben Loyal, concerning the origin of fairies. When Eve was driven out of the Garden of Eden she had many more children, who were rather neglected by their distraught mother, to such an extent that the Lord God warned her that a department angel would visit her in a month and possibly take her brood into care. In a last-moment panic, Eve drove her children into the River Naver but had washed only half of them and their clothes when the angel (I almost said social worker) proclaimed his imminent arrival. Terrified, Eve drove the unwashed into a cave on Ben Loyal and took the clean ones to be shown to the authorities. The poor little dirty ones were forgotten and have been living underground ever since, only daring to come out at night.

As I descended to the road a pair of golden plovers did a marvellous distraction act, flapping and crying to lead me away from their nest. Ann's car appeared on the brae over from Altnaharra as I came in sight of the Inchkinloch bridge. We reached that rendezvous almost simultaneously. The boys were full of their day on Ben Hope, and for much of the evening Ann pored over her records and then yelled in glee that Ben Hope was her 100th Munro. Even the nineteenth-century New Statistical Account raved about Ben Loyal — as have hundreds of visitors in the century since. With a view embracing Orkney, Reay, Assynt, An Teallach, Hope and Klibreck, Morven of Caithness and the Cairngorms, how could it be otherwise?

THE ISLANDS

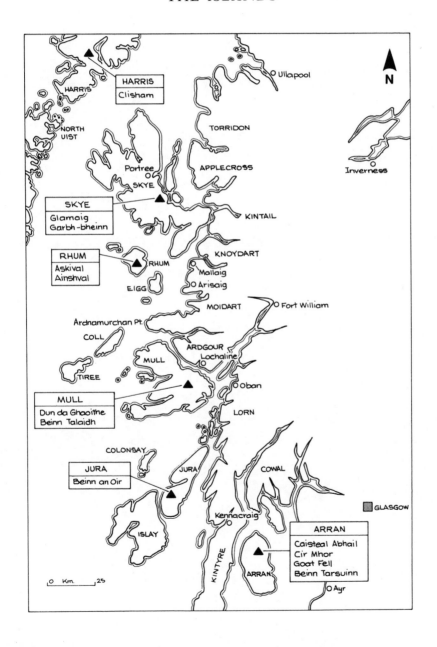

THE WEATHER WAS so wild that the ferry was not operating at the Ballachulish narrows; there were curses and an extra drive round (the long legs of the bridge were being built this November day, 1973), then extra speed had to be found to catch the boat at Kyle. After installing Mother in a B & B at Uig I made another dash, with a laden cycle, to catch the *Hebrides* for Tarbet. The Minch behaved reasonably. Just a modest gale. All the crew, who outnumbered the passengers, were glued to the TV set watching Princess Anne's wedding. The boat more or less took herself across to the Outer Hebrides — that other, saner, uncluttered world where there are still sixty minutes in an hour and the fresh breezes are honey pure. I felt ashamed to be making a mere Corbett-raid, but guilt lay behind it. I was supposed to be giving my mother a tour of Skye.

I puffed westwards, against wind and brae, to set up my bivvy by the Skeaudale River. The shelter was swept periodically by the searchlight beams of passing cars, peppered by showers or glowing eerily in cold moonlight. The moonlight was so bright at 5.30 that I began breakfast, then hid the bivvy and sleeping bag under the bridge and cycled off. I cycled all of 50 yards only to push the bike for the next mile, up to a series of lochans at 600 feet. That was a quarter of Clisham climbed.

Clisham lies less than two miles north of this Tarbet–Stornoway road and by the direct route presents no difficulty. The summit cone rose white with new snow. Grass gave way to boulders and scree and the final approach was on a narrow crest to a trig point standing inside a big cairn on the edge of the crags. I wandered on to another cairn but my allotted time was up. Sadly I romped down through the falling snow, and the run back to Tarbet kept me just ahead of a vicious storm. The crossing to Skye was much rougher than on the previous day. Mother was waiting on the pier.

Just below the top of Clisham I saw an eagle and on the descent I saw two more. I heard rather than saw snow buntings and ravens, and a flock of mixed *turdus* species fought through the storm. There were snipe and other waders, and a curlew very nearly stuck its big beak in my spokes as I hurtled down to sea level. Seton Gordon, writing of Clisham, was bemoaning the lack of bird life, so I must have been lucky.

The highest of the Outer Hebrides has naturally lured me back since, for the hill is a lordly one and can give a grand, natural, day-circuit of about eight miles. There is a daily bus which helps with access but lifts are readily offered. It is probably worth starting, as I did that first time, at the highest point of the road, using the easy ascent to set up the more demanding circuit. The continuation west leads the eye off to an Atlantic horizon where, on a clear day, the sharks'-teeth stacks of St Kilda and the humps of the Flannan Isles can be observed.

The descent westwards from the summit is rocky down to the col then rears up to grassy An t-Isean (not named on the map) with its deep corries to south and north and a narrow ridge off before the steep pull up Mulla-fo-dheas (*lower south summit*, 743 m) where the horseshoe bends slowly to the north over Mulla-fo-thuath (*lower north summit*) and Mullach an Langa. Each step down gives gentler country but the bones are just below the surface. The walking is dry on the whole. Local legend recounts that when the Lord reached the end of the Sixth Day He simply dumped His surplus building material on the earth. The stones landed on the Long Island, and traversing the Clisham you could believe this: the world is very rough, very wild, very bleak. There has not been much change since the day of Creation. There are almost no trees and a limited vegetation; the beauty lies in textures and tones, colours and contrasts and the unique blend of sky, rock and sea.

Our Clisham circuit continues round the northern rim of the Scaladale basin to end on Creag Mo, from whence Ardvourlie can be reached down the east ridge. Creag Mo, like most areas showing crag, is steep cliff and has some rock climbs. Instead of swinging east to Creag Mo, I find it more interesting to skirt above Langadale north to the Bealach na h-Uamba (*Cave pass*) and descent by the impressive path to the A859 at Vigadale Bay. Bus or hitching ends the day. If one has to return to a starting point then Clisham–Mulla-fo-dheas–Mo Buidhe is a good minor circuit.

Harris and Lewis are not separate islands, as one might suppose. What separated them anciently was this barrier of mountains. The Clisham is the most easterly of four wave-crests of hills that seem to storm in from the Atlantic. For centuries no road linked Harris with Lewis. The ice ages feel like just yesterday's work and Creation an event of last week.

Section 18 Skye: 2. GLAMAIG   775 m   OS 32   514300
                       Greedy woman

Section 18 Skye: 3. GARBH-BHEINN   806 m   OS 32   531232
                       Rough hill (garven)

"I drew the blind on a still, lemon-coloured sky and a sight that made me gasp. Right in front of me a tremendous Vesuvius called Glamaig shot up in the air, a colossal cone, with grey-pink ravines searing his gigantic flanks. The rising sun covered him in a weird, reflected light, that hung over his vastness like gold dust. All round were other mountains, vague in morning mists, enormous shadows with white clouds steaming over their crests. Gentler moorlands, brown with heather, formed the reverse slope of that wild valley through which the ice-white stream tumbled beneath a stone bridge towards the waters of Loch Sligachan. No words can tell the strange atmosphere of this place, which is unlike Scotland, unlike Norway, unlike Switzerland, unlike anything else on earth."

Those were the rather rushed words of H. V. Morton, *In Search of Scotland*, but their general tenor is accurate enough. But to practicalities: the 1:25,000 Outdoor Leisure map "The Cuillin and Torridon Hills" is advised for these Skye Corbetts; though Glamaig and much of the crest to Garbh-bheinn is of Red Cuillin character the going is still complex and rough beyond anything on the mainland, while Garbh-bheinn is Black Cuillin in every way. The traverse to Garbh-bheinn from Blaven should only be tackled by rock climbers familiar with Skye ridges, being one of the more complex and technical parts of the Cuillin, and recommended as such. The description belongs in a climbers' rather than a walkers' guidebook so is not given here.

That, however, was the way I first reached Garbh-bheinn. Back in the sixties we often had camping meets by Loch an Athain, and the west faces of Blaven and Clach Glas were a regular playground. One day we did a route up Clach Glas and turned north to add the rest of the *black* hills: Sgurr nan Each, Garbh-bheinn and Belig, a day memorable for alpine flora (Skye is unusually rich, botanically) and for Danny coming out with a classic comment when struggling with one wall of gabbro: "More slack please, Hamish, I want to take a run at it." From Loch an Athain a long but uncomplicated pull leads up to the col south of Garbh-bheinn whence the Corbett can be ascended easily enough, turning any problems on the west. Clach Glas appears as a mini alpine tower from the col.

Loch an Athain is rather remote, and more practical approaches can be made from the north or east. From Loch Slapin head, the obvious Allt Aigeann corrie is boulder-strewn and gives tough going; an easier approach is to follow the path up the Allt na Dunaiche (beaten out as the normal way up Blaven) and then bear up Choire a' Caise to the north west. From the upper bowl of scree take the broad right-hand slope up to the western end of Sgurr nan Each from whence there are about 100 feet down to the col under Garbh-bheinn. Best of all is a circuit from Loch Ainort, which gave me a sparkling day one summer.

Start at the attractive Eas a' Bhradain (*Robbers' Fall*) and work southwards up to the Bealach na Beiste. At least two other falls can be taken in (waterfalls are another Skye speciality) and the walking is easy if a bit damp or heathery at times. Belig is a worthwhile diversion before heading up Garbh-bheinn. This NE Ridge of the Corbett is broad and easy for most of the way, then becomes interestingly rough before popping one out suddenly on to the summit. Descend the North Ridge, with big cliffs on the right, to Druim Eadar Da Choire (*the ridge between the corries*). This ridge can be followed, or Coire nam Bruadaran (*Dream Valley*) and, for the enthusiast, Marsco could also be climbed up and down by the SE Ridge. This is a very pleasant day out and gives something of the "Alternative Skye" which so few discover.

Skye all too often is an infatuation with the main Black Cuillin and the peaks, ridges and routes thereon. Skye generally is magnificent walkers' country and nothing exemplifies this better than a visit to the Red Hills of Glamaig–Marsco across Glen Sligachan. A traverse between the two gives a marvellous panorama of the Black Cuillin in a way you can never enjoy while *on* their cluttered complexities. Glamaig to Garbh-bheinn is even better: a long, hard day which is worth every scree-step of the way.

The screes of the Red Hills are notorious. Glamaig, from Sligachan, looks like a coal-bing of scree yet, by cunning and care, most of it can be avoided in ascent — and utilised in descent. Early this century a Gurkha soldier ran up and down from the hotel in under an hour. My first ascent took a modest three hours one November during my week on Skye holidaying with Mother. I had been up the Clisham two days earlier and then I'd taken her on a walk to the Quirang. Glamaig came as a bonus. At 3 a.m. I came down from the roof bunk in my Dormobile and lowered the roof for I was afraid the wind would tear it off. The storm wrote a new tide-line of snow on Glamaig.

The sheets of ice on the road were the day's main hazard, the heathery moors the day's main effort but they petered out on to grass which petered out on to the screes which were tamed by being glued into place by the new snow. The wind was terrific and the colours were a riot of wine and gold as the sun glittered in below the receding clouds. Glamaig's triangle of shadow lay across Loch Sligachan. The view was reminiscent of looking down on the Kingshouse and Rannoch Moor from the Buachaille. There was a slight easing of the angle and, fighting the wind, I could hardly breathe — the breath was just shoved down my throat again. The trig point of Sgurr Mhairi, the summit of Glamaig, gave a welcome wind-break. I made myself as trig-shaped as I could! Through watering eyes I took in the colossal

panorama: An Teallach, Torridon, Applecross, Kintail, right down
to Mull, peak upon snowy peak, lit by golden fire. Raasay, a favourite
island, made a foreground to the seascape and then there was the
uplifted, classic Sligachan view to the Gillean side of the bold Black
Cuillin.

The ridge on to An Coilleach (the NE Top) was not to be resisted
but I welcomed the chance to turn my back on the wind and angle
down into Coire na h-Airidhe to hit the road at the last house of
Sconser, a quick romp for the scree was either drifted over with snow
or stood brittle on crystals of frozen soil, both giving an efficient
scree-running surface. A few years later came our Glamaig–Marsco
traverse.

That day used up our full ration of superlatives and I'm glad Dave
and Tony, two of my most constant companions, were along. As it
was going to be a scorcher we set off at 6.30 a.m., and were back at
our Sligachan camp at 3.15 p.m. My earlier comments on playing the
screes with cunning were borne out by our experiences. I doubt if we
had fifty feet of real rubbish all day. The early start allowed us to make
the initial ascent in shadow. The Bealach na Sgairde had had cloud
teasing over and when we reached it we gasped with astonishment.
Eastwards, as far as the eye could see, was a blazing white sea of cloud.
The Red Hills alone seemed to be holding back the flood. Every now
and then a stray wisp would sneak through a col but all day we walked
with this white wasteland on the left hand and the sun-delineated
Black Cuillin on the right.

We zigzagged up grass to reach Glamaig by a right-flanking route.
We bombed down to the bealach on the screes. This pattern was
repeated over the big, middling and smaller Beinn Deargs that led
ever-southwards. The last descent to the Mam a' Phobuill was the
worst. The waterfall was reduced to a mere spout but we lunched and
paddled in the burn and filled our hats with water. The banks were
yellow with huge primroses, tormentil, rose-root and globeflower. A
ridge of crack-shattered rocks, reminiscent of Rhum, led right to the
summit. "Poucherseque", was Dave's comment on the view but I
quickly retorted that Poucher had dismissed the Red Hills in a mere
two lines in his *Magic of Skye*. I've also noted that neither that book,
nor his *The Scottish Peaks*, makes any mention of midges!

Section 18 Rhum: 4. ASKIVAL   812 m   OS 39   393952
                       Hill of ash trees

Section 18 Rhum: 5. AINSHVAL   781 m   OS 39   379944
                       Hill of strongholds?

Sir Hugh Munro had a high regard for the Rhum Cuillin and in the
first volume of the *Journal* (1891) put his case: "Only four hills exceed
2,000 feet and these lie in the south east corner which for ruggedness
of mountain outline and boldness of shape, as well as variety and
beauty of distant views, is probably unequalled in Scotland except in
the neighbouring Cuchullins."

Munro ran into the usual Rhum weather mix. "The 4th was not
tempting for climbing so I went out to try for woodcock, accompanied by a keeper with a broad Lancashire accent." (Mr Bullough had,
after all, placed all the resources of the island at his disposal.) The 5th
was a washout but on the next day he had a day which is perhaps so
typical of many people's doings that it is worth quoting in part.

On the 6th, having waited about until 10.30, I determined to profit
by a slight weather improvement, and at any rate climb Allival. I
ascended Coire Dubh in the direction of Barkeval, a fine-shaped
rocky mountain. A very easy ascent led to a flattish ridge between it
and Allival at a height of about 1,500 feet. I was puzzled by the
distance the island appeared to extend but found I was looking at
Canna, the intervening sound being hidden. A quarter of a mile led
to the north west arête of Allival, which although steep, and
continually requiring the use of hands, is not difficult. Reached the
summit at twelve. The top was entirely clear of mist and the views
lovely though, as on the 4th, the summits of the mainland hills were
hidden in cloud.

The ridge connecting this mountain with Askival runs south. It
descends to a col, which falls away steeply both east and west, and
then rises by a very narrow arête to Askival, the summit of which
was now entirely clear of mist. Viewed from Allival, this arête
looked practicable for about half-way up, where a veritable
gendarme appeared entirely to block the way. Both the east and
west faces of the mountain looked inaccessible, and two smaller
blocks within a few feet of the summit seemed insurmountable.
Anyhow, I was only out for a stroll, fully intending to have another
day on these hills; and we all know that although snow slopes are
generally found to be far more formidable than what they appear at

a distance, rocks, on the contrary, which even from a short way off seem inaccessible are often found easy when attacked. It proved so in this case.

I struck an easy way to the col, and a few minutes' ascent by the narrow ridge brought me face to face with the gendarme, which, as anticipated, was quite perpendicular and probably one hundred feet high. The east face, however, though steep presented no particular difficulty. Several attempts to regain the ridge proved abortive, I therefore kept to the face, reaching the summit almost without knowing it at 1.5 p.m.

The clouds had clung persistently to Ainshval and Sgurr nan Gillean, although neither are quite as high as Askival. However, I had plenty of time before me, so determined to descend to the head of Glen Dibidil, the easiest way down from Askival. Reaching Bealach an Oir, I thought I would at least go to the base of Ainshval and have a look, so I skirted the base of Trallval to Bealach an Fhuarain [*the pass of the springs*] between Trallval and Ainshval. There is a very pretty view down a narrow glen and over Loch Fiadh-innis to the sea.

After striking upwards across some uncomfortably steep screes on the north west face, and ascending by a nice bit of real rock-climbing with some rather awkward smooth slabs of rock, I found the slope eased off for the last couple of hundred feet, and the top was reached at 2.50. The last two hundred feet or so had been in thick mist, which now got worse. From here to the top of Sgurr nan Gillean (2,503 feet) is an easy twenty-five minutes' walk along a broad, almost level, and often grassy ridge, with fine corries to the left, which today had some good cornices of snow.

I had been told that Sgurr nan Gillean was anywhere easy on this side; if so, I was unlucky in the mist in striking the one difficult place. I managed to get down into the almost dry bed of a small burn, between cliffs sometimes so close that I could touch them on each side. I had lowered myself down on to a ledge and could not re-ascend, and for half an hour had as steep and disagreeable a piece of climbing as I wish to experience alone; sometimes on rocks at the side, sometimes on loose boulders in the bed of the burn.

I emerged from this gully and from the mist at the same time, at a height of about 1,600 feet, and in half an hour, at 4.30 p.m., reached the track from Loch Scresort, at the foot of Glen Dibidil. This glen, though only a mile and a half long, vies with Glencoe in rugged grandeur, while in its contrasts of glorious sea views it far surpasses it. Right at the head of the glen Trallval stands boldly out; Beinn nan Stac and Askival on the right, Sgurr nan Gillean and

Ainshval on the left. The glen faces to the Sgurr of Eigg and the low-lying green island of Muck. Over this is the long promontory of Ardnamurchan, the westernmost point on the mainland of Britain and behind it again the mountains of Mull, faintly seen in the haze. Towards the mainland there is a grand panorama of sea and mountains.

The distance from Glen Dibidil to the lodge is six miles. The track rises above the sea, with grand cliffs of dark rock, fringed with foam. White-winged gulls float on the waters or a solitary scart skims over them in arrowy flight. As the track rises grand views of Skye, over Soay, open out, then the track descends to Kinloch and Loch Scresort.

The following day it poured in torrents, and on the 8th, profiting by a slight wind and an unlooked-for opportunity, I sailed over in a small open boat to Arisaig. The day was absolutely perfect, without a cloud and I cast many a regretful glance back at the glorious peaks of Rhum.

There is little one need to add to that for, though the island has seen plenty of changes, the hills remain the same. Being an island, however, does present certain logistical problems. The easy answer is to buy a copy of the guidebook to Rhum; as its author I am all for boosting sales! Seriously, the guide provides all the information, not only on the prosaic practical points, but on the lore and history of an unusually interesting island, which is a unique National Nature Reserve. The history of research since the Nature Conservancy Council bought Rhum is fascinating — into red deer, re-afforestation, shearwaters, sea-eagles, archaeology and all sorts of things. Rhum is an island worth some *time*, not just a Corbett raid. Allow a week at least for a first visit.

Being such a special place, access is regulated. You can't just land and bomb off for Askival. For permission write to the Chief Warden, White House, Rhum by Mallaig, or give him a ring: 0687–2026. The staff are very friendly and helpful and contribute much to any visit. Most people camp by Loch Scresort but there is some estate bothy accommodation and a range of residential facilities in Kinloch Castle, the ludicrous mansion of the Bulloughs, and one or two cottagers do B & B. In high summer midges and clegs abound.

Rhum is usually reached by boat from Mallaig, which is the end of the West Highland railway line, and as the *Lochmor* also takes in Eigg, Muck and Canna going, or returning, you have quite a Hebridean sail as well. The views to Rhum and Eigg from the west coast are classic but how few who gaze west over sea actually sail to the Parish of the

Small Isles. Askival is less than $1\frac{1}{2}$ miles from the coast and Sgurr nan Gillean, a Top of Ainshval, is likewise less than a mile. On Bloodstone Hill you feel you could parachute into the waves.

The views *from* Rhum are spacious and grand — Sir Hugh has already said so. Munro does not overstate Rhum's excellence, but you can find the many reasons in the guidebook (*The Island of Rhum*, Cicerone Press). Not many Corbetts are given such extensive background description. Maybe Arran. And that is another island. When you have done all the Corbetts you can start collecting Scottish islands.

Section 18 Mull: 6. BEINN TALAIDH 762 m OS 49 625347
The hill of happiness (cf. Valhalla) or *Hill of good pastures* (talla)

The Island of Mull, third largest of the Hebrides, is an island of inexhaustible attractions. It has something of everything, including a bonus of satellite islands, gems such as Iona and Staffa. Mull is rich in history and lore, is a geologist's and naturalist's paradise, the seaman's delight and the hillgoer's valhalla; indeed, with one Munro, two Corbetts (Talaidh promoted in 1981) and plenty of other hills as well, it is one of the best places in Scotland for walking through glens and round coasts, enough for days on end. We grabbed a bit of everything last time, gluttony perhaps, but we did not suffer indigestion.

"We" were nephew Colin on his Easter holiday, Storm and myself. Our route was worked out in the caravan Mother had taken for the week. We motored round to Glen More (the eastern Glen More) and when the road broke out above the plantings of the Lussa River, Bein Talaidh rose straight ahead in simple symmetry, a cone-shape that is instantly recognisable from as far away as Barra. The peak gives the impression of being much higher than 762 m. At the crook of the road we parked the car and waited for the Craignure–Iona bus.

This corner would give the most direct and quickest ascent of Talaidh but we wanted to approach the peak more graciously. A drift of sheep came out from the low watershed to Glen Forsa, the glen that cuts off the Talaidh–Ben More complex of hills from Dun da Ghaoithe and the Sound of Mull. The road west up Glen More cuts off Ben Buie and Lochbhui to the south — one of the many corners that repay exploration. The early light had fallen well down on Talaidh when the bus came and bore us over that watershed to descend Glen More (the western one). We were dropped off at the bridge over the Allt Teanga Brideig, a couple of miles from Loch Scridain, and wandered upstream to pitch our tents and pass the rest of the day on a leisurely ascent of Ben More. After supper I half-climbed Corra-bheinn, while trying to read a book, as the cold shadow of evening kept chasing me up the hill every few minutes.

In the morning we traversed to find a hollow where we left the tents and then set off up Coir' a Mhaim to a col between two haunches of hill, passing through hind country with beasts grazing on all sides. The Mam Breapadail was a surprise: our long, slow sweat up suddenly led to deep-cut Coire Mor which was a bit like the Devil's Beef Tub near Moffat, which meant a brutal descent; where several burns met we had a break. The sky had clouded over and strange clouds were billowing through the passes but when we smelt them we realised the cloud was the smoke of moor-burning.

We passed a ruined burial ground and a 1910 footbridge which was reduced to two beams. Storm preferred to paddle across. Ben More must have been well alight for smoke was pouring over the hills and when we tramped through to Tomsleibhe above Glen Forsa we found that glen in flames and the shepherds busy taking the beasts down. The circles of flame were still bright in the dark when we had a last look out from the bothy. Our morning's walk placed us at the northern end of Beinn Talaidh. The hill has a gabbro satellite top from whose col a burn, the Allt nam Clar, runs in a deep, straight line down to Glen Forsa. We set off up the burn after lunch. Almost at once we found a piece of twisted metal.

By burning up we eventually came on the main wreckage of an aircraft, the remains of a wartime accident following which the epic winter search and rescue led to several awards. (Quite by chance we learnt something of the story when visiting the church in Salen.) We had to escape as the gorge became too deep-cut, so we zigzagged up the steep east flank to the summit screes. Here a sheep path led along and up on to the North Ridge and we plodded to the summit, which lies 25 yards to the south west of the trig point. The whole island seemed to be on fire, the views hazy, tones upon tones of grey, but a fantastic view, better even than Ben More's because Ben More was part of this panorama that ran from Arran to Skye and from Outer Hebrides to Ben Nevis.

A few flakes of snow fell on top so we didn't linger. By keeping to the grass on the western edge we were able to chunter down the North Ridge easily enough. There were large areas of frost-combing. (The south-east approaches may be shorter but they are steeper and give some crags and roughness. We were in at six. Colin filled some plastic bags with dry grass and we lay on them under the skylight till too dark to read. Storm kept an eye on the hares, hinds and ewes that wandered about outside. I've never seen so many dead sheep on the hills. Quite a few were in the Allt nam Clar — protein enrichment for our water supply.

We walked out along Glen Forsa under our Corbett and arrived at the car with our lower parts filthy with wet, clinging soot from the burnings. Storm had changed from bracken-colour to a uniform black. David Balfour in *Kidnapped* came this way, though his precise route is infuriatingly vague. He, of course, had suffered shipwreck rather than fire.

When we drove over to collect our hidden tents we were horrified to see the whole hillside had been burnt. Burnt too was the flysheet of my Ultimate Tramp but at least its sacrifice had saved the other tent below it. Tents, people and dogs took quite a bit of cleaning. Beinn Talaidh, for us, will always be associated with fire and smoke. Necklaces of flame had been our last view out the bothy skylight, and weeks passed before the lingering smell vanished from our belongings or the car.

Section 18 Mull: 7. DUN DA GHAOITHE   766 m   OS 49   672362
                             Fort of the wind. The castle of the two winds (goe-ee)

Dun da Ghaoithe dominates the Sound of Mull and is the largest hill to be seen when sailing to Craignure from Oban, the most usual approach to Mull. A cheaper car ferry also operates from Lochaline in Morven, crossing to Fishnish. Quite often the impecunious walker compromises by bringing a cycle rather than a car (I've done it myself) but Mull deserves a week and a car simply to begin exploring the island. The magnet of Iona also means that there are buses which can be used if one comes without any means of self-propulsion.

So, from Craignure take the Iona bus round to Torness (ruin) in Glen More and head up, traversing rocky Sgurr Dearg to Mainnir nam Fiadh (*the field of the deer*) and Dun da Ghaoithe, descending by the east ridge to Maol nan Uan with its TV station service road down to the A849 at Torosay Castle. This castle has attractive gardens and, in season, there is a miniature railway to take you back to Craignure. Duart Castle is older and set in a commanding site overlooking the Sound of Mull. There is time to enjoy both the hill and the castles on a summer's outing. Another day of high walking can be had by taking the Tobermory bus to Fishnish Bay, wandering up Maol Buide, then along by the Beinn Chreagachs and Beinn Mheadhon to reach the Corbett. Or you could traverse the lot — but that is not so easily fitted in to a day trip from Oban! A simple circuit from Craignure is probably the most popular expedition, if popular is the right word for the uncrowded hills of Mull. At least I've met accounts of Dun da Ghaoithe; Beinn Talaidh seems to lie under a strange moratorium.

Campbell Steven's *The Island Hills* has a description of Dun da Ghaoithe and, as the book takes in Arran, Jura, Rhum and Skye as well as Mull (plus plenty of islands without Corbetts), those bent on the Corbett quest would enjoy reading it. Campbell Steven describes two ascents of the hill, both from the Craignure side, circuits similar to one I made on a frantic Corbetts tour during a Sabbatical year spent in mountains all round the world. My notes were a bit sparse but they can recapture the day in a way unaided memory cannot do. The briefest of hill logs is better than none.

28.6.72 Dun da Ghaoithe. Crazy pace still. A week ago in the Alps, then the flight to Benbecula unable to land so this week of unplanned Corbett-bagging instead. Up at 4 a.m. to do Leum Uilleim before morning train to Glasgow, collect the car from the airport, collect the dog from Dollar and motor to Oban and a night in the Dormobile by Loch Nell. Body not keen on rising today. Just a cuppa and in for 6.30 sailing to Craignure. Breakfast on *Columba* till out to watch Duart Castle. Motor a couple of miles along to Scallastle Bay. Skirt bracken bump of Cnoc Bhacain and then curling ridge to the summit, overlooking Coire na Circe. Neat shelter for one shower: laid two posts against the fence and roofed it with space blanket. Regular outbursts and then into cloud for the last gravelly steps. Slaggy corries of grey. And a big cairn. Pause naturally, and it cleared, instantly. Great. Romp round the rim of Coire Mor to the peakier pap of Mainnir nam Fiadh. Sgurr Dearg an attractive peak, too. West of it all was blotted out in cloud. As so often the view *down* rewarding on islands. Clutch of islands' Corbetts too. Continue on down the curve of east ridge: chips laid down in regular stripes like a patterned carpet. Bale off into Coire nan Dearc but come on a deer fence for new tree planting. The Scallastle River a succession of falls and pools. Mull rivers are made for swimming. Not today though. Cut across before house to the Dormobile. Lunch of toasted cheese. Road works but fine tarred surface (silver straight after rain) up Glen More. Time to relax. Corbetts will take a long time yet — but a pleasing prospect with more islands and breaking new ground; the delights of discovery. Ben More cleared but last memory of the calling curlews, oyster catchers and snipe, the Mull magic.

Section 18 Jura: 8. BEINN AN OIR   784 m   OS 61   498749
    Hill of Gold

We had come to know the north end of Jura from several school visits, an exciting coast with huge caves and the great Sound of Corrie-vreckan, but we had always sailed there from Loch Craignish. The three Paps of Jura (such odd symmetrical cones) were at the other end of the island, alluring but out of reach. They became "someday hills".

The Outer Hebrides and western seaboard had been keeping me occupied. Regretfully the time came to return home but as I sailed from Mull back to Oban I decided the west could have one more fling: we'd end with the Hill of Gold on Jura. The 4.30 p.m. ferry took us to Port Askaig and ten minutes later the "landing-craft" ferry was slap-slapping into the waves across the Sound of Islay to Feolin on Jura. A stuffy south wind rose in the night; it was almost a pleasure to set off early.

All I knew of Beinn an Oir was its reputation of being a pile of "loose and shifty", boot-destroying quartzite, so I wore my oldest pair and decided feet could just become wet. The walk up the Corran River therefore came as a pleasant surprise, the wind had dried the grass and the going, by the burn, was pleasant. My only excitement was when a big boulder supporting the bank gave way when I stood on it. The dog's excitement was the large number of deer all day. A cuckoo, down to one syllable, "cucked" at us regularly on the way up to Loch an t-Siob under Beinn Shiantaich. I was thinking the loch would be a likely place for divers when a pair started cackling on its wind-whipped surface. The heat was boiling up for a storm and streamers were already touching the grey peaks. Thoughts of a long day over the three Paps vanished and I had to race to win the summit of Jura.

The cloud was down to the beallach by the time we had been blown up to it. I started up right and a brief break showed a stormy sea round Rhuvaal light at the northern end of Islay. Bad quartz was not good in those conditions. Gusts were apt to throw me off balance and the greasy rock caused several slithers. The dog, as ever, seemed quite unaffected. A lot of the scree could not be dodged and we ended on a surprisingly narrow crest. I left the odd wee marker cairn as I went so that I could backtrack quickly without the rigmarole of compass work. A final rocky cone landed us beside the trig point. We were there just long enough to eat some chocolate before retreating as we'd come. We kept higher across the moors, cut corners, and had a great tussle with the wind. We crossed back to Islay all right, but the ferry to the mainland was hours late. The deluge began on the crossing. I suppose I had been lucky.

Jura's hills are not climbed very often I'm sure, but the unusual nature of the peaks seems to drive ascensionists into print. One of the few *Journal* notes by J. Rooke Corbett was about his visit to the Paps in 1931. The ferry crossing cost him six shillings return, then he took the direct route from the ferry to the Paps over the moors, rounded Beinn a' Chaolais (*the hill of the sound*) to ascend Beinn an Oir by its easiest, most vegetated line, the NW Ridge. The NW side of Beinn Shiantaidh (*the consecrated hill*) is also its easiest, grassiest; he went up and down it that way. Beinn a' Chaolais was tackled by its East Ridge and, as in my case, Corbett lost a race to have the summit clear. Quite a few accounts I've read tell of these sudden changes of weather. The Paps seem to cull clouds out of any sky. On their tops you certainly "stumble between the immensities".

A new bulldozed track heading northwards from the ferry helps the direct moorland approach. Charles, on an appalling day, was glad to use the footpath to Glen Batrick for easy access. Charles also pointed out to me that both sheets 60 and 61 have Beinn an Oir on them but each gives a different height. The Islay sheet gives 785 m.

Corbett, on Beinn an Oir, commented about two huts in a dip to the north of the summit with a causeway leading to the top, and Inkson McConnochie (1914) described a hut by the lochan north east of the hill. The summit had a huge survey cairn. Recent visitors have sometimes mentioned the causeway, an odd man-made intrusion into the stark, bony landscape, and these remains point back to the Ordnance Survey's original great triangulation of the country. They pinpointed peaks as far distant as Slieve Snacht in Donegal, Beinn Mhor in South Uist, Ben Nevis, Lawers and The Merrick.

The Paps are often mentioned by the early "tourers": Pennant, Grierson, Maccullough and others. The last, usually a loquacious enthusiast, girned, "Intimate as I am with Jura, I have little to say of it, and much less to say in its favour." However, commenting on the striking, and unique, appearance of the symmetrical Paps and, of the view from the top, he recorded, "the skeleton and structure of Jura, which seems atomized to its very foundations". Grierson found the ascent "very abrupt" and commented on "loose blocks so troublesome that much care was required to escape broken bones", yet there were "blaeberries, crawberries, junipers and braelics". Several people note the thrift which grows as happily on the rocks by the sea as on the rocks on the barren heights. Thomas Pennant, who was no mountain man, scaled Beinn an Oir on his 1772 tour, "a task of much labour and difficulty". He, at least, had a view:

Find our fatigues fully recompenced by the prospect from this sublime spot: *Jura* itself afforded a stupendous scene of rock, varied with little lakes innumerable. The depth below was tremendous on every side.

To the South appeared *Ilay*, extended like a map beneath us; and beyond that, the North of *Ireland*; to the East, *Gigha* and *Cara*, *Cantyre* and *Arran*, and the Firth of *Clyde*, bounded by *Airshire*; an amazing tract of mountains to the north east as far as *Ben-lomond*; *Skarba* finished the Northern view; and over the Western ocean were scattered *Colonsay* and *Oransay*, *Mull*, *Iona* and still further the long extents of *Tirey* and *Col* just apparent.

On the summit are several lofty *cairns*, the work of idle herds, or curious travellers. A hind passed along the sides full speed, and a brace of *Ptarmigans* often favored us. The other *paps* are seen very distinctly; all of the same figure, perfectly mamillary.

An Englishman, a Scotsman and an Irishman had been marooned in the hut on Beinn an Oir one long day of storm when one of them noticed an old bottle lying in the debris on the floor. He picked up the bottle and began rubbing the dirt off, then uncorked it to have a sniff only to recoil as a cloud poured out and quickly took the form of a genie. The genie offered them a wish each. The Englishman, who had been thinking of home comforts in soft Sussex, at once blurted out, "I wish I was back home" — and promptly vanished. The others goggled, then the Scotsman half-suggested, "I wish I was comfy and dry in the *Ranger's Rest* in Glasgow with a *Jura* in my hand." He too vanished. The Irishman looked at the blowing rain and cloud outside and shuddered. What a miserable place! "Bejabers this is a desolate place. I wish me two friends were back here with me now."

Section 18 Arran: 9. GOAT FELL   874 m   OS 69   991415
Hill of the wind

"Arran is magic", was the reaction of one lad I spoke to recently. He had taken his cycle over and explored the island thoroughly by road, by tramping and camping the glens and ridges and enjoying several rock climbs. Few places can give such a variety of good things; and my own list would add prehistoric monuments, wildlife, seashore and garden interests. That lad had, unprompted, commented on the "bonny bright bushes" at Brodick Castle — having been there at rhododendron time. The moment one lands on the pier at Brodick, Goat Fell catches the eye; the peak rises behind the castle across the bay as gracefully as Fuji Yama and, as Pennant said of Lochranza, "the whole is environed with a theatre of mountains."

All the Corbetts can be traversed in a day, something of a marathon; but Arran should be savoured, selectively and sensitively, rather than gulped down, a whole menu in one binge. The peaks break down into two logical and immensely enjoyable expeditions: you can have your cake and eat it.

Glen Rosa and Glen Sannox reach into the big granite hills as if they were trying to remove Goat Fell from the rest of the peaks. Goat Fell is really a solitary summit and, being the highest, both dominates the scenery from Brodick Bay and gives a huge view from its trig point. I can still remember the thrill of reaching the top the first time, as a boy, and seeing the Clyde glittering in the sun, and Tarsuinn, Cir Mhor and Caisteal Abhail ranged raggedly against the sunset colours.

Arran attracted me first as an island. I had never heard of Corbetts or Munros though the visit was to double my tally of the former. Arran was reached by cycling from home in Dollar and staying in Brodick Youth Hostel (a bad gap now without a hostel) and, like the youth I was speaking to thirty years on, I explored thoroughly, besides traversing all the ridges and getting gripped on the granite crags. Arran was magic, all right. Some things don't change.

There is a well marked path for Goat Fell from Brodick, leaving the lushness of the castle grounds up by the Cnocan Burn. On the moors the map shows this burn splitting into two and I remember going to inspect it and being disappointed to find the split was caused by an old mill dam. The path curves up from the SE corrie to reach the summit via the East Ridge. The panoramic view is "One of the most entrancing in Scotland" (Poucher). "A marvellous combination of fantastic mountain scenery so near, sunlit seas far below, and the isles away to the west makes this prospect unique."

One of the few mountain books I have read over and over again is Janet Adam Smith's *Mountain Holidays*. The book opens with a chapter on Arran, where she climbed Goat Fell at the age of nine, having been blasted off the East Ridge the year before. Those were family holiday visits, under the care of the poet and mountaineer W. P. Ker (whose telling influence is gently described), and they led to many of the participants going on to climb and explore in other parts of the world. The book continues with Alpine holidays and I found it quite infectious. Even the Alps could be fun, as Goat Fell was fun. A fun based on acquired skills, but still fun. Where grim-faced Whymper had left me gasping, Janet Adam Smith beguiled me to the Alps — and beyond.

I'd already read about Arran's ridges, for Dollar was the home of W. K. Holmes and his sister, who were kind to the maverick youth who already ran wild on the Ochils. W.K.H.'s modest book *Tramping Scottish Hills* has a chapter on the Goat Fell Horseshoe. That book I knew almost by heart. W.K.H. and W.P.K. I suspect were very alike in many ways. Their quiet, solid, yet visionary approach to the hills I feel is sadly lacking today when big egos seem to want instant trips. Thank God we have had these peers, these poets and philosophers whose love is of the hills themselves, for themselves. Read them, friends, and also read Tom Weir and W. H. Murray and Seton Gordon. Arran was special for all of them.

Arran has a mention in just about every general book on the Scottish hills, and scores of entries in journals and magazines. Hamish MacInnes's *West Highland Walks*, Vol. 3, gives a good general coverage of the island while Poucher's *The Scottish Peaks* and Bennet's *Scottish Mountain Climbs* have interesting photographs of its mountains.

I cannot remember how I descended on that first visit — it was probably by the "tourist path" I'd ascended — but I can recall the next descent, to Sannox, and this, with the ascent from Brodick, is the classic traverse. From the trig point head north along the castellated ridge of the Stacach to North Goat Fell which is the real hub of the mountain with ridges radiating in three directions, that to the north west dropping to the Saddle linking Goat Fell with the other granite giants while the NE Ridge is the continuation of the traverse, edging down along the cliffs of Coire nam Fuaran. (In 1889 a young man was murdered and his body found below these cliffs.) The ridge levels off over Mullach Buidhe (819 m) then becomes a rocky crest, sheer on the east (Coire na Ciche) side and super-steep above Glen Sannox. Cioch na h-Oighe (*the Maiden's breast*) is 661 m. There is a path all the way, now, down into Glen Sannox. For a young lad on his own this descent was quite exciting: a first taste of exposure and the friendly adhesiveness of granite.

During the early to mid 1970s I was to see plenty of young men react to Arran's hills: we went there several times with trainees from the *Captain Scott* and had a survival camp in Glen Rosa on one occasion. Some of the townies found the wind on Goat Fell quite frightening, it periodically knocked whole groups to the ground at once. On another occasion we backpacked over Goat Fell to camp on the Saddle with a view down Glen Rosa and the wind and cloud racing harmlessly up Cir Mhor from Glen Sannox. Those winter months on a tall ship are an unforgettable experience — and what an approach to the hills!

Section 18 Arran: 10. BEINN TARSUINN   825 m   OS 69   959412
Transverse hill

Section 18 Arran: 11. CIR MHOR   798 m   OS 69   973432
Big comb (keer vor)

Section 18 Arran: 12. CAISTEAL ABHAIL   859 m   OS 69   969444
Ptarmigan stronghold (cash-tyal-avil)

W. Douglas, of Douglas Boulder fame, produced the first SMC *Journal* article on Arran in 1896. He extensively quotes Alexander Nicolson, the Skye enthusiast who, nevertheless, had much to say about Arran which he considered the most beautiful island in Scotland. He in turn quotes someone else in describing the view of these hills from Goat Fell: a "terrible congregation of jagged ridges and fantastic peaks". Douglas delves back with several quotations, which mirror the changing view people had of mountains.

In 1628 "Lugless Willie Lithgow" commented on "Goatfield which, with wide eyes, overlooketh the western continent and the northern country of Ireland, the Isle of Man and the higher coast of Cumberland. A larger prospect no mountain in the world can show, pointing out three kingdoms at one sight; neither is there any isle like it for brave gentry, good archers, and hill hovering hunters."

Maccullough (1811) found the "high and serrated forms peculiarly striking, presenting a rugged mountainous character unequalled in Scotland except by the Cuchullin in Sky". He was a geologist, of course, and keen on all sorts of studies. Science was becoming *the* reason for climbing hills at home, or abroad, so he was at a loss over the ascent by a minister who, having climbed up, "just went down again". I suspect more people made ascents for fun, even in those days. No one wrote about them, that's all.

The Rev. Thomas Grierson in his *Autumnal Rambles among the Scottish Mountains* (1850) is delightful with his "thrills of horror", Lord Cockburn broke into his "Circuit Journeys" to climb Goat Fell (a $5\frac{1}{2}$-hour round trip), Hugh M'cullough looks at these hills as "such a wild storm of mountains" and is tempted to quote a Paisley weaver on top of Ben Lomond turning to a friend with, "Man, Jock, are the works of God no devilish?"

Walkers are sometimes put off the Arran hills by reports of difficulties, of unavoidable climbing, of Bad Steps, of cyclopean rocks and boiler-plate slabs, which is a pity: Arran is a great place for walkers and for backpacking. The young *Captain Scott* trainees quite happily carried their gear over Goat Fell to that camp on the Saddle and the next day traversed Cir Mhor and Caisteal Abhail to camp by Loch Tanna west of Glen Iorsa before climbing Beinn Bharran above the west coast and rejoining ship off Lochranza Castle. Distances are not great in the Arran hills, there are many paths and plenty of grassy slopes and easy valleys, besides the dramatic upsurge of peaks. The traverse of these peaks is a classic expedition.

The walk begins from Glen Rosa and follows up the Garbh Allt (*rough burn*) which drains Coire a' Bhradain to gain Beinn Nuis (*face hill*) from the south east, an easy tramp with a final steep pull. The walk north to Beinn Tarsuinn presents no difficulty though the east face is an amazing world of granite slabs and pinnacles. Tarsuinn has perhaps the best panoramic view for it includes Goat Fell soaring over its scoured, rocky base. Rock, heather and boulders quickly lead down to the Bowmen's Pass, Bealach an Fhir-bhogha, where decisions have to be made, for the A' Chir Ridge lies ahead. This can be outflanked on the west below the overlapping rocks, and both the Coire a' Bhradain and Glen Iorsa sides of the pass can be descended, but the crest is not as difficult as appearances suggest and it is worth "having a look". Most of the day's route has been worn into a path, and even on the rocks the way is usually visible from the marks of passing feet. A rising line up the slabs on the west side leads to the crest.

Exposed but easy scrambling leads along to the summit of A' Chir (*The comb*: Ah keer), the top being a large, undercut boulder which is a minor challenge in itself. Beyond the summit, on the descent, lies the notorious *mauvais pas*, which is basically unavoidable so has to be faced. The exposure rather than any technical difficulty gives the Bad Step its reputation. A cairn shows where the ridge has to be left to descend a twelve-foot wall on the east face to a ledge angling along to easier ground. Some people claim this is not the actual Bad Step but just a difficult section of ridge. That name they would keep for a feature met not long before, at the foot of the initial descent off A' Chir, where a foot-wide col (the narrowest part of the whole ridge) is cleft through so that you have to make "a step across space", so to speak. You can allocate the name as you choose.

Beyond these adrenalin-boosting spots there is one further granite tower and then easy grass slopes which lead up to Cir Mhor, famous for the Rosa Pinnacle, a soaring, curving buttress of granite on the right. (The best view of the pinnacle is from the Fionn Choire, reached by walking up Glen Rosa.) The summit of this *aiguille*-like peak is a superb situation for such an easy ascent, the central position giving views in all directions, both down the glens and to the other peaks, but my favourite view is from Caisteal Abhail. There, the view takes in Cir Mhor as well. The crest from Cir Mhor to Caisteal Abhail is easy.

There is a welcome spring on the shoulder, as one pulls up to the *Ptarmigan's castles*, which is a good resting place. Cir Mhor appears to lean over into Glen Sannox and its jagged shape is echoed in Goat Fell behind and, distantly, in the thrust of Holy Island opposite Lamlash. The Castles are a collection of summit boulders and tors, as is the route's continuation eastwards for the next mile. Careful navigation is required not to stray on to secondary ridges — and then there is the Witch's Step, the Carlin's Leap, Ceum na Caillich.

These are either the deep gash in the ridge caused by the weathering away of a whin dyke, or the tricky exit up the far side — opinion again does not agree — but everything can be avoided by descending a short way from the gap and traversing along the northern flanks. (Sheep have long ago worn paths under all the crags, and these are usually clear.) The far side of the gap appears intimidating but "goes" with just one awkward place — the sloping slab from which a bulge of granite tries to push you off. This leads to a gully which runs up to easier ground, the top being another claimant for the actual title of the Witch's Step. I reckon the Step names, on both hills, belong to the gaps where there is a step across. (The name Ceum na Caillich on the 1:50,000 map is much misplaced.)

The ridge runs out over a rise (634 m) to the prow of Suidhe Fhearghas (Soo-ee Fergus, *Fergus's Seat*) from which the descent can be made to the nineteenth hole of the Sannox Golf Course. Fergus was the bard of the Fiana, who often hunted in Arran according to Irish legends. Or Fergus was the king who came up here to survey his domains. Again, take your pick.

If simply seeking the Corbetts and wishing to avoid the Bad Insteps, Witches' Hiccups and so on I'd recommend the following. Reach Beinn Tarsuinn as above and then, from the Bealach an Fhirbhogha, take the pavement-like crest of Beinn a' Chiabhain to descend by Crioc Breac back to Glen Rosa. For Cir Mhor walk up Glen Rosa and gain the A' Chir–Cir Mhor saddle. Perhaps add Caisteal Abhail and return the same way or cross the Saddle to descend Glen Sannox; or, best of all, from the castles, head for Loch na Davie and Lochranza.

When I took the dog to Arran for his Corbetts we did the three together by going up by Beinn a' Chiabhain, adding Tarsuinn, along A' Chir, out to Caisteal Abhail, back to Cir Mhor and down Fionn Choire to Glen Rosa. The dog's exuberance was rather alarming. On the tricky wall I tied clothes together to make a rope to lower Storm in the rucksack, but he decided to jump out half-way down. As often as not when I was struggling he'd be peering down at me, mocking my incompetence. He's very hard to live up to.

On Goat Fell there is a good path off Meall Breac down to Corrie, giving a traverse that can be made without difficulty. These are all recommendable routes. Perhaps they will help bring you back to Arran again. Once you have got the Corbetts out of your system you still have to do something. As Robert Louis Stevenson said: ". . . where we have discovered a continent or crossed a chain of mountains [or done the Corbetts] it is only to find another ocean or another plain upon the farther side. Even in one corner the weather and the seasons keep so deftly changing that, though we walk there for a lifetime, there will be always something new to startle and delight. Little do you know your blessedness; for to travel hopefully is a better thing than to arrive . . .

"You lean from the window, your last pipe reeking whitely into the darkness, your body full of delicious pains, your mind enthroned in the seventh circle of content; when suddenly the mood changes, the weathercock goes about, and you ask yourself one question more: whether [Corbetts done] you have been wise, or the most egregious of donkeys? But at least you have had a fine moment, and looked down upon all the kingdoms of the earth. And whether it was wise or foolish, tomorrow's travel will carry you body, and mind, into some different parish of the infinite."

APPENDICES

BIBLIOGRAPHICAL NOTES

SOME BOOKS MENTIONED IN THE TEXT

Bennet, Donald, *Scottish Mountain Climbs*, Batsford 1979
Bord, Janet & Colin, *Sacred Waters*, Granada 1985
Borthwick, Alistair, *Always a Little Further*, Faber 1939, repr. Diadem 1983
Brown, Hamish M., *Hamish's Mountain Walk*, Gollancz 1978, paperback Paladin 1980
——*Hamish's Groats End Walk*, Gollancz 1981, paperback Paladin 1983
——*The Island of Rhum*, Milnthorpe, Cicerone Press 1988
——*Travels*, Edinburgh, The Scotsman 1986
Corbett, J. Rooke, see *SMC Journal*
Crockett, S. R., *The Raiders*, T. Fisher Unwin 1894, repr. Ernest Benn 1947
Ellice, E. C., *Place Names of Glengarry and Glenquoich*, Routledge 1931
Firsoff, V. A., *In the Hills of Breadalbane*, Hale 1954
Grierson, Rev. Thomas, *Autumnal Rambles among the Scottish Mountains*, Edinburgh, Paton & Ritchie 1850
Hall, Rev. James, *Travels in Scotland*, London, J. Johnson 1807
Hogg, James, *A Tour in the Highlands in 1803*, Paisley, A. Gardner 1888
Holmes, W. K., *Tramping Scottish Hills*, Stirling, Eneas Mackay 1946, repr. as *On Scottish Hills*, Oliver & Boyd 1962
Jeffrey, Alan, *Scotland Underground*, A. Oldham, Rhychydwr, Crymych, Dyfed
Maccullough, J., *A Description of the Western Islands (1811–21)* extracted in *SMC Journal*
—— *Highlands and Western Islands of Scotland* extracted in *SMC Journal*
McGill, Patrick, *Children of the Dead End*, Herbert Jenkins 1914, paperback Caliban Books 1985
MacInnes, Hamish, *West Highlands Walks*, 3 vols. Hodder 1979–84
McOwan, Rennie, *Walks in the Trossachs and Rob Roy Country*, Edinburgh, The Saint Andrew Press 1983
Macrow, Brenda, *Torridon Highlands*, Hale 1950
Miles, Hamish, *Fair Perthshire*, Bodley Head 1930
Morton, H. V., *In Search of Scotland*, Methuen 1930, paperback Methuen 1984
Mould, D. D. C. Pochin, *Roads from the Isles*, Oliver & Boyd 1950
Munro's Tables and other Tables of Lesser Heights, Edinburgh, SMC 1984 edit.
Munro, H., see also *SMC Journal*
Plumb, Charles, *Walking in the Grampians*, A. Maclehose 1935
Poucher, W. A., *The Scottish Peaks*, Constable 1965, 6th ed. 1982
——*The Magic of Skye*, Constable 1949

Robertson, Rev. A. E., see *SMC Journal*

Smith, Janet Adam, *Mountain Holidays*, Dent 1946

Smith, Robert, *Grampian Ways*, Melven Press 1980

Steven, Campbell, *The Island Hills*, Hurst & Blackett 1955

Stevenson, Robert Louis, "El Dorado" in *Virginibus Puerisque*, Kegan Paul 1881, paperback Penguin 1946

Stott, Louis, *Waterfalls of Scotland*, Aberdeen University Press 1987

Victoria, Queen, *More Leaves from the Journal of a Life in the Highlands*, Smith, Elder & Co. 1884, extracted in *Our Life in the Highlands*, Wm Kimber 1968

Wilson, Ken, and Gilbert, Richard, *The Big Walks*, Diadem 1980

——*Classic Walks*, Diadem 1982

Young, Geoffrey Winthrop, *Collected Poems*, Methuen 1936

JOURNALS AND GUIDES

Cairngorm Club *Journal*

Getting Around the Highlands and Islands, F. H. G. Publications, Abbey Mill Centre, Seedhill, Paisley PA1 1JN (or from Tourist Offices)

Grampian Club *Bulletin*

SMC District Guides

SMC Journal

Scottish Postbus Timetable (can be ordered from any Post Office)

MUNROS WITH ADJACENT CORBETTS

Munro Section & Number	Munro Name	Corbett Section & Number	Corbett Name
1: 2	Beinn Narnain and	2: 4	The Cobbler and
1: 3	Beinn Ime	2: 5	Beinn Luibhean, & others
1: 7	Beinn Bhuidhe	2: 8	Meall an Fhudair
1: 9	Ben Lui	3: 2	Beinn Chuirn
1:24	Ben Vorlich and	2:15	Meall na Fearna and
1:25	Stuc a' Chroin	2:14	Beinn Each
1:26	Ben Chonzie	4:13	Auchnafree Hill
2: 8	Carn Gorm	4:12	Beinn Dearg
2: 9	Stuchd an Lochain	4: 9, 10	Sron a' Choire Chnapanich & Meall Buidhe
2:11	Meall Buidhe	4:11	Cam Chreag
2:19	Meall a' Choire Leith	4: 6	Meall Luaidhe
2:20	Meall nan Tarmachan	4: 7	Beinn nan Oighreag
2:24	Meall Ghaordie	4: 7	Beinn nan Oighreag
	and	4: 8	Meall nan Subh
2:26	Creag Mhor	3: 8	Cam Chreag
2:28	Ben Challum	3: 8	Cam Chreag
	and	3: 7	Beinn Chaorach
2:30	Meall Glas	4: 1	Beinn nan Imirean
2:40	Beinn Mhanach	3:10	Beinn nam Fuaran
3: 5	Stob Diamh, Cruachan	3: 1	Beinn a' Bhuiridh
3:16	Meall nan Eun	3:13	Stob Dubh, Beinn Ceitlein
3:23	Creise	5: 4	Beinn Mhic Chasgaig
3:33	Bidean nam Bian	5: 3	Beinn Maol Chaluim
3:41	Meall Dearg	5: 6	Garbh Bheinn
3:43	Sgorr na h-Ulaidh	5: 2	Meall Ligiche
3:46	Beinn Sgulaird	3:11	Creach Bheinn
4:40	Stob Ban	5:10, 11	Sgurr Innse, Cruach Innse
4:41	Stob Coire Easain	5:10, 11	Sgurr Innse, Cruach Innse
4:47	Beinn na Lap	5: 9	Leum Uilleim
4:48	Carn Dearg	6: 1	Meall na Meoig
5: 1	Sgairneach Mhor	6: 6	Sow of Atholl
5: 6	Carn na Caim	6: 8	An Dun
6: 1	Carn an Fhidhleir	7: 6	Beinn Bhreac
6: 3	Beinn Dearg	7: 5	Beinn Mheadhonach
	or	7: 6	Beinn Bhreac
		7: 5	Beinn Mheadhonach
6: 4	Carn a' Chlamain	7:11	Conachraig
7:20	Lochnagar	8: 1	Creag Mhor
8:29	Bynach More	8: 1	Creag Mhor
8:41	Beinn a' Chaorainn		

THE CORBETTS IN ORDER OF ALTITUDE

Metres

914 Beinn Dearg (Torridon 13:4)
    Sgurr a' Choire-bheithe

912 Beinn Bhreac
    Leathad an Taobhain

911 The Fara

909 Streap
    Beinn nan Oighreag

908 Ganu Mor, Foinaven
    Beinn Dearg Mor

907 Fuar Tholl
    Meall Buidhe

906 Leum Uilleim

904 Beinn Maol Chaluim

903 Ben Vuirich

902 Beinn Damh

901 Ben Tee
    Beinn Mheadhonach
    Sgurr an Fhuarain
    Beinn an Lochain

900 Culardoch
    Beinn Odhar

899 Aonach Buidhe

897 Beinn a' Bhuiridh
    Corrieyairack Hill

896 Gairbeinn
    Beinn Bhan (Applecross 13:2)
    Ruadh-stac Beag
    Ben Tirran

895 Creag Mhor

894 Sgurr nan Eugalt

892 Beinn a' Chuallaich
    An Ruadh-stac

889 Beinn Enaiglair
    Aonach Shasuinn

888 Sgurr Dhomhnuill

887 Ben Aden
    Creagan na Beinne

885 Sgurr a' Bhac Chaolais
    Garbh Bheinn (Ardgour 10:3)
    Cam Chreag (Auch 3:8)
    Beinn a' Chaisteil (Auch 3:9)

884 The Cobbler

883 Stob Dubh, Beinn Ceitlein

882 Rois-Bheinn
    Beinn Odhar Bheag

880 Beinn Chuirn
    Sgurr Mhurlagain

c.880 Meall a' Ghiubhais

879 Ben Ledi
    Creag Uchdag
    Fraochaidh
    Sguman Coinntich
    Sgurr a' Mhuilinn

878 Carn an Fhreiceadain

876 Craig an Loch

875 Baosbheinn

874 Sgurr na Ba Glaise
    Goat Fell

873 Sgurr nan Lochan Uaine
    Ben Hee

871 Morven

868 Faochaig
    Meall na Meoig of Ben Pharlagain

867 Sgurr na h-Aide
    Garbh Bheinn (L. Leven 5:6)

865 Conachcraig
    Stob a' Choin

863 Carn a' Choire Ghairbh
    Beinn Tharsuinn (Sheasgaich 14:8)

862 Cam Chreag (Glen Lyon 4:11)
Beinn Mhic Chasgaig
Meall na h-Aisre
Sgurr na Feartaig
Creag an Dail Bheag (Carn Liath)
Beinn a' Bha'ach Ard

860 Beinn Lair

859 Morrone
Caisteal Abhail

858 Beinn Luibhean
Fraoch Bheinn

857 Beinn a' Chrulaiste
Cruach Innse
Carn Dearg Mor
Beinn a' Chaisgein Mor

855 Stob an Aonaich Mhoir
Beinn Bhuidhe
Beinn an Eoin

853 Creach Bheinn (Ardgour 10:2)

852 Meall an t-Seallaidh

849 Cul Mor
Bac an Eich
Sgurr Ghiubhsachain

847 Ben Donich

846 Canisp

845 Carn Ban
Beinn Resipol

844 Beinn nan Imirean

843 The Merrick

841 Sgurr an Airgid
Ben Vrackie
Beinn Mholach

840 Broad Law
Meallan nan Uan
Ben Rinnes
Beinn Udlaidh

*c.*840 Beinn Trilleachan

838 Carn Chuinneag
Meall na h-Eilde

*c.*838 Sgurr Gaorsaic

837 Sron a' Choire Chnapanich

835 Sgurr Cos na Breachd-laoidh

834 Creag nan Gabhar

830 Beinn Dearg (Glen Lyon 4:12)
Carn Dearg (S of Glen Roy 9:2)

829 Brown Cow Hill
Carn Mor (Glen Pean 11:1)

827 An Dun

825 Beinn Tarsuinn (Arran 18:10)

824 Geal-charn Mor

822 White Coomb

821 Geal Charn (Caiplich 8:3)
Benvane

818 Beinn Chaorach
Carn na Drochaide
Sgorr na Diollaid
Beinn Dearg Bheag

817 Binnein an Fhidhleir

816 Carn a' Chuilinn

815 Carn Dearg (N of Gleann Eachach
9:5)

814 Corserine
An Stac
An Sidhean
Creag Liath, Breabag

813 Beinn Each
Sgor Mor

812 Askival

811 Carn na Saobhaidhe

810 Creach Bheinn (Loch Creran 3:11)
Meall a' Bhuachaille

809 Creag MacRanaich
Meall na Fearna

808 Sail Gharbh, Quinag
Sgurr Innse
Hart Fell

807 Beinn nam Fuaran
Craig Rainich
Monamenach

806 Ben Gulabin
Garbh-bheinn (Skye 18:3)

804 Geal Charn (Arkaig 12:2)
Beinn na h-Eaglaise
Carn Mor (Ladder Hills 8:5)
Meall nan Subh

803 The Sow of Atholl
Beinn Bhreach-liath

801   Meallan Liath Coire Mhic
         Dhughaill

800   Cranstackie

c.800   Beinn Iaruinn

799   Clisham

798   Am Bathach
         Cir Mhor

797   Cairnsmore of Carsphairn
         Beinn Dronaig

796   Sgurr an Utha
         Mam na Gualainn
         Sgurr Coire Choinnichean
         Beinn Bhan (Great Glen 12:1)

792   Carn Ealasaid
         Beinn Mhic-Mhonaidh
         Sgurr a' Chaorachain
         Beinn Leoid

791   Beinn Airigh Charr

790   Druim nan Cnamh

789   Auchnafree Hill
         Glas Bheinn (Blackwater 5:8)

788   Meall Dubh

787   The Brack
         Meall Tairneachan
         Beinn a' Chaisteil (Strath Vaich 15:14)
         Arkle

786   Carn na Nathrach

785   Beinn na Caillich

784   Beinn an Oir

783   Beinn Mhic Cedidh

782   Sgurr Dubh

781   Sgurr Mhic Bharraich
         Corryhabbie Hill
         Ainshval

780   Meall Luaidhe
         Farragon Hill

779   Beinn Bheula

778   Mount Battock

777   Meall Horn

776   Sail Gorm, Quinag
         Glas Bheinn (Assynt 16:5)

775   Meall na Leitreach
         Glamaig
         Sgorr Craobh a' Chaorainn

774   Meall a' Phubuill
         Cook's Cairn

773   Beinn nan Caorach

772   Meall Lighiche
         Beinn Spionnaidh

771   Ceann na Baintighearna
         Stob Coire a' Chearcaill

770   Druim Tarsuinn
         Beinn a' Choin

769   Cul Beag
         Meallach Mhor

768   Shalloch on Minnoch
         Carn Dearg (N of Glen Roy 9:4)

767   Sail Mhor

766   Beinn Liath Mhor a' Ghiubhais Li
         Dun da Ghaoithe
         Fuar Bheinn

765   Braigh nan Uamhachan

764   Meall an Fhudair
         Little Wyvis
         Spidean Coinich, Quinag
         Ben Loyal

762   Beinn Talaidh
         Beinn na h-Uamha

INDEX OF CORBETTS

References given are to section numbers